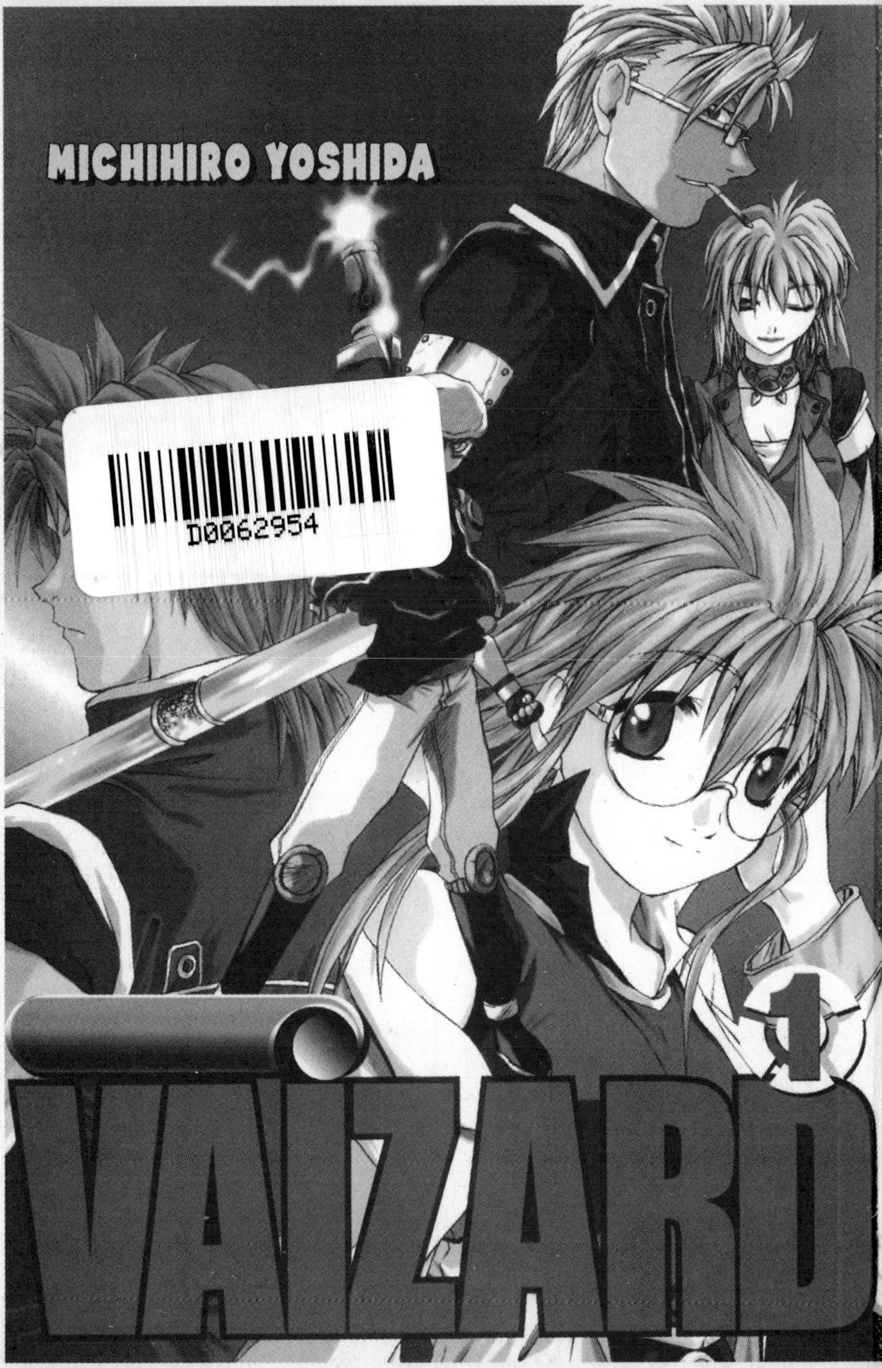
MICHIHIRO YOSHIDA
VAIZARD
1

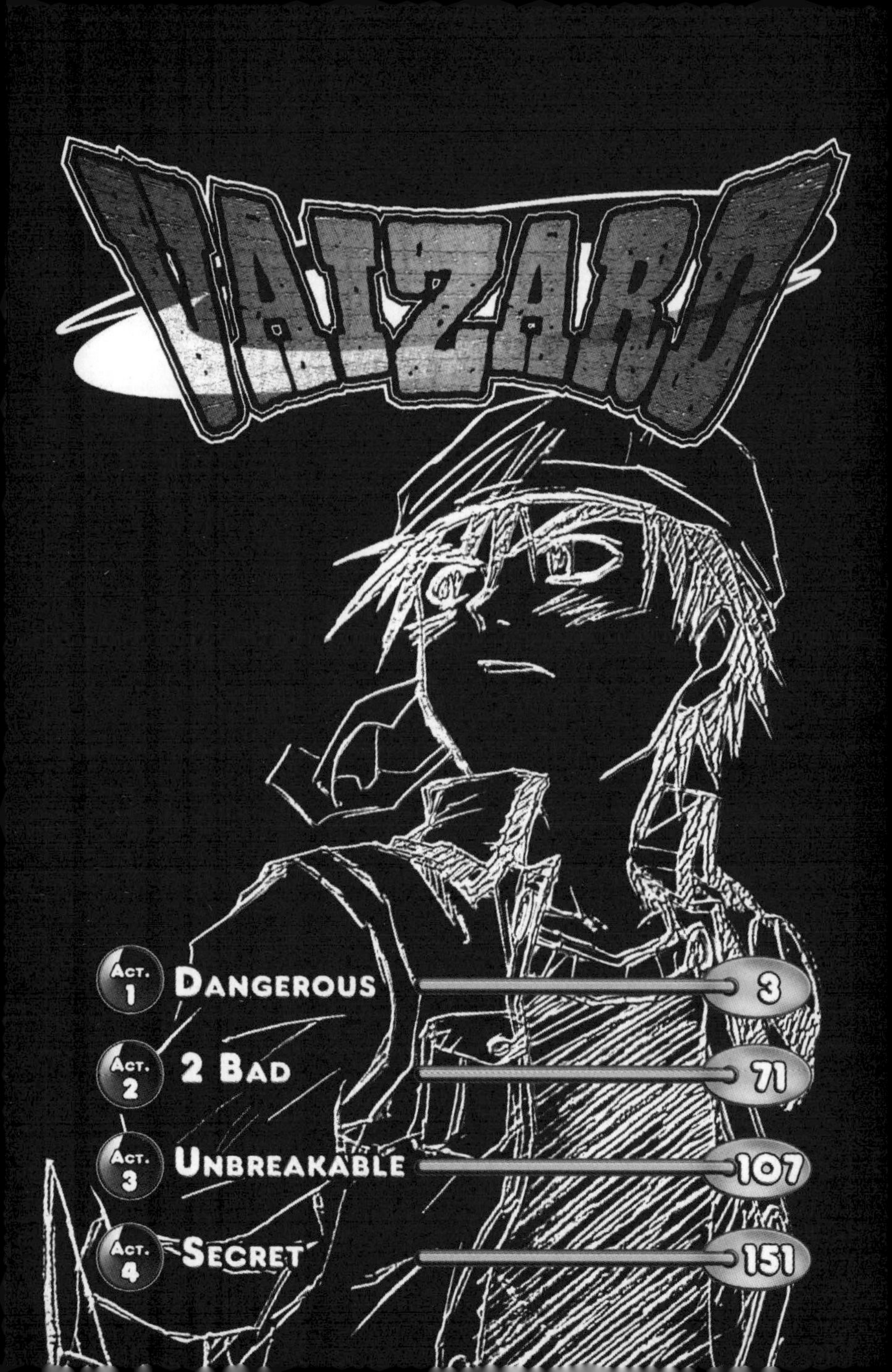
VAIZARD

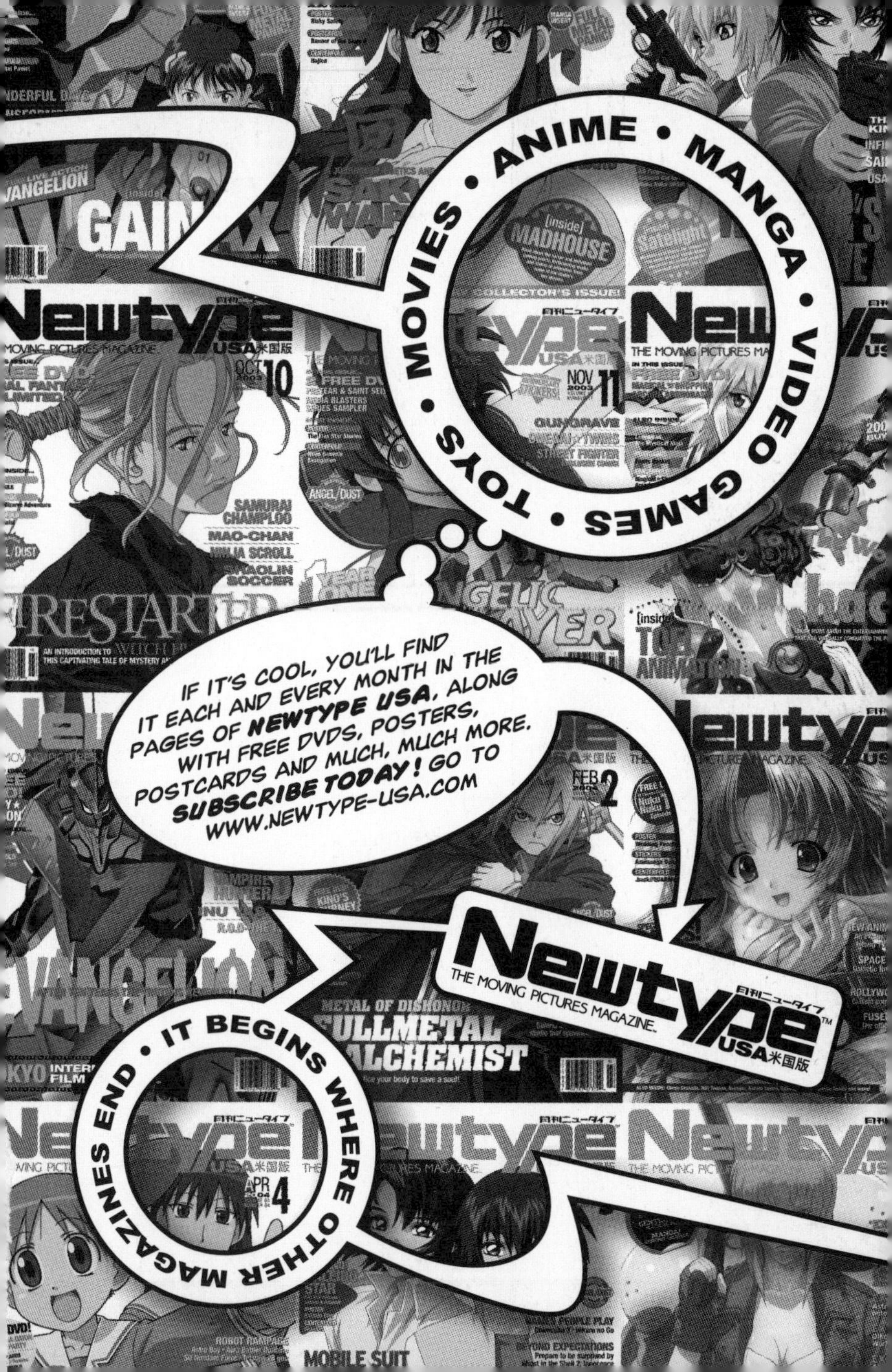
MOVIES • ANIME • MANGA • VIDEO GAMES • TOYS
IF IT'S COOL, YOU'LL FIND IT EACH AND EVERY MONTH IN THE PAGES OF NEWTYPE USA, ALONG WITH FREE DVDS, POSTERS, POSTCARDS AND MUCH, MUCH MORE. SUBSCRIBE TODAY! GO TO WWW.NEWTYPE-USA.COM
Newtype USA 月刊ニュータイプ 米国版
THE MOVING PICTURES MAGAZINE.
IT BEGINS WHERE OTHER MAGAZINES END •

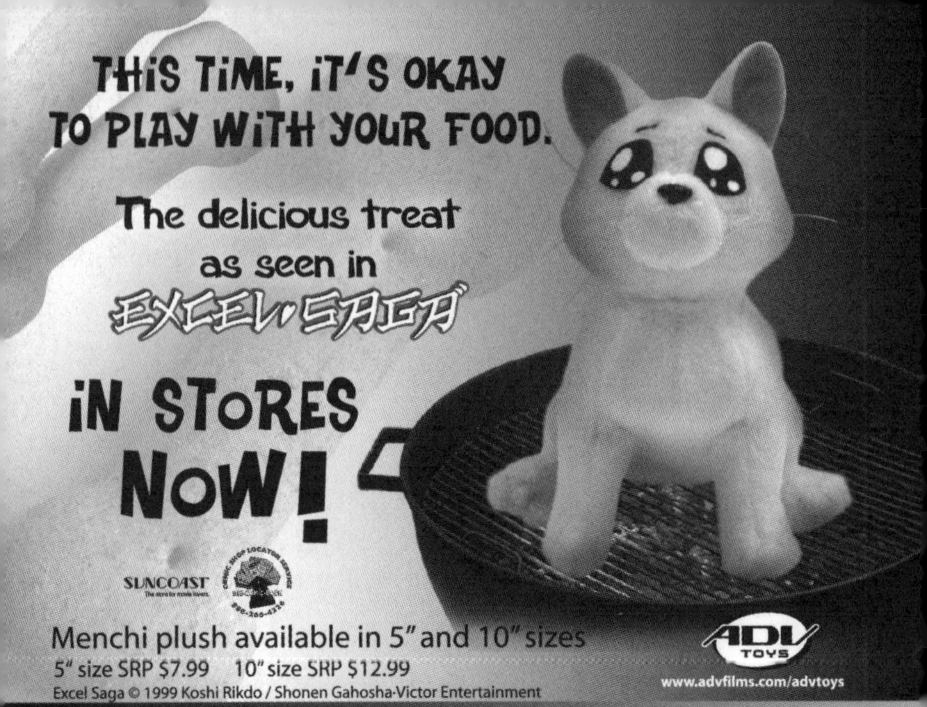
THIS TIME, IT'S OKAY
TO PLAY WITH YOUR FOOD.
The delicious treat
as seen in
EXCEL SAGA
IN STORES
NOW!
SUNCOAST
Menchi plush available in 5" and 10" sizes
5" size SRP $7.99 10" size SRP $12.99
Excel Saga © 1999 Koshi Rikdo / Shonen Gahosha-Victor Entertainment
ADV TOYS
www.advfilms.com/advtoys

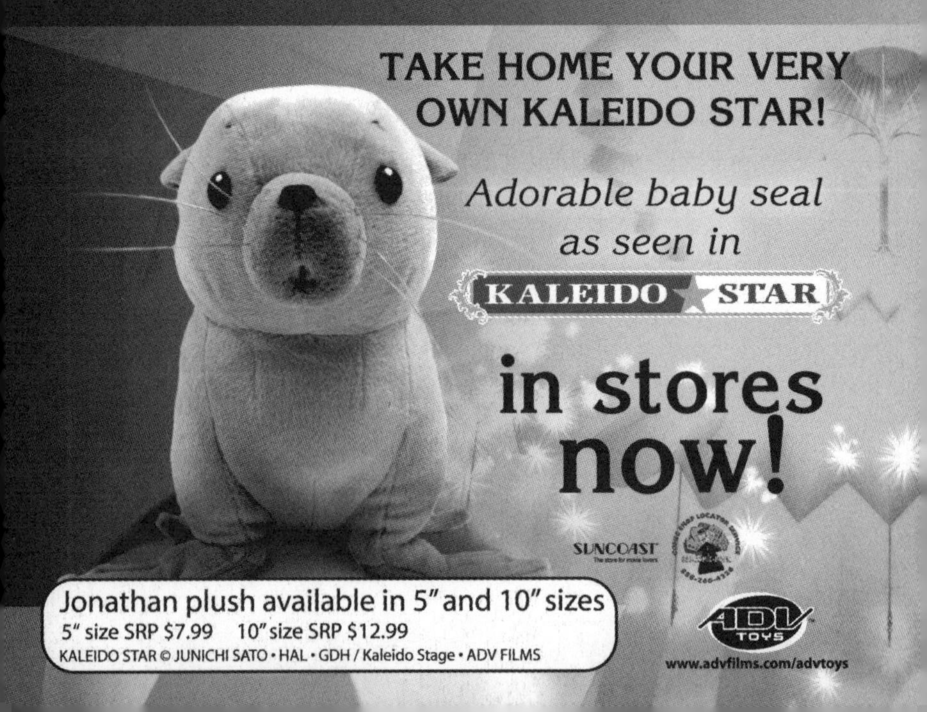
TAKE HOME YOUR VERY
OWN KALEIDO STAR!
Adorable baby seal
as seen in
KALEIDO STAR
in stores
now!
SUNCOAST
Jonathan plush available in 5" and 10" sizes
5" size SRP $7.99 10" size SRP $12.99
KALEIDO STAR © JUNICHI SATO • HAL • GDH / Kaleido Stage • ADV FILMS
ADV TOYS
www.advfilms.com/advtoys

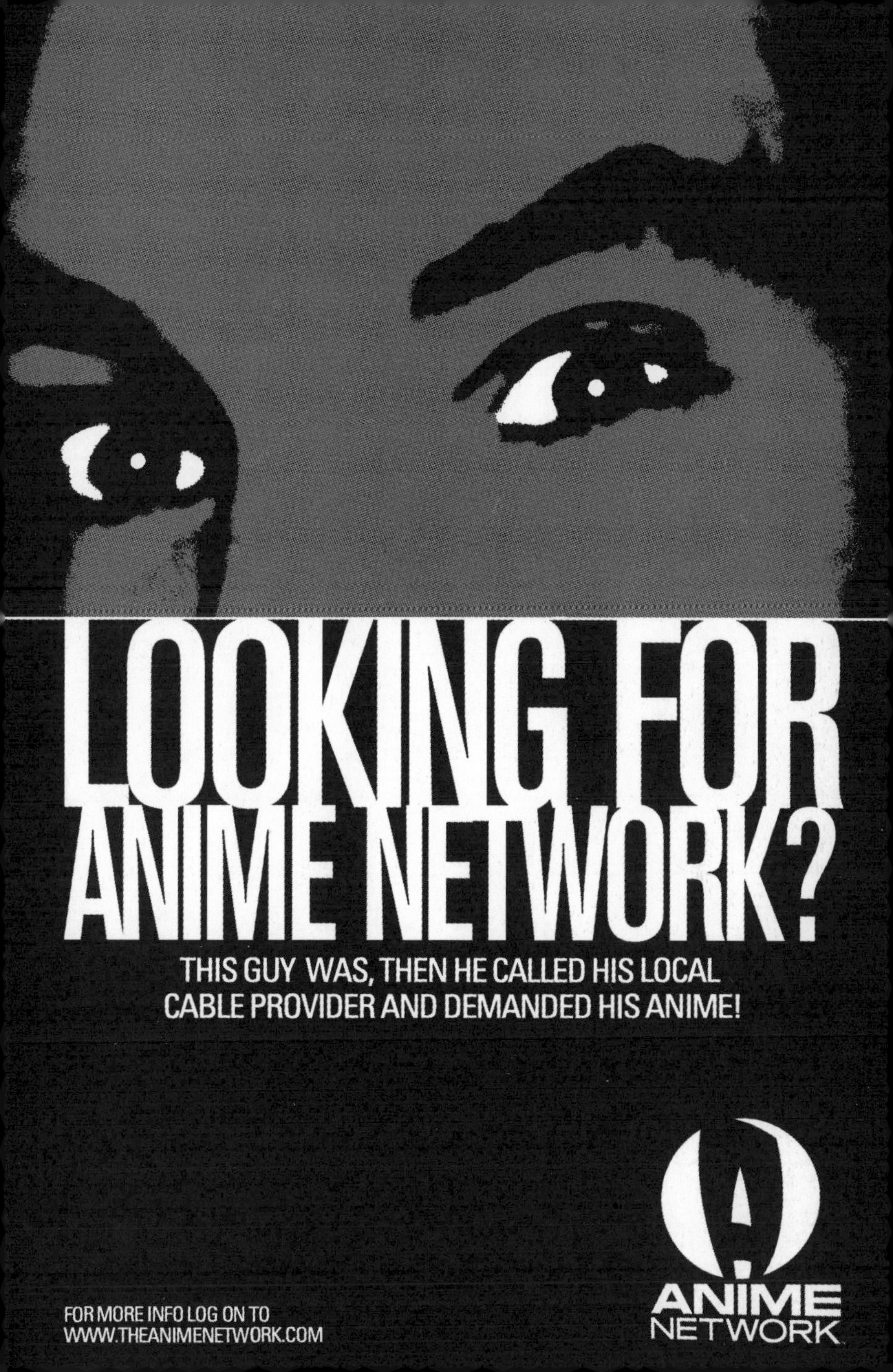
LOOKING FOR ANIME NETWORK?
THIS GUY WAS, THEN HE CALLED HIS LOCAL CABLE PROVIDER AND DEMANDED HIS ANIME!
FOR MORE INFO LOG ON TO WWW.THEANIMENETWORK.COM
ANIME NETWORK

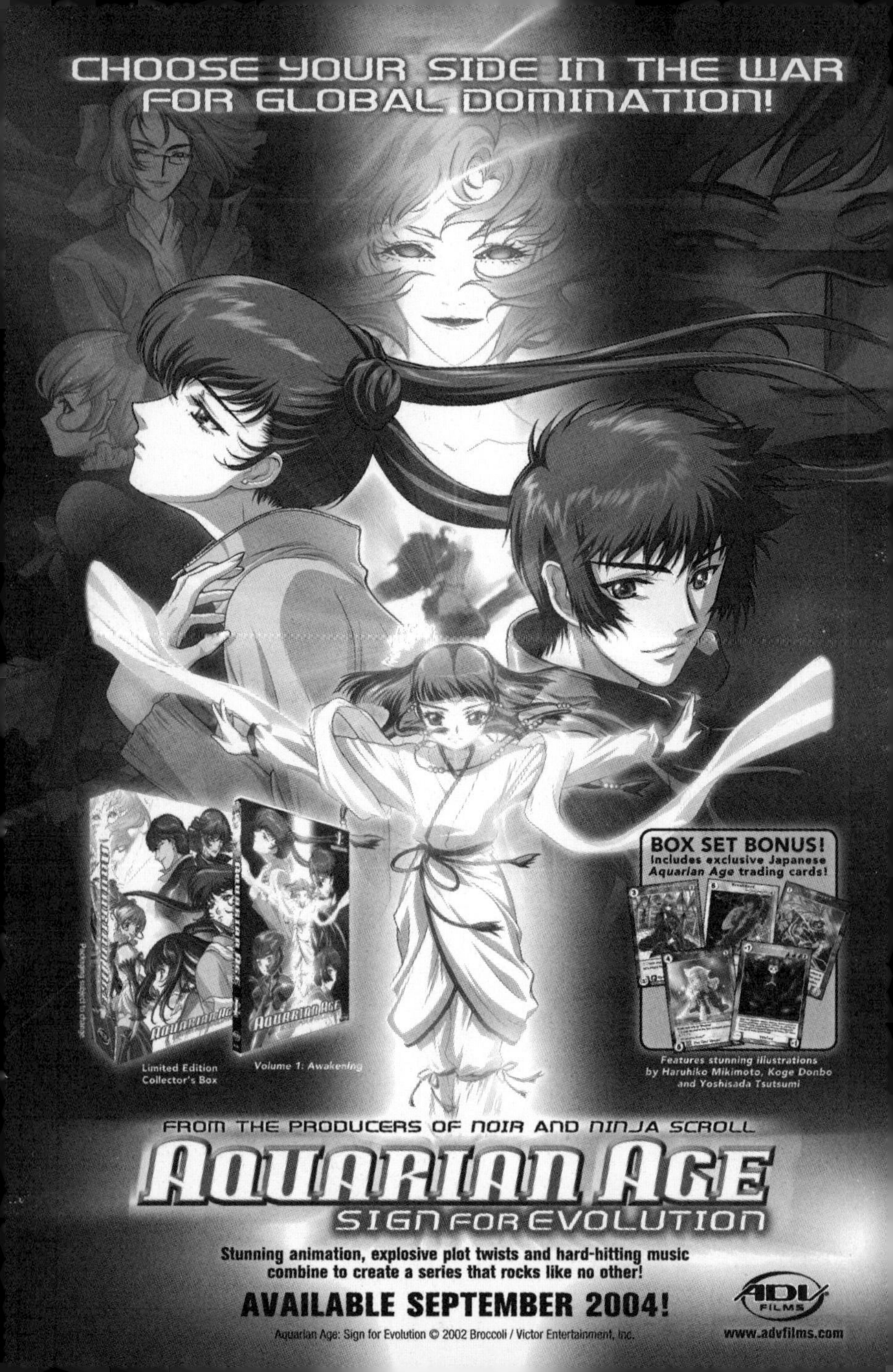

CHOOSE YOUR SIDE IN THE WAR
FOR GLOBAL DOMINATION!
Limited Edition
Collector's Box
Volume 1: Awakening
BOX SET BONUS!
Includes exclusive Japanese
Aquarian Age trading cards!
Features stunning illustrations
by Haruhiko Mikimoto, Koge Donbo
and Yoshisada Tsutsumi
FROM THE PRODUCERS OF NOIR AND NINJA SCROLL
AQUARIAN AGE
SIGN FOR EVOLUTION
Stunning animation, explosive plot twists and hard-hitting music
combine to create a series that rocks like no other!
AVAILABLE SEPTEMBER 2004!
ADV FILMS
Aquarian Age: Sign for Evolution © 2002 Broccoli / Victor Entertainment, Inc.
www.advfilms.com

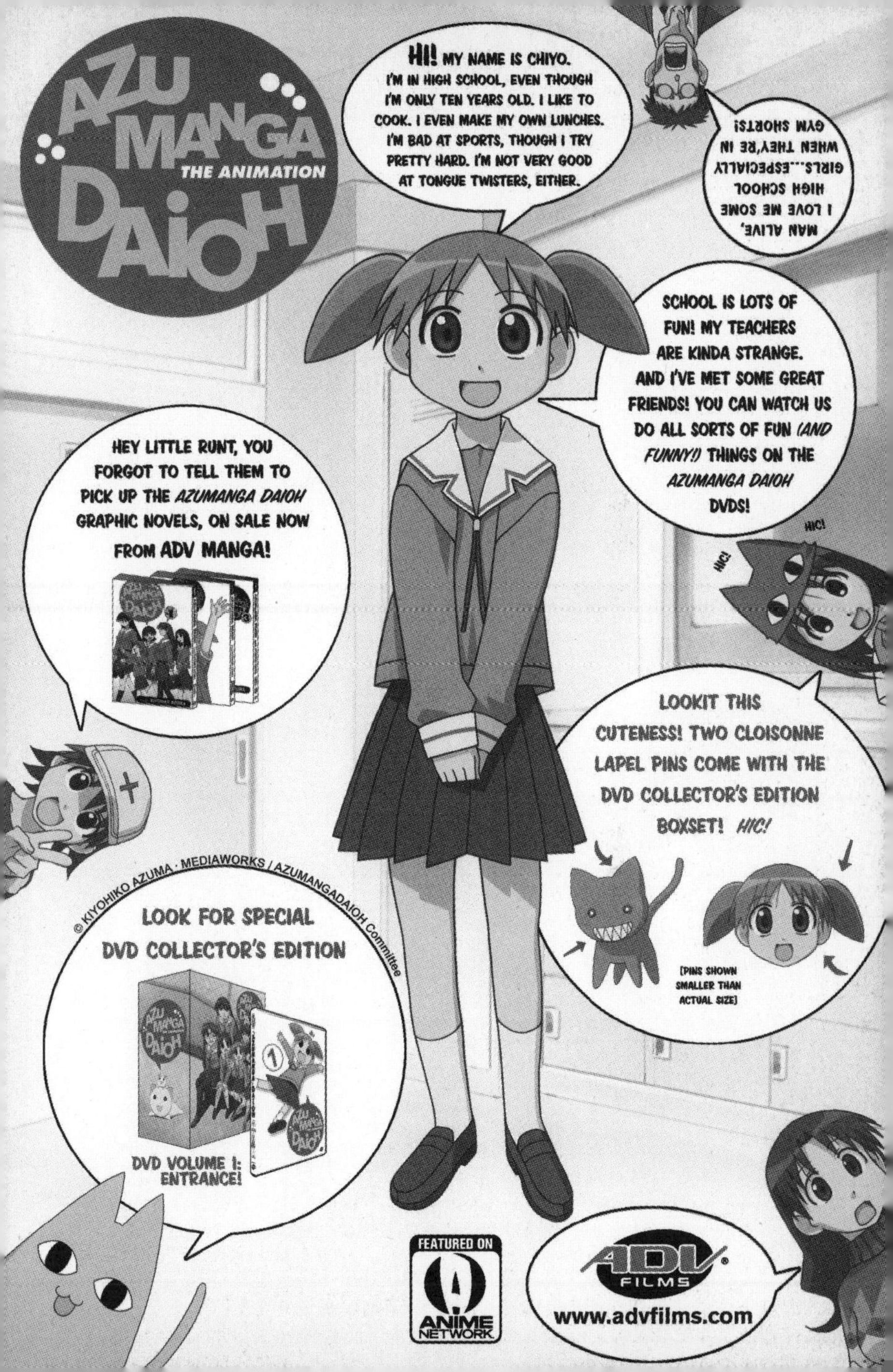
AZUMANGA DAIOH
THE ANIMATION
HI! MY NAME IS CHIYO. I'M IN HIGH SCHOOL, EVEN THOUGH I'M ONLY TEN YEARS OLD. I LIKE TO COOK. I EVEN MAKE MY OWN LUNCHES. I'M BAD AT SPORTS, THOUGH I TRY PRETTY HARD. I'M NOT VERY GOOD AT TONGUE TWISTERS, EITHER.
MAN ALIVE, I LOVE ME SOME HIGH SCHOOL GIRLS...ESPECIALLY WHEN THEY'RE IN GYM SHORTS!
SCHOOL IS LOTS OF FUN! MY TEACHERS ARE KINDA STRANGE. AND I'VE MET SOME GREAT FRIENDS! YOU CAN WATCH US DO ALL SORTS OF FUN (AND FUNNY!) THINGS ON THE AZUMANGA DAIOH DVDS!
HEY LITTLE RUNT, YOU FORGOT TO TELL THEM TO PICK UP THE AZUMANGA DAIOH GRAPHIC NOVELS, ON SALE NOW FROM ADV MANGA!
HIC!
HIC!
LOOKIT THIS CUTENESS! TWO CLOISONNE LAPEL PINS COME WITH THE DVD COLLECTOR'S EDITION BOXSET! HIC!
[PINS SHOWN SMALLER THAN ACTUAL SIZE]
© KIYOHIKO AZUMA · MEDIAWORKS / AZUMANGADAIOH Committee
LOOK FOR SPECIAL DVD COLLECTOR'S EDITION
DVD VOLUME 1: ENTRANCE!
FEATURED ON ANIME NETWORK
ADV FILMS
www.advfilms.com

EDITOR'S

PICKS

PICK 1

NAJICA BLITZ TACTICS

Najica is a skilled perfumer for CRI Cosmetics, but her talents include more than creating sweet fragrances—she is actually a special operative for the secret intelligence organization behind CRI. Her mission: travel the world in search of evildoers and along the way, rescue a few girls like Lila, her undercover partner. Lila is in fact one of a group of rare individuals called Humaritts, and the mysteries of these extraordinary beings are about to lead Najica, along with her super-skilled sidekick, on a mission of their own...

© 2002 by Takuya Tashiro/STUDIO FANTASIA·AFW/NAJICA Project/Media Factory

PICK 2

RAY

Ray is a grown woman with a troubled past and a superhuman gift—she has X-Ray vision! Raised on an organ-donor farm, her own eyes were taken and sold on the black market. Then the gift of sight came to her unexpectedly, and once again she could see the world—only, she saw a lot more of it! Now, working as a nurse and moonlighting as a surgeon, Ray is ready to face her past and the horrible place she had to call home, and finally destroy the underground group that robbed her of her sight and her childhood.

PICK 3

STEEL ANGEL KURUMI

Designed for military use, the Steel Angel Kurumi is a fearsome android warrior. Constructed with an Angel Heart, the ultra-megawatt cosmic power source of the angels, Kurumi answers only to the person who activated her—a young, sweet boy named Nakahito. Poor Nakahito is in store for quite a ride, not only because the military desperately wants Kurumi back, but also because they both discover that she is not alone. Accompanied by the other steel angels, Kurumi must rescue a kidnapped Nakahito, play for her life in a "Steel Fight" tournament, and sing her heart out as a teen-idol singer. The adventures never stop for these adorable little warriors!

CHECK'EM OUT TODAY!

www.adv-manga.com

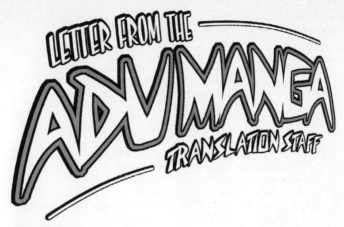

LETTER FROM THE ADV MANGA TRANSLATION STAFF

Dear Reader,

On behalf of the ADV Manga translation team, thank you for purchasing an ADV book. We are enthusiastic and committed to our work, and strive to carry our enthusiasm over into the book you hold in your hands.

Our goal is to retain the spirit of the original Japanese book. While great care has been taken to render a true and accurate translation, some cultural or readability issues may require a line to be adapted for greater accessibility to our readers. At times, manga titles that include culturally-specific concepts will feature a "Translator's Notes" section, which explains noteworthy references to the original text.

We hope our commitment to a faithful translation is evident in every ADV book you purchase.

Sincerely,

Javier Lopez
Lead Translator

Madoka Moroe

Haruka Kaneko-Smith

Eiko McGregor

Kay Bertrand

Joshua M. Cole

Brendan Frayne

Amy Forsyth

VAIZARD VOLUME 1

© Michihiro Yoshida 2003
All rights reserved.
First published in 2003 by MAG Garden Corporation.
English translation rights arranged with MAG Garden Corporation.

Translator **HARUKA KANEKO-SMITH**
Lead Translator/Translation Supervisor **JAVIER LOPEZ**
ADV Manga Translation Staff **KAY BERTRAND, JOSH COLE,
AMY FORSYTH, BRENDAN FRAYNE, EIKO MCGREGOR
AND MADOKA MOROE**

Print Production/ Art Studio Manager **LISA PUCKETT**
Pre-press Manager **KLYS REEDYK**
Art Production Manager **RYAN MASON**
Sr. Designer/Creative Manager **JORGE ALVARADO**
Graphic Designer/Group Leader **SCOTT SAVAGE**
Graphic Designer **CHY LING**
Graphic Artists **NATALIA MORALES, LISA RAPER, CHRIS LAPP
AND NANAKO TSUKIHASHI**
Graphic Intern **MARK MEZA**

International Coordinator **TORU IWAKAMI**
International Coordinator **ATSUSHI KANBAYASHI**

Publishing Editor **SUSAN ITIN**
Assistant Editor **MARGARET SCHAROLD**
Editorial Assistant **VARSHA BHUCHAR**
Proofreaders **SHERIDAN JACOBS AND STEVEN REED**
Editorial Intern **JENNIFER VACCA**

Research/ Traffic Coordinator **MARSHA ARNOLD**

Executive VP, CFO, COO **KEVIN CORCORAN**

President, CEO & Publisher **JOHN LEDFORD**

Email: editor@adv-manga.com
www.adv-manga.com
www.advfilms.com

For sales and distribution inquiries please call **1.800.282.7202**

 is a division of A.D. Vision, Inc.
10114 W. Sam Houston Parkway, Suite 200, Houston, Texas 77099

ISBN: 1-4139-0168-9
First printing, November 2004
10 9 8 7 6 5 4 3 2 1
Printed in Canada

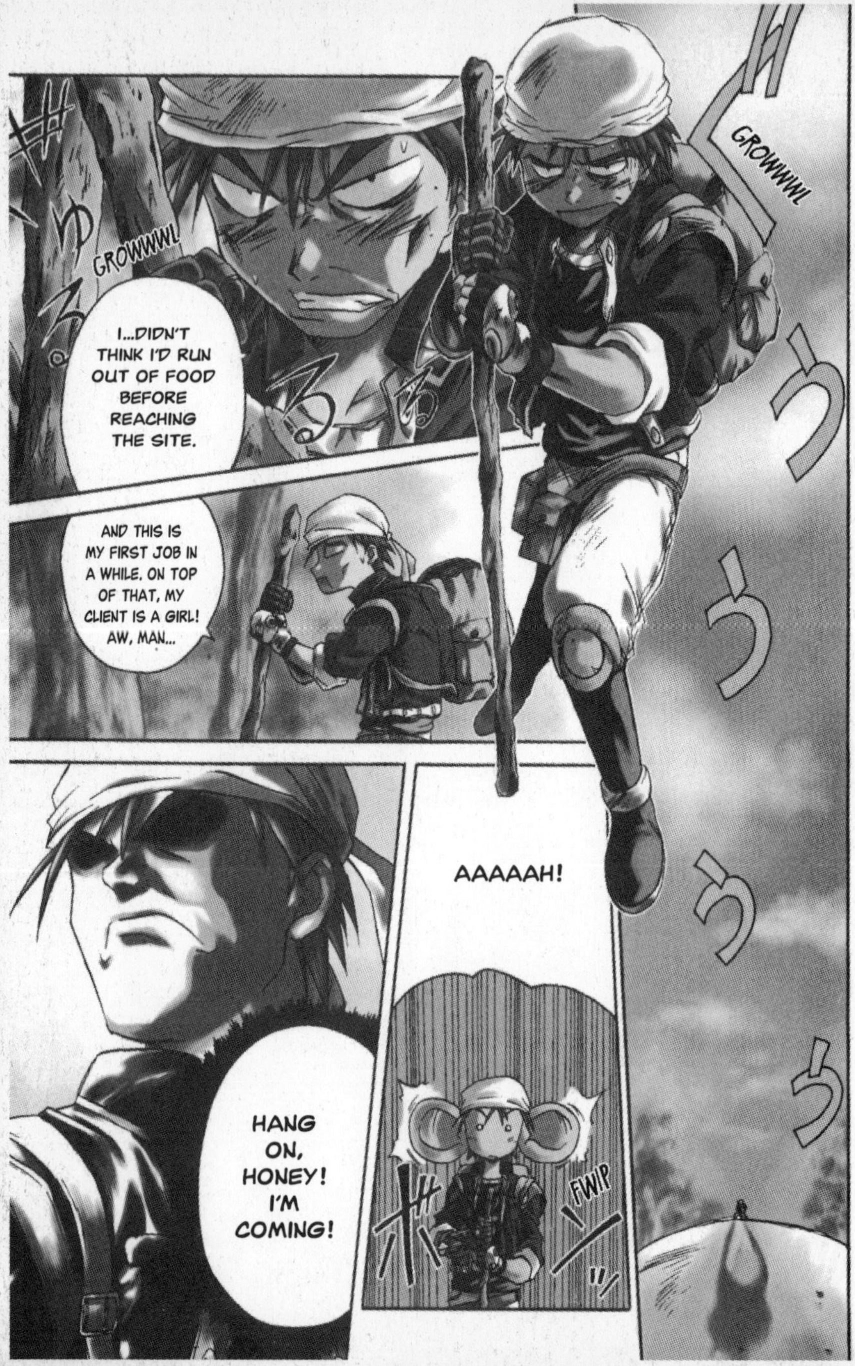
GROWWWL
GROWWWL
I...DIDN'T THINK I'D RUN OUT OF FOOD BEFORE REACHING THE SITE.
AND THIS IS MY FIRST JOB IN A WHILE. ON TOP OF THAT, MY CLIENT IS A GIRL! AW, MAN...
AAAAAH!
FWIP
HANG ON, HONEY! I'M COMING!

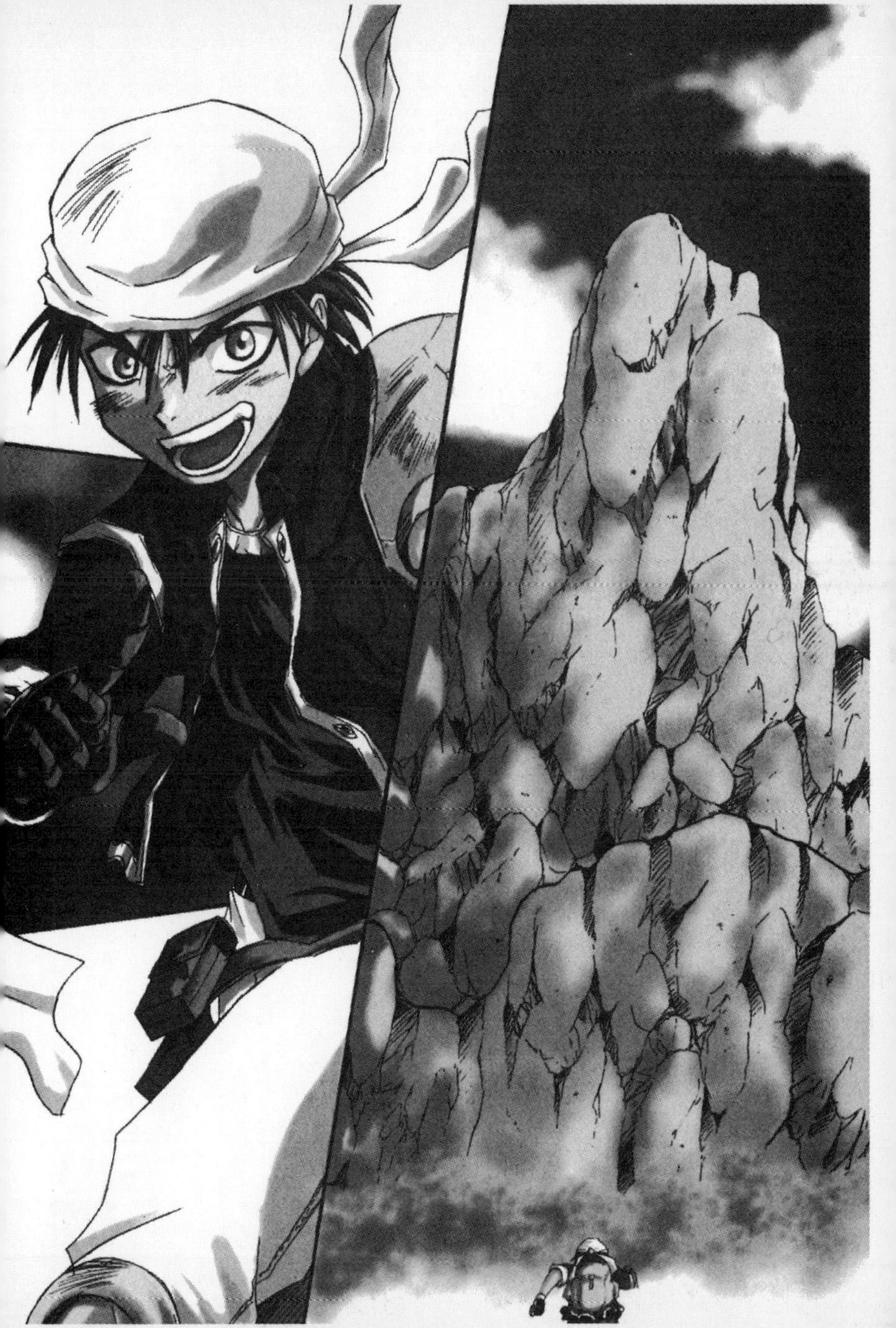

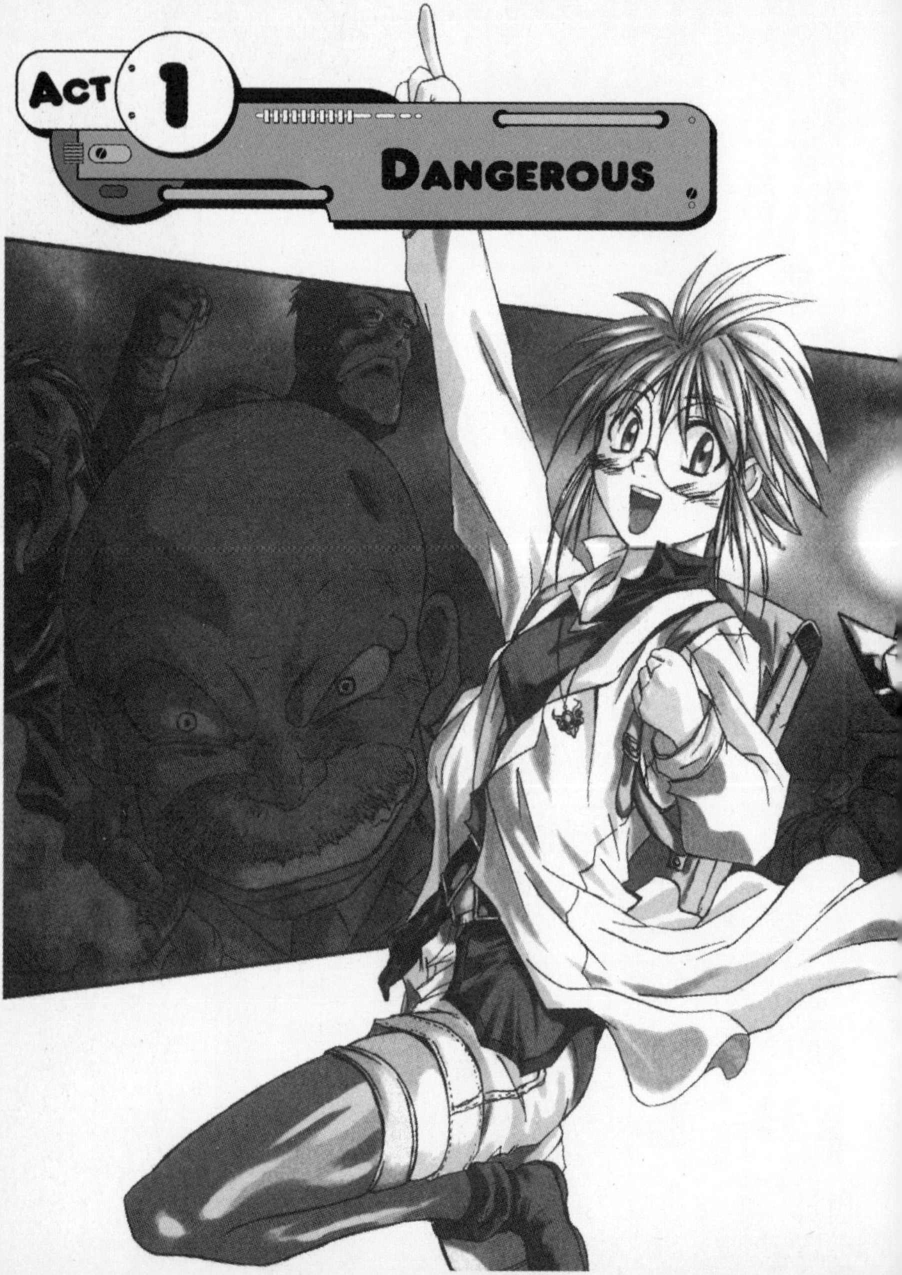
ACT 1
DANGEROUS

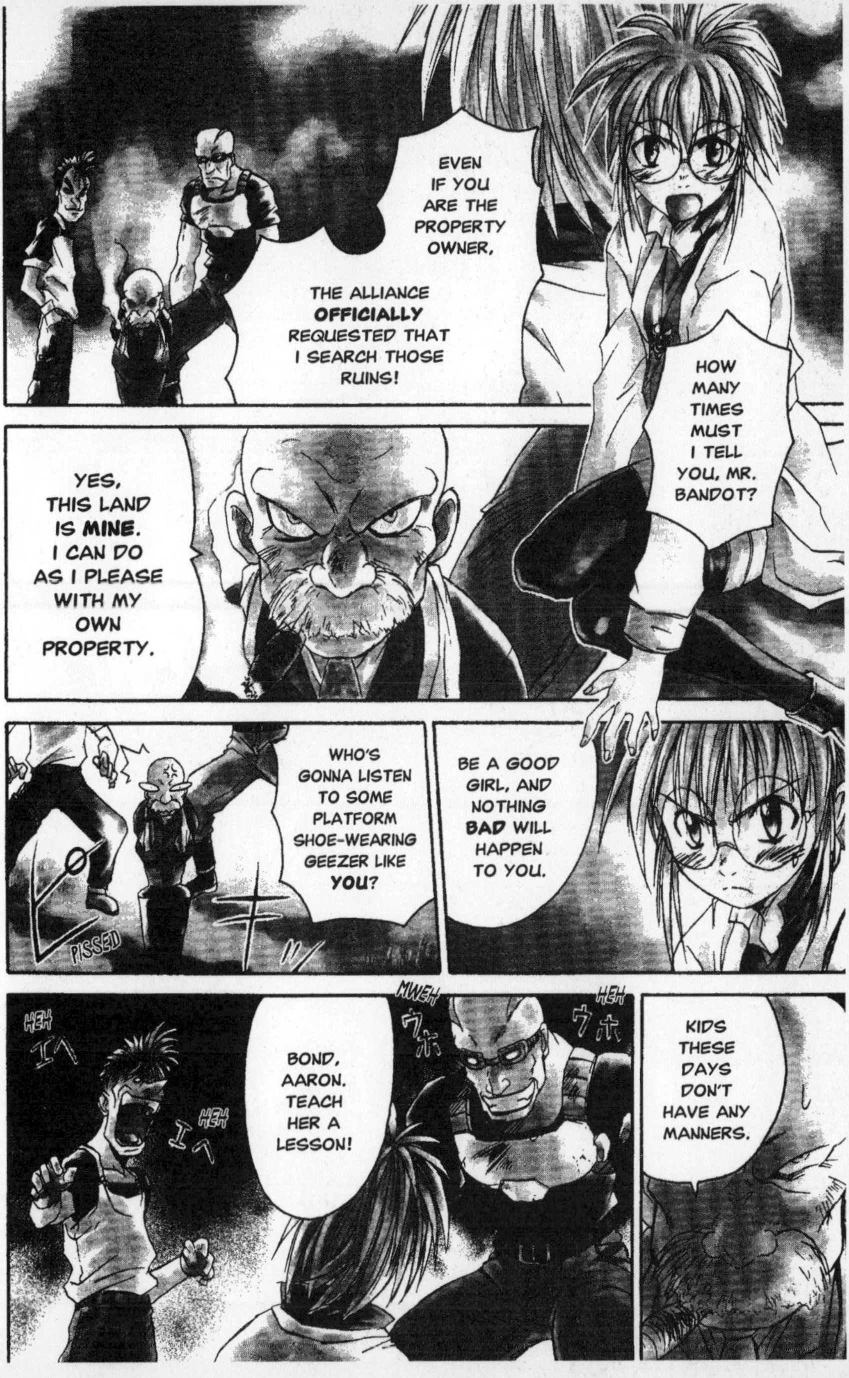
EVEN IF YOU ARE THE PROPERTY OWNER,
THE ALLIANCE **OFFICIALLY** REQUESTED THAT I SEARCH THOSE RUINS!
HOW MANY TIMES MUST I TELL YOU, MR. BANDOT?
YES, THIS LAND IS **MINE**. I CAN DO AS I PLEASE WITH MY OWN PROPERTY.
BE A GOOD GIRL, AND NOTHING **BAD** WILL HAPPEN TO YOU.
WHO'S GONNA LISTEN TO SOME PLATFORM SHOE-WEARING GEEZER LIKE **YOU**?
PISSED
KIDS THESE DAYS DON'T HAVE ANY MANNERS.
HEH
MWEH
BOND, AARON. TEACH HER A LESSON!
HEH
HEH

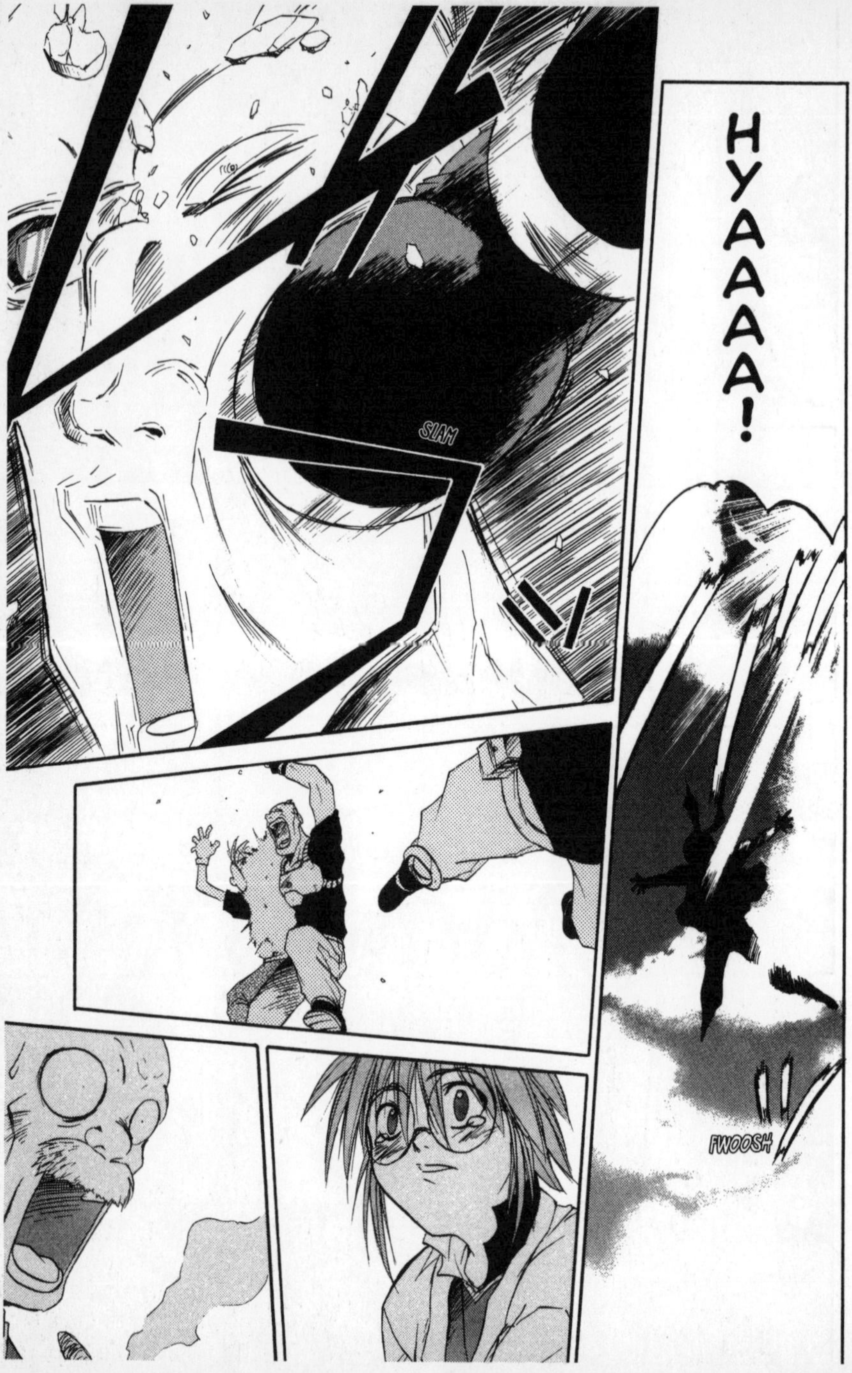
HYAAAAA!
SLAM
FWOOSH

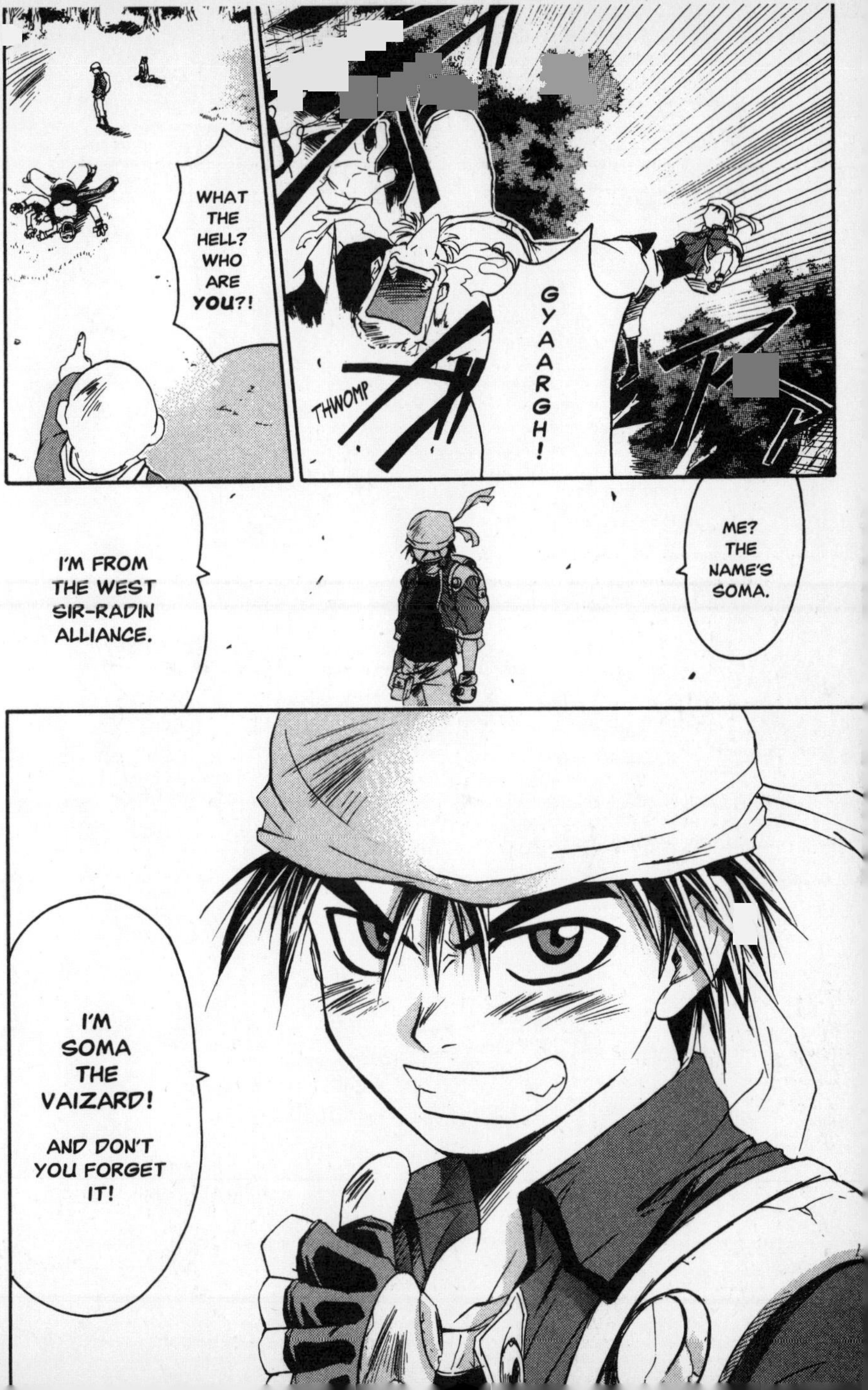
THWOMP
GYAARGH!
WHAT THE HELL? WHO ARE YOU?!
ME? THE NAME'S SOMA.
I'M FROM THE WEST SIR-RADIN ALLIANCE.
I'M SOMA THE VAIZARD!
AND DON'T YOU FORGET IT!

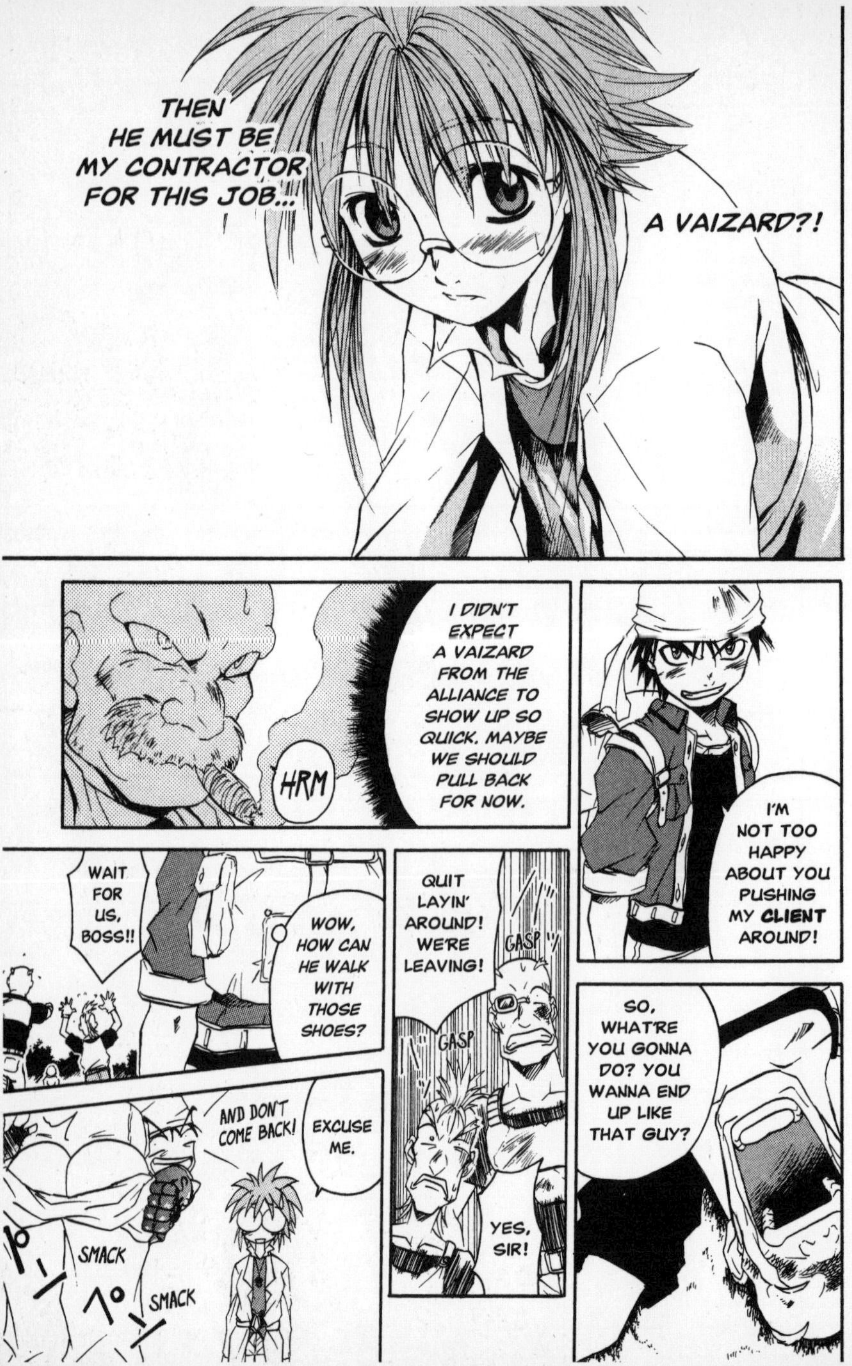
THEN HE MUST BE MY CONTRACTOR FOR THIS JOB...
A VAIZARD?!
HRM
I DIDN'T EXPECT A VAIZARD FROM THE ALLIANCE TO SHOW UP SO QUICK. MAYBE WE SHOULD PULL BACK FOR NOW.
I'M NOT TOO HAPPY ABOUT YOU PUSHING MY **CLIENT** AROUND!
WAIT FOR US, BOSS!!
WOW, HOW CAN HE WALK WITH THOSE SHOES?
QUIT LAYIN' AROUND! WE'RE LEAVING!
GASP
GASP
YES, SIR!
SO, WHAT'RE YOU GONNA DO? YOU WANNA END UP LIKE THAT GUY?
AND DON'T COME BACK!
EXCUSE ME.
SMACK
SMACK

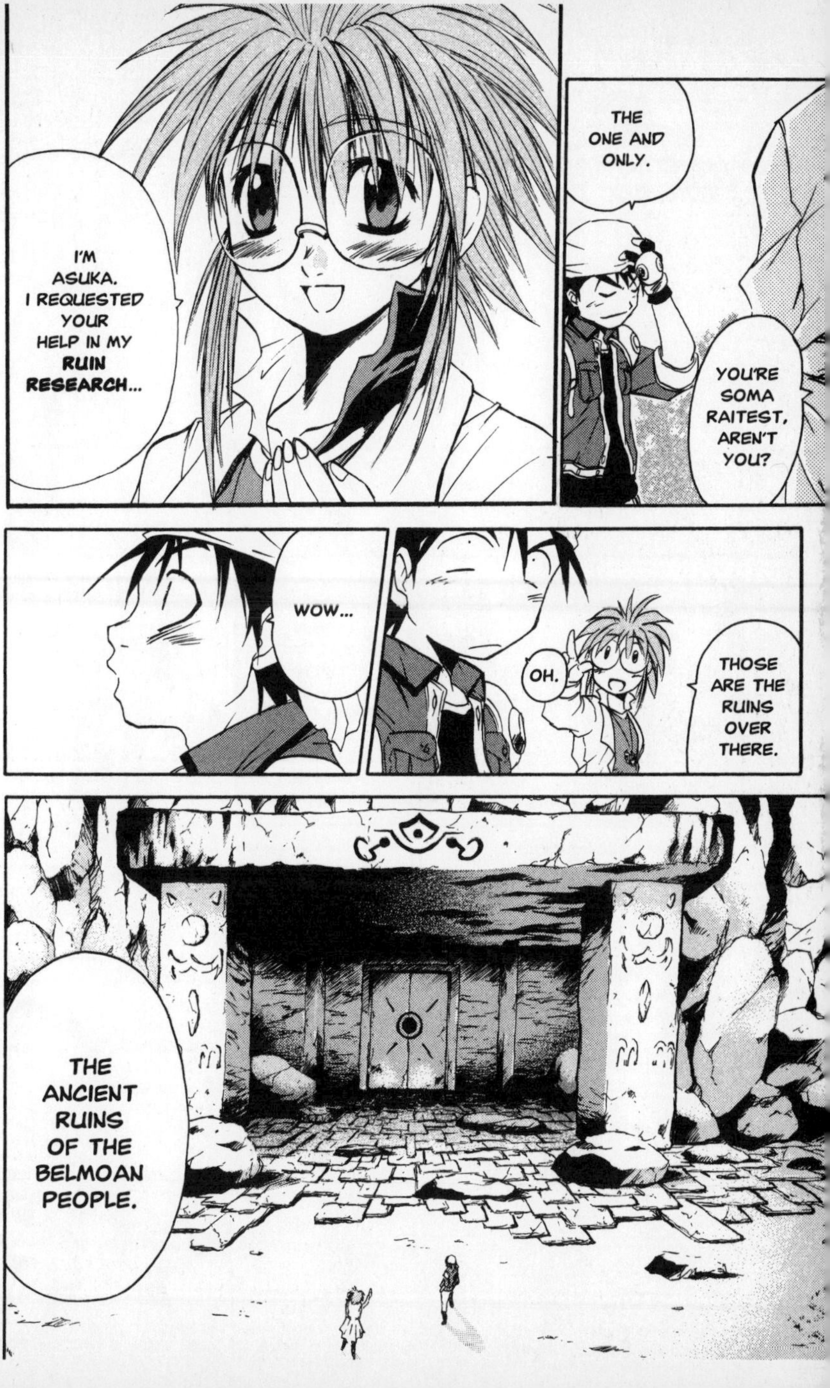
YOU'RE SOMA RAITEST, AREN'T YOU?
THE ONE AND ONLY.
I'M ASUKA. I REQUESTED YOUR HELP IN MY RUIN RESEARCH...
OH.
THOSE ARE THE RUINS OVER THERE.
WOW...
THE ANCIENT RUINS OF THE BELMOAN PEOPLE.

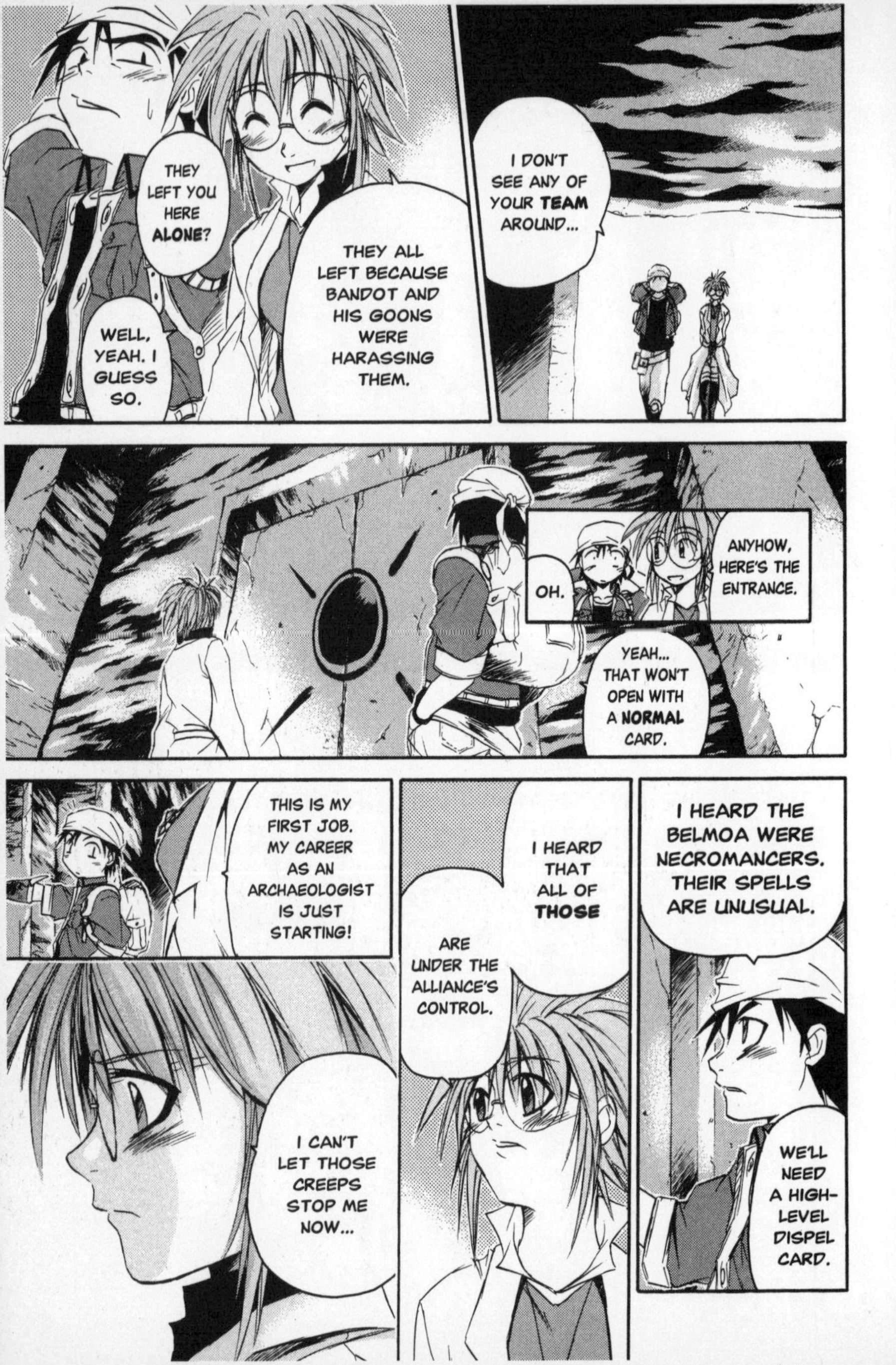
I DON'T SEE ANY OF YOUR TEAM AROUND...
THEY ALL LEFT BECAUSE BANDOT AND HIS GOONS WERE HARASSING THEM.
THEY LEFT YOU HERE ALONE?
WELL, YEAH. I GUESS SO.
ANYHOW, HERE'S THE ENTRANCE.
OH.
YEAH... THAT WON'T OPEN WITH A NORMAL CARD.
I HEARD THE BELMOA WERE NECROMANCERS. THEIR SPELLS ARE UNUSUAL.
WE'LL NEED A HIGH-LEVEL DISPEL CARD.
I HEARD THAT ALL OF THOSE
ARE UNDER THE ALLIANCE'S CONTROL.
THIS IS MY FIRST JOB. MY CAREER AS AN ARCHAEOLOGIST IS JUST STARTING!
I CAN'T LET THOSE CREEPS STOP ME NOW...

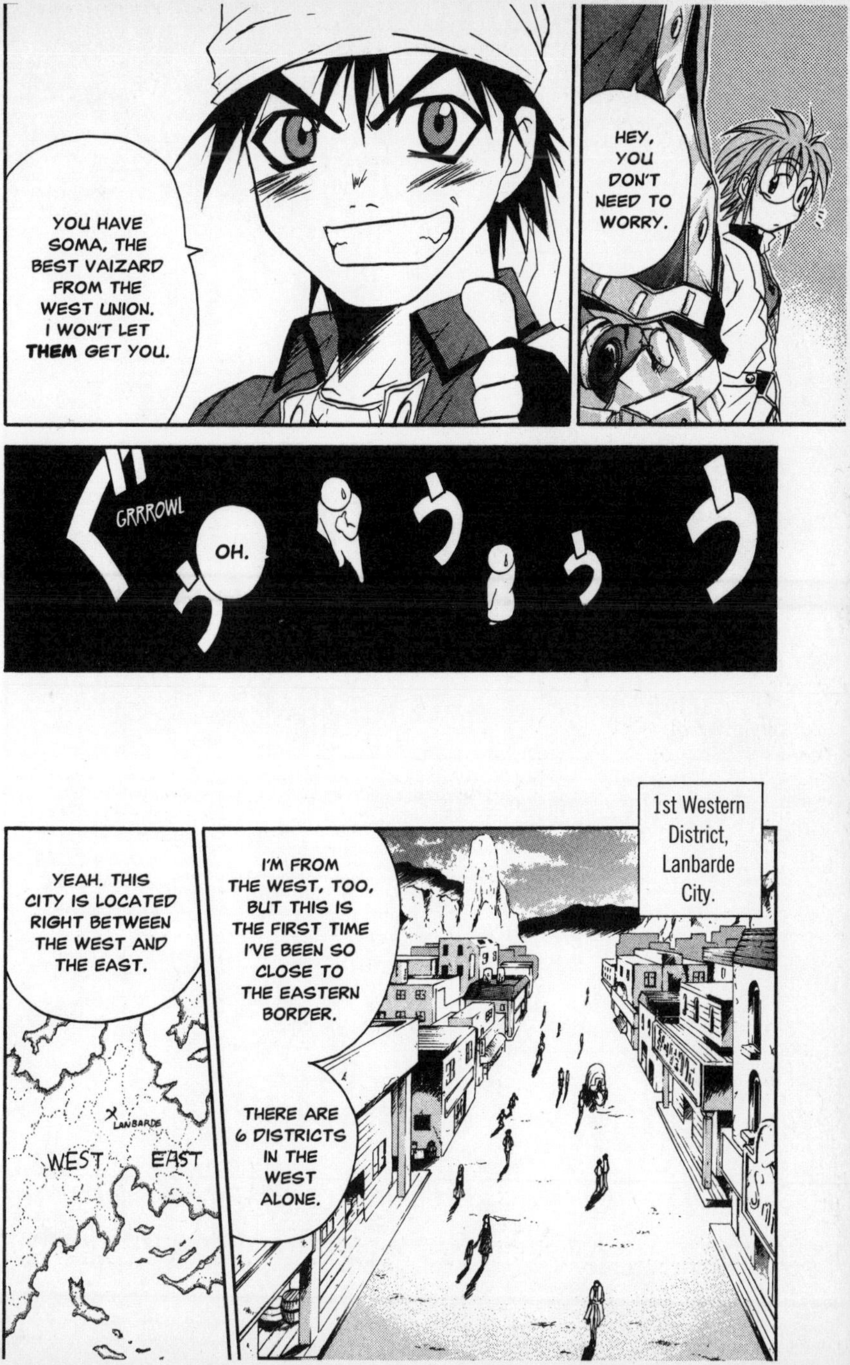
HEY, YOU DON'T NEED TO WORRY.
YOU HAVE SOMA, THE BEST VAIZARD FROM THE WEST UNION. I WON'T LET **THEM** GET YOU.
ぐぅうぅう
GRRROWL
OH.
1st Western District, Lanbarde City.
I'M FROM THE WEST, TOO, BUT THIS IS THE FIRST TIME I'VE BEEN SO CLOSE TO THE EASTERN BORDER.
THERE ARE 6 DISTRICTS IN THE WEST ALONE.
YEAH. THIS CITY IS LOCATED RIGHT BETWEEN THE WEST AND THE EAST.
LANBARDE
WEST
EAST

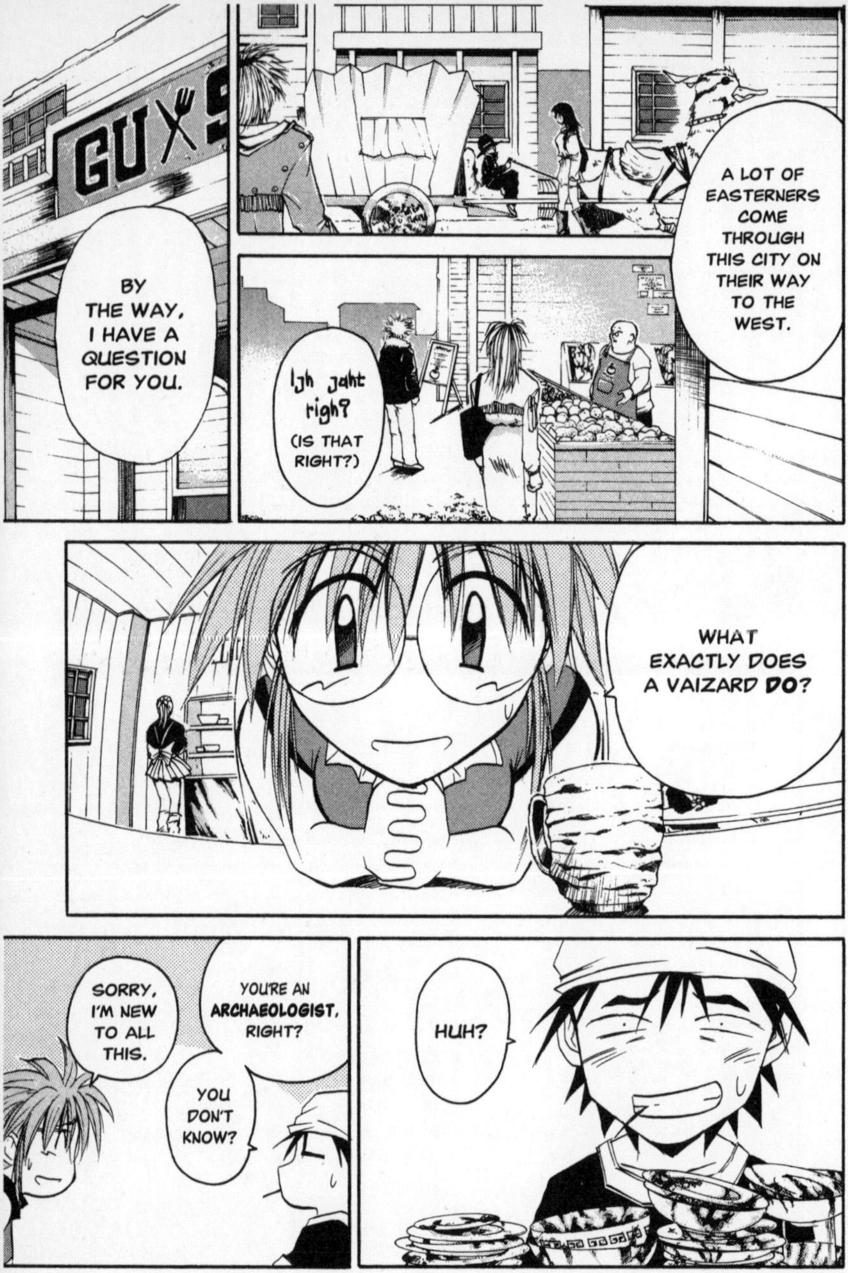
A LOT OF EASTERNERS COME THROUGH THIS CITY ON THEIR WAY TO THE WEST.
Ijh jaht righ? (IS THAT RIGHT?)
BY THE WAY, I HAVE A QUESTION FOR YOU.
GU X S
WHAT EXACTLY DOES A VAIZARD DO?
HUH?
YOU'RE AN ARCHAEOLOGIST, RIGHT?
YOU DON'T KNOW?
SORRY, I'M NEW TO ALL THIS.

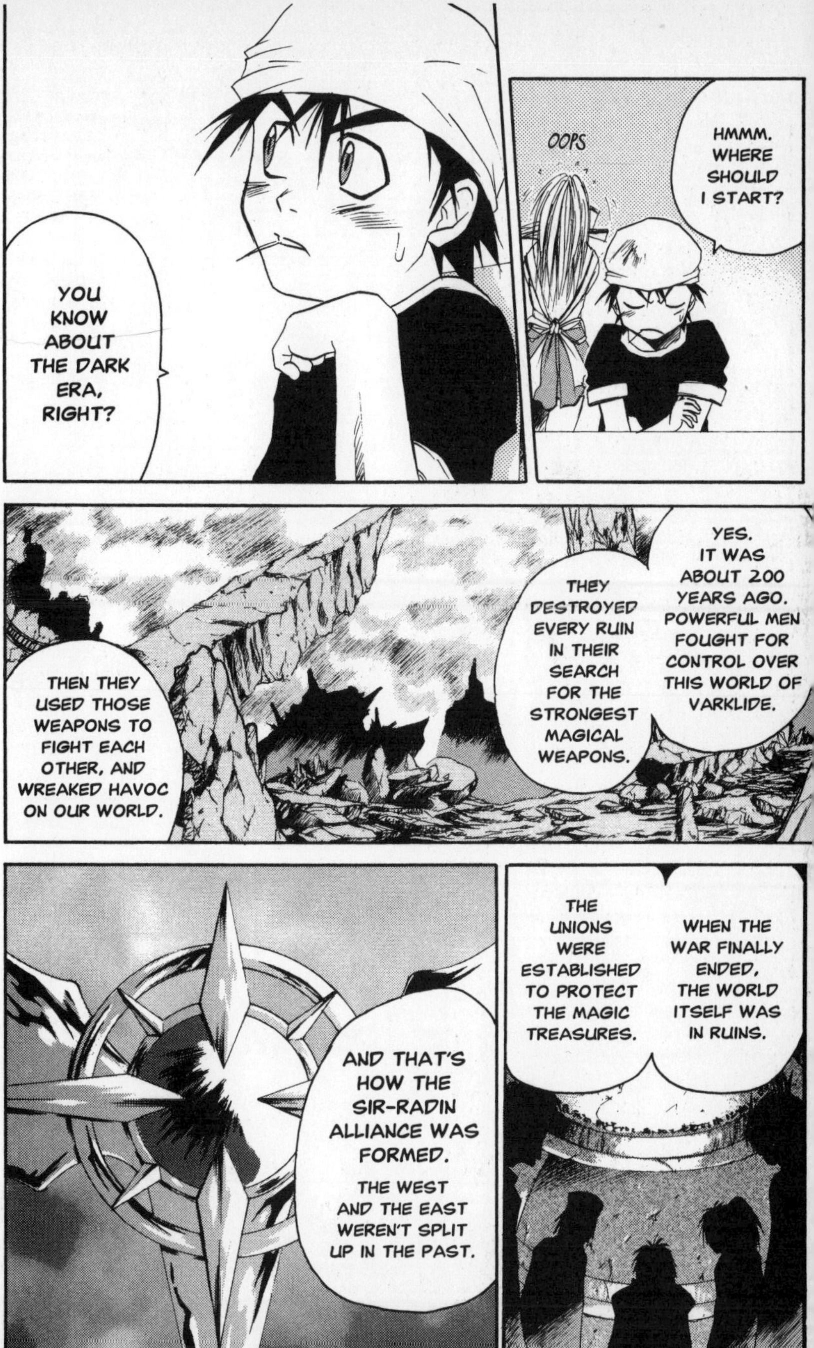
HMMM. WHERE SHOULD I START?
OOPS
YOU KNOW ABOUT THE DARK ERA, RIGHT?
YES. IT WAS ABOUT 200 YEARS AGO. POWERFUL MEN FOUGHT FOR CONTROL OVER THIS WORLD OF VARKLIDE.
THEY DESTROYED EVERY RUIN IN THEIR SEARCH FOR THE STRONGEST MAGICAL WEAPONS.
THEN THEY USED THOSE WEAPONS TO FIGHT EACH OTHER, AND WREAKED HAVOC ON OUR WORLD.
WHEN THE WAR FINALLY ENDED, THE WORLD ITSELF WAS IN RUINS.
THE UNIONS WERE ESTABLISHED TO PROTECT THE MAGIC TREASURES.
AND THAT'S HOW THE SIR-RADIN ALLIANCE WAS FORMED.
THE WEST AND THE EAST WEREN'T SPLIT UP IN THE PAST.

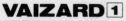

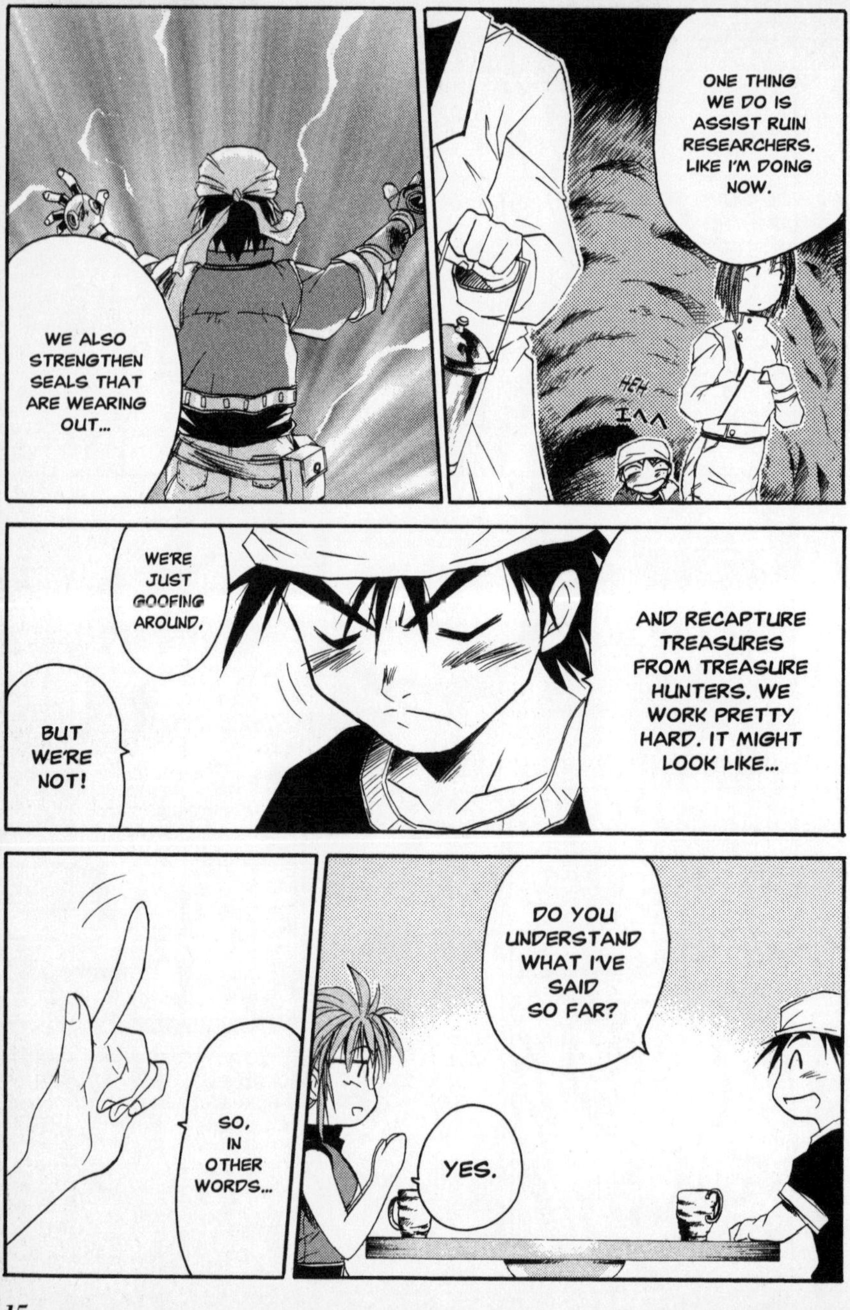
ONE THING WE DO IS ASSIST RUIN RESEARCHERS. LIKE I'M DOING NOW.
HEH
WE ALSO STRENGTHEN SEALS THAT ARE WEARING OUT...
AND RECAPTURE TREASURES FROM TREASURE HUNTERS. WE WORK PRETTY HARD. IT MIGHT LOOK LIKE...
WE'RE JUST GOOFING AROUND,
BUT WE'RE NOT!
DO YOU UNDERSTAND WHAT I'VE SAID SO FAR?
YES.
SO, IN OTHER WORDS...

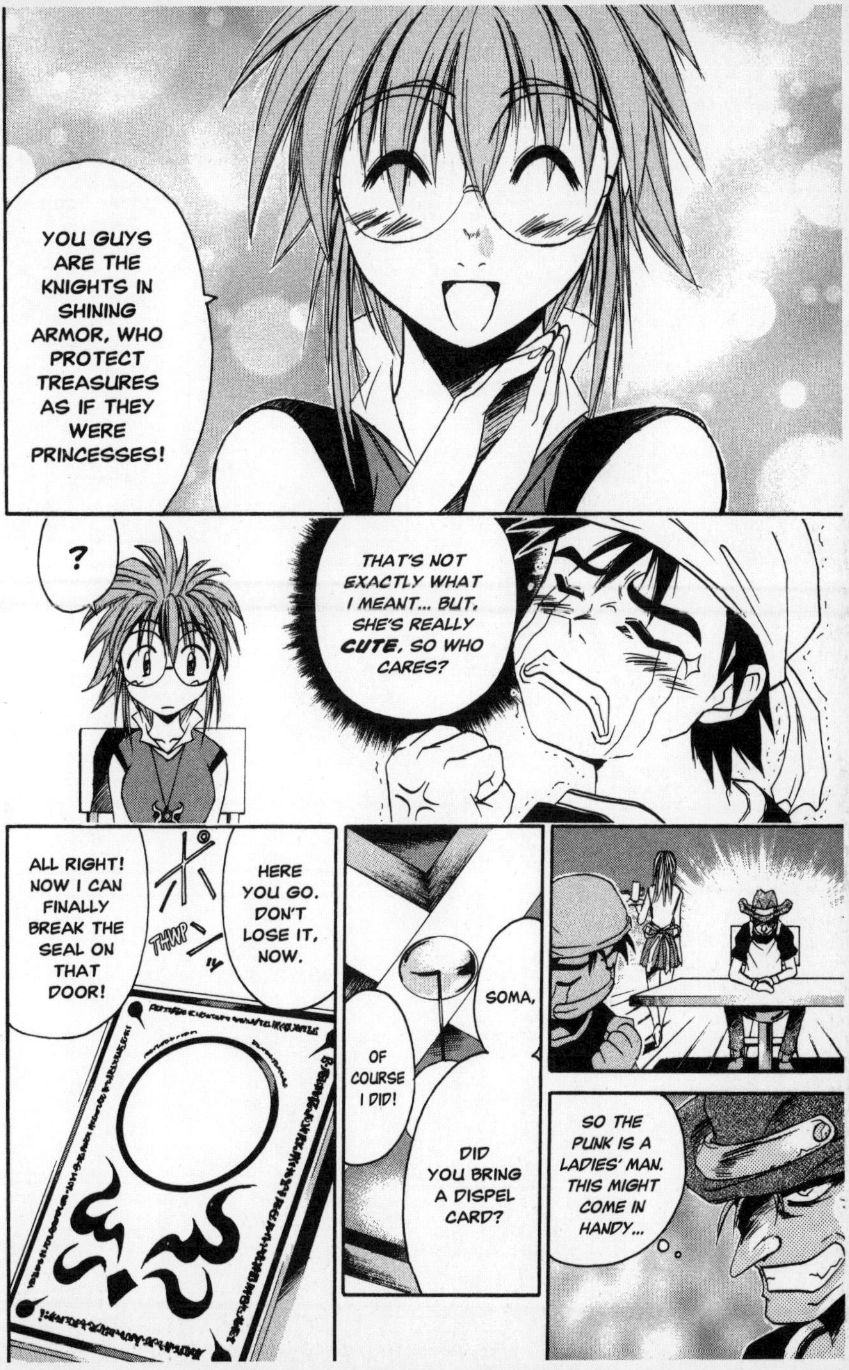
YOU GUYS ARE THE KNIGHTS IN SHINING ARMOR, WHO PROTECT TREASURES AS IF THEY WERE PRINCESSES!
THAT'S NOT EXACTLY WHAT I MEANT... BUT, SHE'S REALLY CUTE, SO WHO CARES?
?
SO THE PUNK IS A LADIES' MAN. THIS MIGHT COME IN HANDY...
SOMA,
DID YOU BRING A DISPEL CARD?
OF COURSE I DID!
HERE YOU GO. DON'T LOSE IT, NOW.
THWP
ALL RIGHT! NOW I CAN FINALLY BREAK THE SEAL ON THAT DOOR!

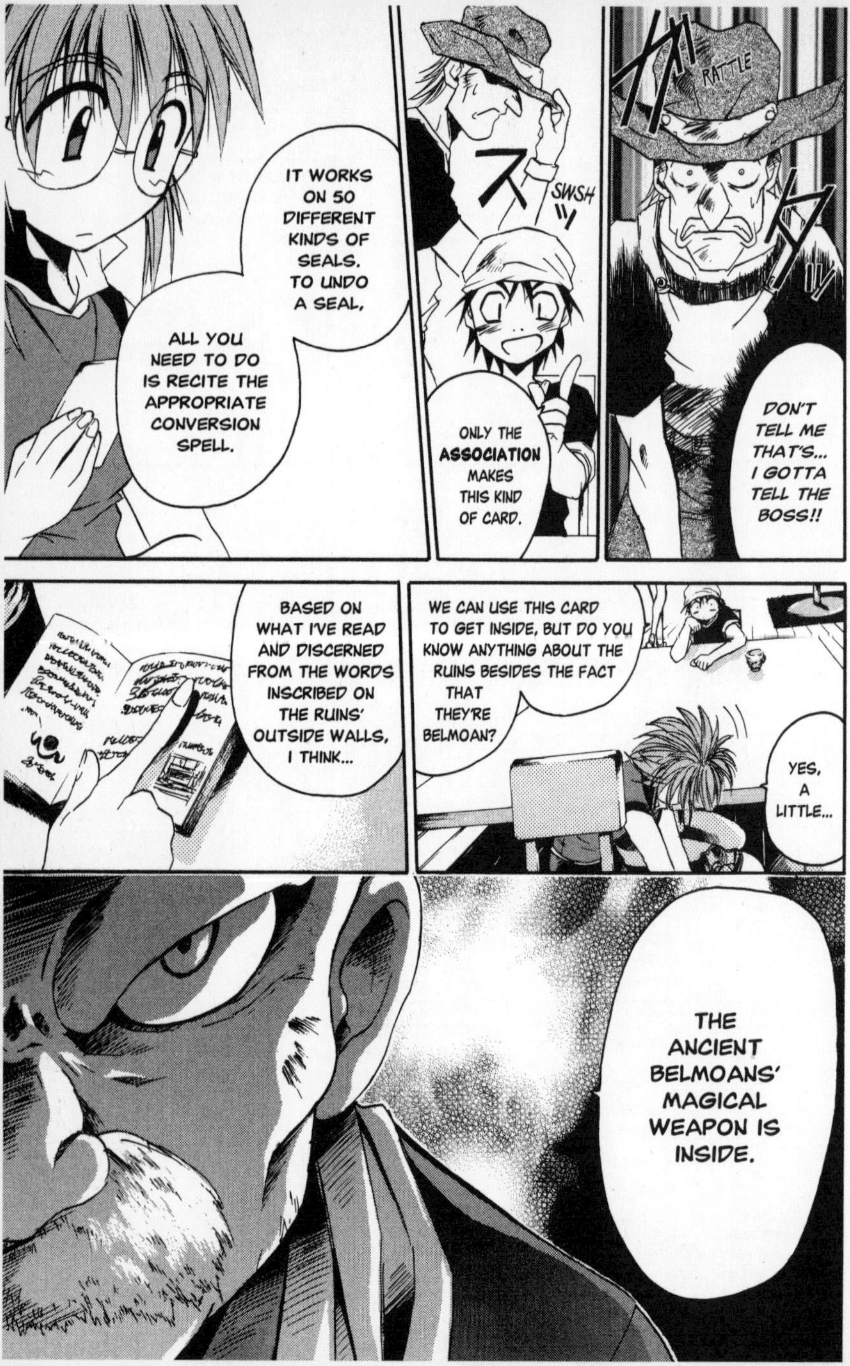
IT WORKS ON 50 DIFFERENT KINDS OF SEALS. TO UNDO A SEAL,
ALL YOU NEED TO DO IS RECITE THE APPROPRIATE CONVERSION SPELL.
SWSH
ONLY THE **ASSOCIATION** MAKES THIS KIND OF CARD.
RATTLE
DON'T TELL ME THAT'S... I GOTTA TELL THE BOSS!!
BASED ON WHAT I'VE READ AND DISCERNED FROM THE WORDS INSCRIBED ON THE RUINS' OUTSIDE WALLS, I THINK...
WE CAN USE THIS CARD TO GET INSIDE, BUT DO YOU KNOW ANYTHING ABOUT THE RUINS BESIDES THE FACT THAT THEY'RE BELMOAN?
YES, A LITTLE...
THE ANCIENT BELMOANS' MAGICAL WEAPON IS INSIDE.

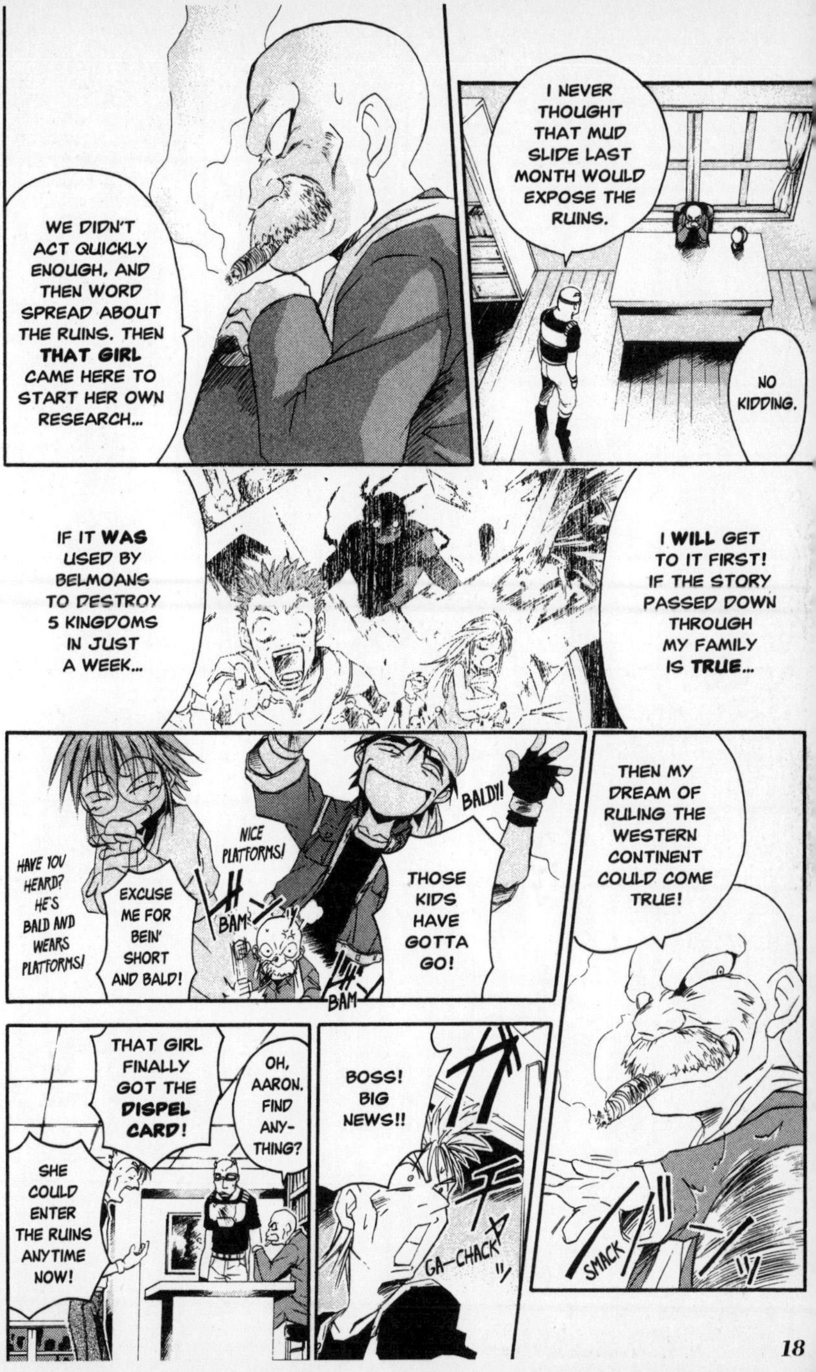
I NEVER THOUGHT THAT MUD SLIDE LAST MONTH WOULD EXPOSE THE RUINS.
NO KIDDING.
WE DIDN'T ACT QUICKLY ENOUGH, AND THEN WORD SPREAD ABOUT THE RUINS. THEN THAT GIRL CAME HERE TO START HER OWN RESEARCH...
I WILL GET TO IT FIRST! IF THE STORY PASSED DOWN THROUGH MY FAMILY IS TRUE...
IF IT WAS USED BY BELMOANS TO DESTROY 5 KINGDOMS IN JUST A WEEK...
THEN MY DREAM OF RULING THE WESTERN CONTINENT COULD COME TRUE!
THOSE KIDS HAVE GOTTA GO!
BALDY!
NICE PLATFORMS!
BAM
BAM
EXCUSE ME FOR BEIN' SHORT AND BALD!
HAVE YOU HEARD? HE'S BALD AND WEARS PLATFORMS!
SMACK
GA-CHACK
BOSS! BIG NEWS!!
OH, AARON. FIND ANYTHING?
THAT GIRL FINALLY GOT THE DISPEL CARD!
SHE COULD ENTER THE RUINS ANYTIME NOW!

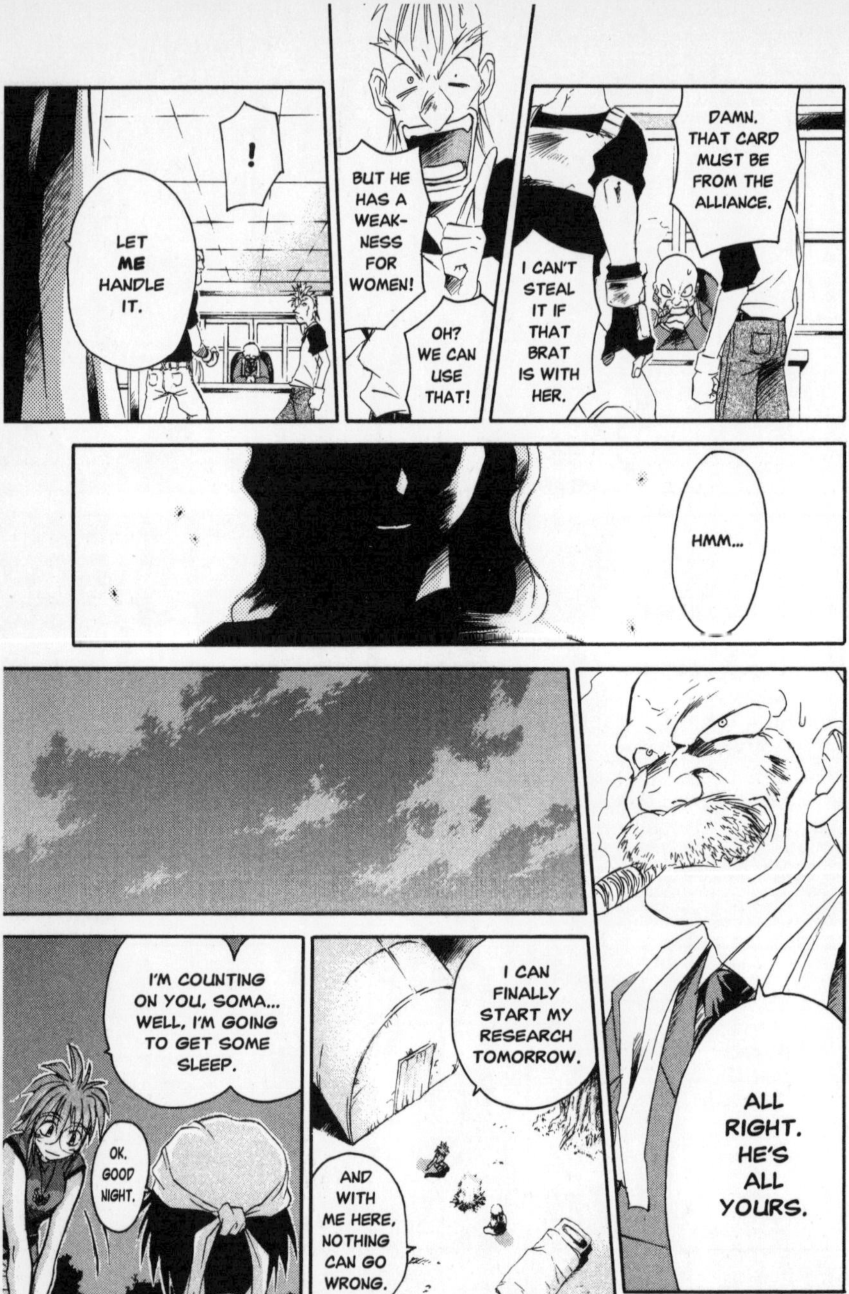
DAMN. THAT CARD MUST BE FROM THE ALLIANCE.
I CAN'T STEAL IT IF THAT BRAT IS WITH HER.
BUT HE HAS A WEAKNESS FOR WOMEN!
OH? WE CAN USE THAT!
!
LET ME HANDLE IT.
HMM...
ALL RIGHT. HE'S ALL YOURS.
I CAN FINALLY START MY RESEARCH TOMORROW.
AND WITH ME HERE, NOTHING CAN GO WRONG.
I'M COUNTING ON YOU, SOMA... WELL, I'M GOING TO GET SOME SLEEP.
OK. GOOD NIGHT.

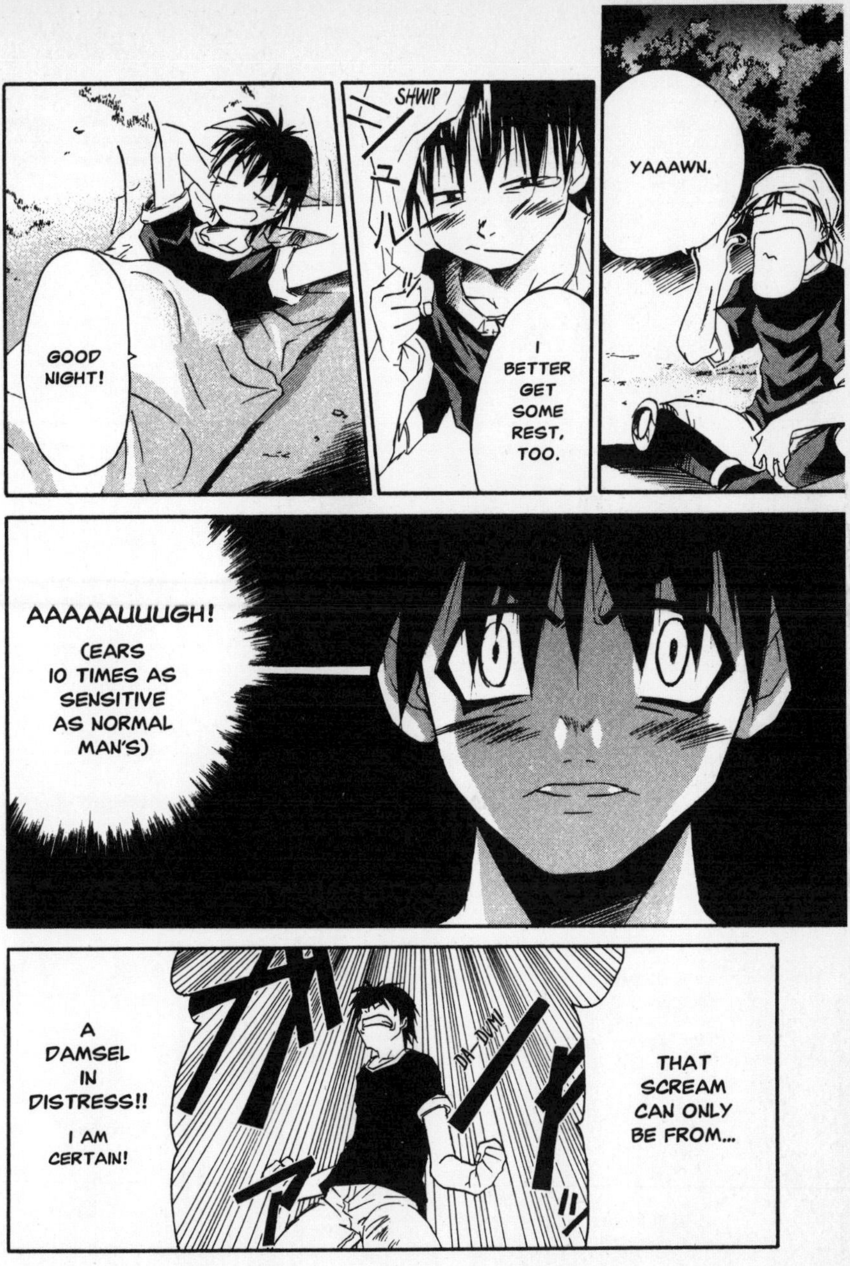
YAAAWN.
SHWIP
I BETTER GET SOME REST, TOO.
GOOD NIGHT!
AAAAAUUUGH!
(EARS 10 TIMES AS SENSITIVE AS NORMAL MAN'S)
THAT SCREAM CAN ONLY BE FROM...
DA-DUM!
A DAMSEL IN DISTRESS!!
I AM CERTAIN!

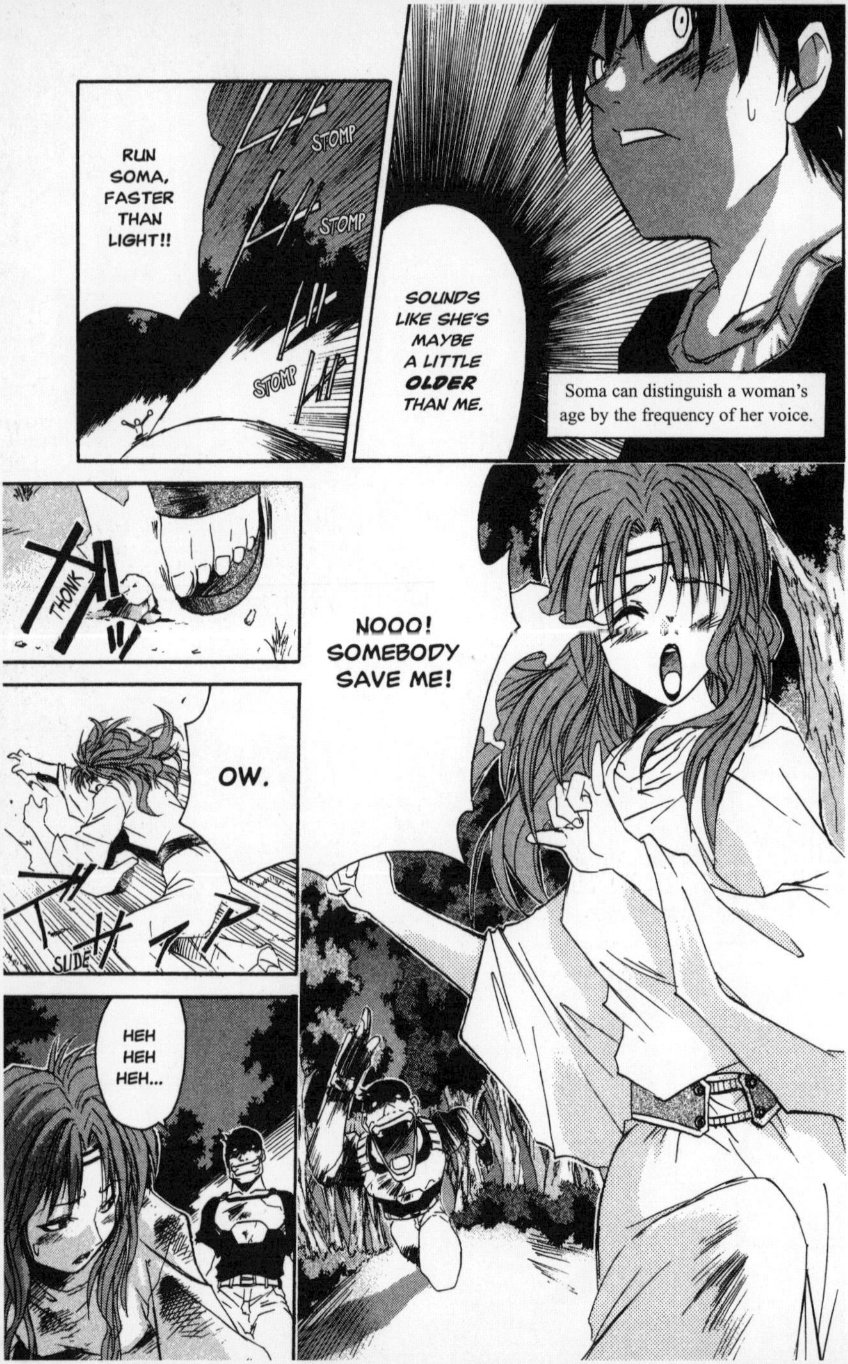
Soma can distinguish a woman's age by the frequency of her voice.
SOUNDS LIKE SHE'S MAYBE A LITTLE OLDER THAN ME.
RUN SOMA, FASTER THAN LIGHT!!
STOMP
STOMP
STOMP
NOOO! SOMEBODY SAVE ME!
THONK
OW.
SLIDE
HEH HEH HEH...

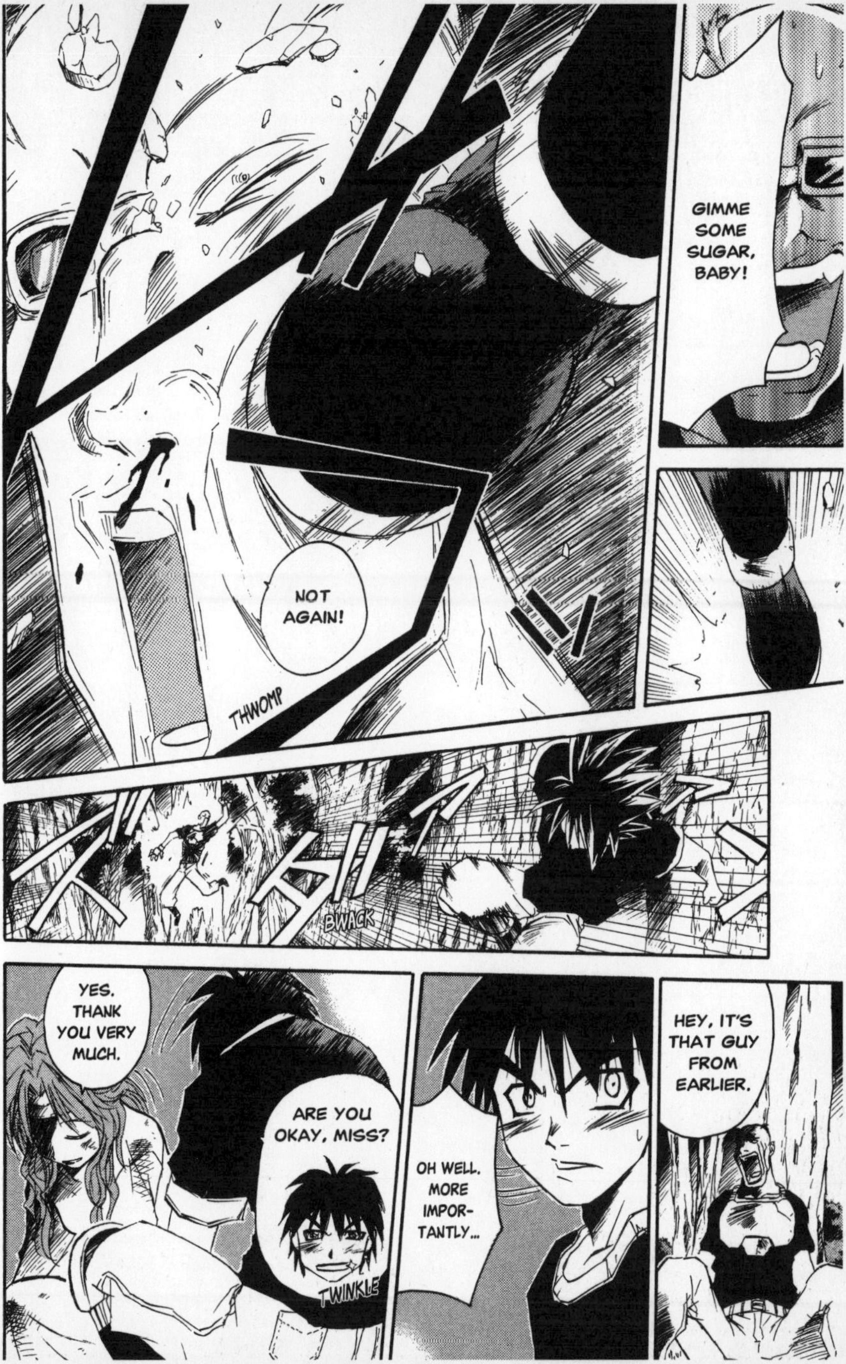
GIMME SOME SUGAR, BABY!
NOT AGAIN!
THWOMP
BWACK
HEY, IT'S THAT GUY FROM EARLIER.
OH WELL. MORE IMPOR-TANTLY...
YES. THANK YOU VERY MUCH.
ARE YOU OKAY, MISS?
TWINKLE

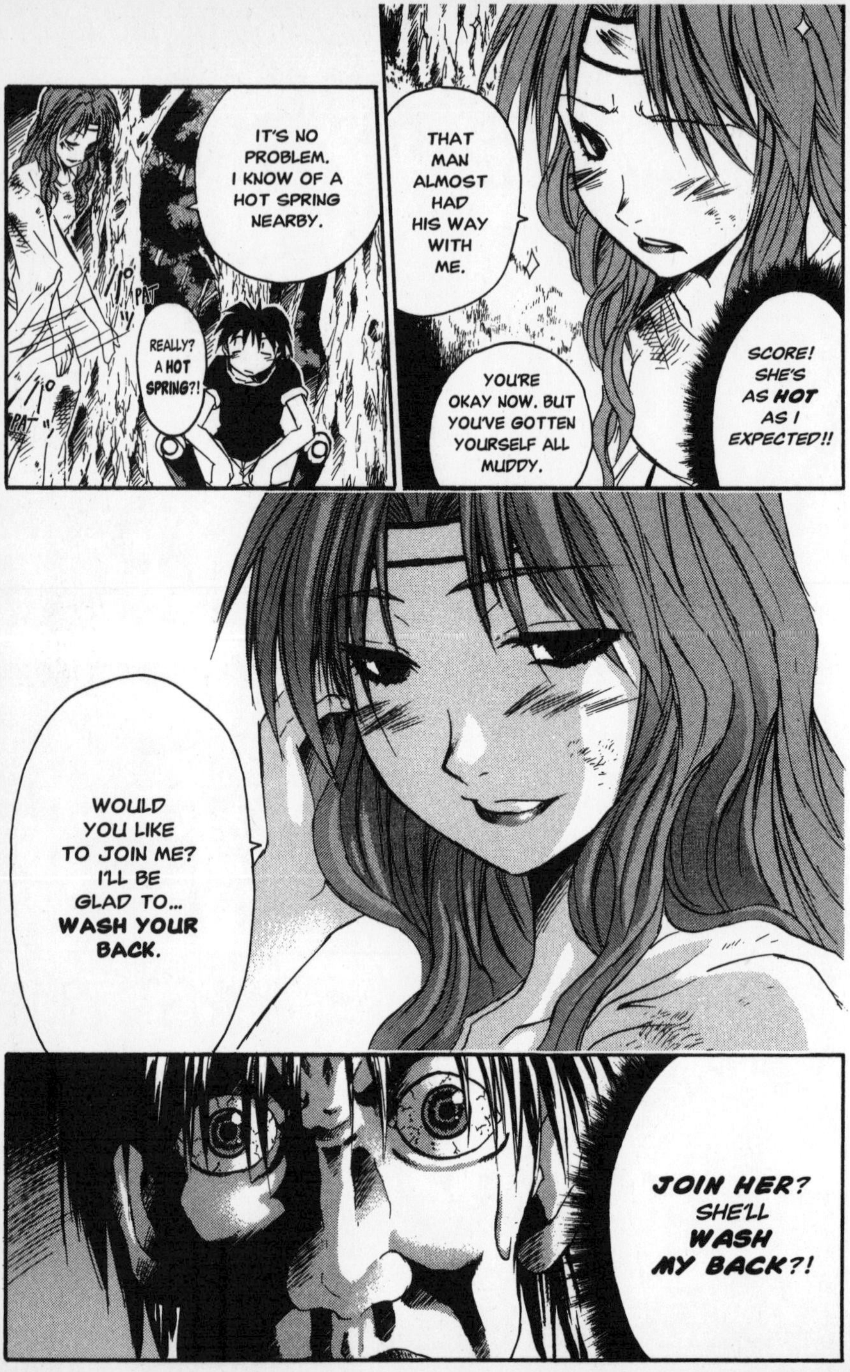
THAT MAN ALMOST HAD HIS WAY WITH ME.
YOU'RE OKAY NOW. BUT YOU'VE GOTTEN YOURSELF ALL MUDDY.
SCORE! SHE'S AS HOT AS I EXPECTED!!
IT'S NO PROBLEM. I KNOW OF A HOT SPRING NEARBY.
REALLY? A HOT SPRING?!
PAT
PAT
WOULD YOU LIKE TO JOIN ME? I'LL BE GLAD TO... WASH YOUR BACK.
JOIN HER? SHE'LL WASH MY BACK?!

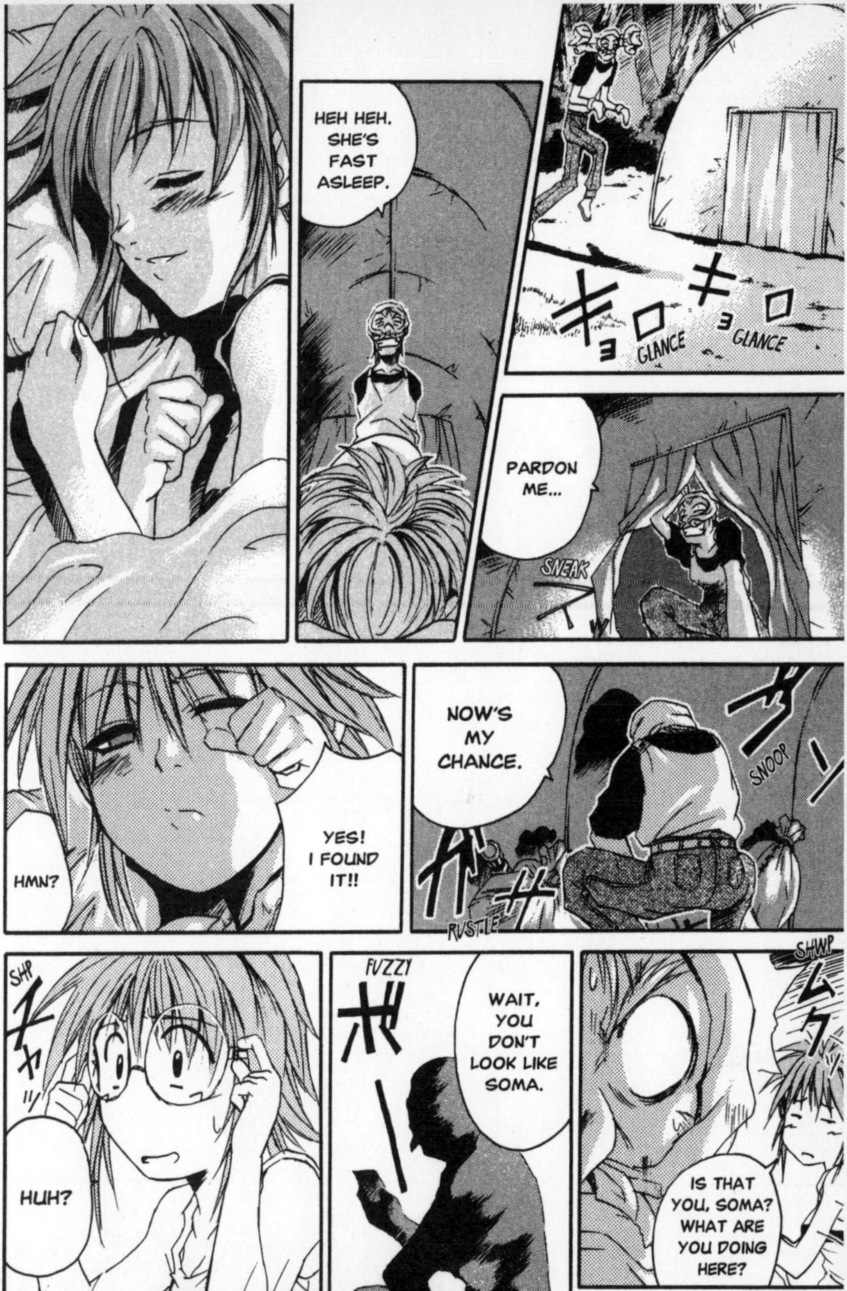

キョロ GLANCE
キョロ GLANCE
HEH HEH. SHE'S FAST ASLEEP.
PARDON ME...
SNEAK
NOW'S MY CHANCE.
SNOOP
RUSTLE
YES! I FOUND IT!!
HMN?
SHWP
IS THAT YOU, SOMA? WHAT ARE YOU DOING HERE?
FUZZY
WAIT, YOU DON'T LOOK LIKE SOMA.
SHP
HUH?

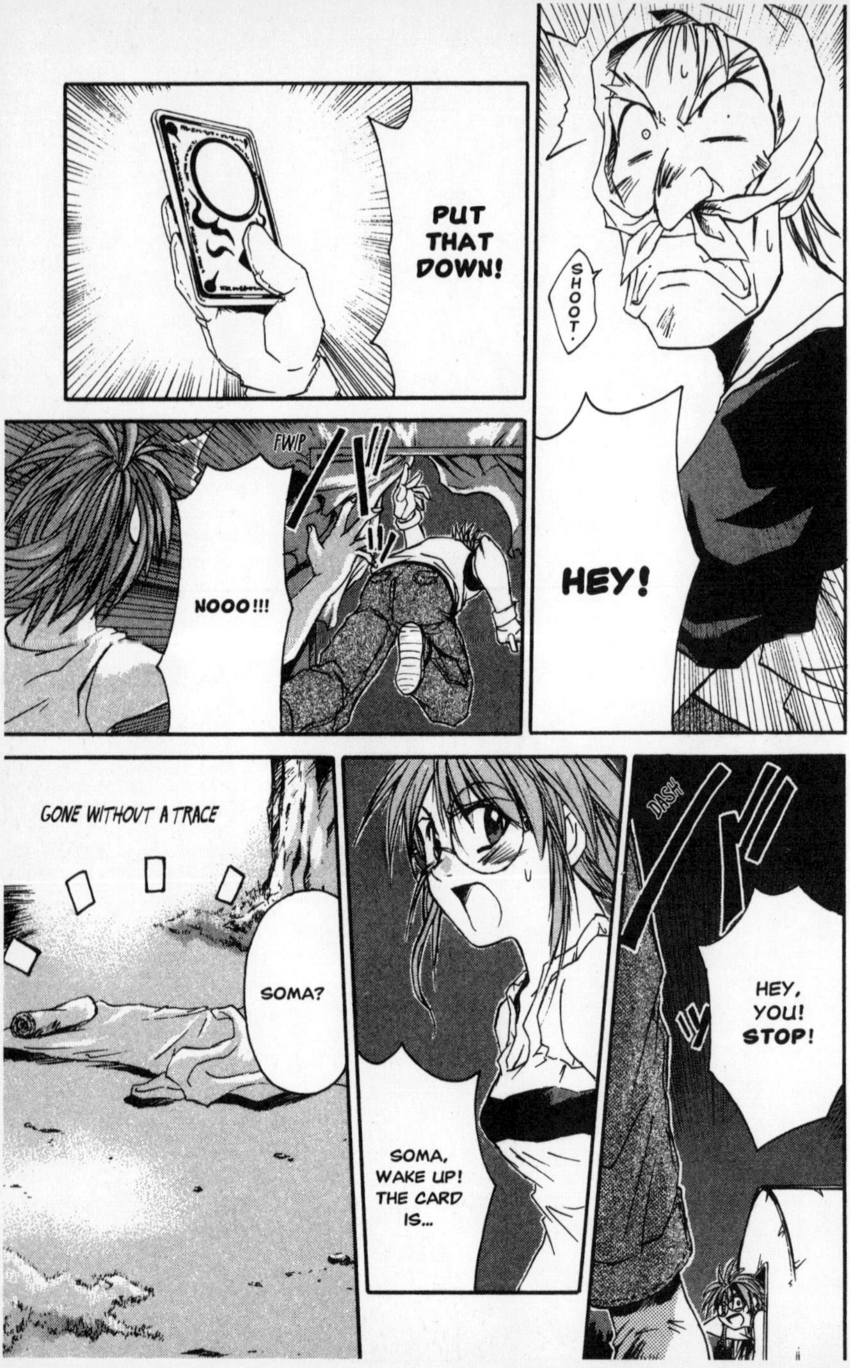
SHOOT.
HEY!
PUT THAT DOWN!
FWIP
NOOO!!!
DASH
HEY, YOU! STOP!
SOMA, WAKE UP! THE CARD IS...
GONE WITHOUT A TRACE
SOMA?

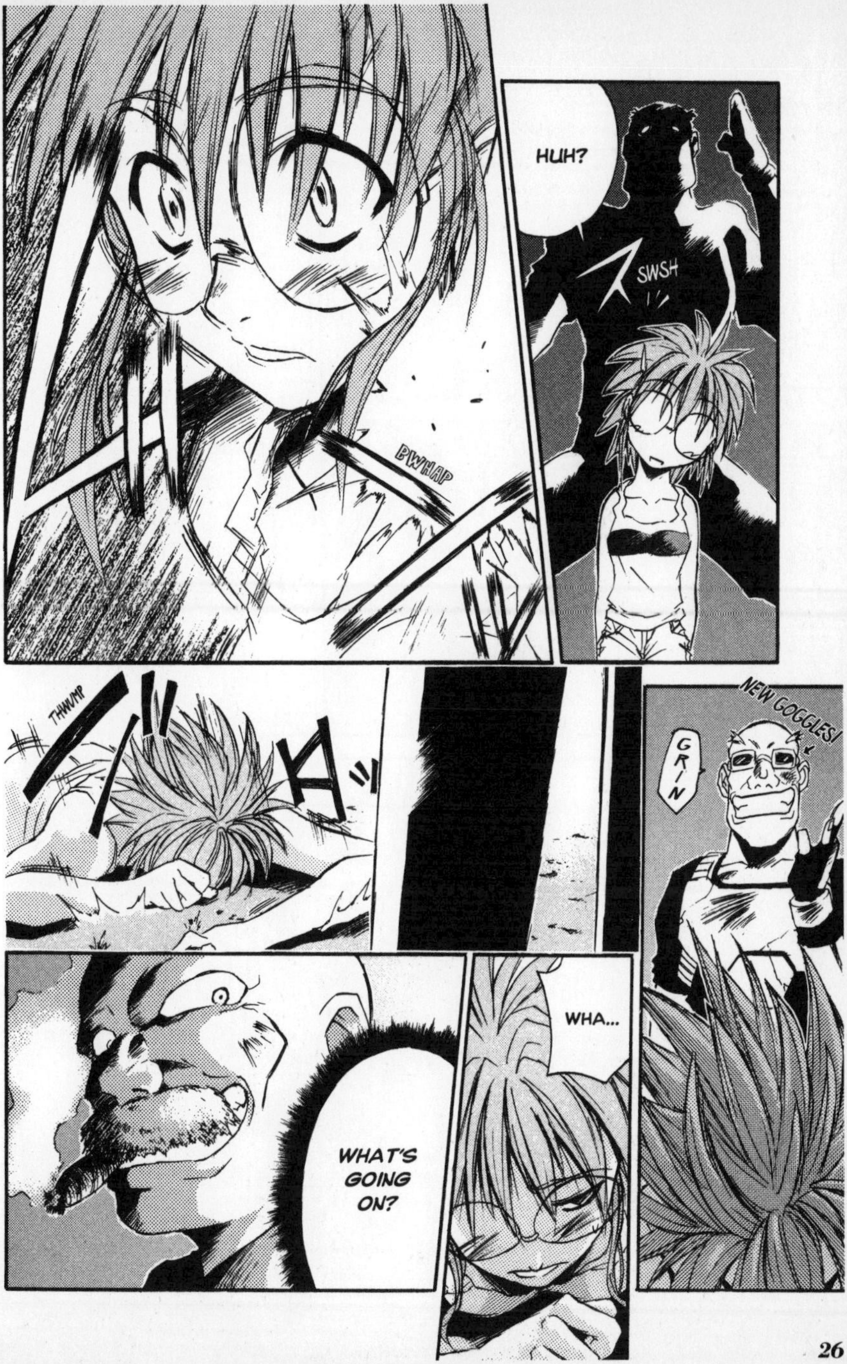
HUH?
SWSH
BWHAP
THWUMP
NEW GOGGLES!
GRIN
WHA...
WHAT'S GOING ON?

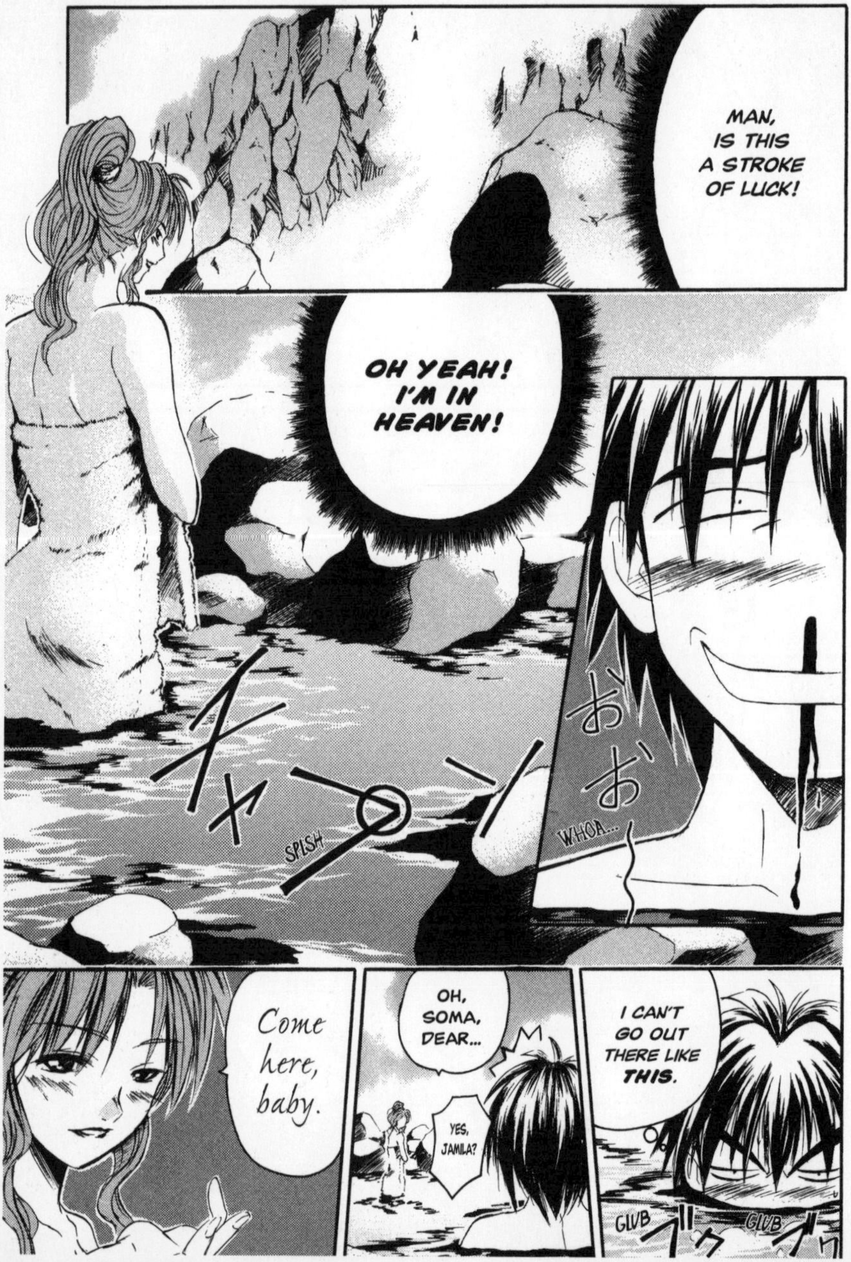
MAN, IS THIS A STROKE OF LUCK!
OH YEAH! I'M IN HEAVEN!
おお
WHOA...
SPISH
I CAN'T GO OUT THERE LIKE **THIS.**
GLUB
GLUB
OH, SOMA, DEAR...
YES, JAMILA?
Come here, baby.

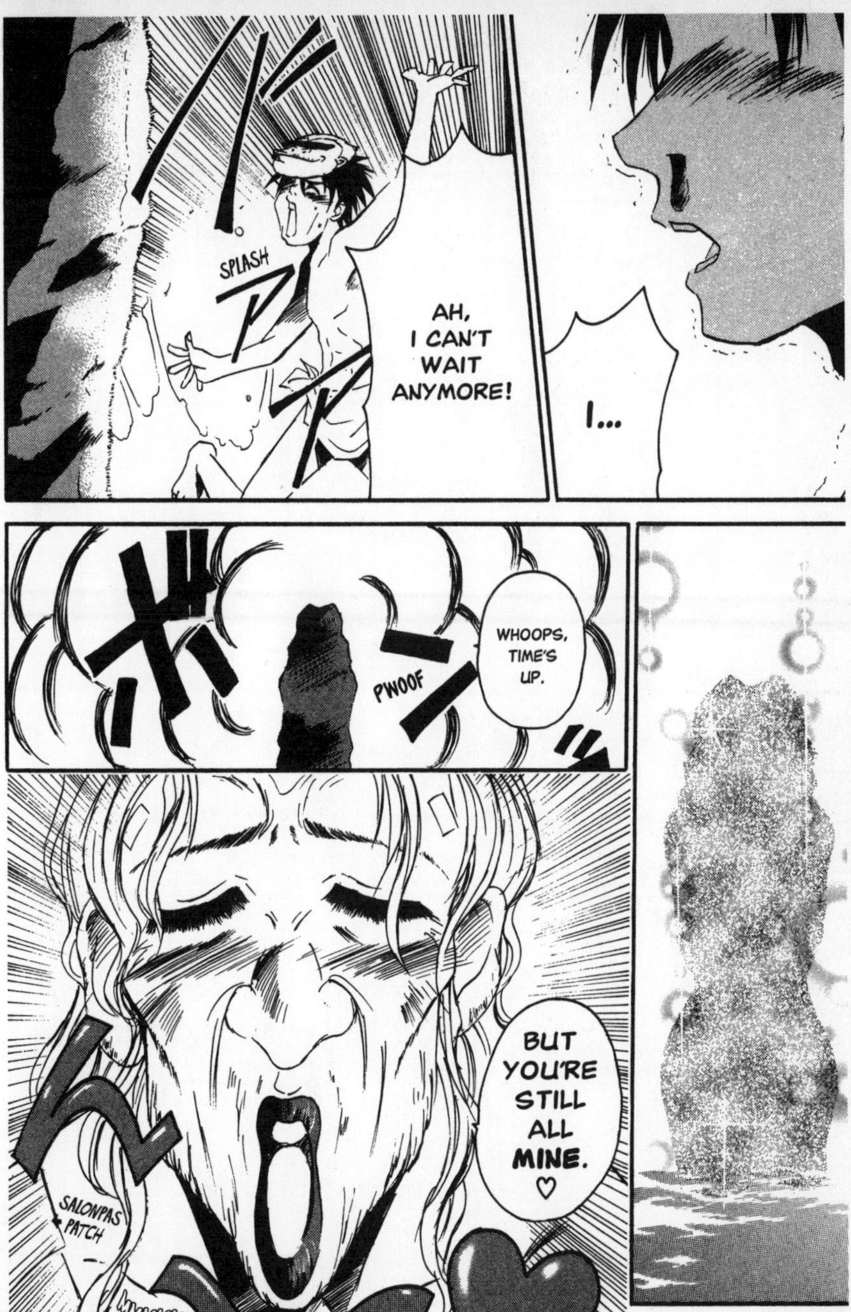
I...
AH, I CAN'T WAIT ANYMORE!
SPLASH
WHOOPS, TIME'S UP.
PWOOF
BUT YOU'RE STILL ALL MINE. ♡
SALONPAS PATCH
MMMMMNN

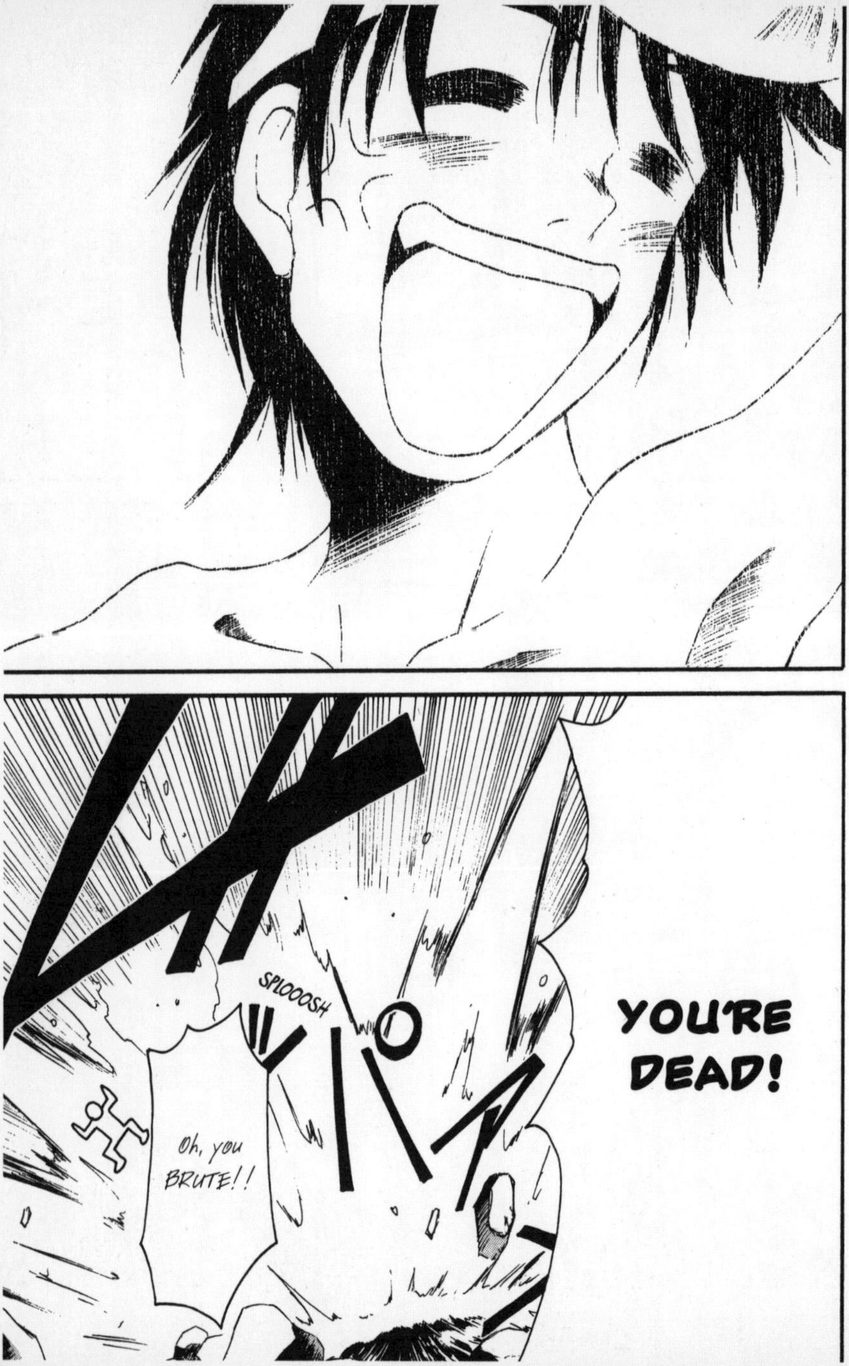
YOU'RE DEAD!
SPLOOOSH
Oh, you BRUTE!!

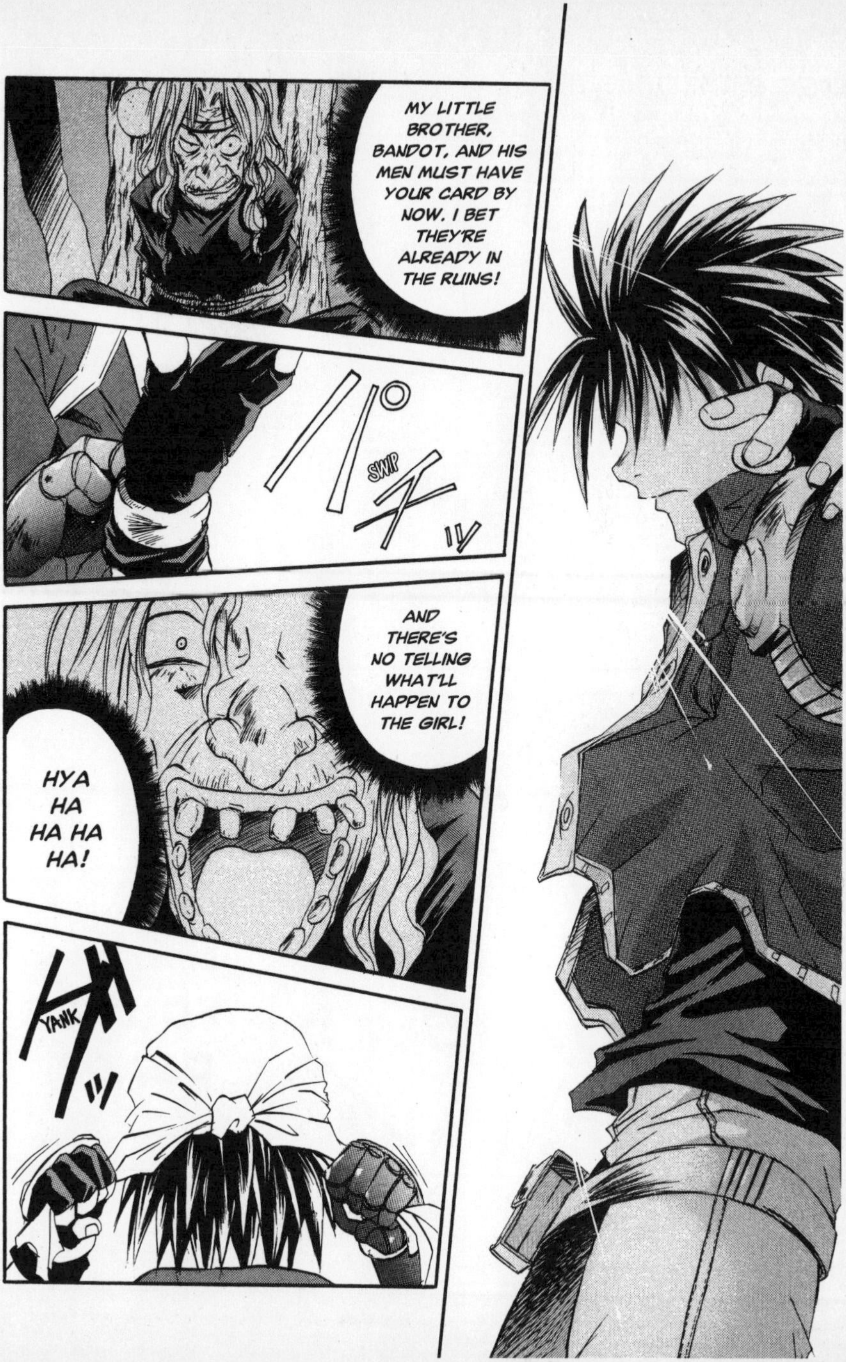

MY LITTLE BROTHER, BANDOT, AND HIS MEN MUST HAVE YOUR CARD BY NOW. I BET THEY'RE ALREADY IN THE RUINS!
SWIP
AND THERE'S NO TELLING WHAT'LL HAPPEN TO THE GIRL!
HYA HA HA HA HA!
YANK

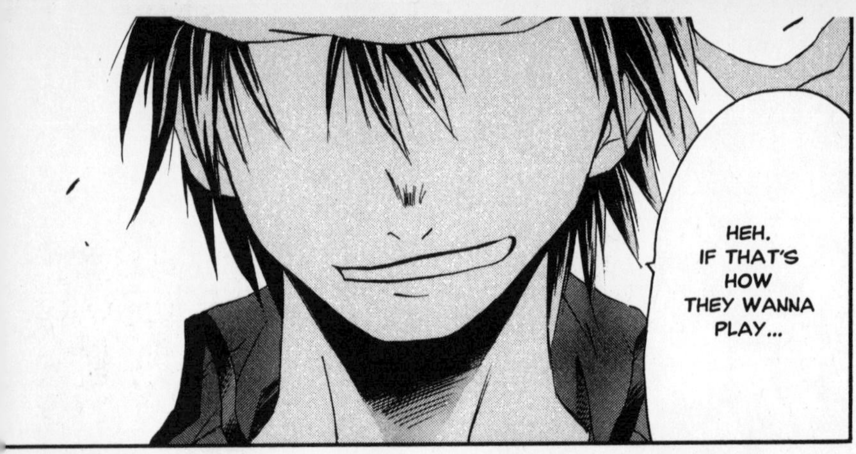
HEH.
IF THAT'S HOW THEY WANNA PLAY...

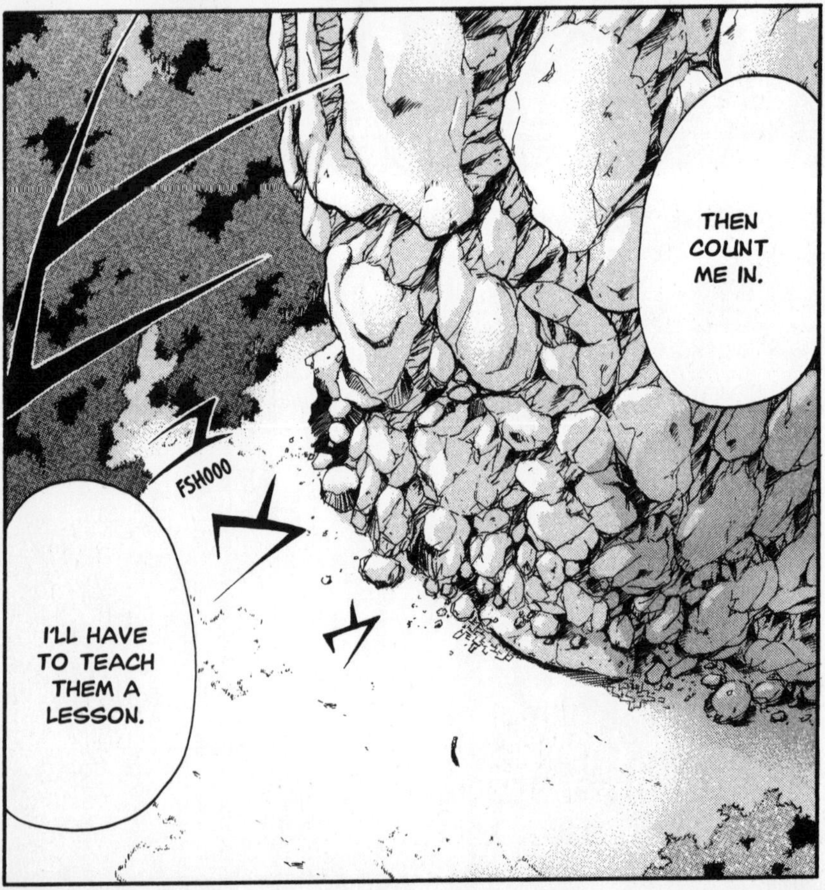
THEN COUNT ME IN.
FSHOOO
I'LL HAVE TO TEACH THEM A LESSON.

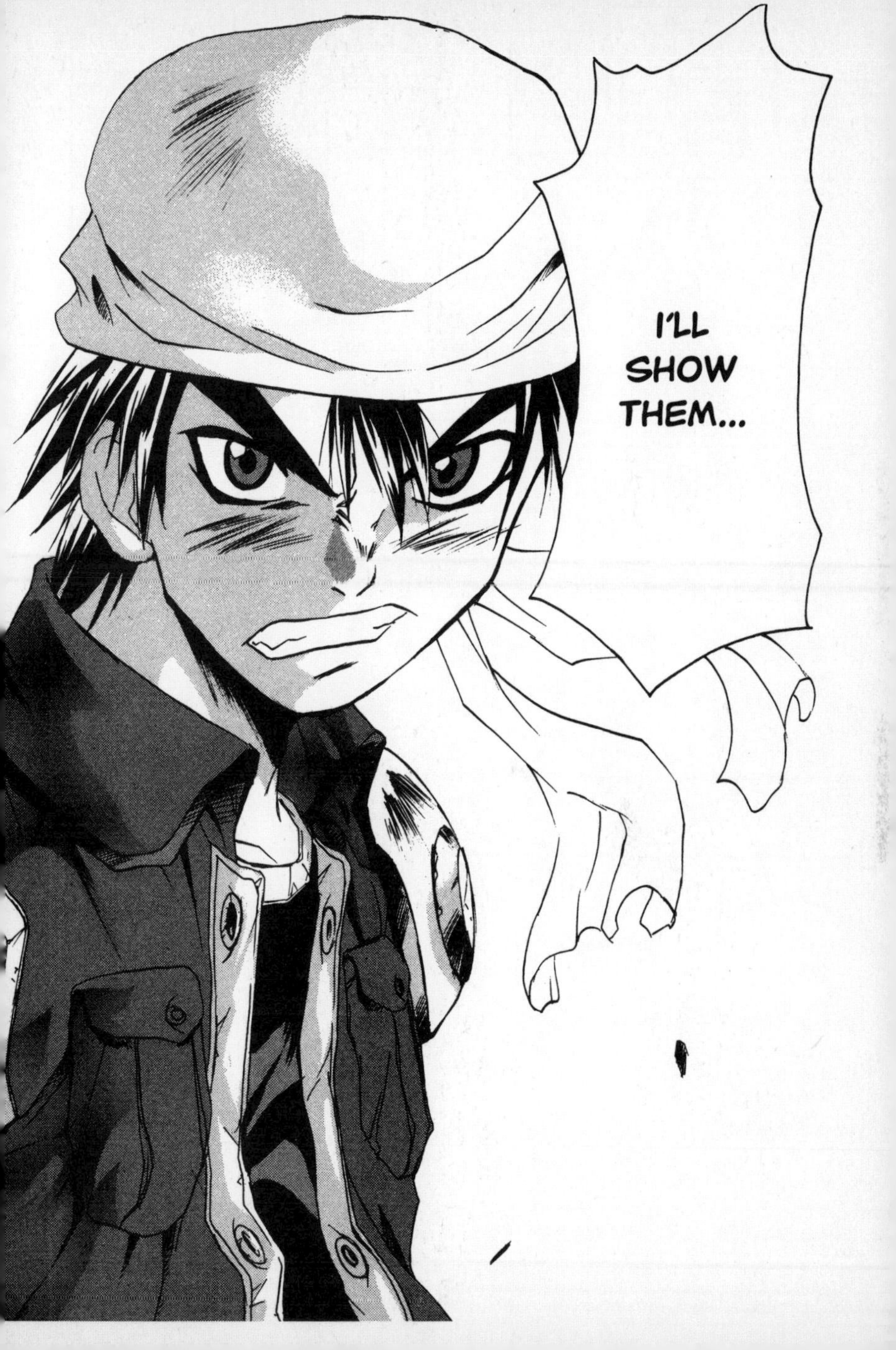
I'LL SHOW THEM...

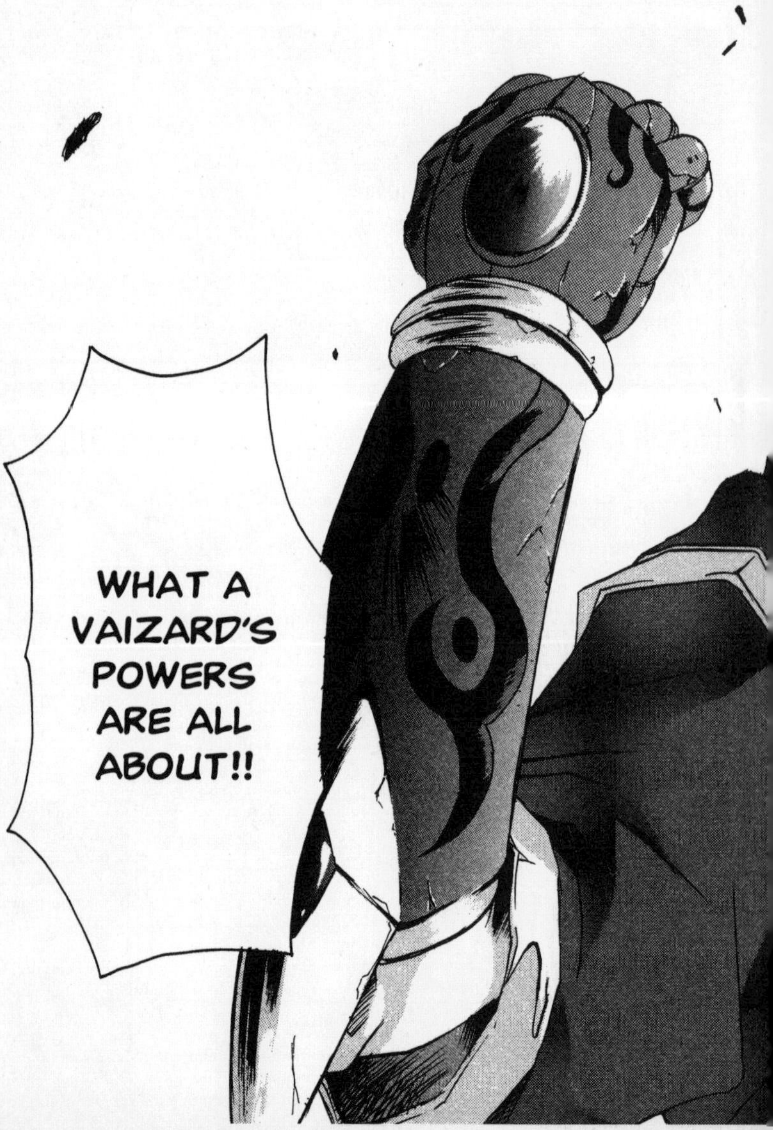
WHAT A VAIZARD'S POWERS ARE ALL ABOUT!!

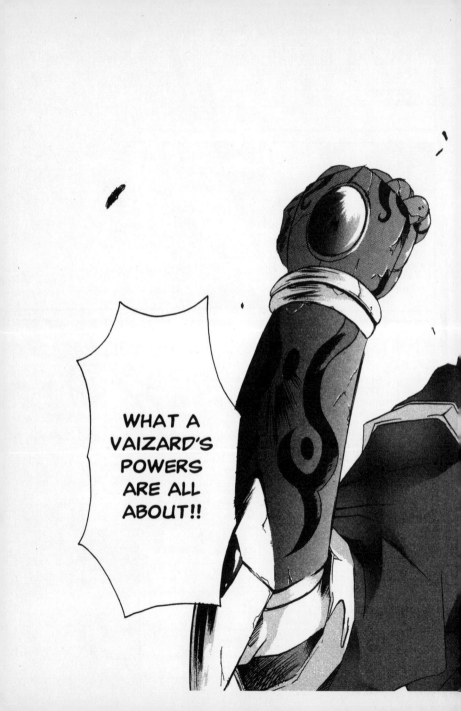

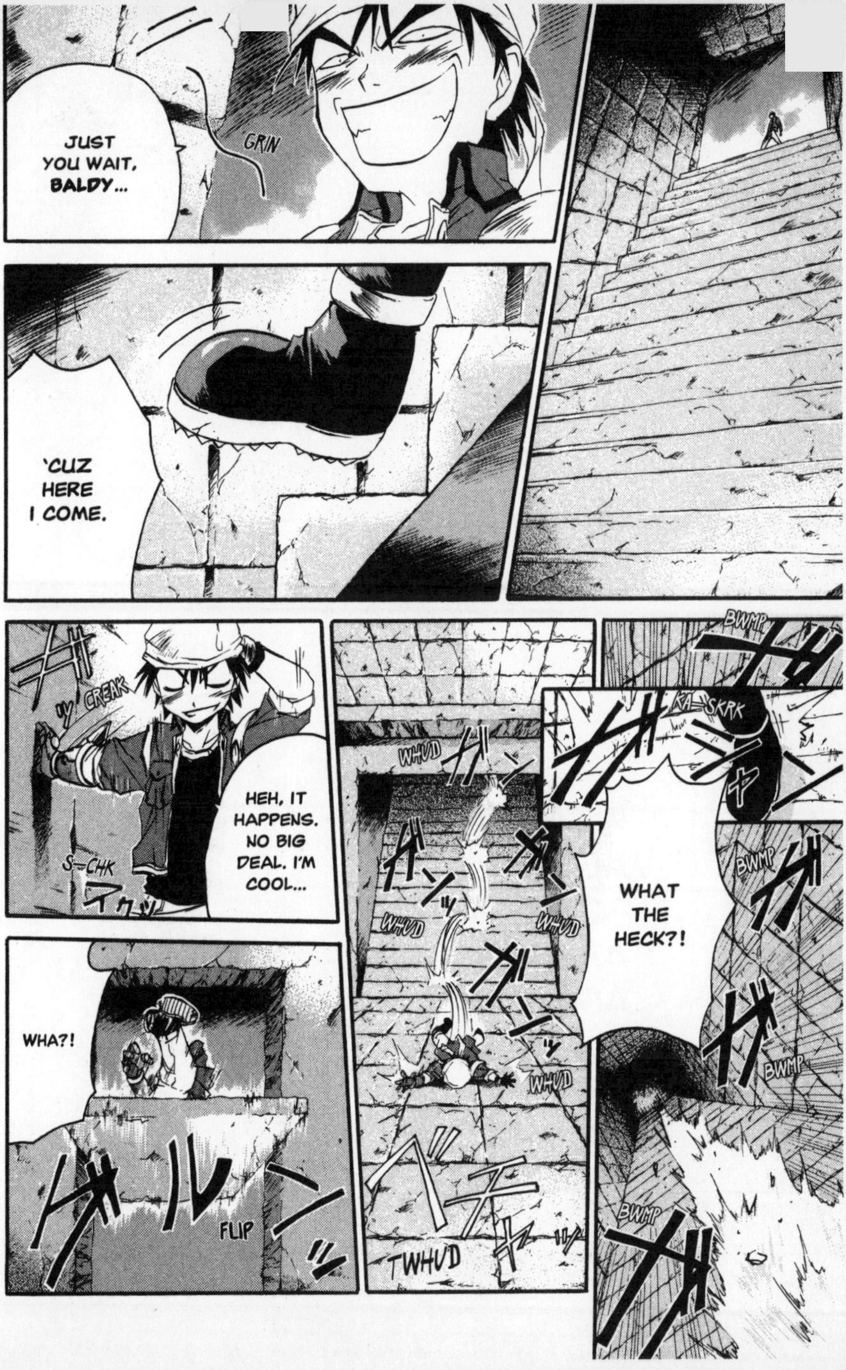

JUST YOU WAIT, BALDY...
GRIN
'CUZ HERE I COME.
BWMP
KA-SKRK
WHAT THE HECK?!
BWMP
BWMP
BWMP
WHUD
WHUD
WHUD
WHUD
TWHUD
CREAK
HEH, IT HAPPENS. NO BIG DEAL. I'M COOL...
S-CHK
WHA?!
FLIP

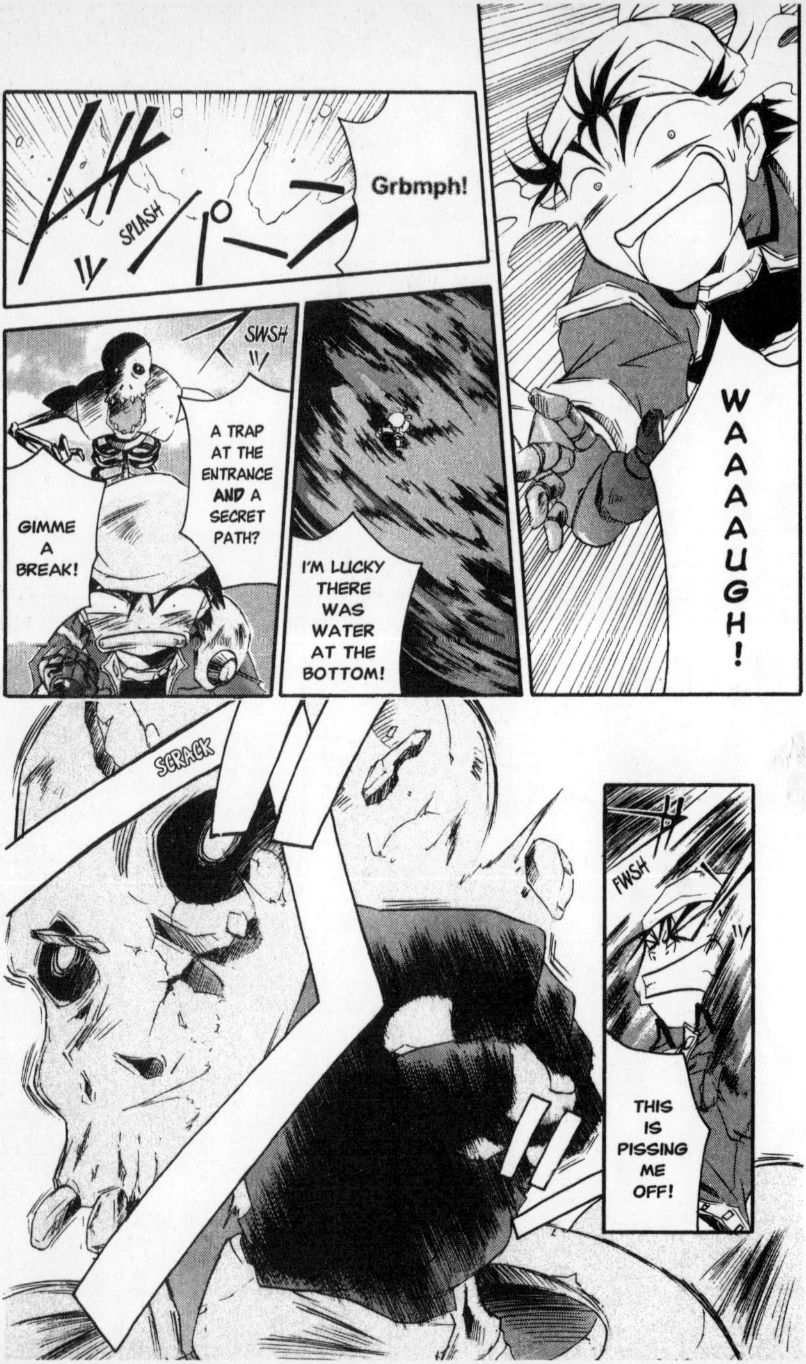
WAAAAAUGH!
SPLASH
Grbmph!
I'M LUCKY THERE WAS WATER AT THE BOTTOM!
SWSH
A TRAP AT THE ENTRANCE AND A SECRET PATH?
GIMME A BREAK!
FWSH
THIS IS PISSING ME OFF!
SCRACK

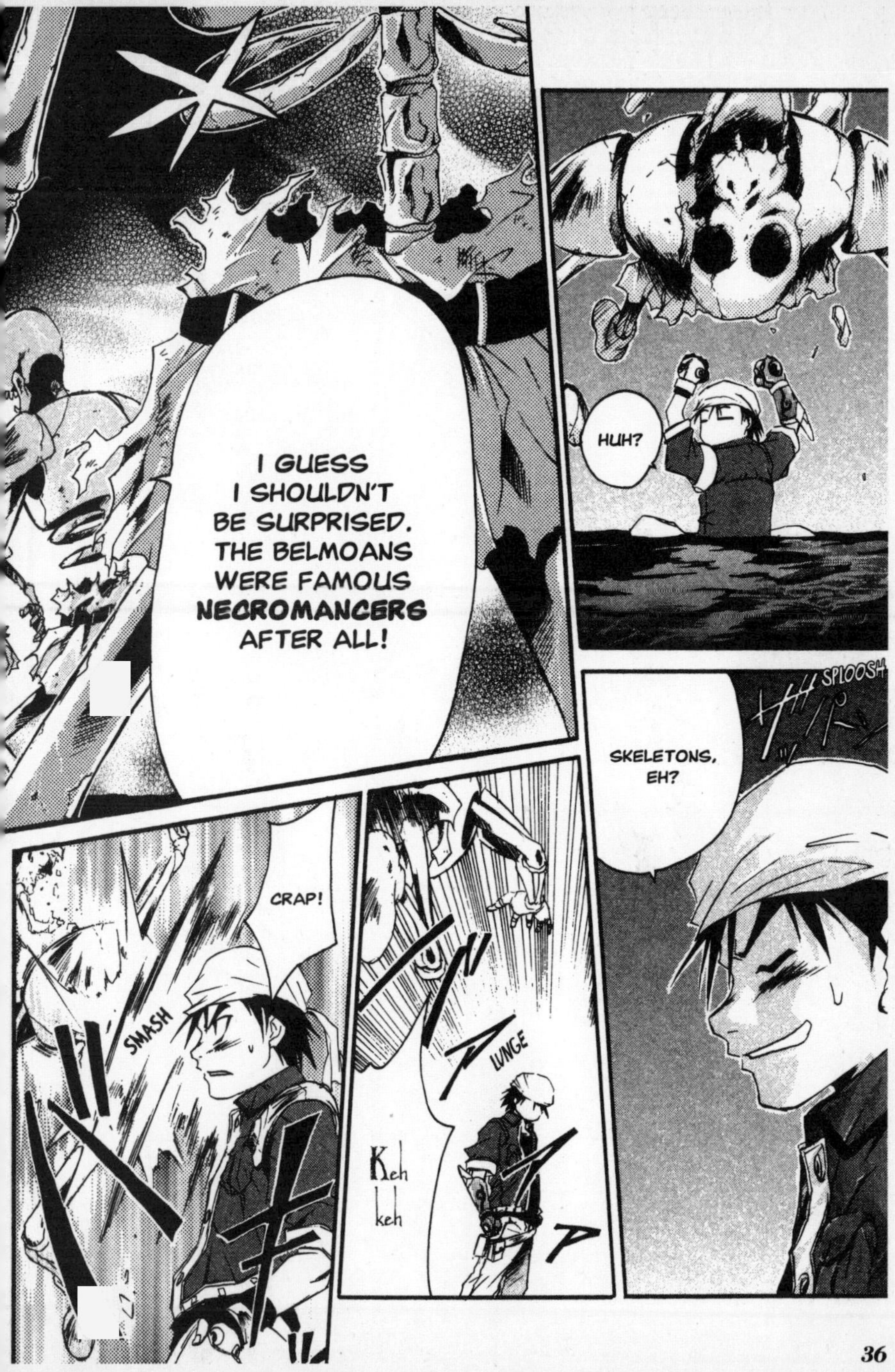

I GUESS I SHOULDN'T BE SURPRISED. THE BELMOANS WERE FAMOUS NECROMANCERS AFTER ALL!
HUH?
SPLOOSH
SKELETONS, EH?
LUNGE
Keh keh
CRAP!
SMASH

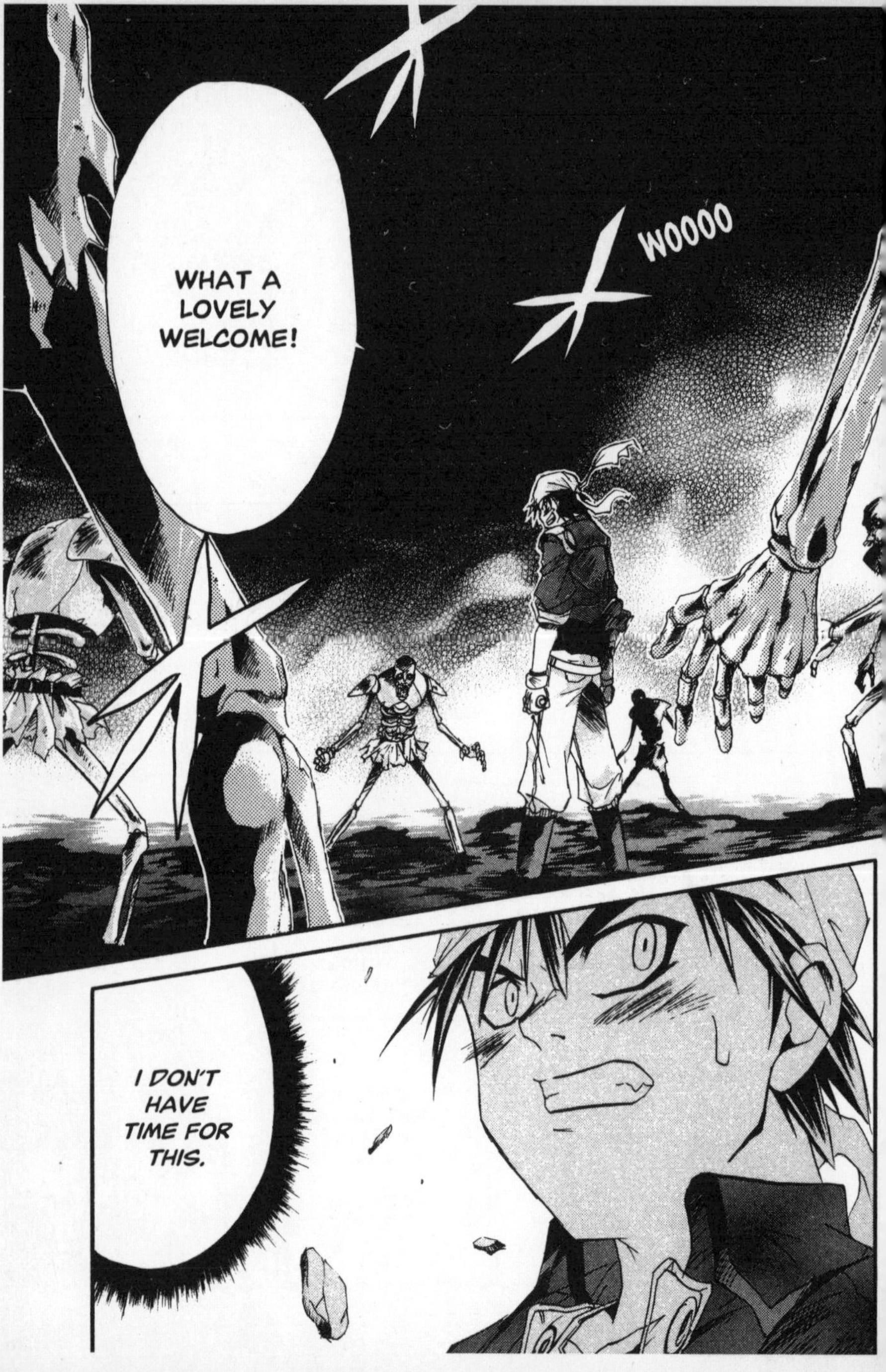
WOOOO
WHAT A LOVELY WELCOME!
I DON'T HAVE TIME FOR THIS.

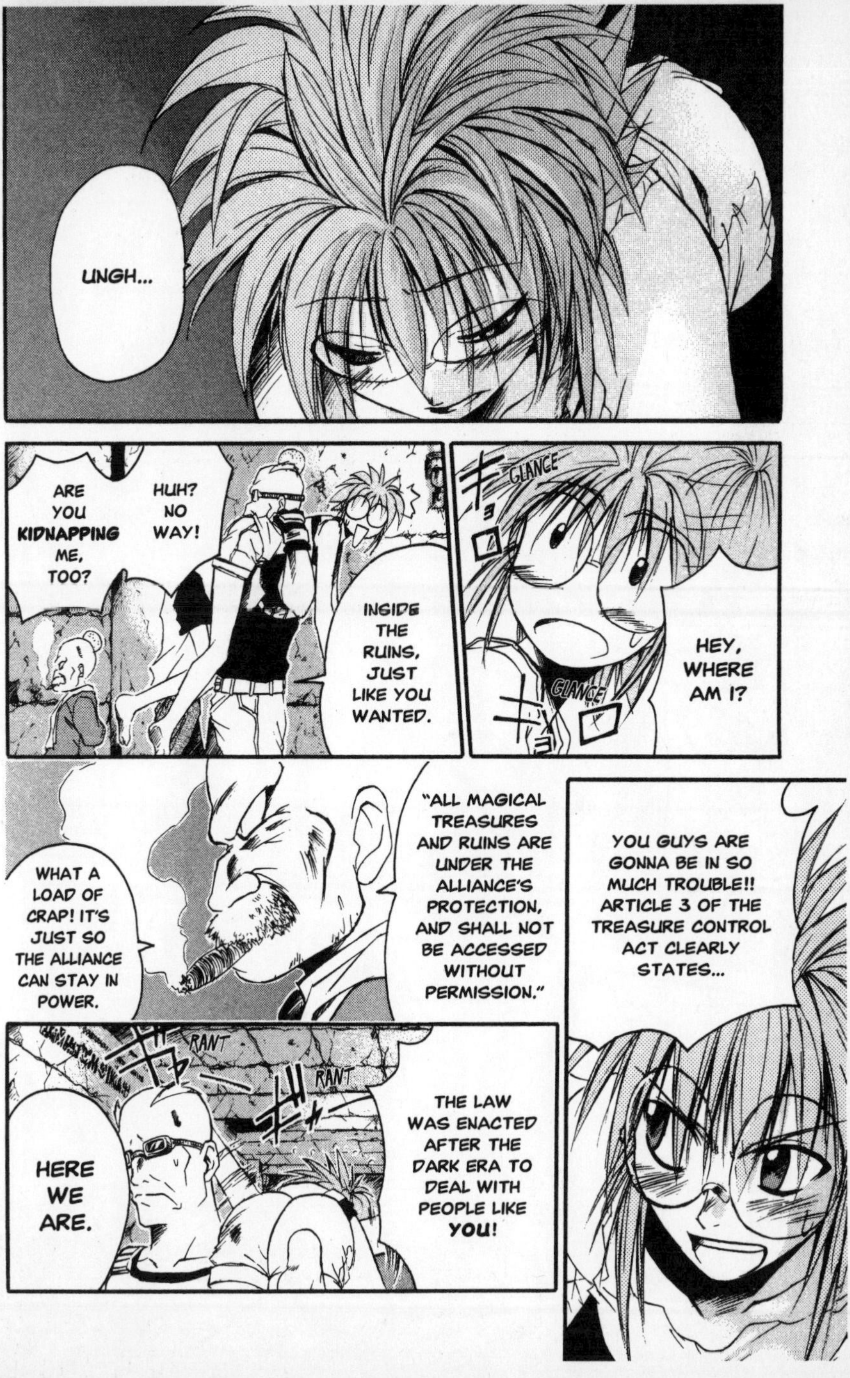
UNGH...
GLANCE
GLANCE
HEY, WHERE AM I?
INSIDE THE RUINS, JUST LIKE YOU WANTED.
ARE YOU KIDNAPPING ME, TOO?
HUH? NO WAY!
YOU GUYS ARE GONNA BE IN SO MUCH TROUBLE!! ARTICLE 3 OF THE TREASURE CONTROL ACT CLEARLY STATES...
"ALL MAGICAL TREASURES AND RUINS ARE UNDER THE ALLIANCE'S PROTECTION, AND SHALL NOT BE ACCESSED WITHOUT PERMISSION."
WHAT A LOAD OF CRAP! IT'S JUST SO THE ALLIANCE CAN STAY IN POWER.
RANT
RANT
THE LAW WAS ENACTED AFTER THE DARK ERA TO DEAL WITH PEOPLE LIKE YOU!
HERE WE ARE.

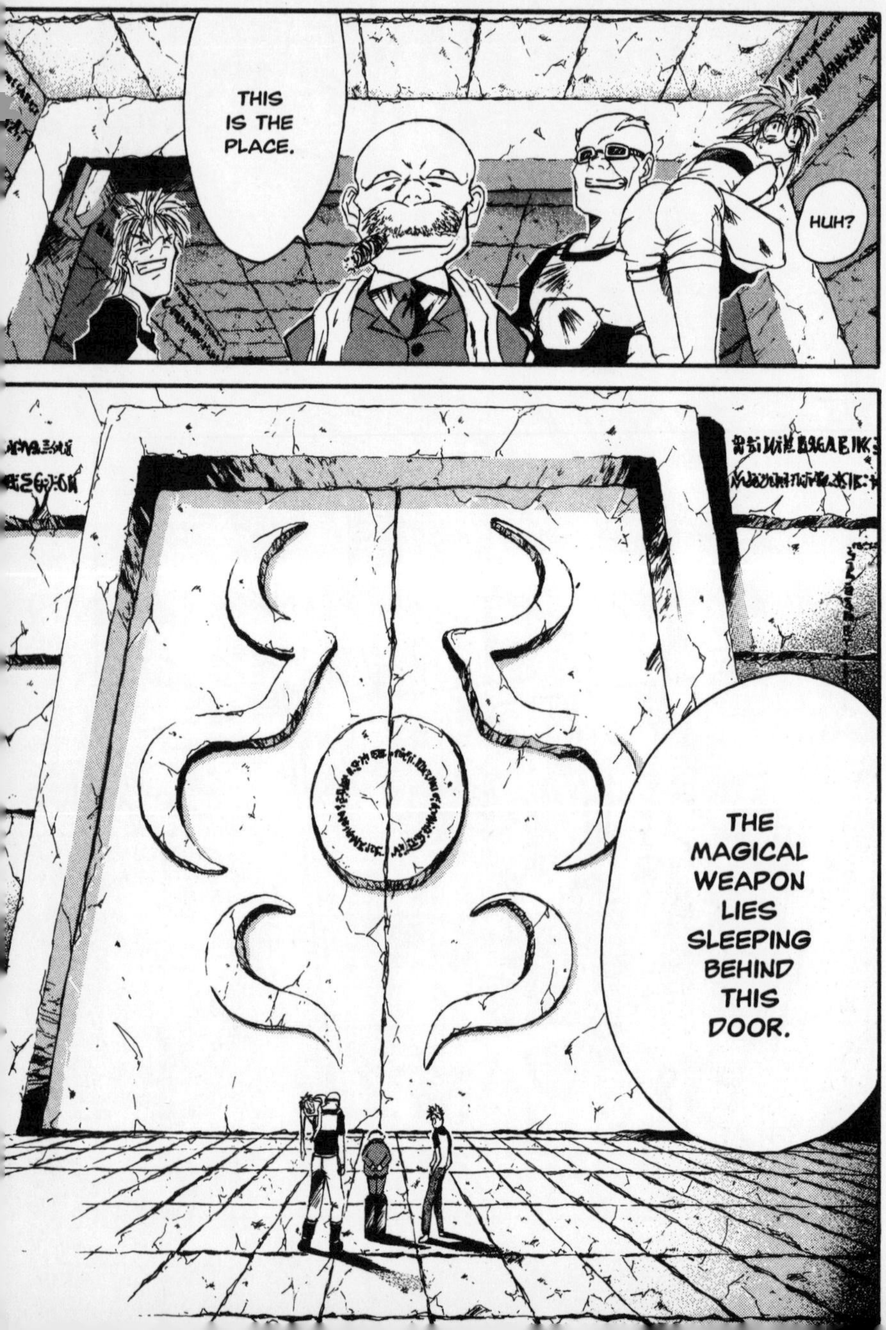
HUH?
THIS IS THE PLACE.
THE MAGICAL WEAPON LIES SLEEPING BEHIND THIS DOOR.

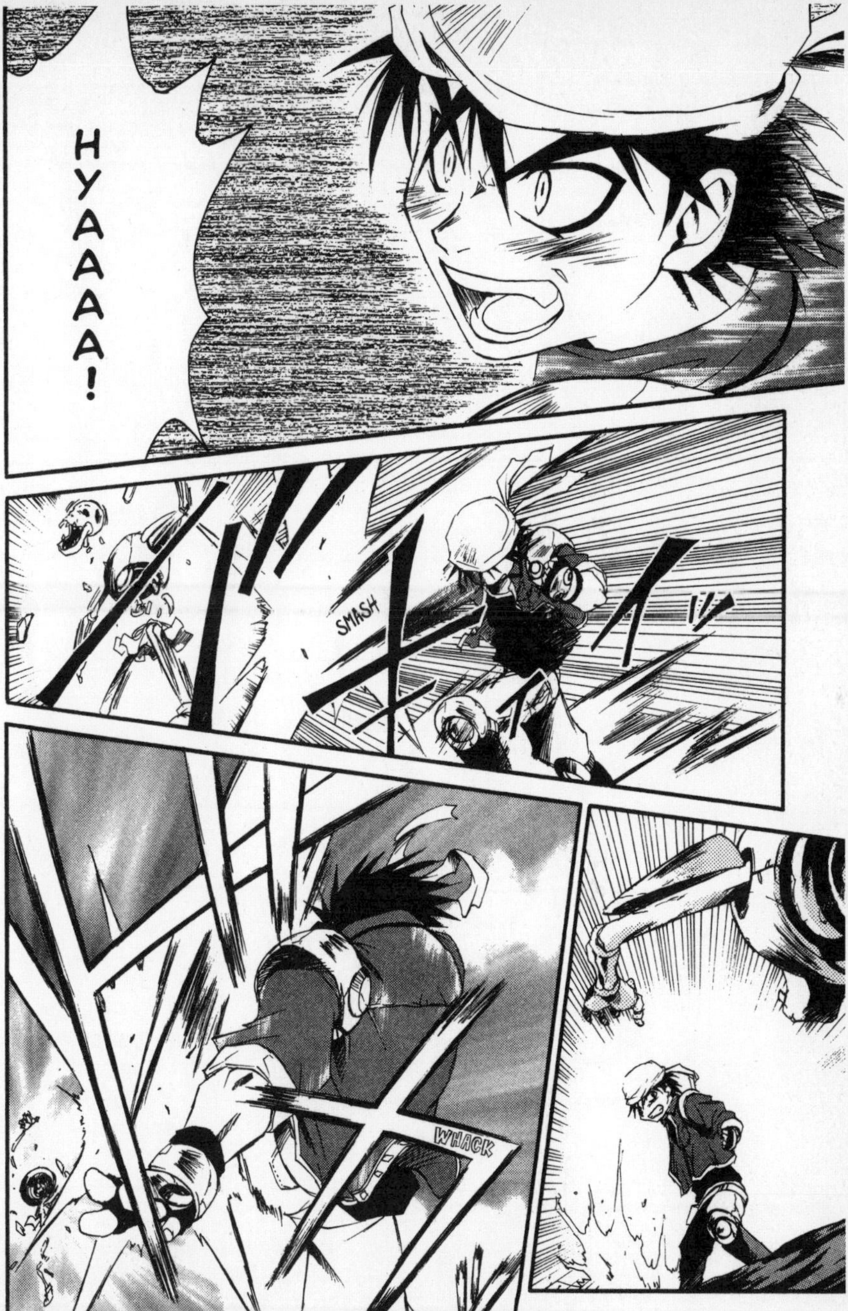
HYAAAAA!
SMASH
WHACK

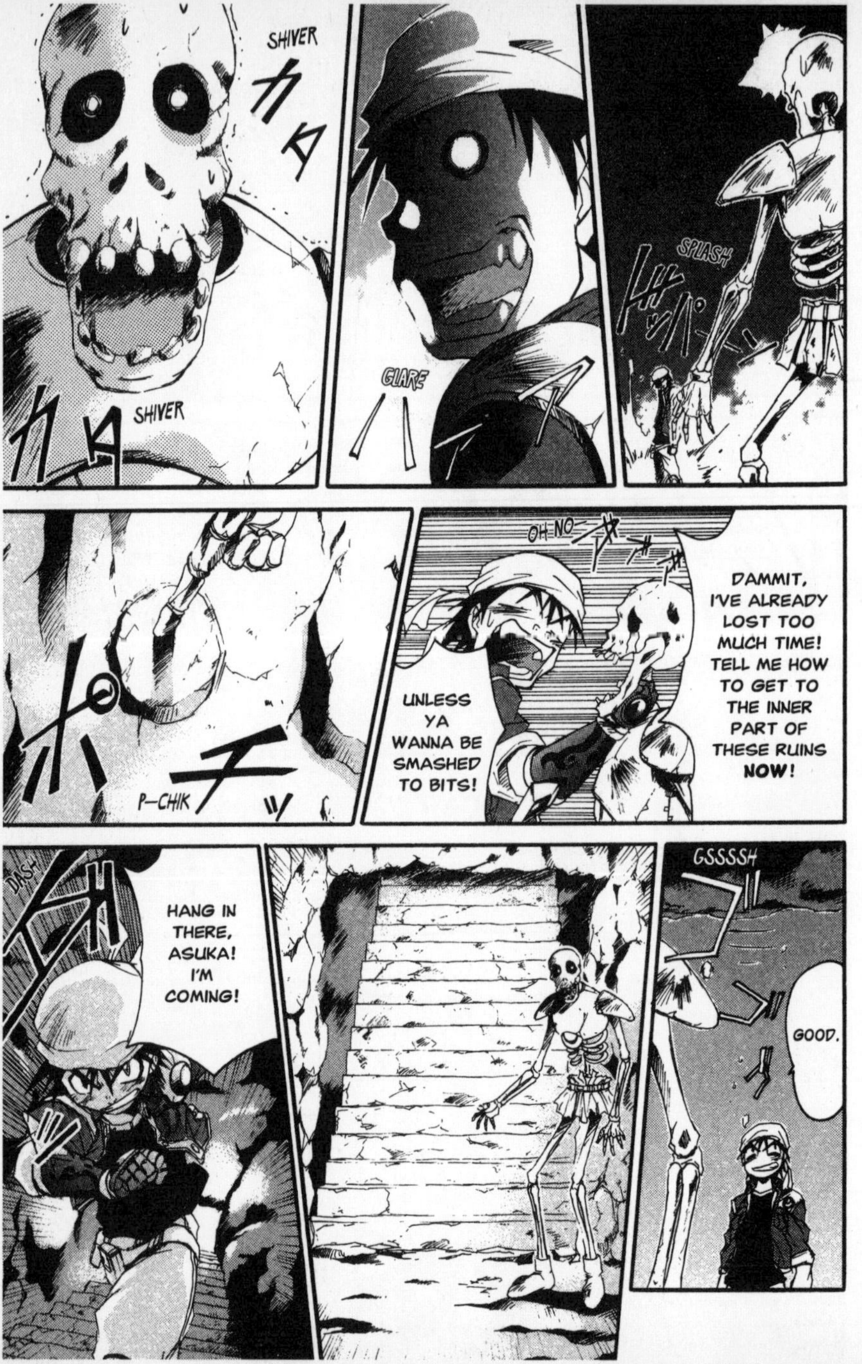
SPLASH
GLARE
SHIVER
SHIVER
OH-NO
DAMMIT, I'VE ALREADY LOST TOO MUCH TIME! TELL ME HOW TO GET TO THE INNER PART OF THESE RUINS **NOW**!
UNLESS YA WANNA BE SMASHED TO BITS!
P-CHIK
GSSSSH
GOOD.
DASH
HANG IN THERE, ASUKA! I'M COMING!

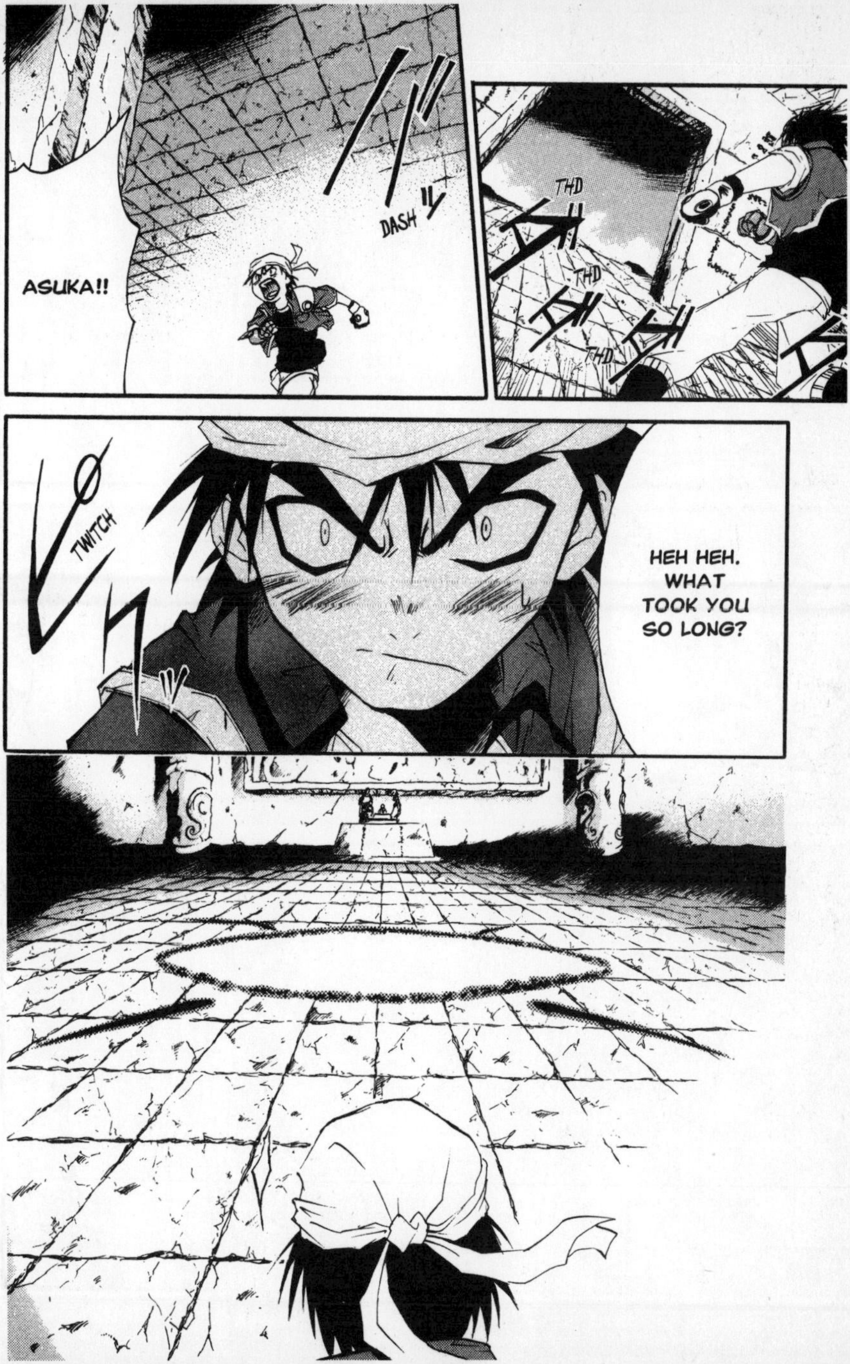
ASUKA!!
DASH
THD
THD
THD
TWITCH
HEH HEH. WHAT TOOK YOU SO LONG?

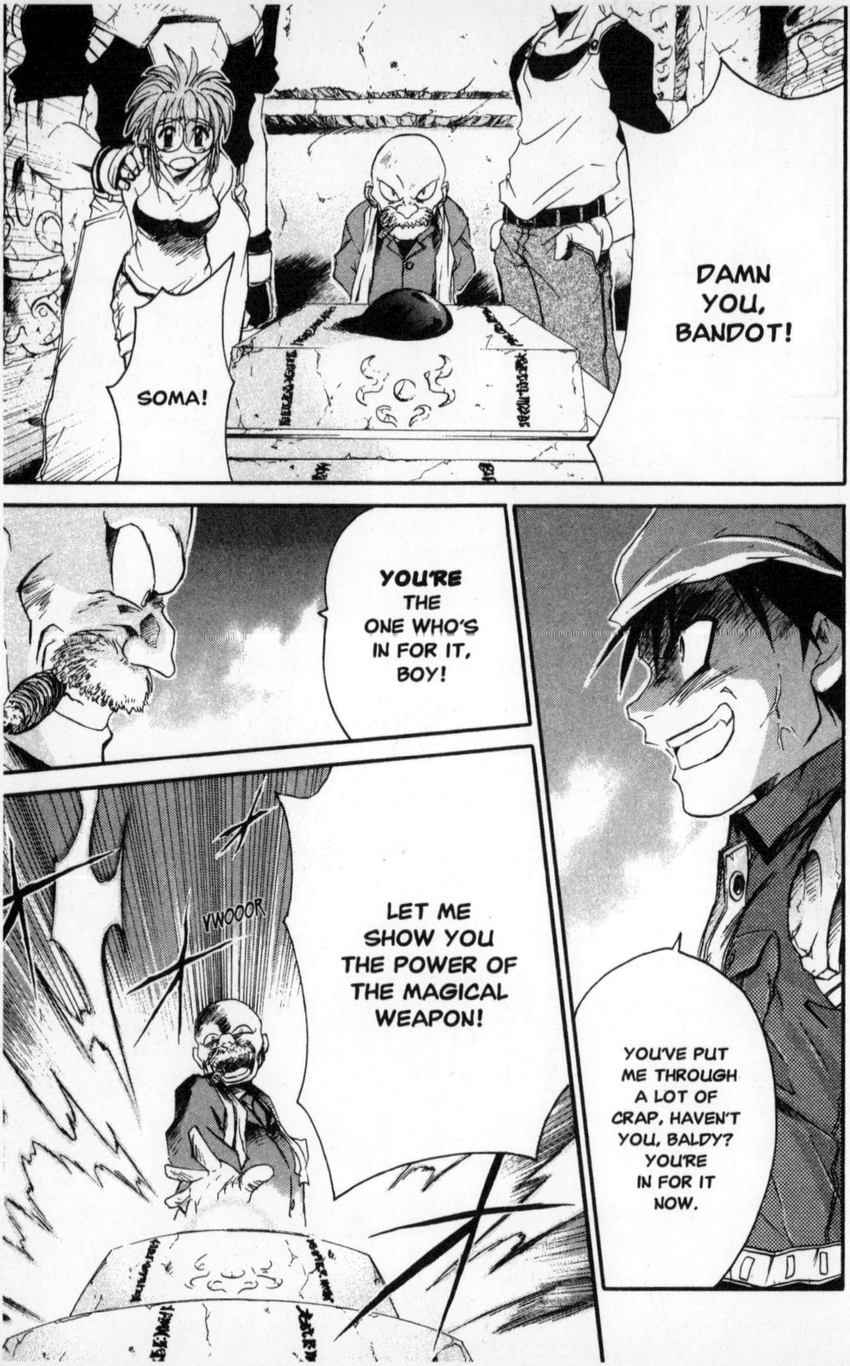

DAMN YOU, BANDOT!
SOMA!
YOU'VE PUT ME THROUGH A LOT OF CRAP, HAVEN'T YOU, BALDY? YOU'RE IN FOR IT NOW.
YOU'RE THE ONE WHO'S IN FOR IT, BOY!
LET ME SHOW YOU THE POWER OF THE MAGICAL WEAPON!
YWOOOR

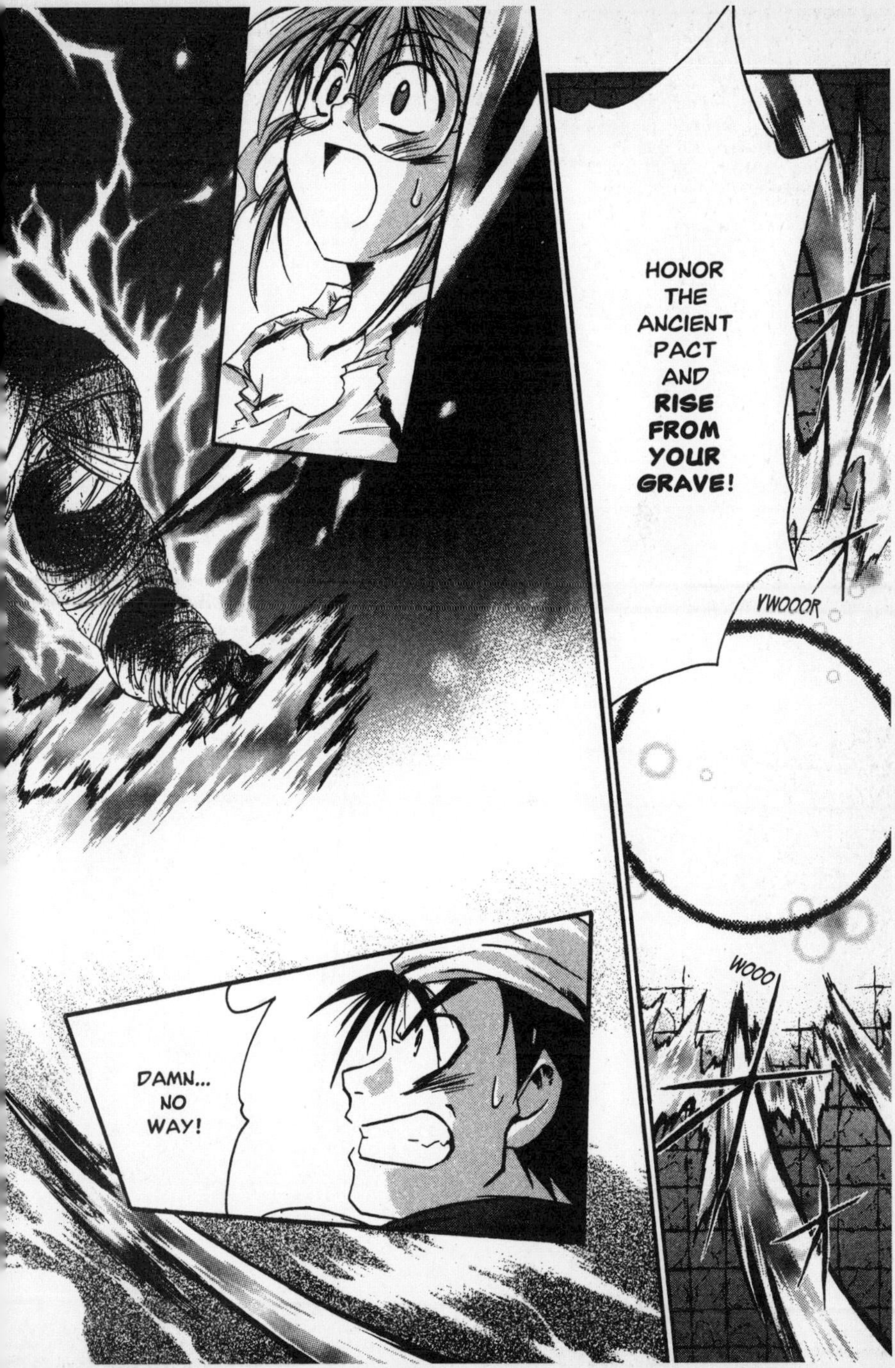
HONOR THE ANCIENT PACT AND RISE FROM YOUR GRAVE!
VWOOOR
WOOO
DAMN... NO WAY!

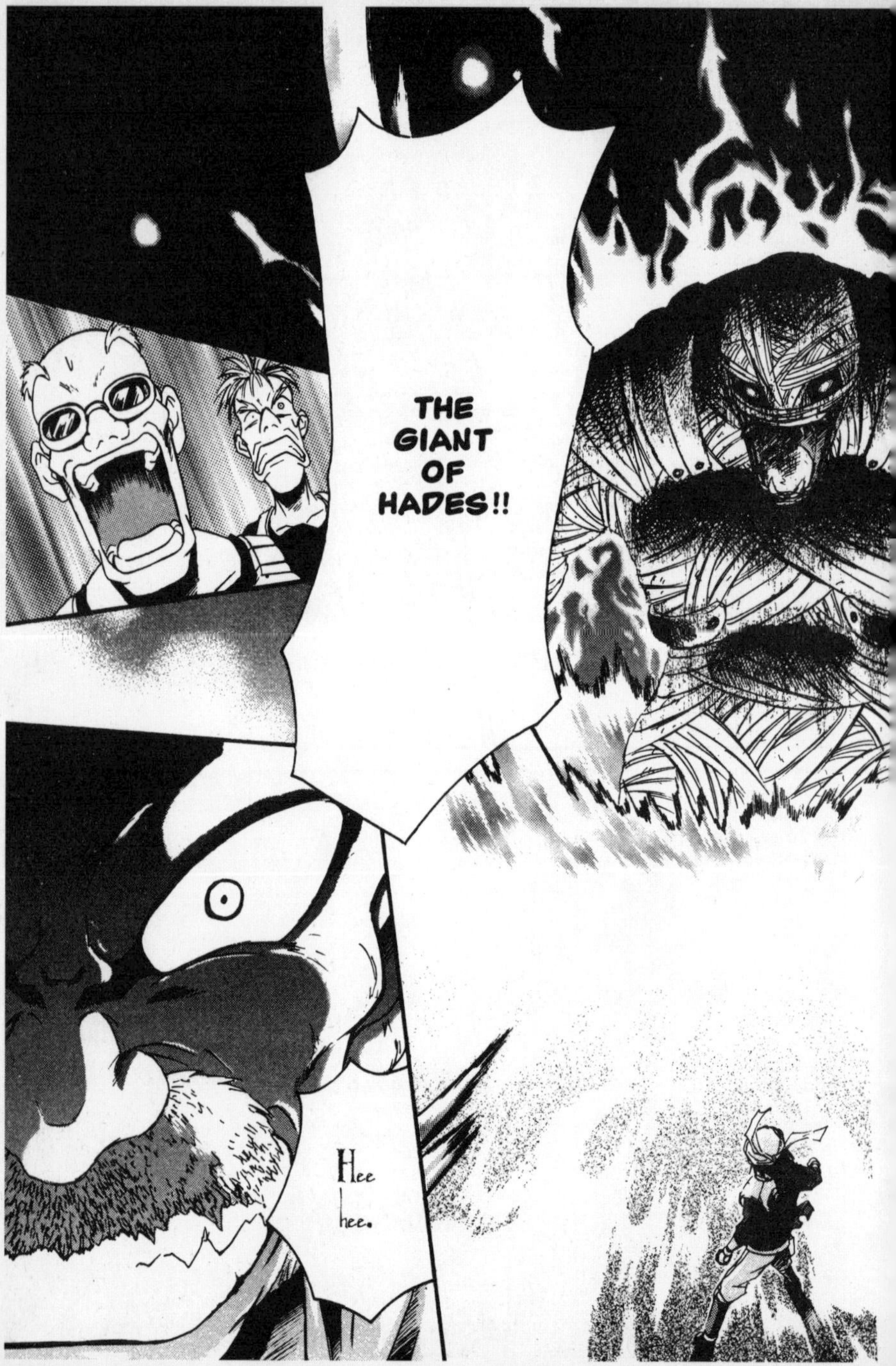
THE GIANT OF HADES!!
Hee hee.

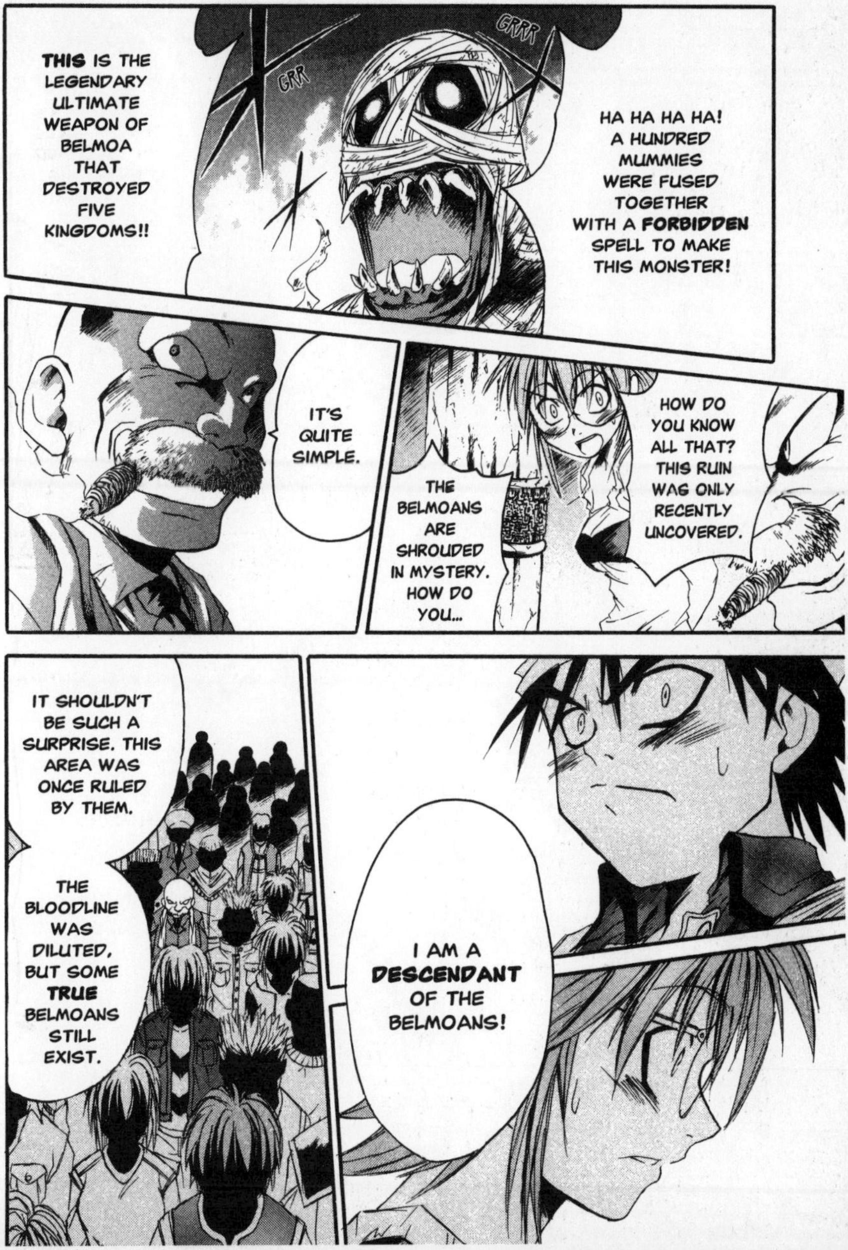
GRR
GRRR
HA HA HA HA! A HUNDRED MUMMIES WERE FUSED TOGETHER WITH A FORBIDDEN SPELL TO MAKE THIS MONSTER!
THIS IS THE LEGENDARY ULTIMATE WEAPON OF BELMOA THAT DESTROYED FIVE KINGDOMS!!
HOW DO YOU KNOW ALL THAT? THIS RUIN WAS ONLY RECENTLY UNCOVERED.
THE BELMOANS ARE SHROUDED IN MYSTERY. HOW DO YOU...
IT'S QUITE SIMPLE.
IT SHOULDN'T BE SUCH A SURPRISE. THIS AREA WAS ONCE RULED BY THEM.
THE BLOODLINE WAS DILUTED, BUT SOME TRUE BELMOANS STILL EXIST.
I AM A DESCENDANT OF THE BELMOANS!

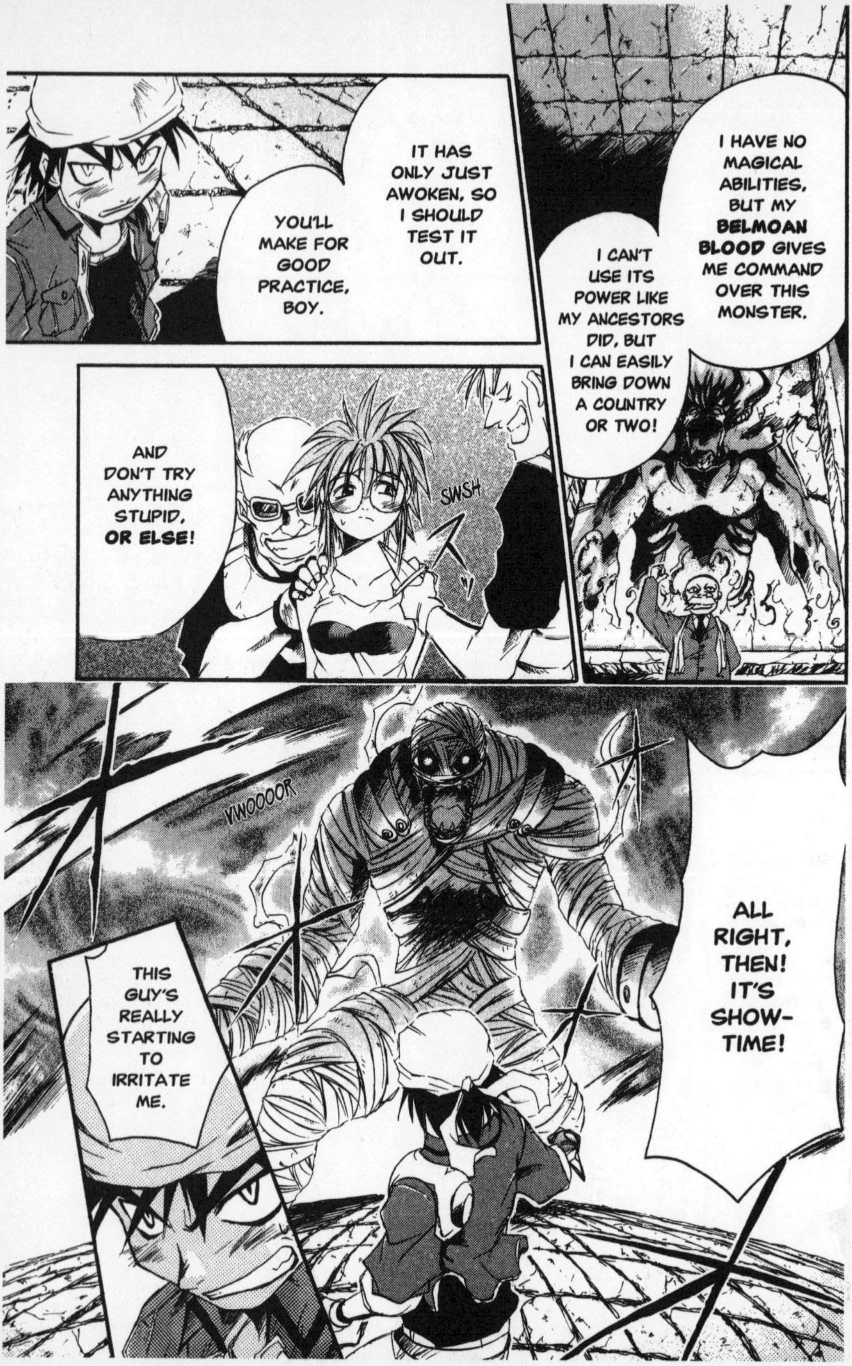
I HAVE NO MAGICAL ABILITIES, BUT MY **BELMOAN BLOOD** GIVES ME COMMAND OVER THIS MONSTER.
I CAN'T USE ITS POWER LIKE MY ANCESTORS DID, BUT I CAN EASILY BRING DOWN A COUNTRY OR TWO!
IT HAS ONLY JUST AWOKEN, SO I SHOULD TEST IT OUT.
YOU'LL MAKE FOR GOOD PRACTICE, BOY.
SWSH
AND DON'T TRY ANYTHING STUPID, **OR ELSE!**
ALL RIGHT, THEN! IT'S SHOW-TIME!
YWOOOOR
THIS GUY'S REALLY STARTING TO IRRITATE ME.

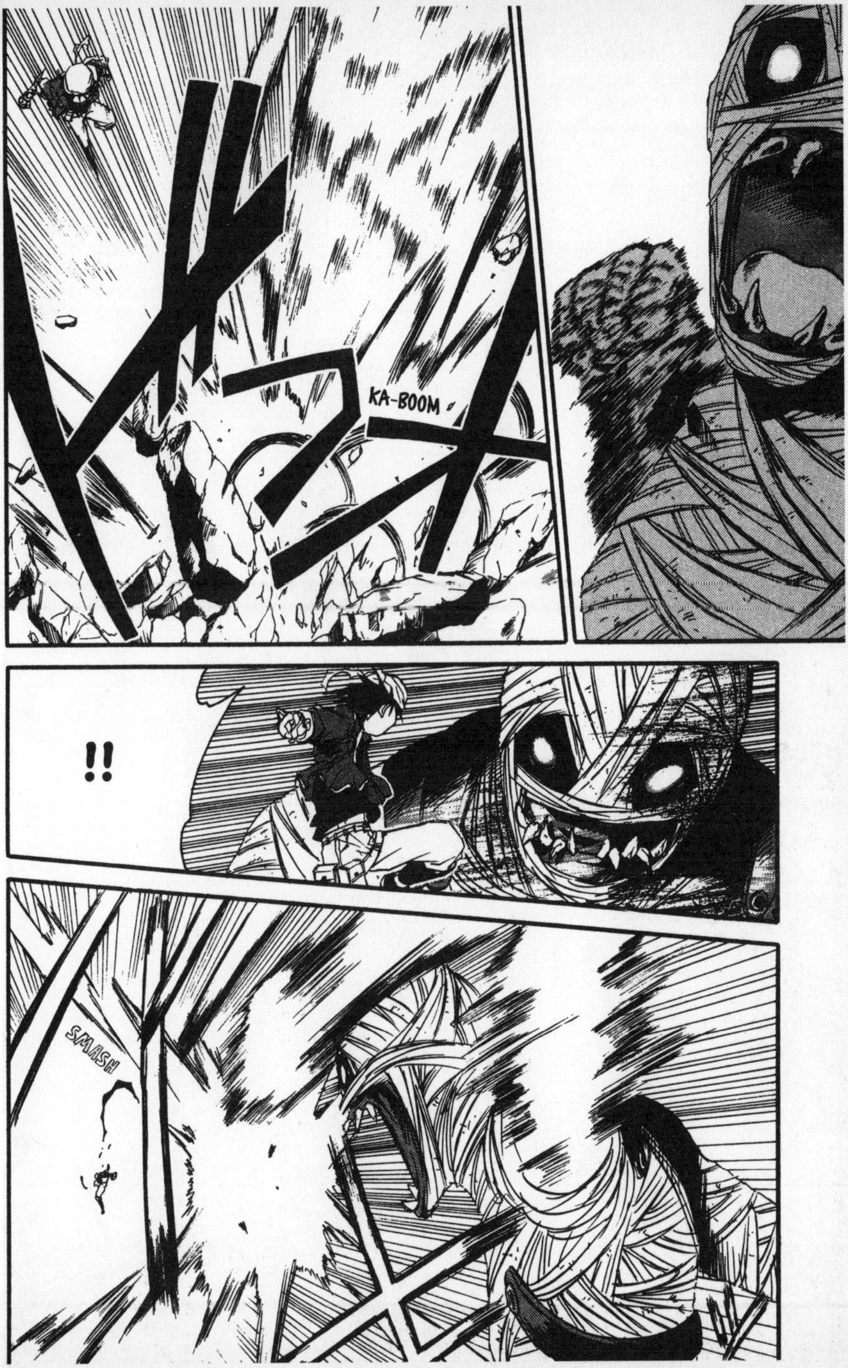
KA-BOOM
!!
SMASH

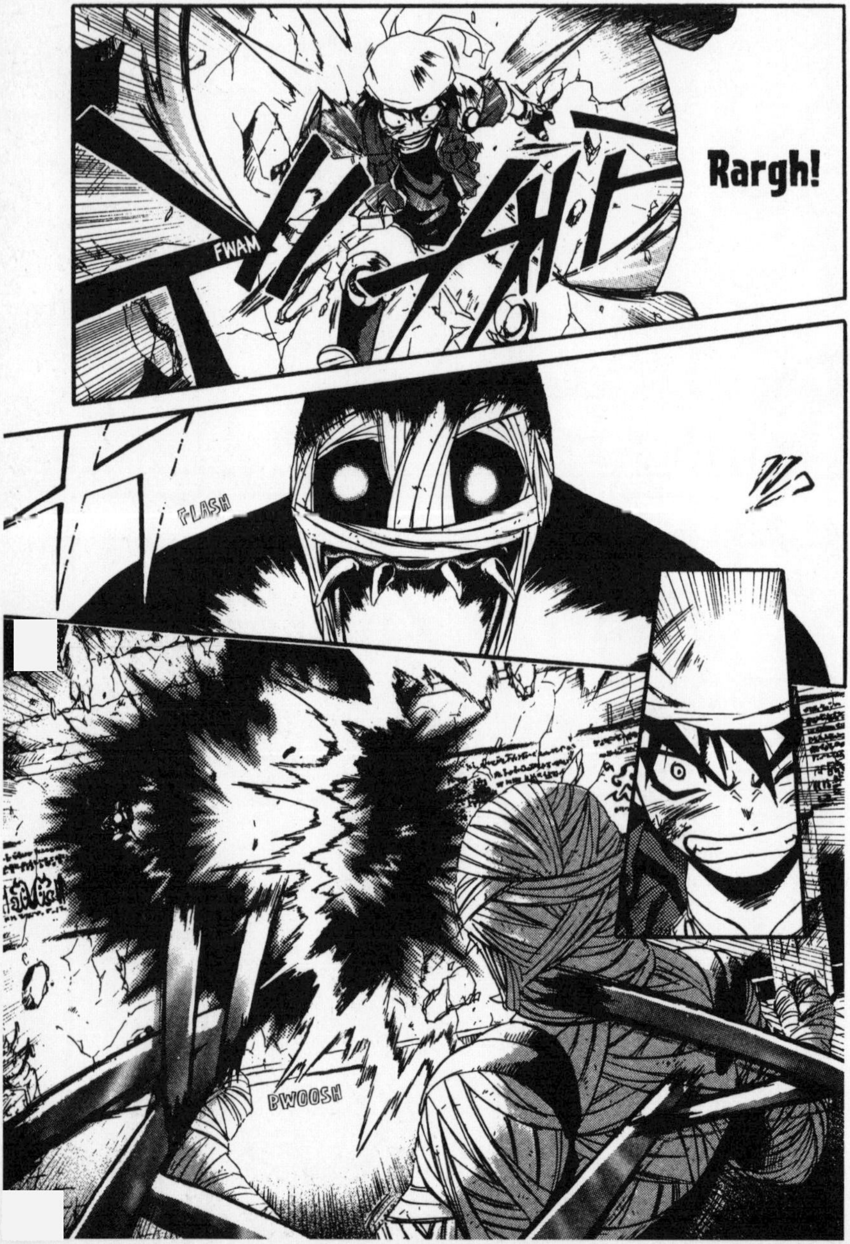
Rargh!
FWAM
FLASH
BWOOSH

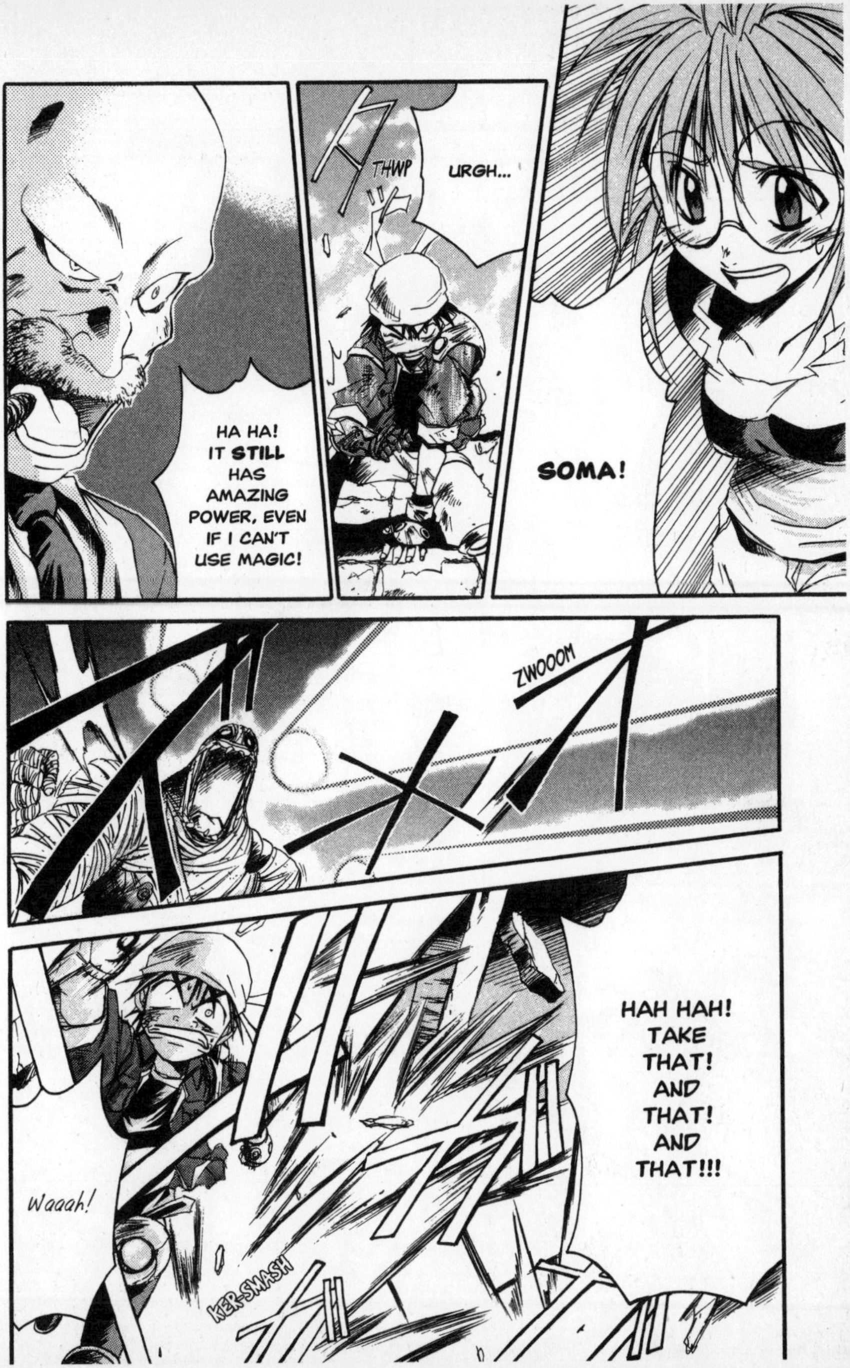
SOMA!
URGH...
THWP
HA HA! IT STILL HAS AMAZING POWER, EVEN IF I CAN'T USE MAGIC!
ZWOOOM
HAH HAH! TAKE THAT! AND THAT! AND THAT!!!
Waaah!
KER-SMASH

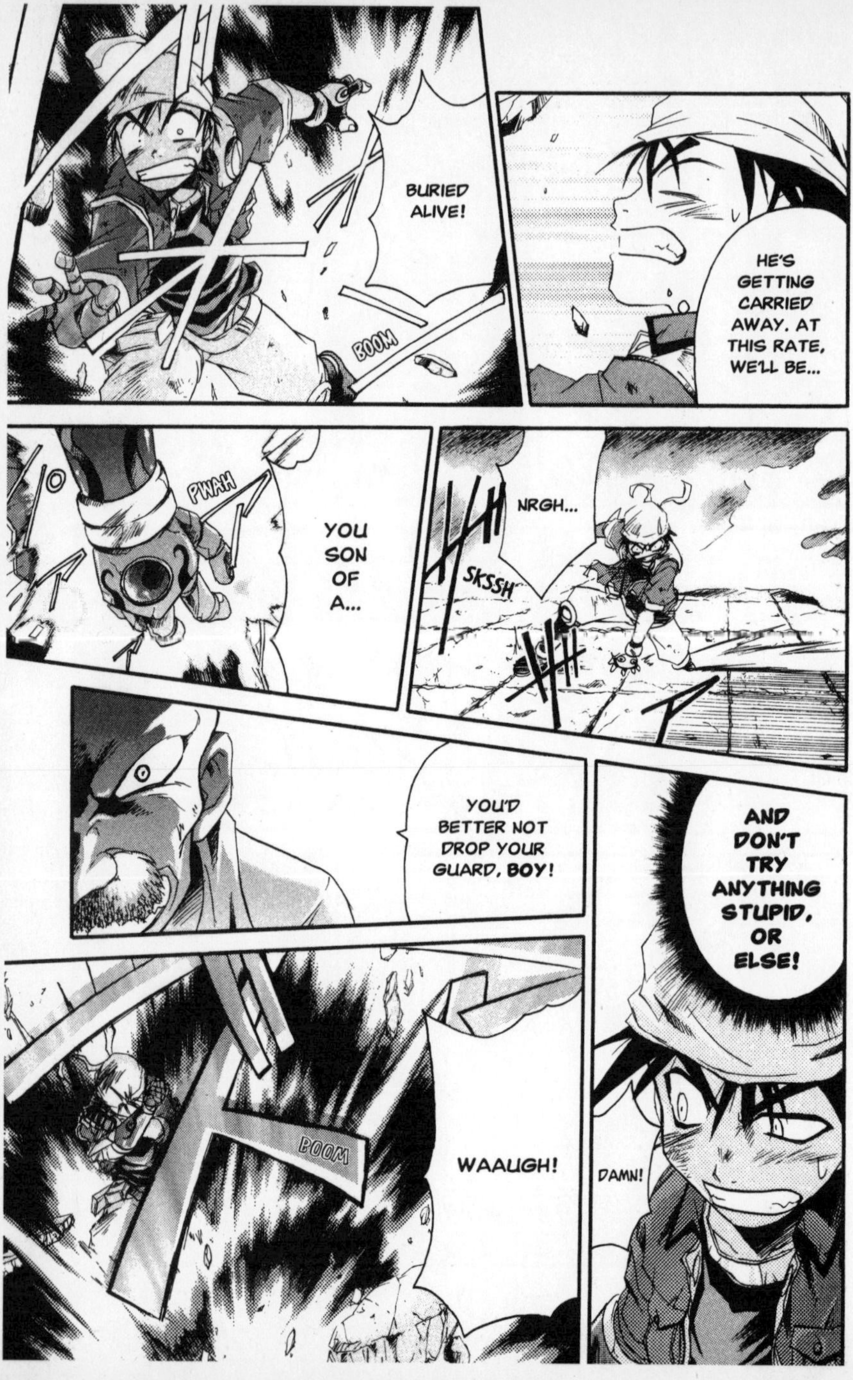
HE'S GETTING CARRIED AWAY. AT THIS RATE, WE'LL BE...
BURIED ALIVE!
BOOM
PWAH
YOU SON OF A...
NRGH...
SKSSH
YOU'D BETTER NOT DROP YOUR GUARD, BOY!
AND DON'T TRY ANYTHING STUPID, OR ELSE!
BOOM
WAAUGH!
DAMN!

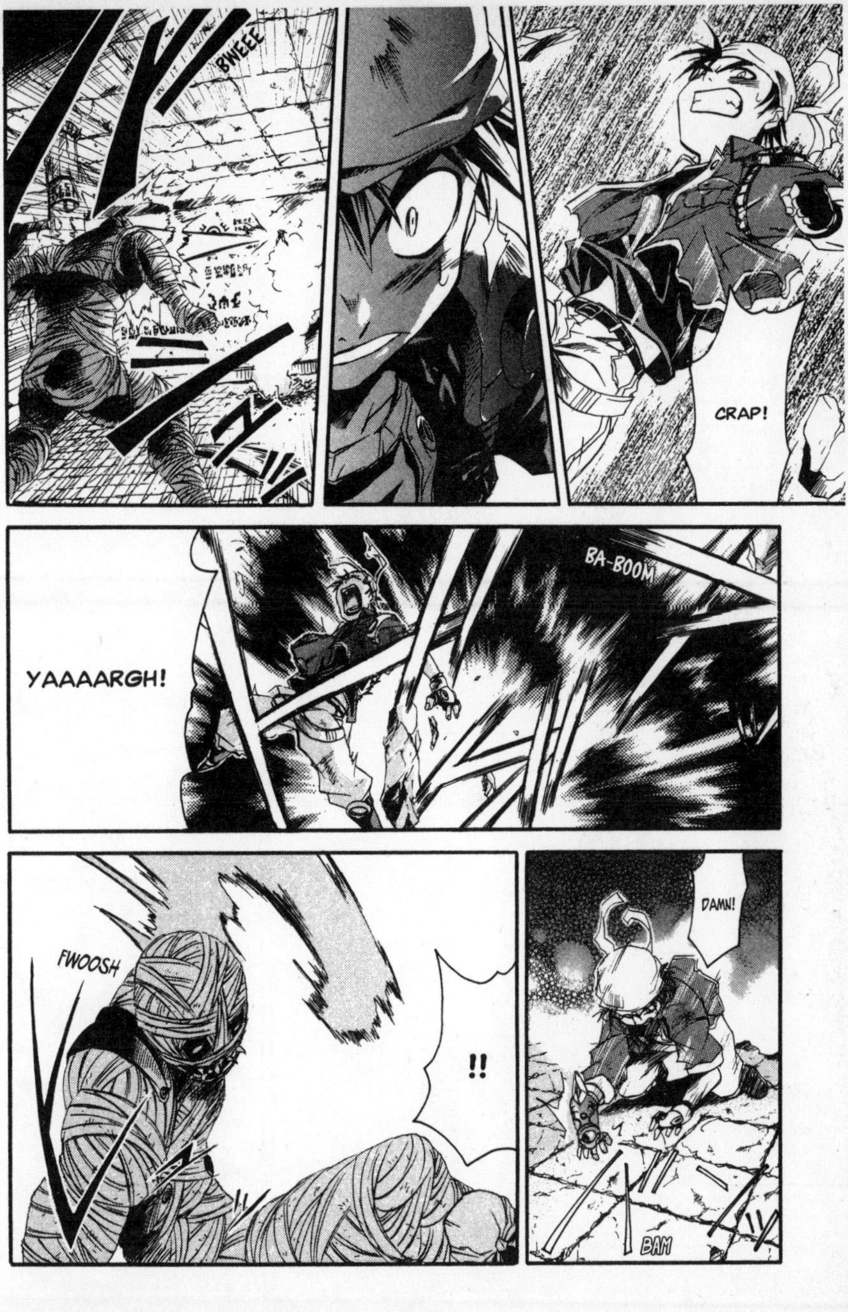
BWEEE
CRAP!
BA-BOOM
YAAAARGH!
FWOOSH
!!
DAMN!
BAM

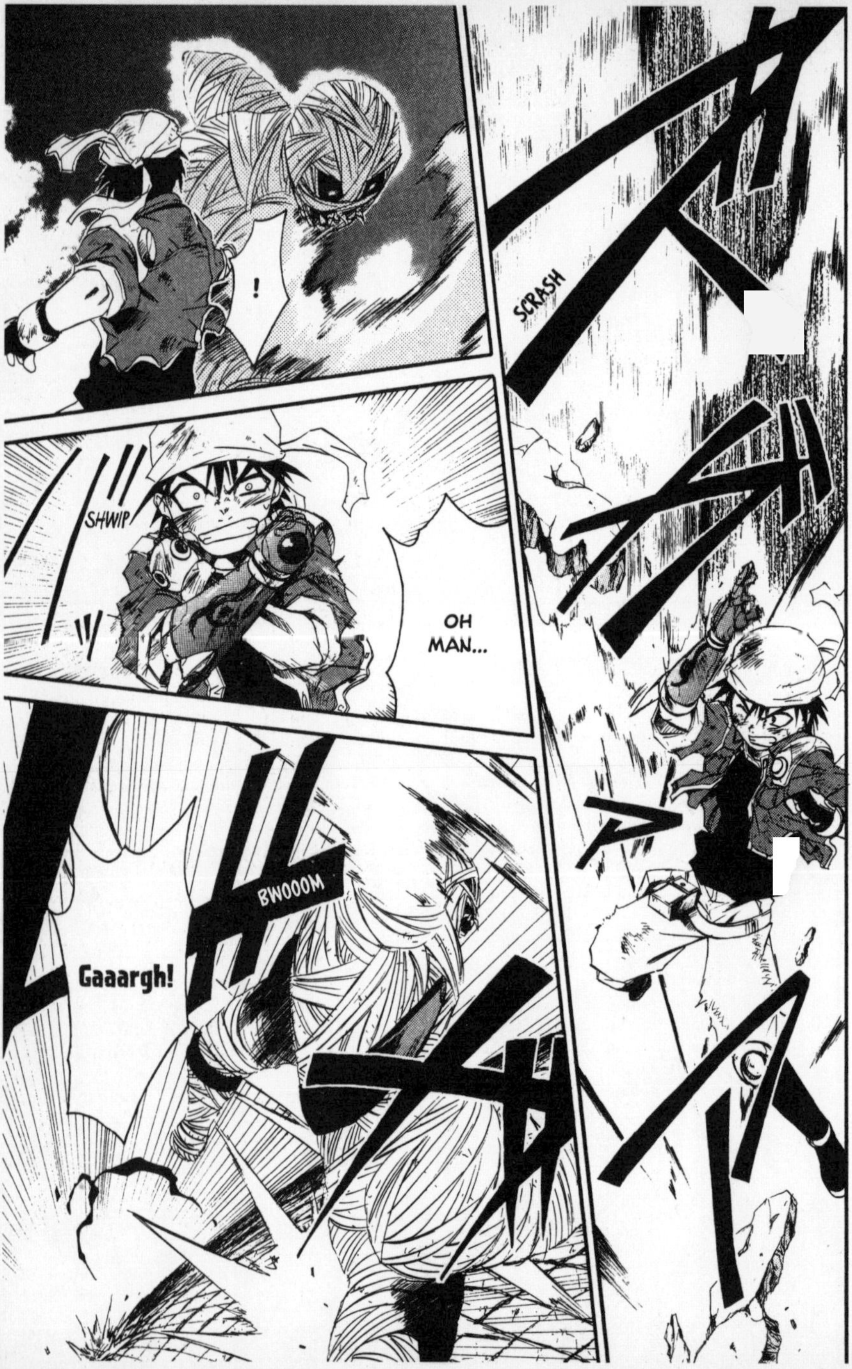
SCRASH
!
SHWIP
OH MAN...
BWOOOM
Gaaargh!

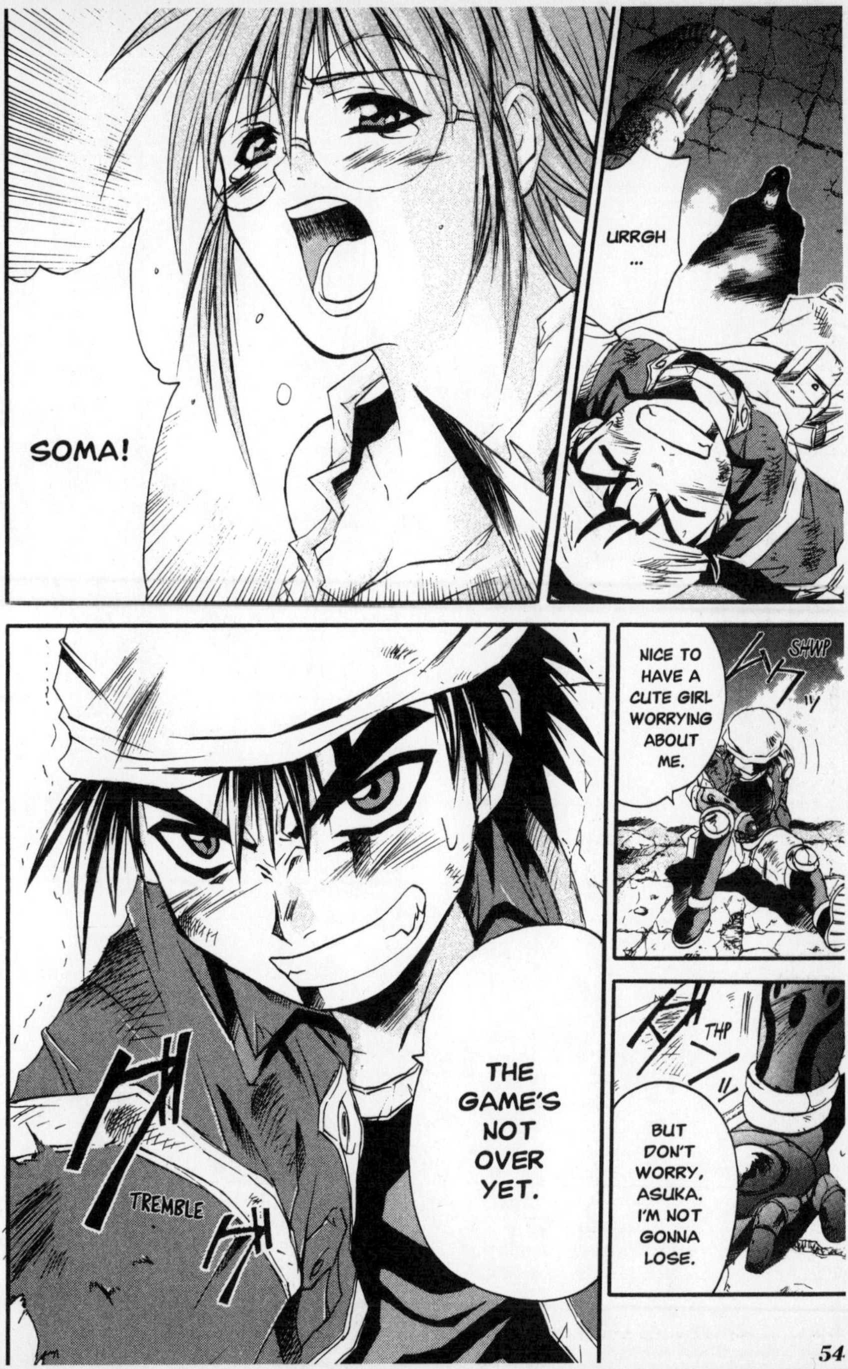
URRGH ...
SOMA!
SHWP
NICE TO HAVE A CUTE GIRL WORRYING ABOUT ME.
THP
BUT DON'T WORRY, ASUKA. I'M NOT GONNA LOSE.
THE GAME'S NOT OVER YET.
TREMBLE

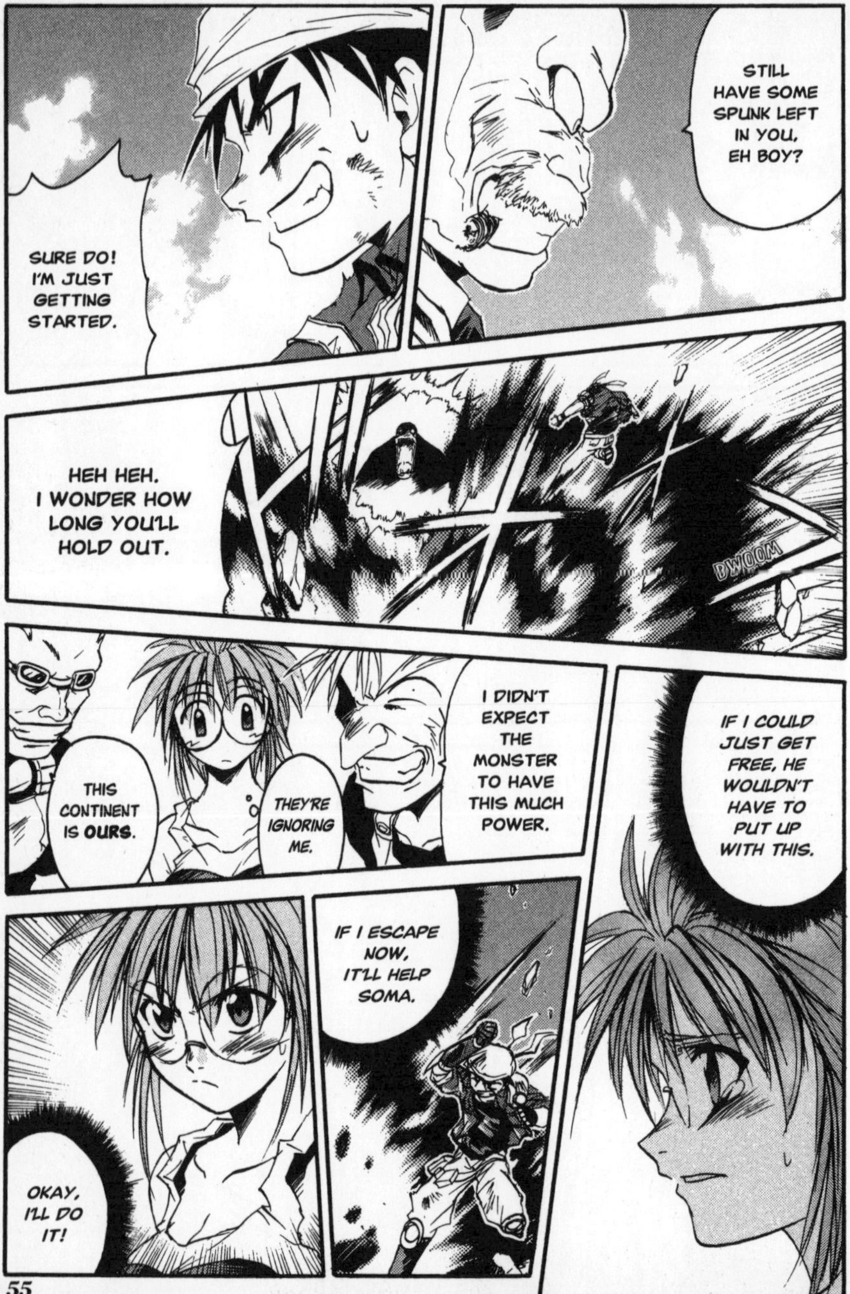
STILL HAVE SOME SPUNK LEFT IN YOU, EH BOY?
SURE DO! I'M JUST GETTING STARTED.
HEH HEH. I WONDER HOW LONG YOU'LL HOLD OUT.
DWOOM
IF I COULD JUST GET FREE, HE WOULDN'T HAVE TO PUT UP WITH THIS.
I DIDN'T EXPECT THE MONSTER TO HAVE THIS MUCH POWER.
THEY'RE IGNORING ME.
THIS CONTINENT IS OURS.
IF I ESCAPE NOW, IT'LL HELP SOMA.
OKAY, I'LL DO IT!

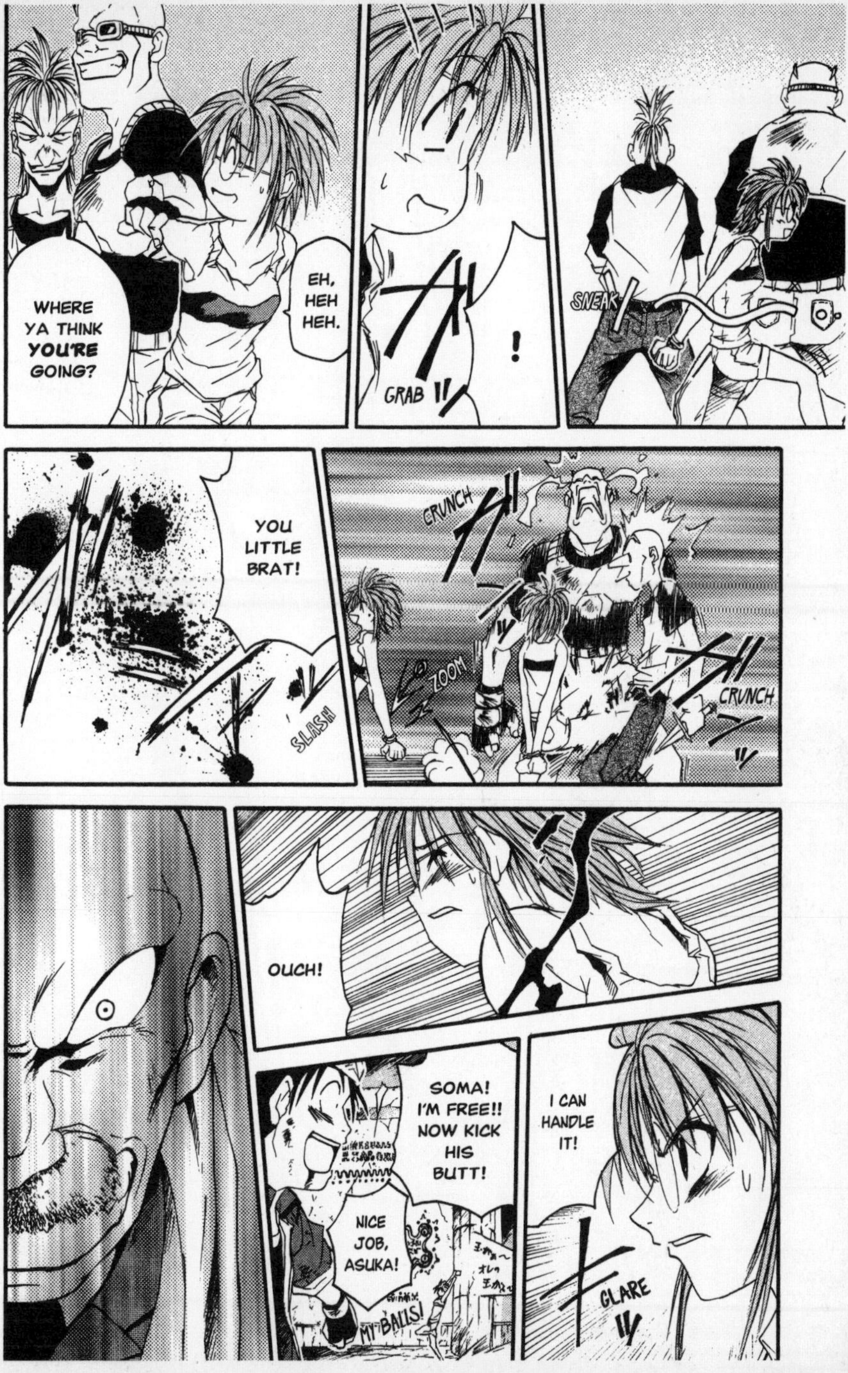
SNEAK
GRAB
!
WHERE YA THINK YOU'RE GOING?
EH, HEH HEH.
CRUNCH
ZOOM
CRUNCH
YOU LITTLE BRAT!
SLASH
OUCH!
I CAN HANDLE IT!
GLARE
SOMA! I'M FREE!! NOW KICK HIS BUTT!
NICE JOB, ASUKA!
MY BALLS!

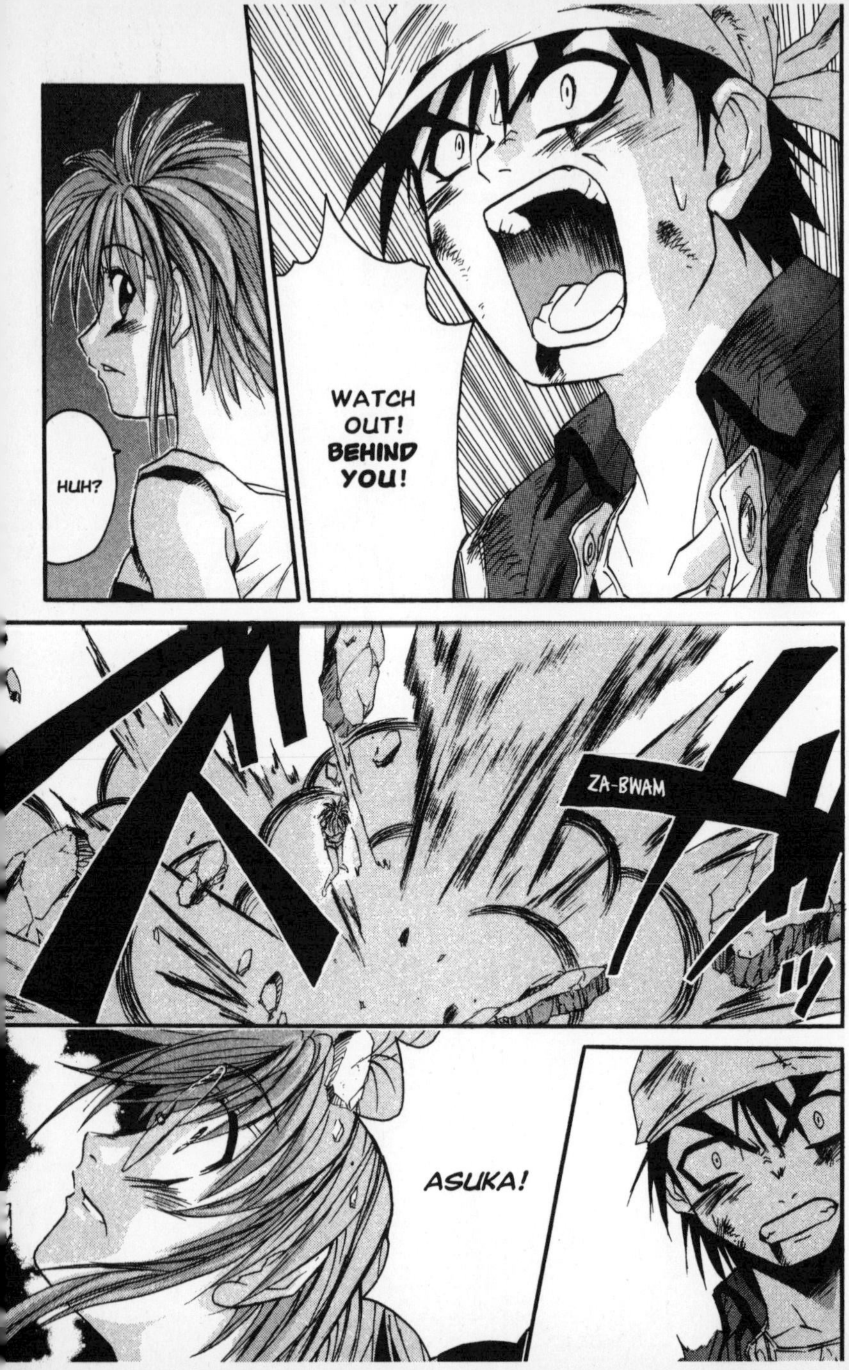
WATCH OUT! BEHIND YOU!
HUH?
ZA-BWAM
ASUKA!

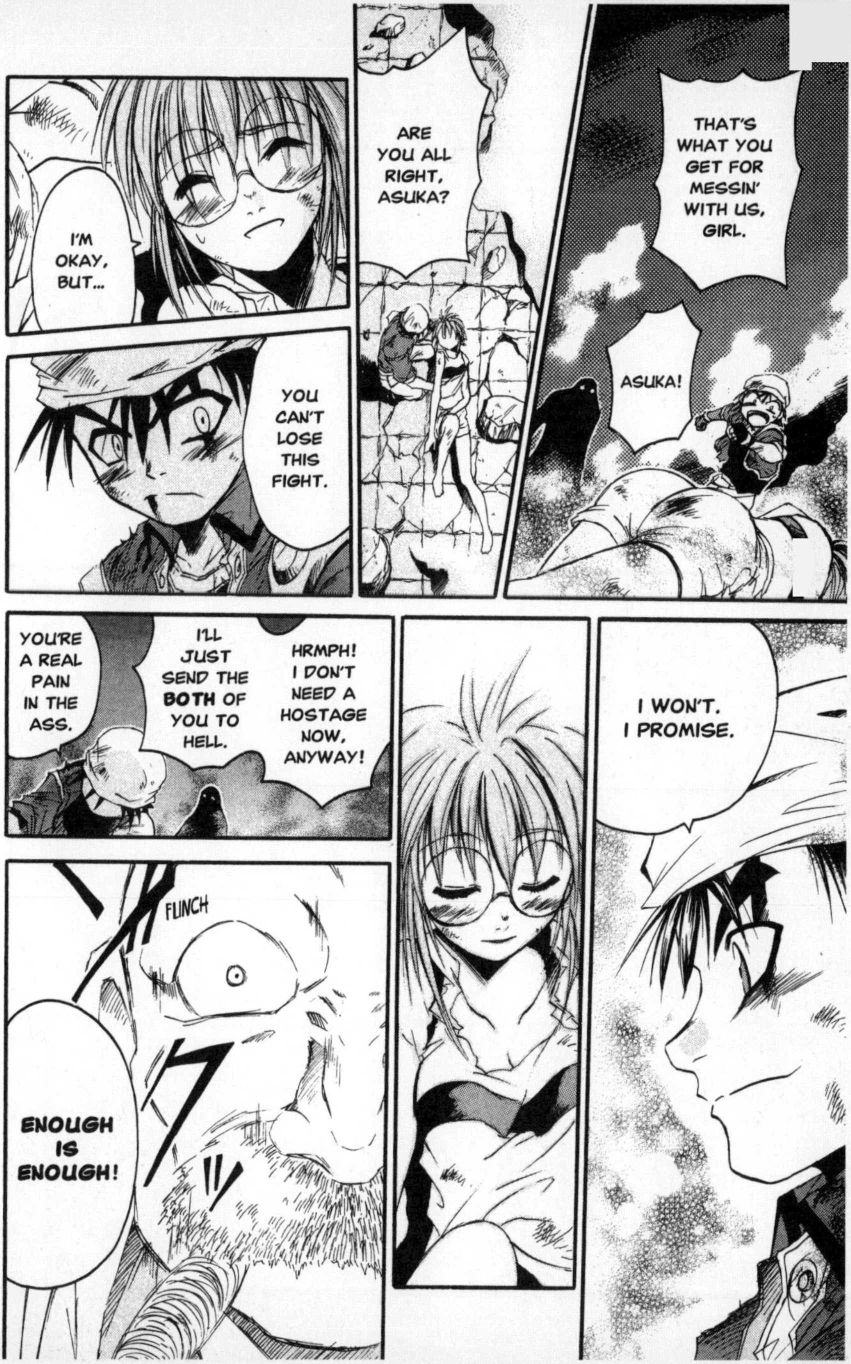
THAT'S WHAT YOU GET FOR MESSIN' WITH US, GIRL.
ASUKA!
ARE YOU ALL RIGHT, ASUKA?
I'M OKAY, BUT...
YOU CAN'T LOSE THIS FIGHT.
HRMPH! I DON'T NEED A HOSTAGE NOW, ANYWAY!
I'LL JUST SEND THE BOTH OF YOU TO HELL.
YOU'RE A REAL PAIN IN THE ASS.
I WON'T. I PROMISE.
FLINCH
ENOUGH IS ENOUGH!

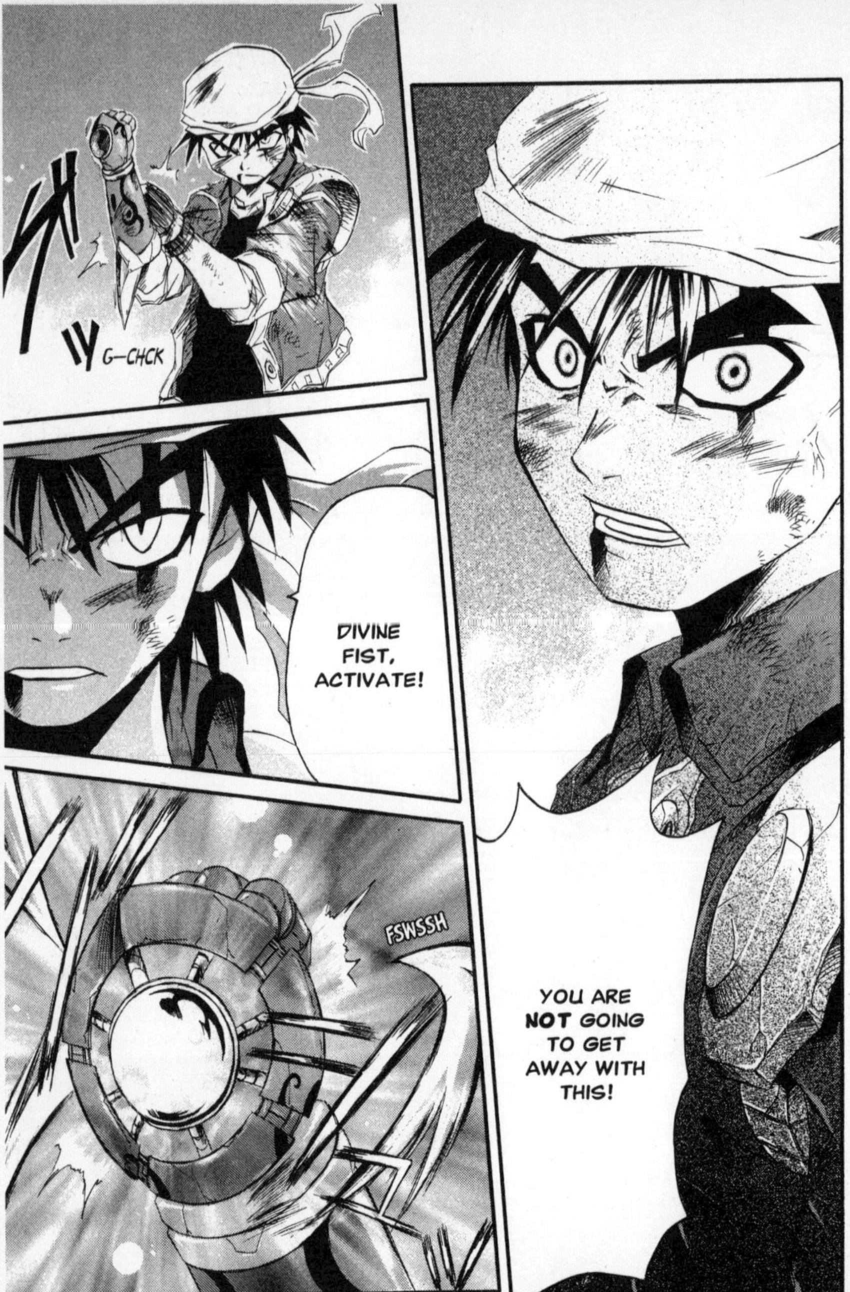
YOU ARE NOT GOING TO GET AWAY WITH THIS!
G-CHCK
DIVINE FIST, ACTIVATE!
FSWSSH

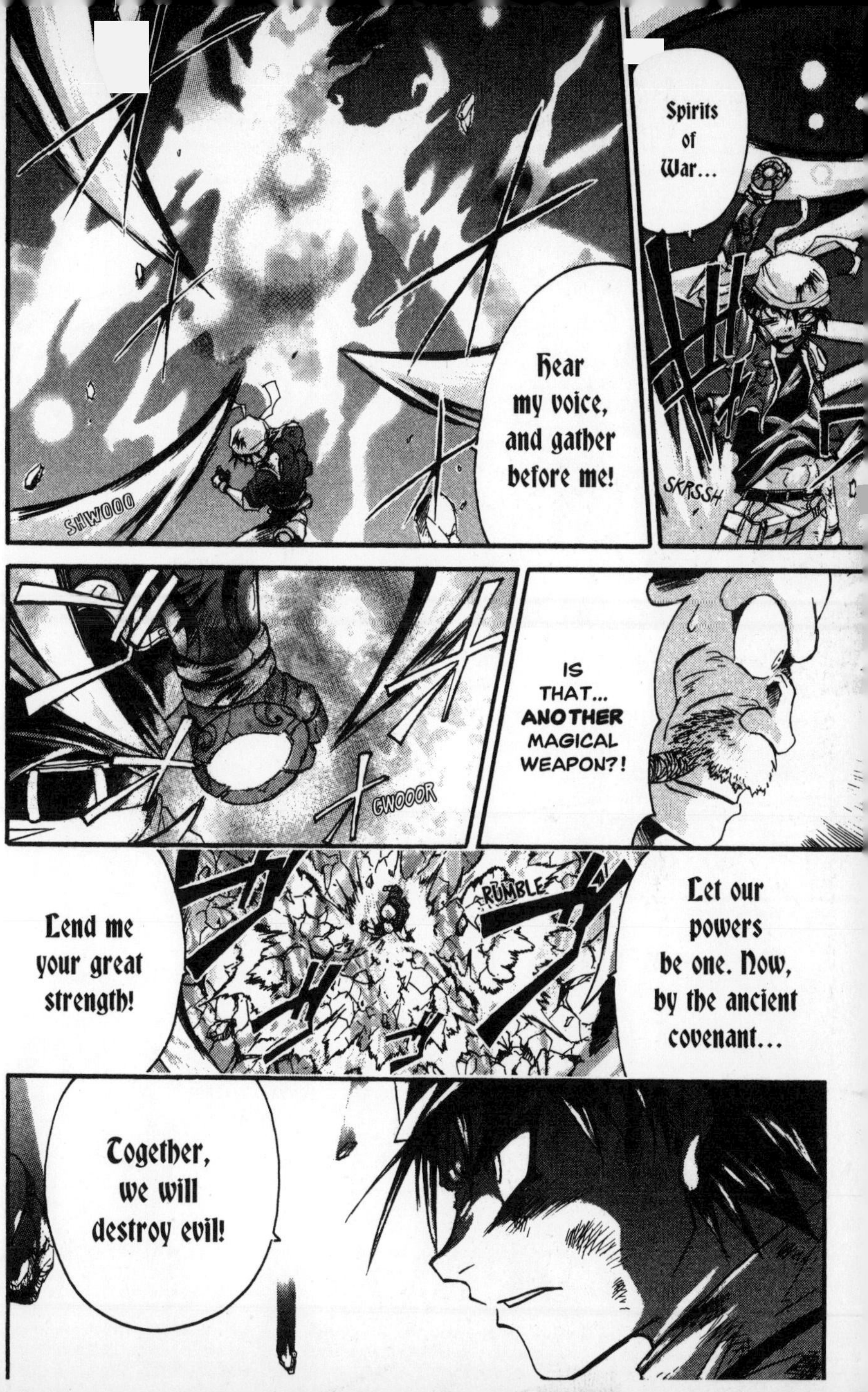
Spirits of War...
SKRSSH
Hear my voice, and gather before me!
SHWOOO
IS THAT... ANOTHER MAGICAL WEAPON?!
GWOOOR
Let our powers be one. Now, by the ancient covenant...
RUMBLE
Lend me your great strength!
Together, we will destroy evil!

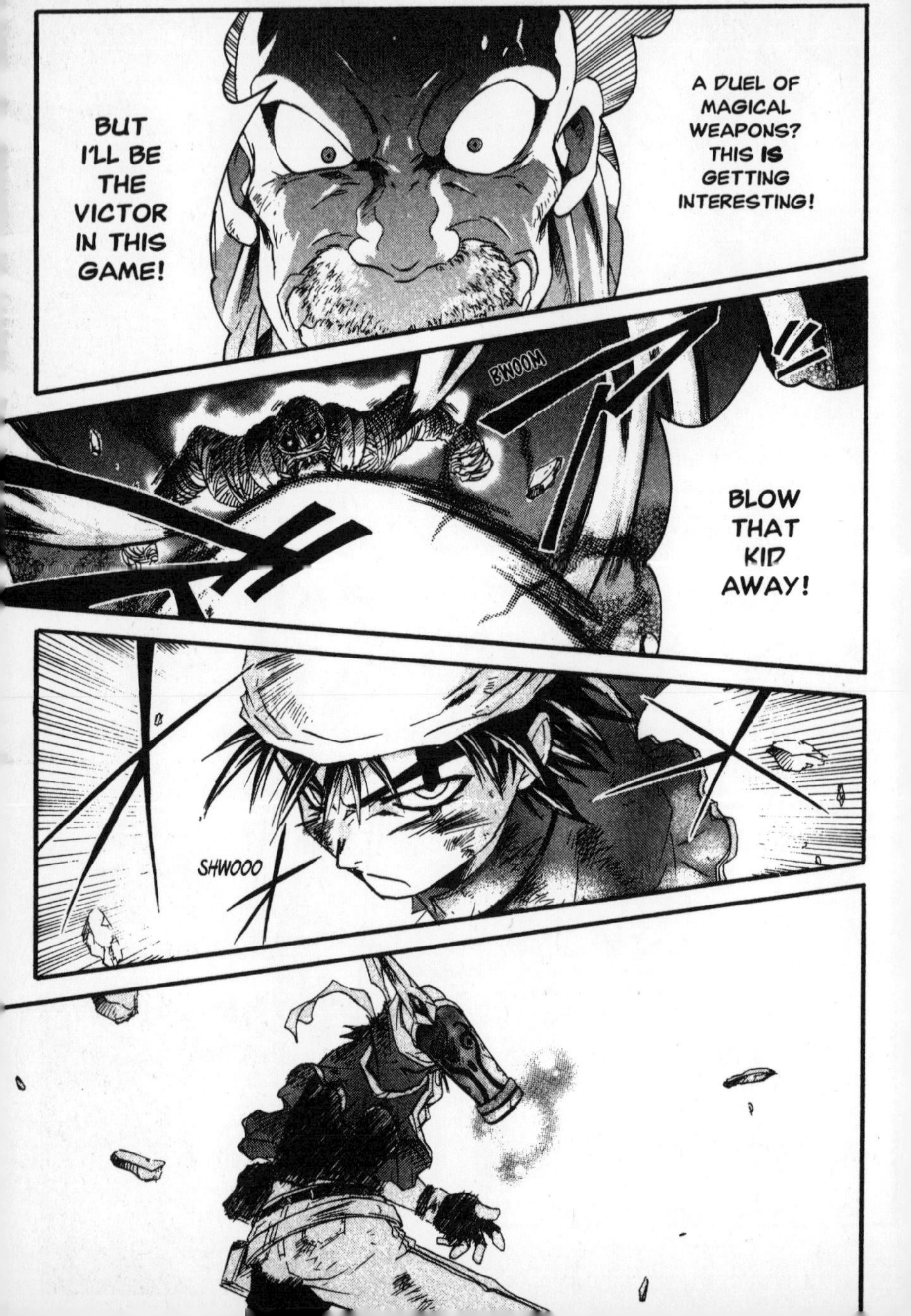
A DUEL OF MAGICAL WEAPONS? THIS IS GETTING INTERESTING!
BUT I'LL BE THE VICTOR IN THIS GAME!
BWOOM
BLOW THAT KID AWAY!
SHWOOO

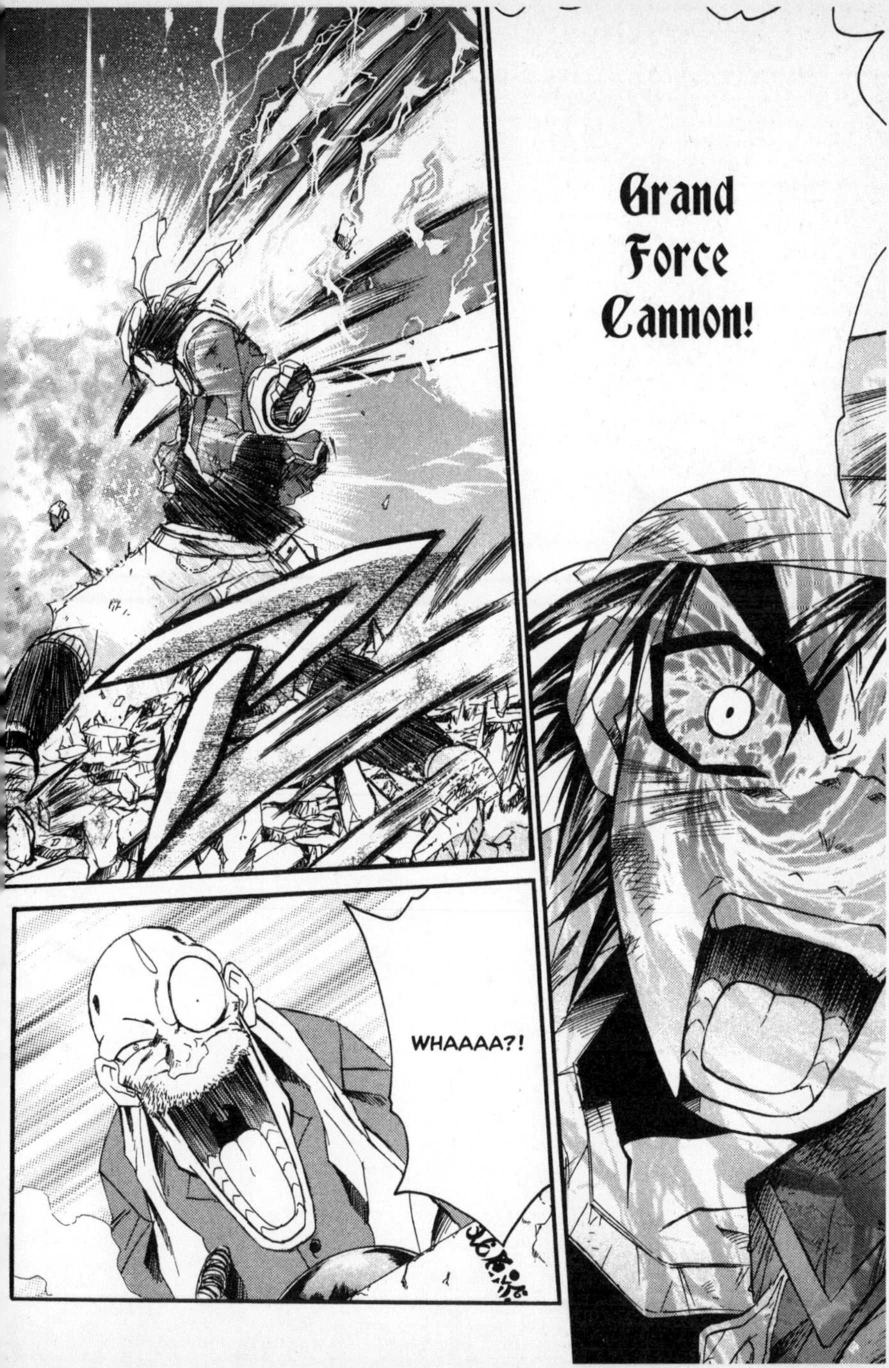
Grand Force Cannon!
WHAAAA?!

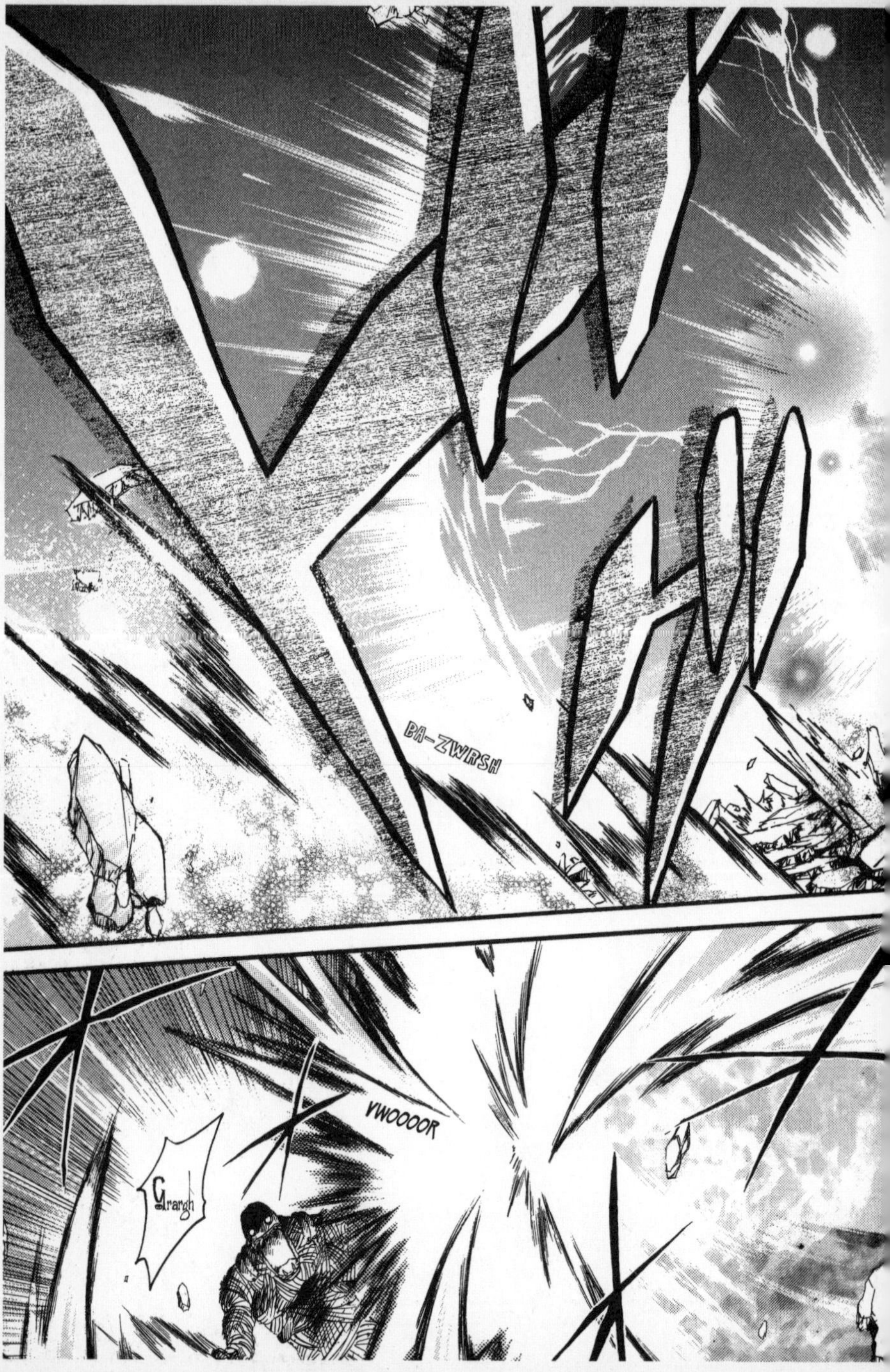
BA-ZWRSH
VWOOOR
Grargh

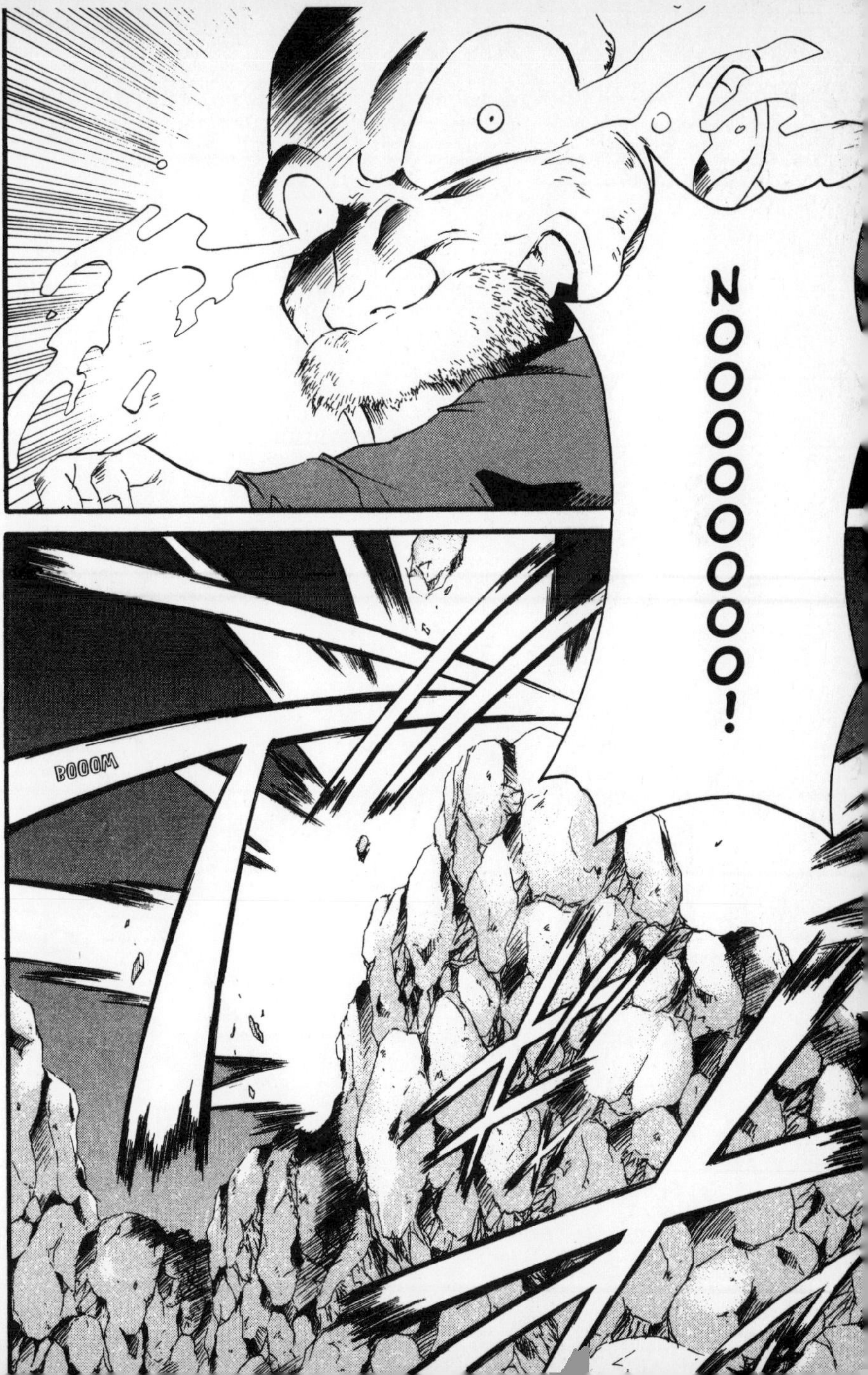
NOOOOOOOO!
BOOOM

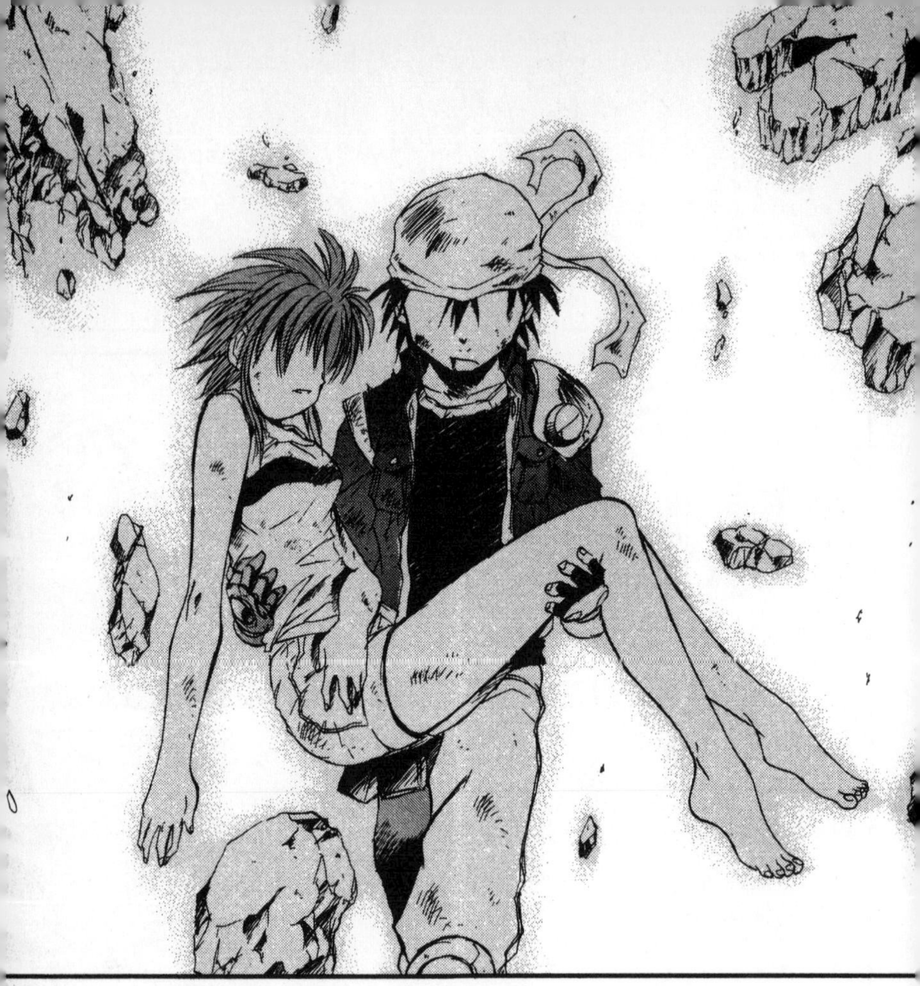

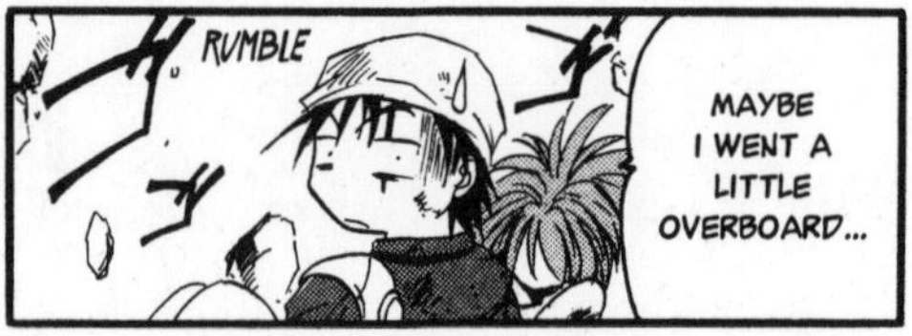
RUMBLE
MAYBE I WENT A LITTLE OVERBOARD...

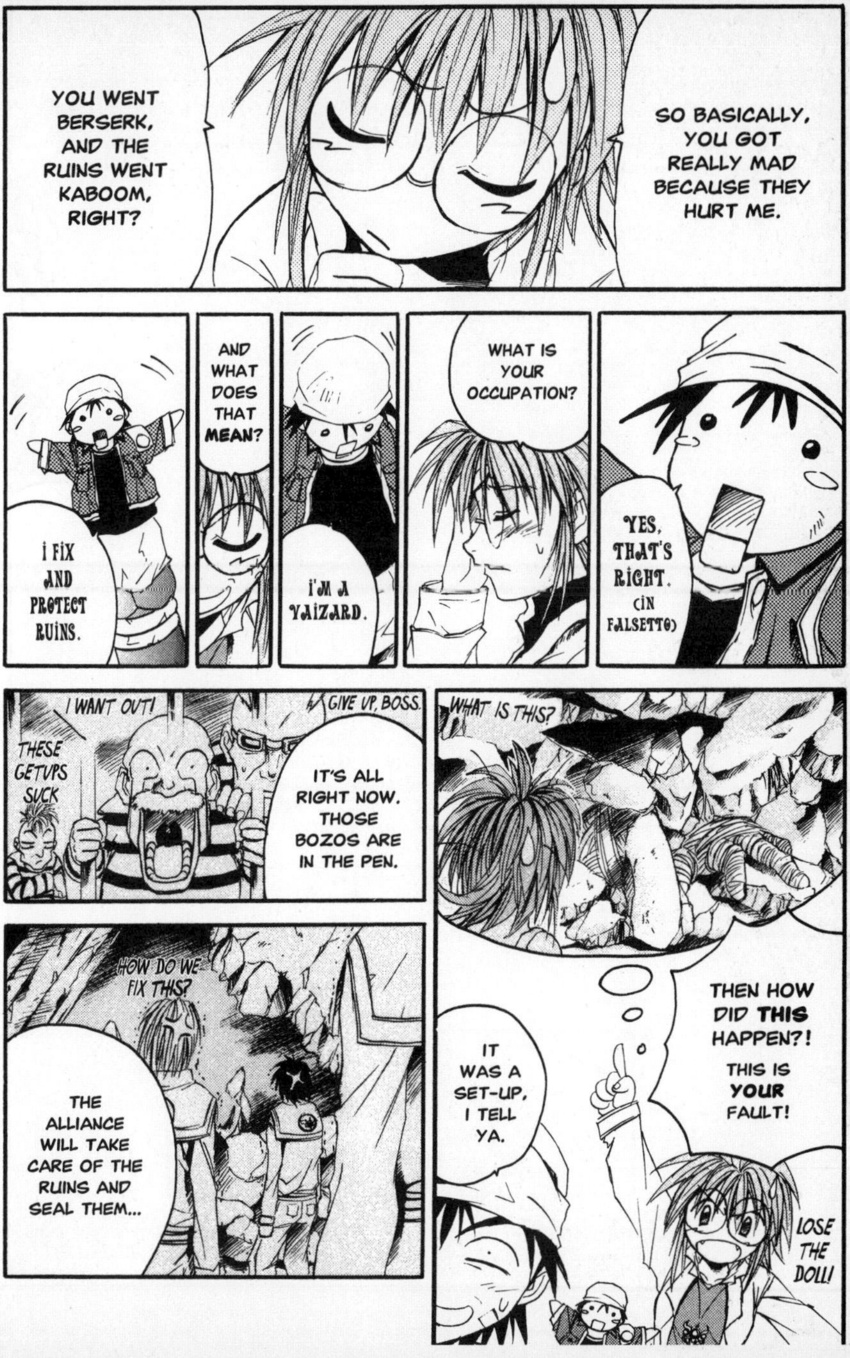

SO BASICALLY, YOU GOT REALLY MAD BECAUSE THEY HURT ME.
YOU WENT BERSERK, AND THE RUINS WENT KABOOM, RIGHT?
YES, THAT'S RIGHT. (IN FALSETTO)
WHAT IS YOUR OCCUPATION?
I'M A YAIZARD.
AND WHAT DOES THAT MEAN?
I FIX AND PROTECT RUINS.
WHAT IS THIS?
IT'S ALL RIGHT NOW. THOSE BOZOS ARE IN THE PEN.
GIVE UP, BOSS.
I WANT OUT!
THESE GETUPS SUCK
THE ALLIANCE WILL TAKE CARE OF THE RUINS AND SEAL THEM...
HOW DO WE FIX THIS?
THEN HOW DID THIS HAPPEN?!
THIS IS YOUR FAULT!
IT WAS A SET-UP, I TELL YA.
LOSE THE DOLL!

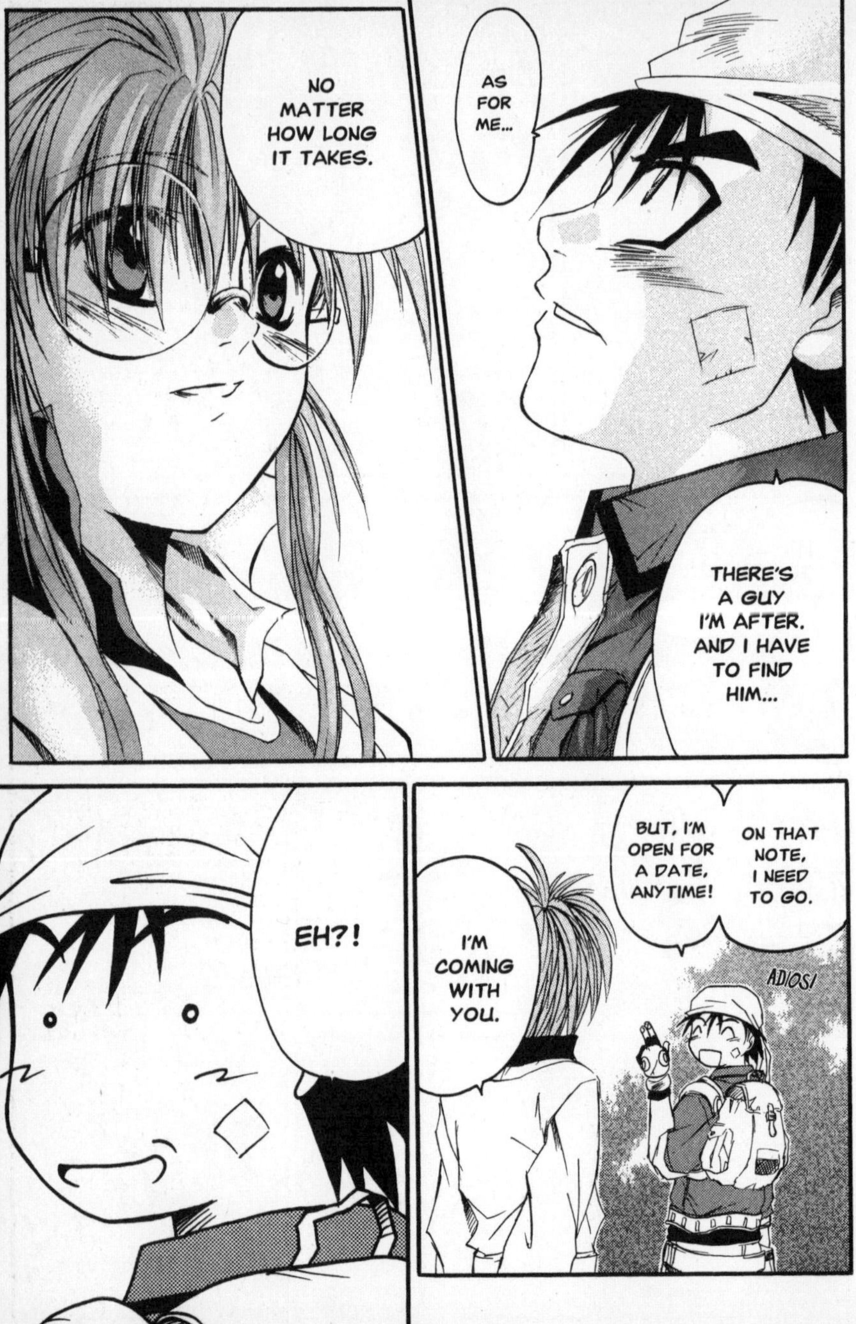
AS FOR ME...
THERE'S A GUY I'M AFTER. AND I HAVE TO FIND HIM...
NO MATTER HOW LONG IT TAKES.
ON THAT NOTE, I NEED TO GO.
BUT, I'M OPEN FOR A DATE, ANYTIME!
ADIOS!
I'M COMING WITH YOU.
EH?!

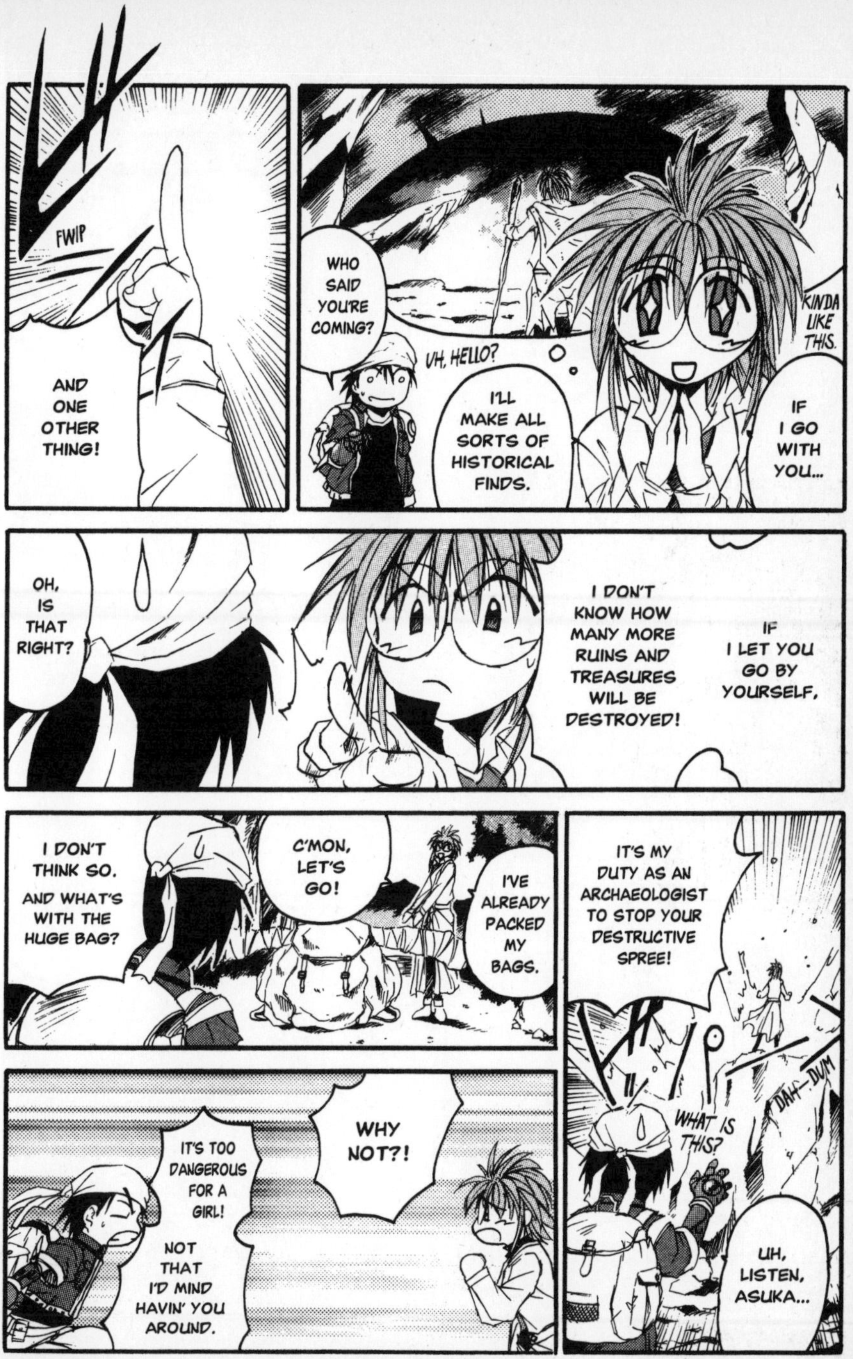
IF I GO WITH YOU...
KINDA LIKE THIS.
I'LL MAKE ALL SORTS OF HISTORICAL FINDS.
UH, HELLO?
WHO SAID YOU'RE COMING?
FWIP
AND ONE OTHER THING!
IF I LET YOU GO BY YOURSELF,
I DON'T KNOW HOW MANY MORE RUINS AND TREASURES WILL BE DESTROYED!
OH, IS THAT RIGHT?
IT'S MY DUTY AS AN ARCHAEOLOGIST TO STOP YOUR DESTRUCTIVE SPREE!
DAH-DUM
WHAT IS THIS?
UH, LISTEN, ASUKA...
I'VE ALREADY PACKED MY BAGS.
C'MON, LET'S GO!
I DON'T THINK SO.
AND WHAT'S WITH THE HUGE BAG?
WHY NOT?!
IT'S TOO DANGEROUS FOR A GIRL!
NOT THAT I'D MIND HAVIN' YOU AROUND.

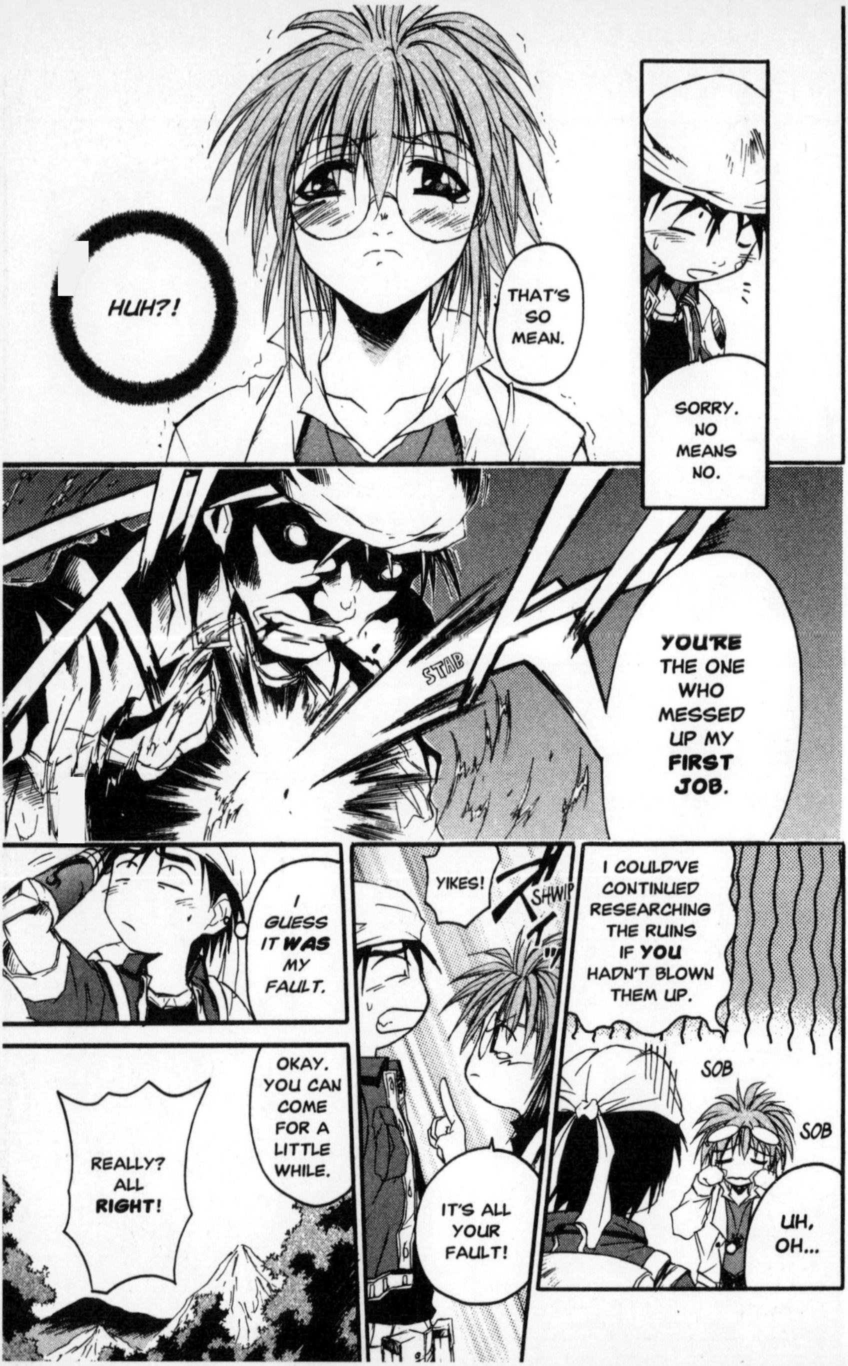
SORRY. NO MEANS NO.
THAT'S SO MEAN.
HUH?!
YOU'RE THE ONE WHO MESSED UP MY FIRST JOB.
STAB
I COULD'VE CONTINUED RESEARCHING THE RUINS IF YOU HADN'T BLOWN THEM UP.
SOB
SOB
UH, OH...
YIKES!
SHWIP
IT'S ALL YOUR FAULT!
I GUESS IT WAS MY FAULT.
OKAY. YOU CAN COME FOR A LITTLE WHILE.
REALLY? ALL RIGHT!

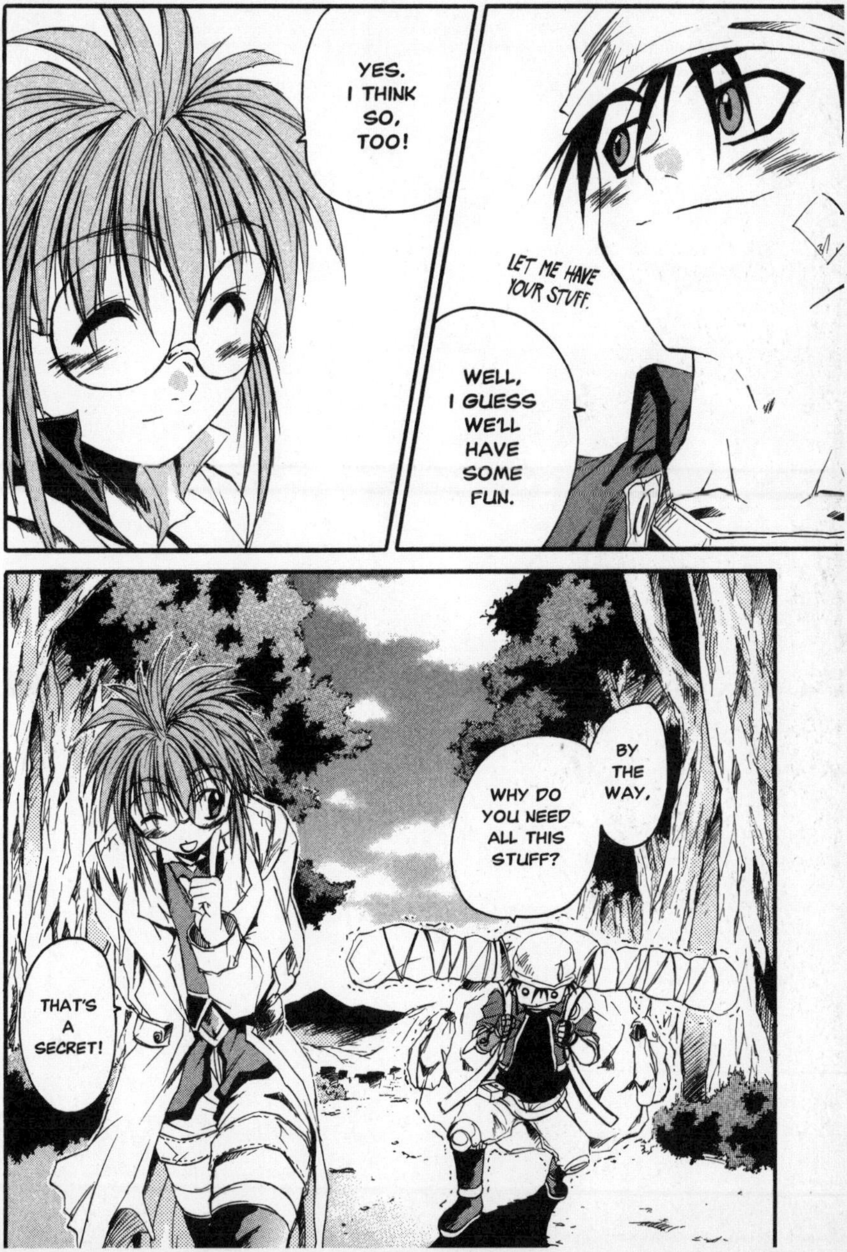
LET ME HAVE YOUR STUFF.
WELL, I GUESS WE'LL HAVE SOME FUN.
YES. I THINK SO, TOO!
BY THE WAY,
WHY DO YOU NEED ALL THIS STUFF?
THAT'S A SECRET!

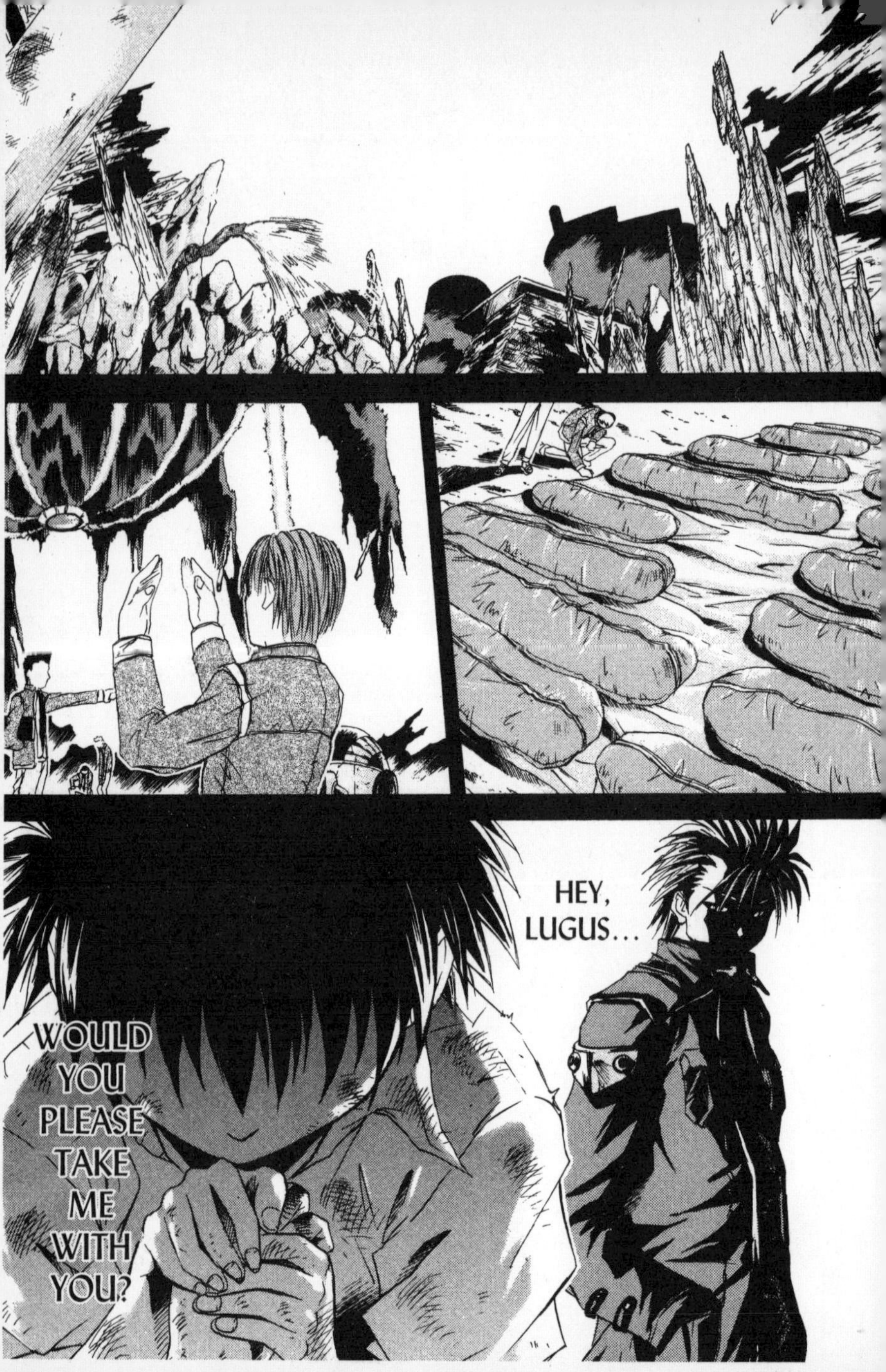
HEY, LUGUS...
WOULD YOU PLEASE TAKE ME WITH YOU?

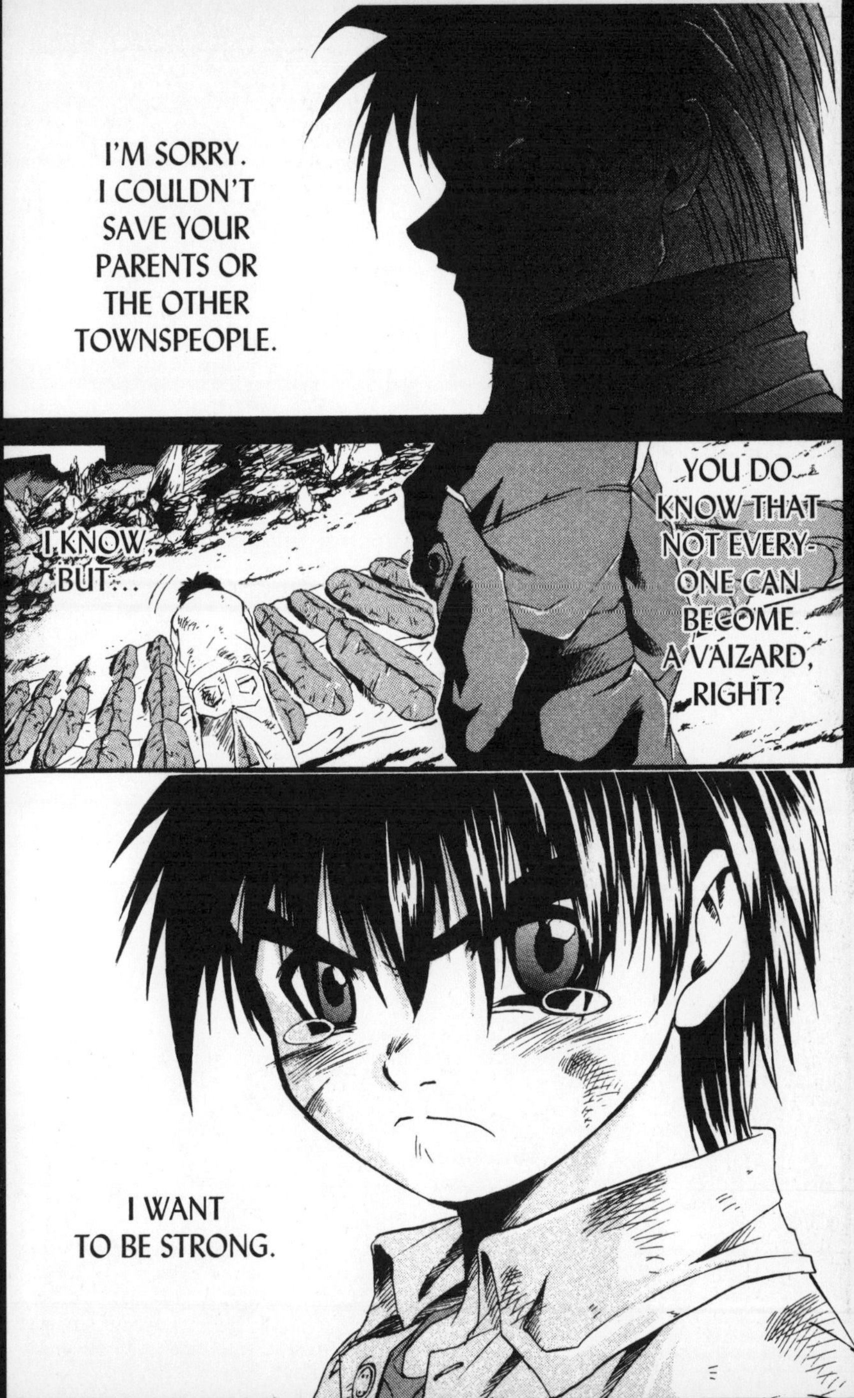
I'M SORRY. I COULDN'T SAVE YOUR PARENTS OR THE OTHER TOWNSPEOPLE.
YOU DO KNOW THAT NOT EVERY-ONE CAN BECOME A VAIZARD, RIGHT?
I KNOW, BUT...
I WANT TO BE STRONG.

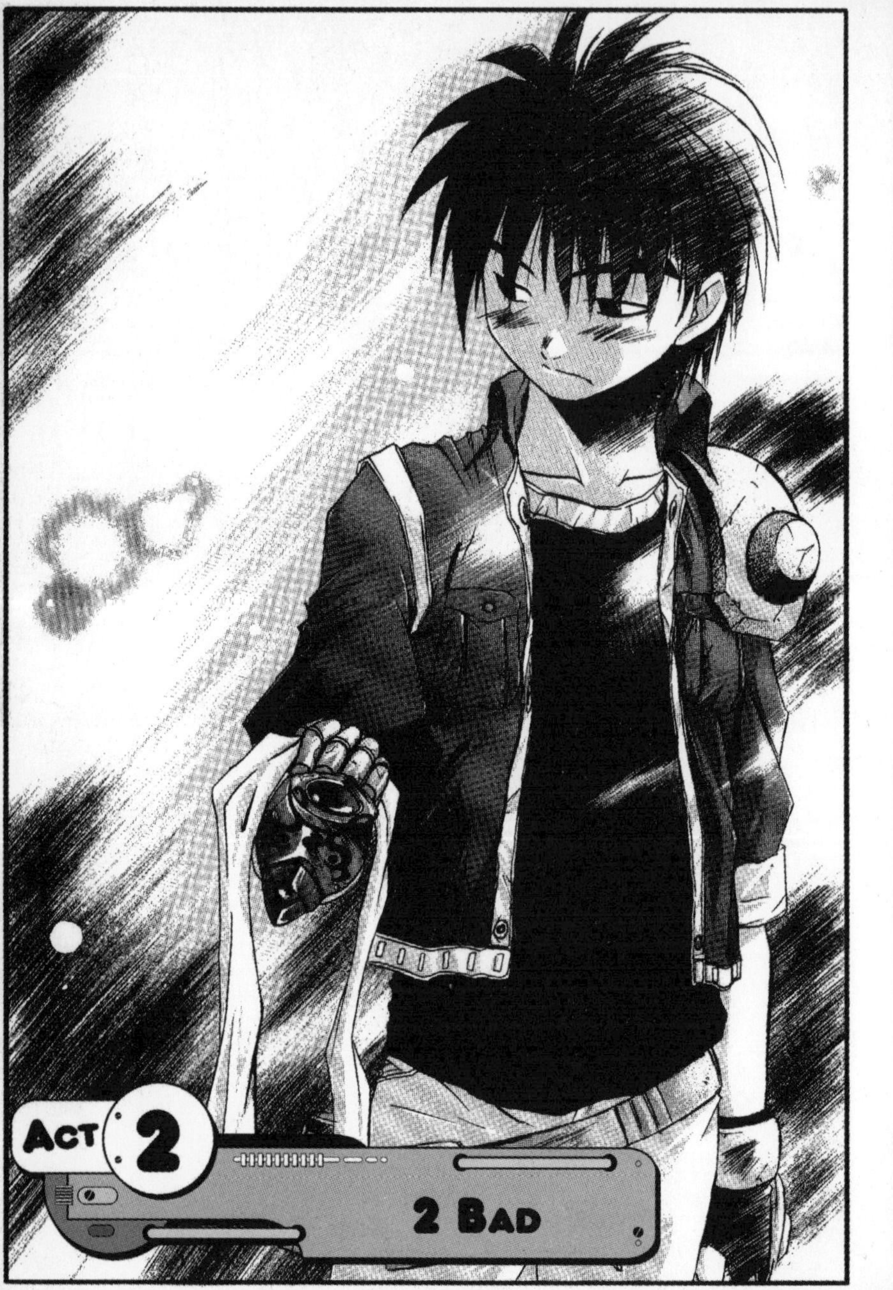
ACT 2
2 BAD

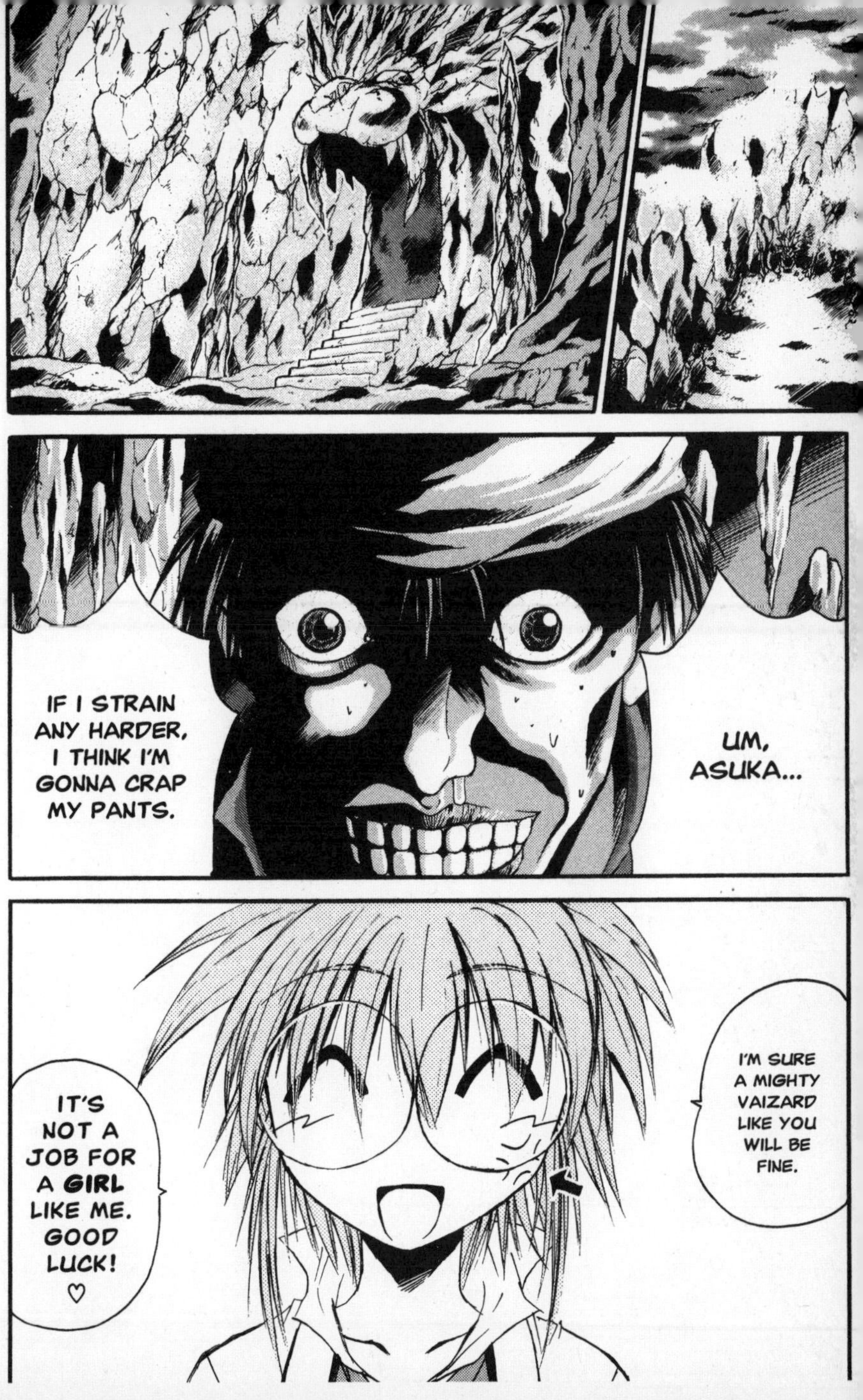
UM, ASUKA...
IF I STRAIN ANY HARDER, I THINK I'M GONNA CRAP MY PANTS.
I'M SURE A MIGHTY VAIZARD LIKE YOU WILL BE FINE.
IT'S NOT A JOB FOR A **GIRL** LIKE ME. GOOD LUCK! ♡

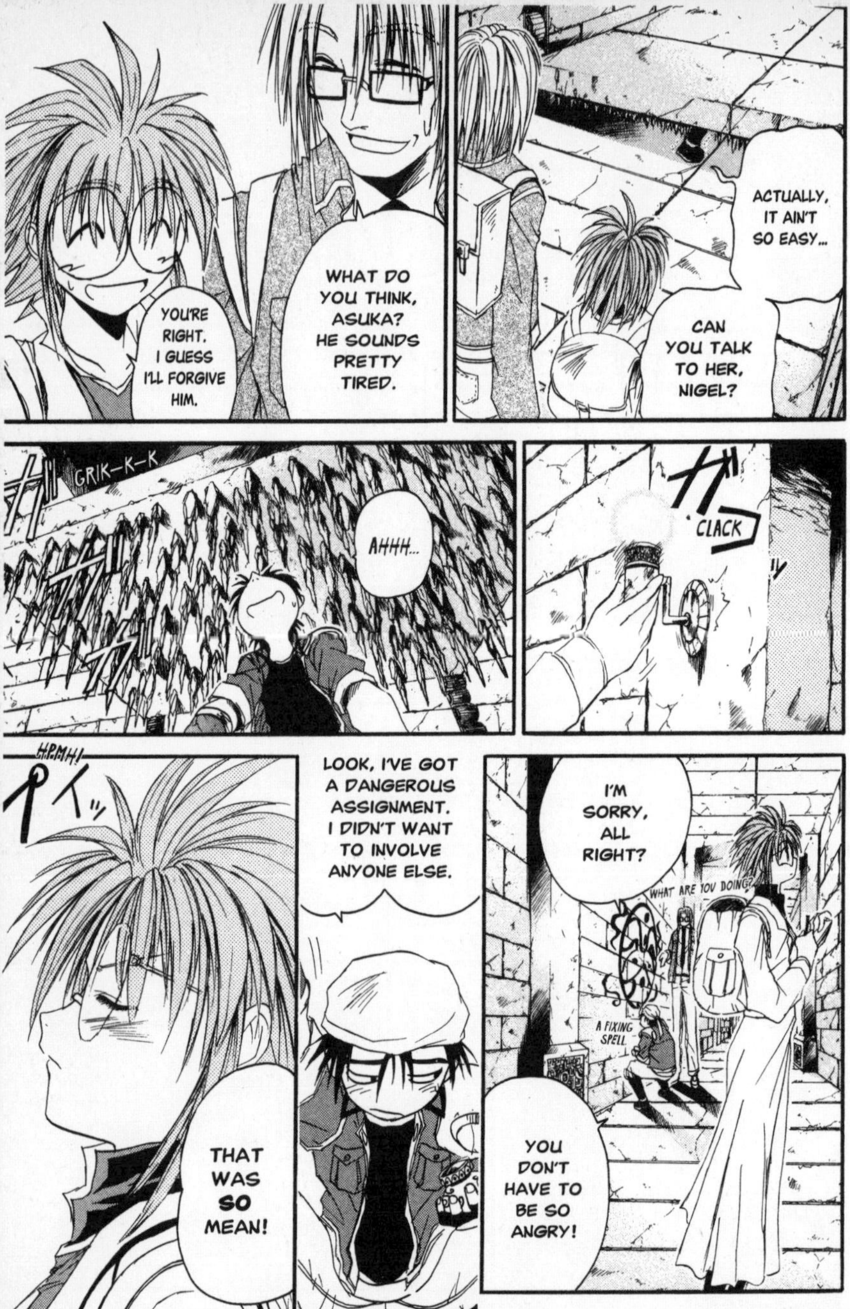
ACTUALLY, IT AIN'T SO EASY...
CAN YOU TALK TO HER, NIGEL?
WHAT DO YOU THINK, ASUKA? HE SOUNDS PRETTY TIRED.
YOU'RE RIGHT. I GUESS I'LL FORGIVE HIM.
CLACK
GRIK-K-K
AHHH...
I'M SORRY, ALL RIGHT?
WHAT ARE YOU DOING?
A FIXING SPELL
YOU DON'T HAVE TO BE SO ANGRY!
HPMH!
LOOK, I'VE GOT A DANGEROUS ASSIGNMENT. I DIDN'T WANT TO INVOLVE ANYONE ELSE.
THAT WAS SO MEAN!

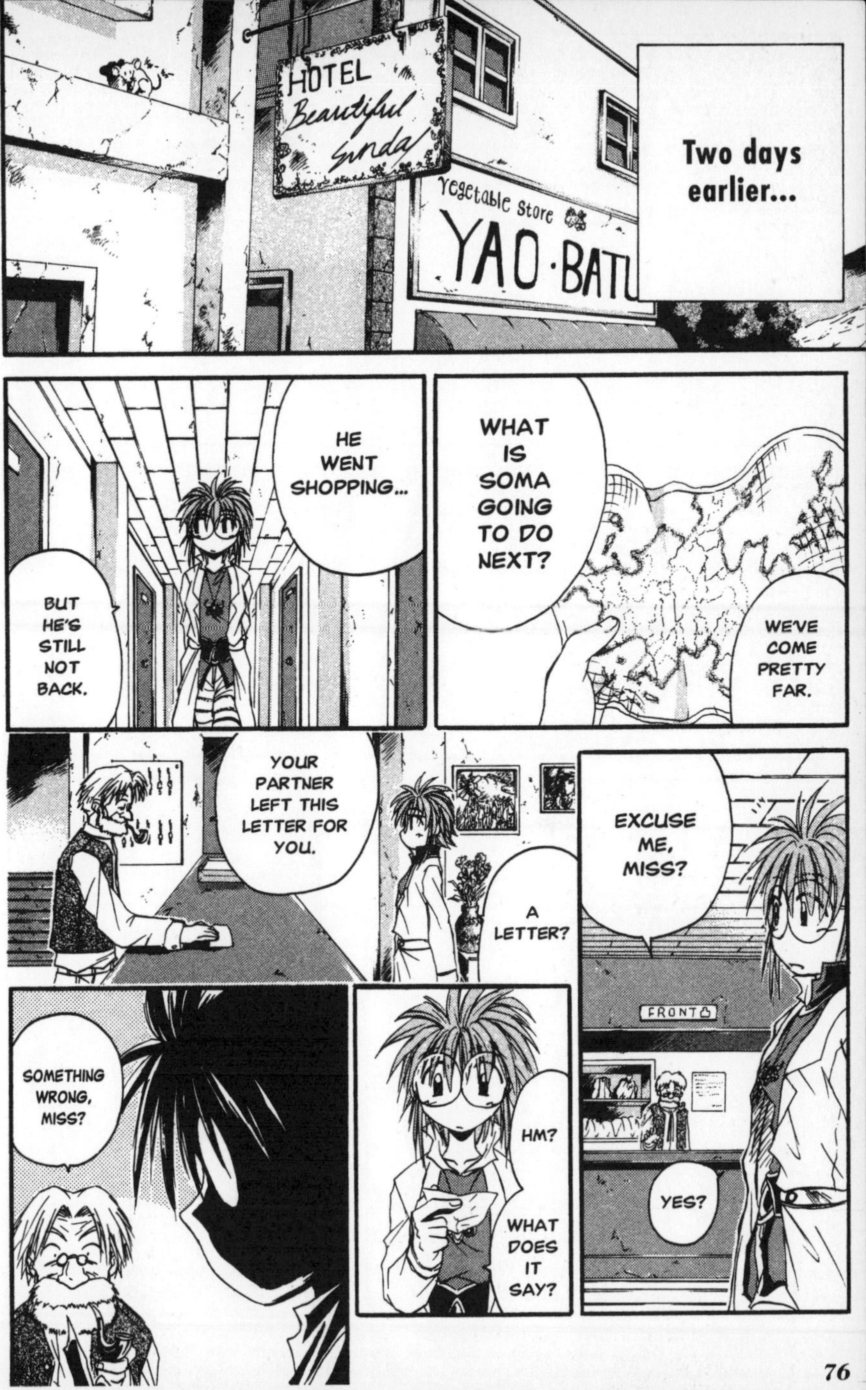
HOTEL
Beautiful
Sunda
Vegetable Store
YAO·BATU
Two days earlier...
WHAT IS SOMA GOING TO DO NEXT?
WE'VE COME PRETTY FAR.
HE WENT SHOPPING...
BUT HE'S STILL NOT BACK.
EXCUSE ME, MISS?
YES?
FRONT
YOUR PARTNER LEFT THIS LETTER FOR YOU.
A LETTER?
HM?
WHAT DOES IT SAY?
SOMETHING WRONG, MISS?

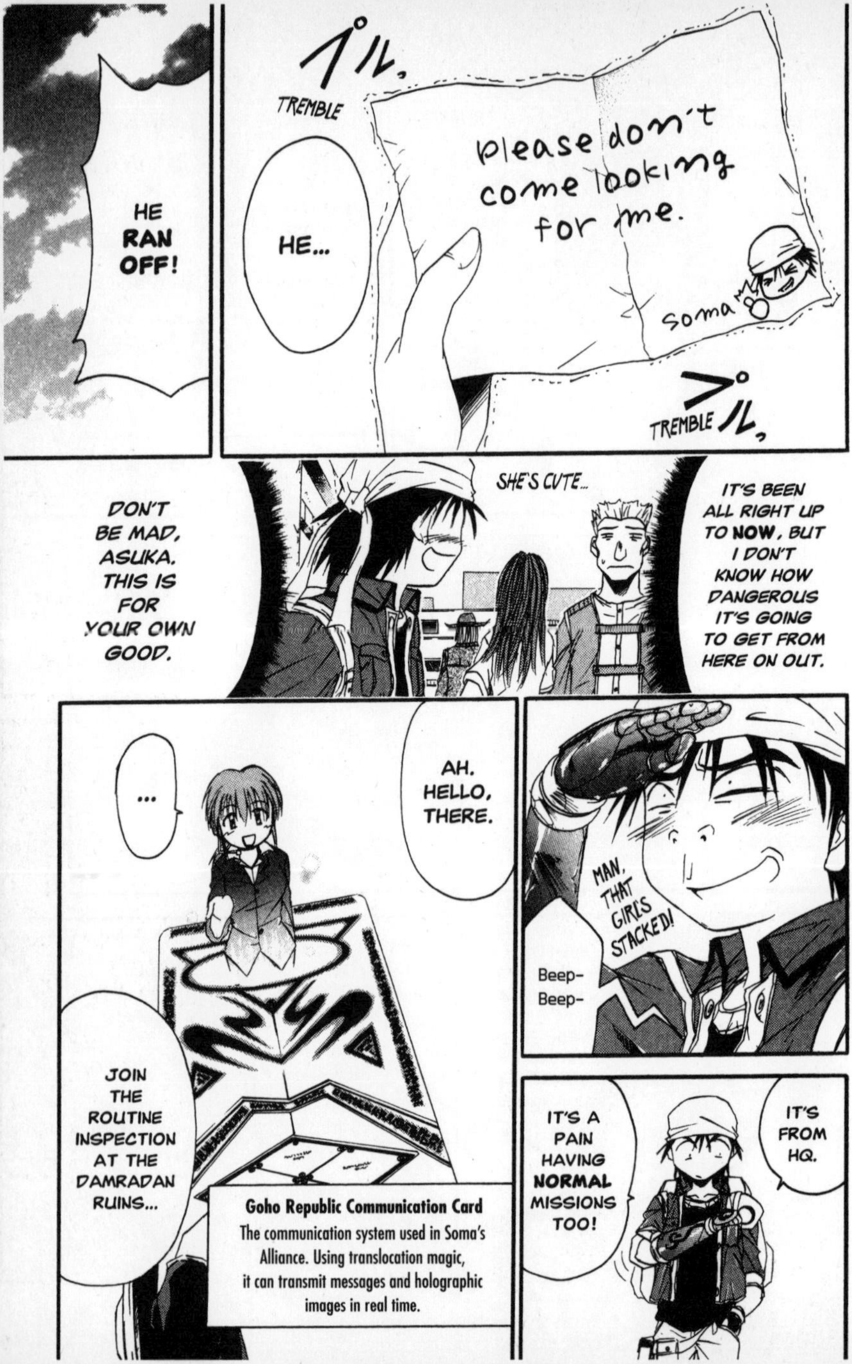
TREMBLE
HE...
please don't come looking for me.
Soma
TREMBLE
HE RAN OFF!
IT'S BEEN ALL RIGHT UP TO NOW, BUT I DON'T KNOW HOW DANGEROUS IT'S GOING TO GET FROM HERE ON OUT.
SHE'S CUTE...
DON'T BE MAD, ASUKA. THIS IS FOR YOUR OWN GOOD.
Beep-Beep-
MAN, THAT GIRL'S STACKED!
IT'S FROM HQ.
IT'S A PAIN HAVING NORMAL MISSIONS TOO!
AH. HELLO, THERE.
...
JOIN THE ROUTINE INSPECTION AT THE DAMRADAN RUINS...
Goho Republic Communication Card
The communication system used in Soma's Alliance. Using translocation magic, it can transmit messages and holographic images in real time.

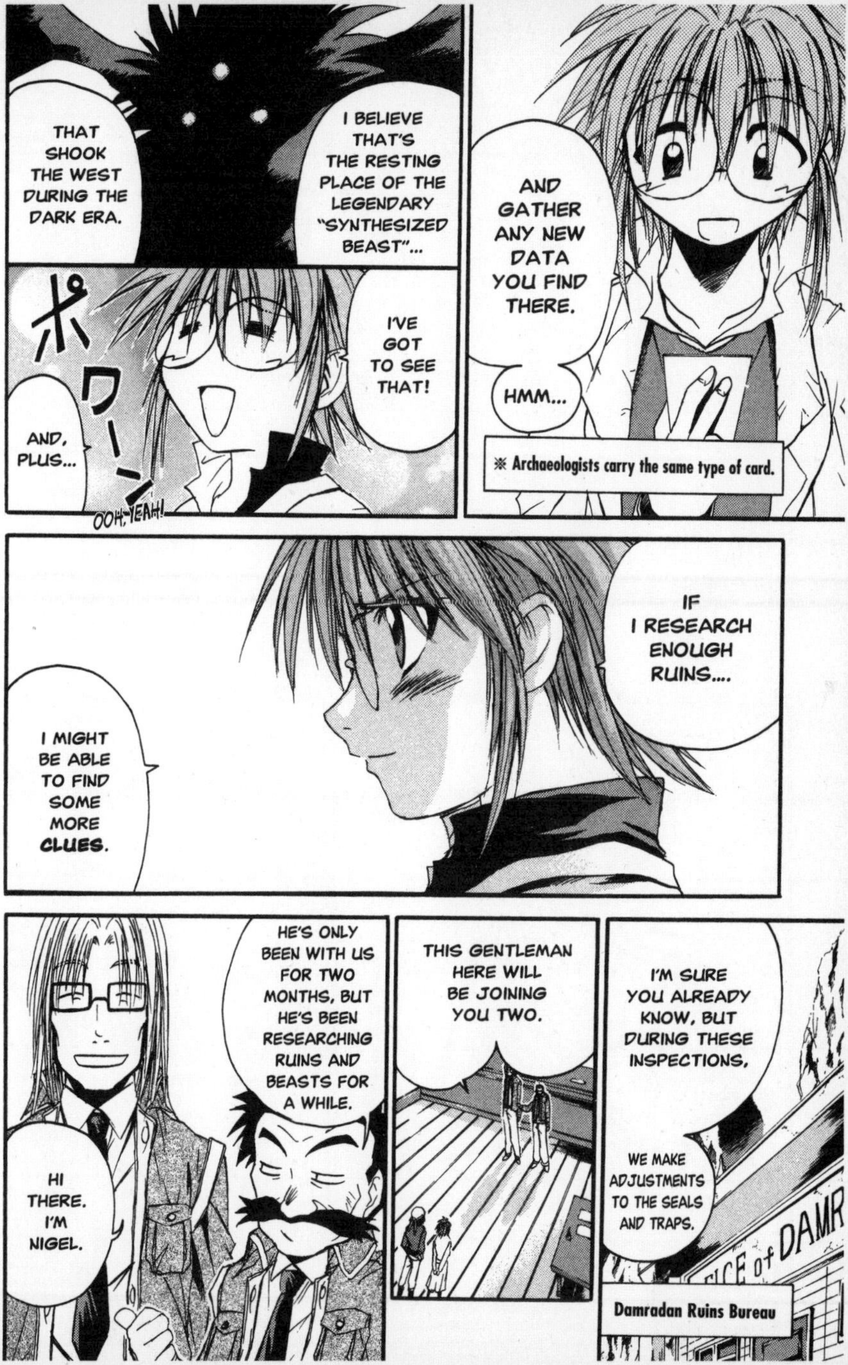

AND GATHER ANY NEW DATA YOU FIND THERE.
HMM...
※ Archaeologists carry the same type of card.
I BELIEVE THAT'S THE RESTING PLACE OF THE LEGENDARY "SYNTHESIZED BEAST"...
THAT SHOOK THE WEST DURING THE DARK ERA.
I'VE GOT TO SEE THAT!
ポワーン
OOH, YEAH!
AND, PLUS...
IF I RESEARCH ENOUGH RUINS....
I MIGHT BE ABLE TO FIND SOME MORE CLUES.
Damradan Ruins Bureau
I'M SURE YOU ALREADY KNOW, BUT DURING THESE INSPECTIONS,
WE MAKE ADJUSTMENTS TO THE SEALS AND TRAPS.
THIS GENTLEMAN HERE WILL BE JOINING YOU TWO.
HE'S ONLY BEEN WITH US FOR TWO MONTHS, BUT HE'S BEEN RESEARCHING RUINS AND BEASTS FOR A WHILE.
HI THERE. I'M NIGEL.

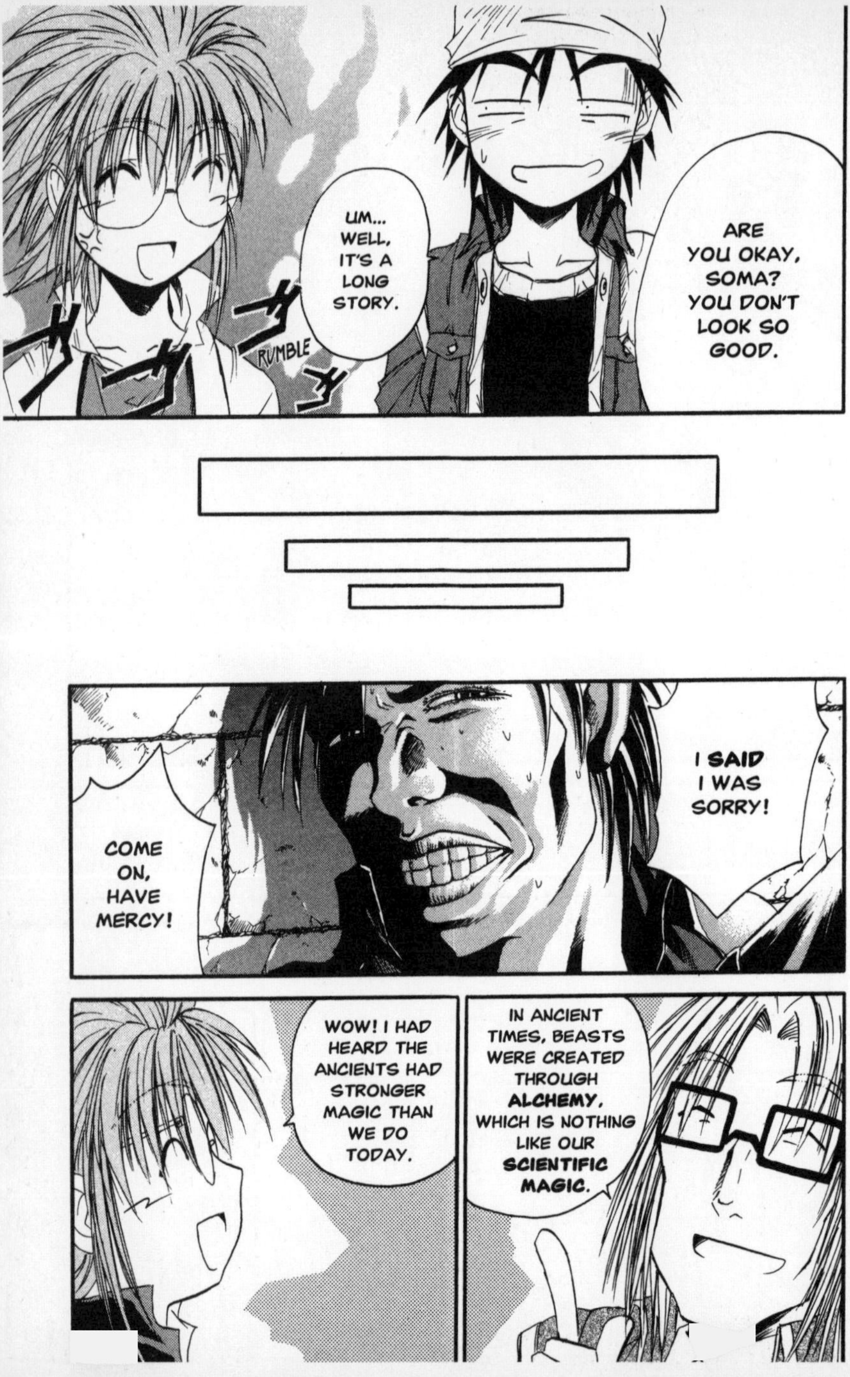
ARE YOU OKAY, SOMA? YOU DON'T LOOK SO GOOD.
UM... WELL, IT'S A LONG STORY.
RUMBLE
I SAID I WAS SORRY!
COME ON, HAVE MERCY!
WOW! I HAD HEARD THE ANCIENTS HAD STRONGER MAGIC THAN WE DO TODAY.
IN ANCIENT TIMES, BEASTS WERE CREATED THROUGH ALCHEMY, WHICH IS NOTHING LIKE OUR SCIENTIFIC MAGIC.

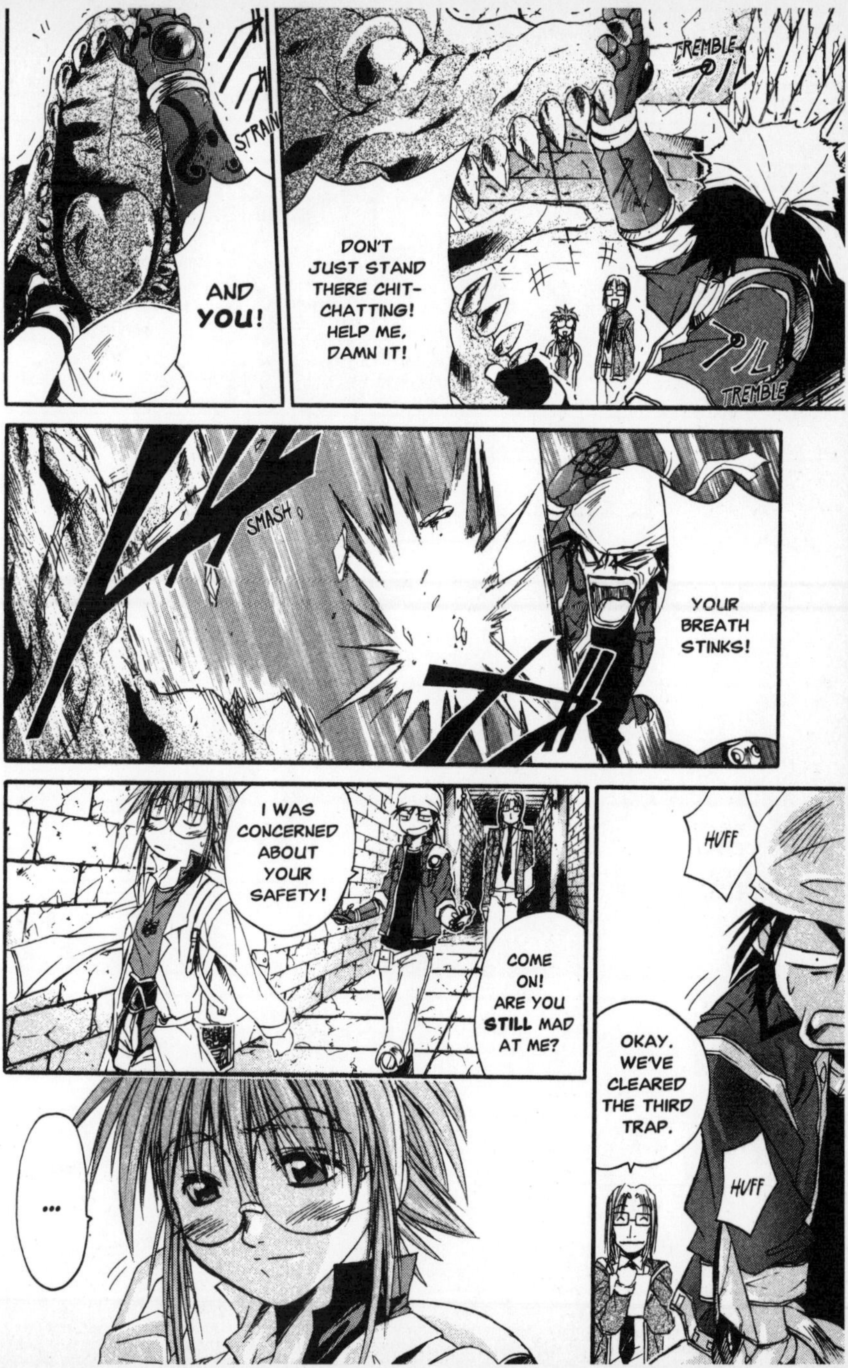

TREMBLE
DON'T JUST STAND THERE CHIT-CHATTING! HELP ME, DAMN IT!
TREMBLE
STRAIN
AND YOU!
SMASH
YOUR BREATH STINKS!
HUFF
OKAY. WE'VE CLEARED THE THIRD TRAP.
HUFF
I WAS CONCERNED ABOUT YOUR SAFETY!
COME ON! ARE YOU STILL MAD AT ME?
...

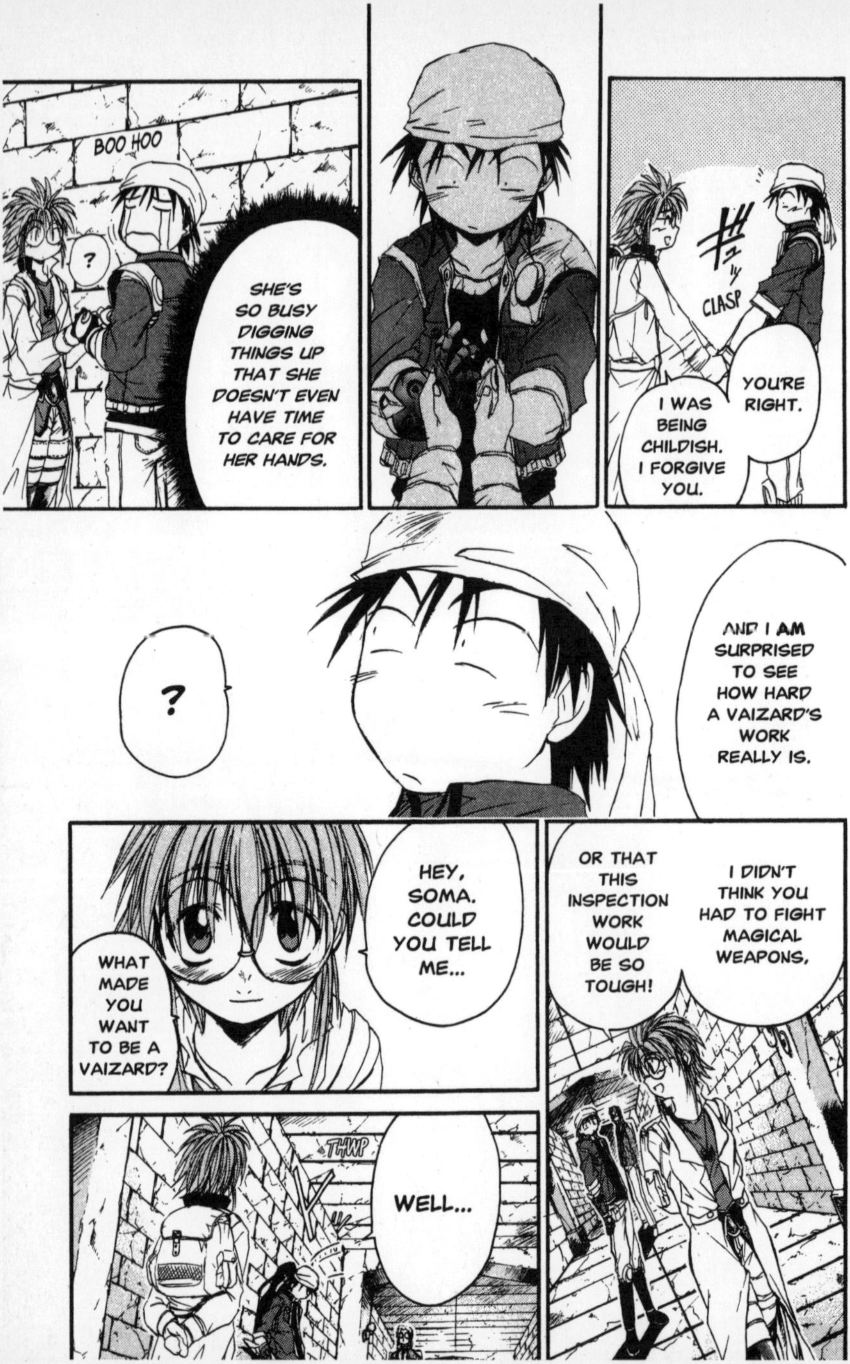
BOO HOO
?
SHE'S SO BUSY DIGGING THINGS UP THAT SHE DOESN'T EVEN HAVE TIME TO CARE FOR HER HANDS.
CLASP
YOU'RE RIGHT.
I WAS BEING CHILDISH. I FORGIVE YOU.
?
AND I AM SURPRISED TO SEE HOW HARD A VAIZARD'S WORK REALLY IS.
I DIDN'T THINK YOU HAD TO FIGHT MAGICAL WEAPONS,
OR THAT THIS INSPECTION WORK WOULD BE SO TOUGH!
HEY, SOMA. COULD YOU TELL ME...
WHAT MADE YOU WANT TO BE A VAIZARD?
THWP
WELL...

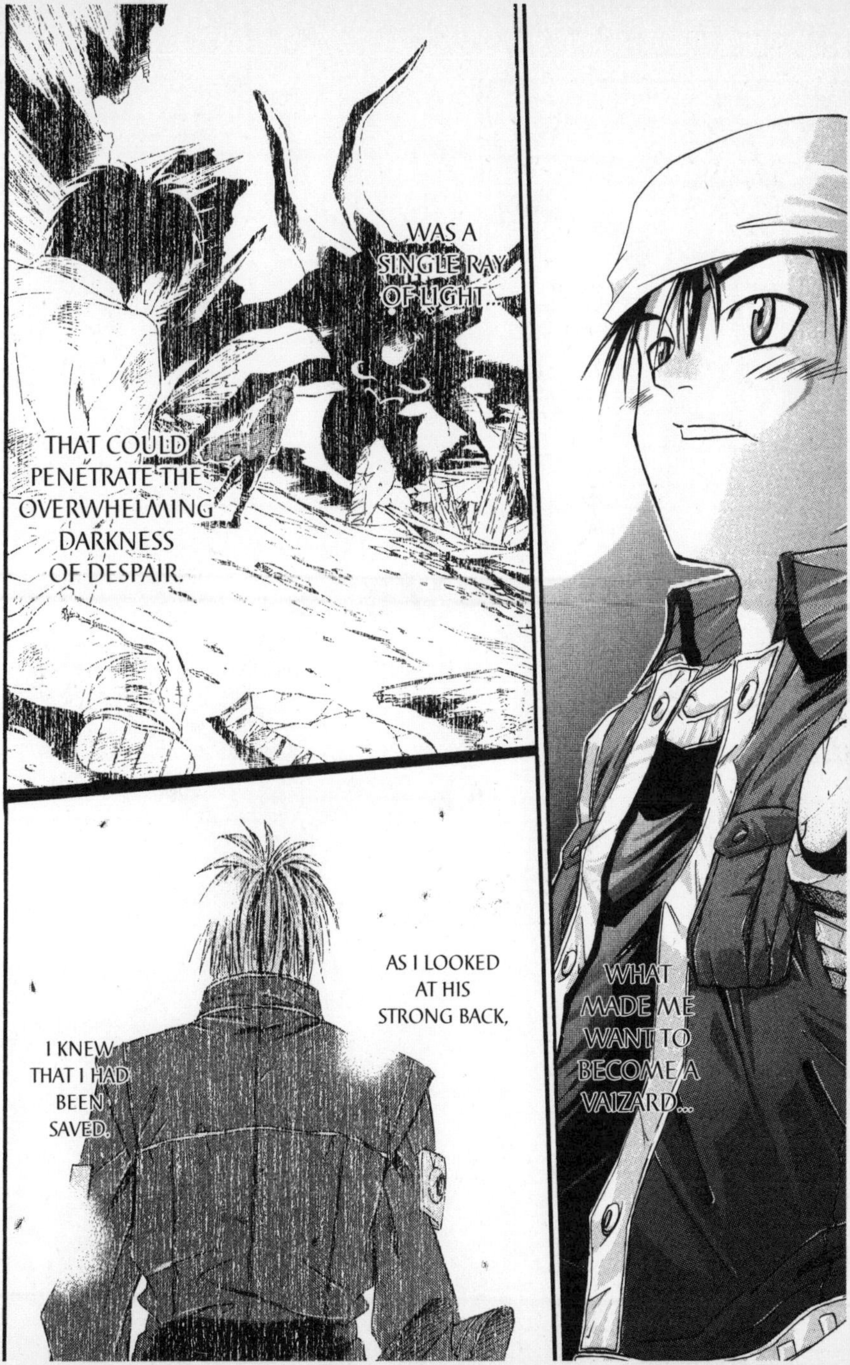
WHAT MADE ME WANT TO BECOME A VAIZARD...
WAS A SINGLE RAY OF LIGHT...
THAT COULD PENETRATE THE OVERWHELMING DARKNESS OF DESPAIR.
AS I LOOKED AT HIS STRONG BACK,
I KNEW THAT I HAD BEEN SAVED.

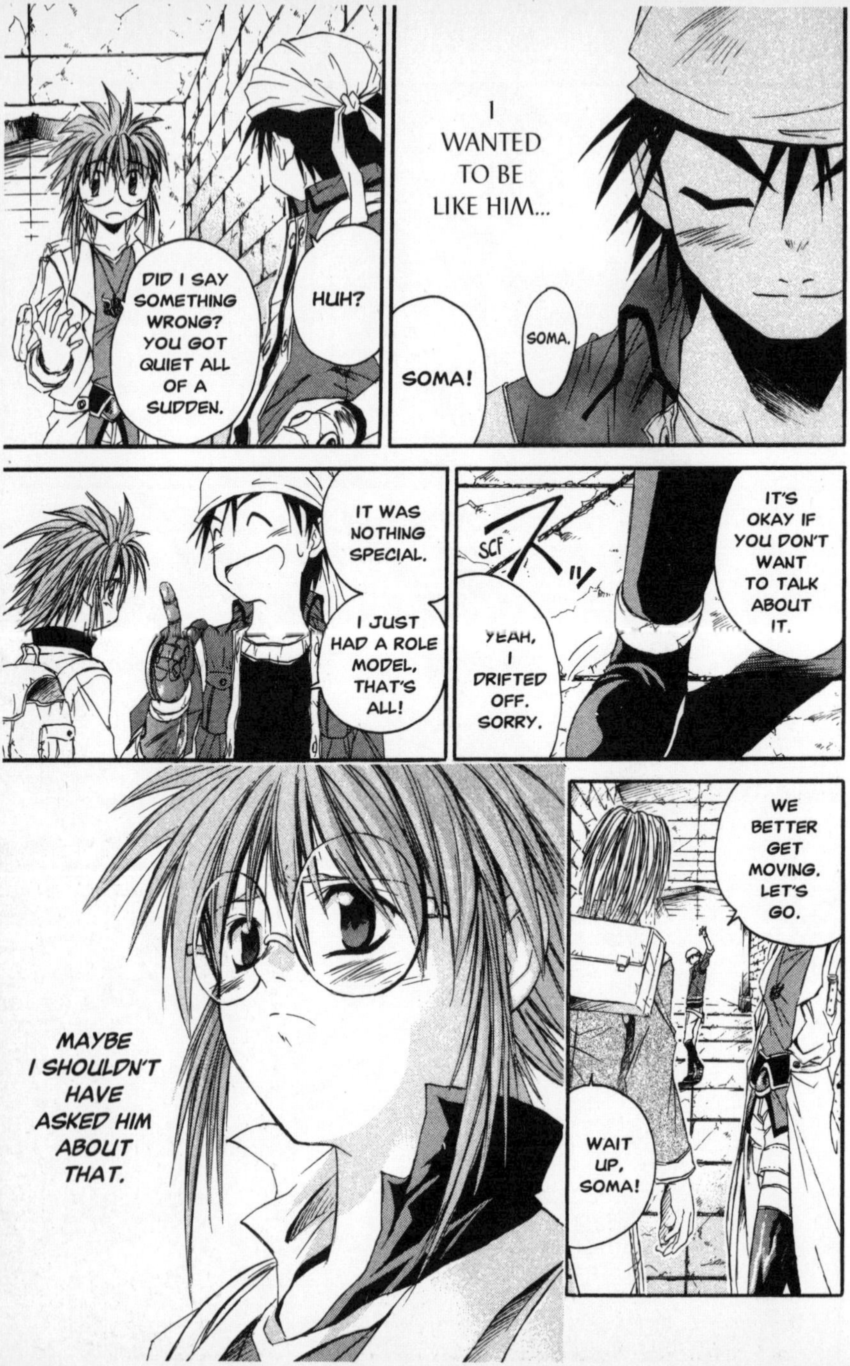
I WANTED TO BE LIKE HIM...
SOMA.
SOMA!
HUH?
DID I SAY SOMETHING WRONG? YOU GOT QUIET ALL OF A SUDDEN.
IT'S OKAY IF YOU DON'T WANT TO TALK ABOUT IT.
SCF
YEAH, I DRIFTED OFF. SORRY.
IT WAS NOTHING SPECIAL.
I JUST HAD A ROLE MODEL, THAT'S ALL!
WE BETTER GET MOVING. LET'S GO.
WAIT UP, SOMA!
MAYBE I SHOULDN'T HAVE ASKED HIM ABOUT THAT.

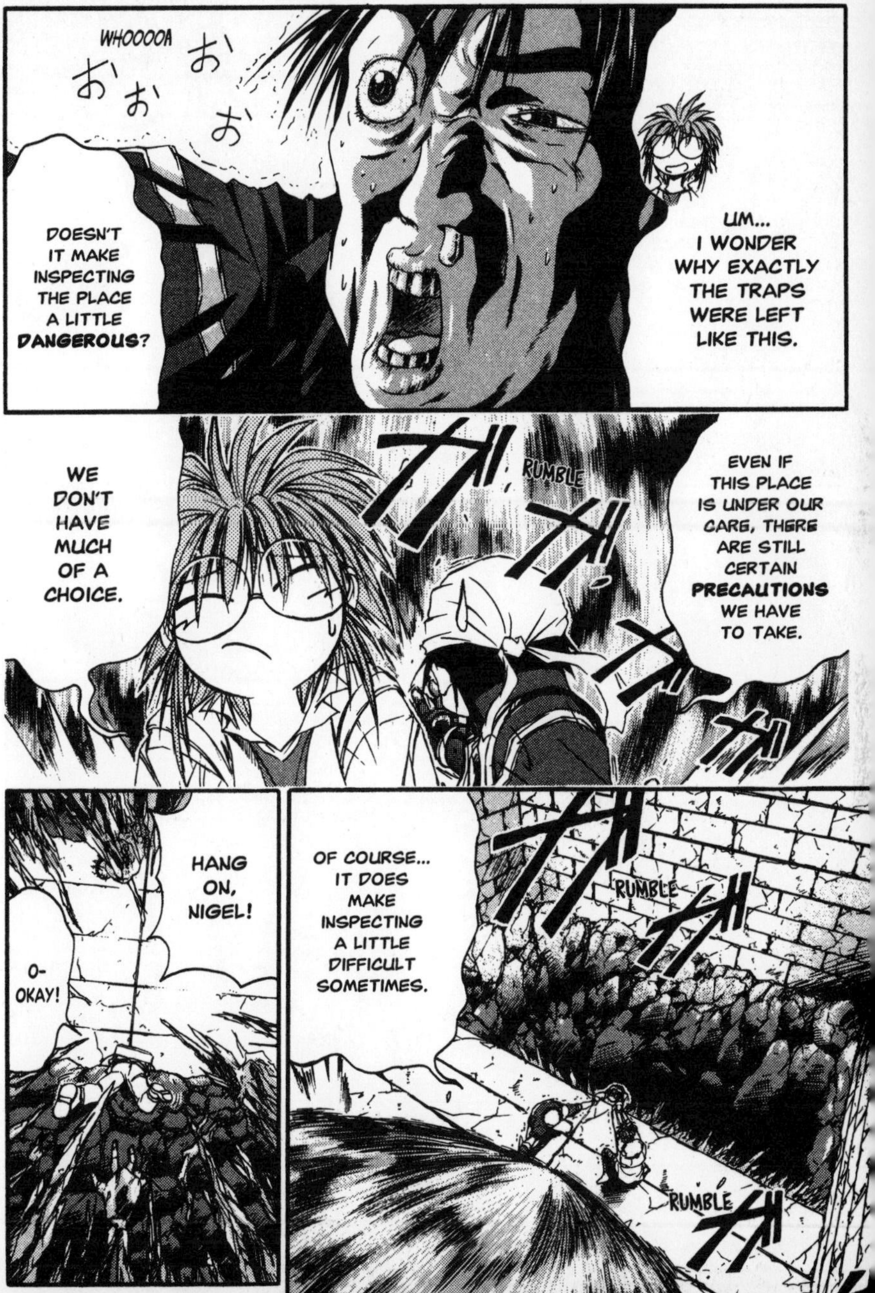

UM... I WONDER WHY EXACTLY THE TRAPS WERE LEFT LIKE THIS.
WHOOOOA
おぉぉぉ
DOESN'T IT MAKE INSPECTING THE PLACE A LITTLE **DANGEROUS**?
EVEN IF THIS PLACE IS UNDER OUR CARE, THERE ARE STILL CERTAIN **PRECAUTIONS** WE HAVE TO TAKE.
RUMBLE
WE DON'T HAVE MUCH OF A CHOICE.
RUMBLE
OF COURSE... IT DOES MAKE INSPECTING A LITTLE DIFFICULT SOMETIMES.
RUMBLE
HANG ON, NIGEL!
O-OKAY!

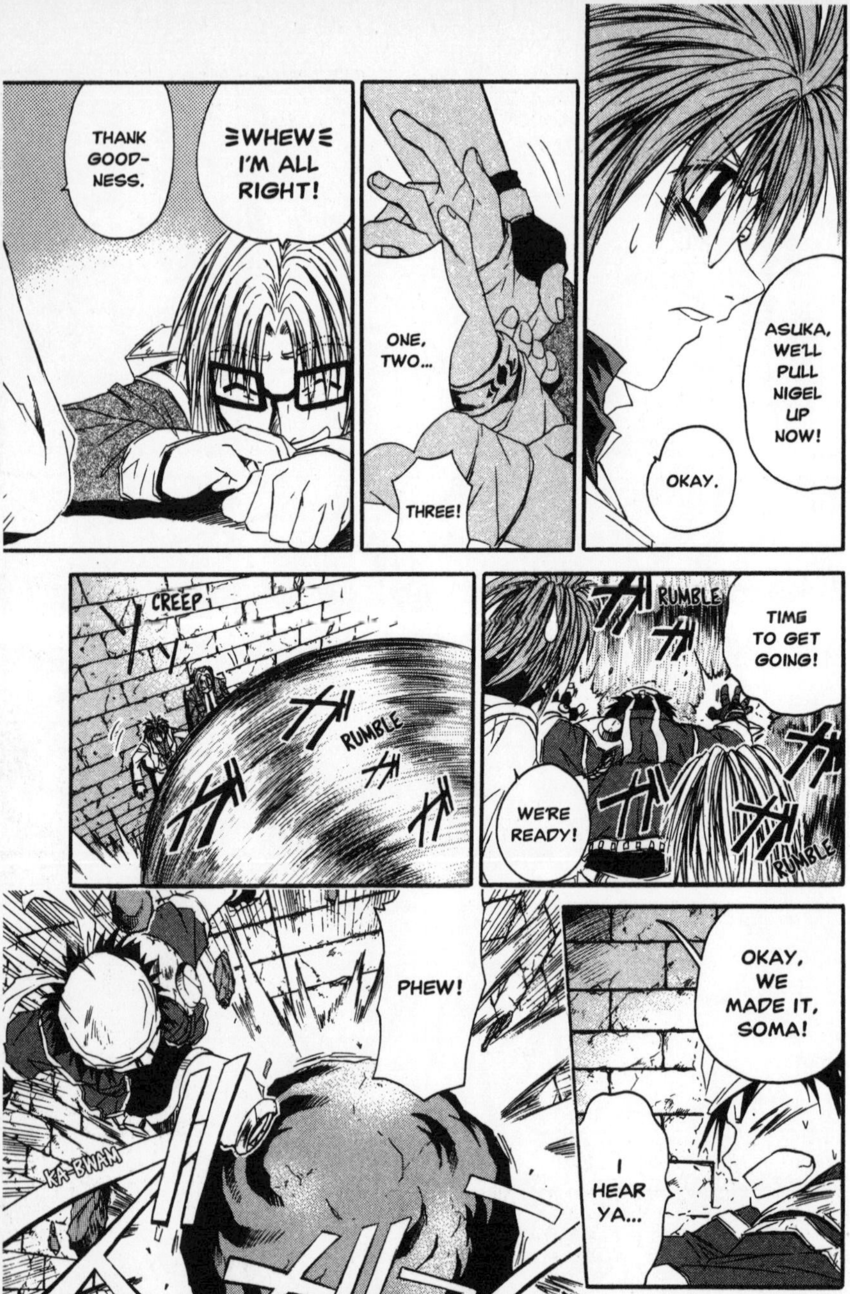
ASUKA, WE'LL PULL NIGEL UP NOW!
OKAY.
ONE, TWO...
THREE!
≡WHEW≡ I'M ALL RIGHT!
THANK GOODNESS.
RUMBLE
TIME TO GET GOING!
WE'RE READY!
RUMBLE
CREEP
RUMBLE
OKAY, WE MADE IT, SOMA!
I HEAR YA...
PHEW!
KA-BWAM

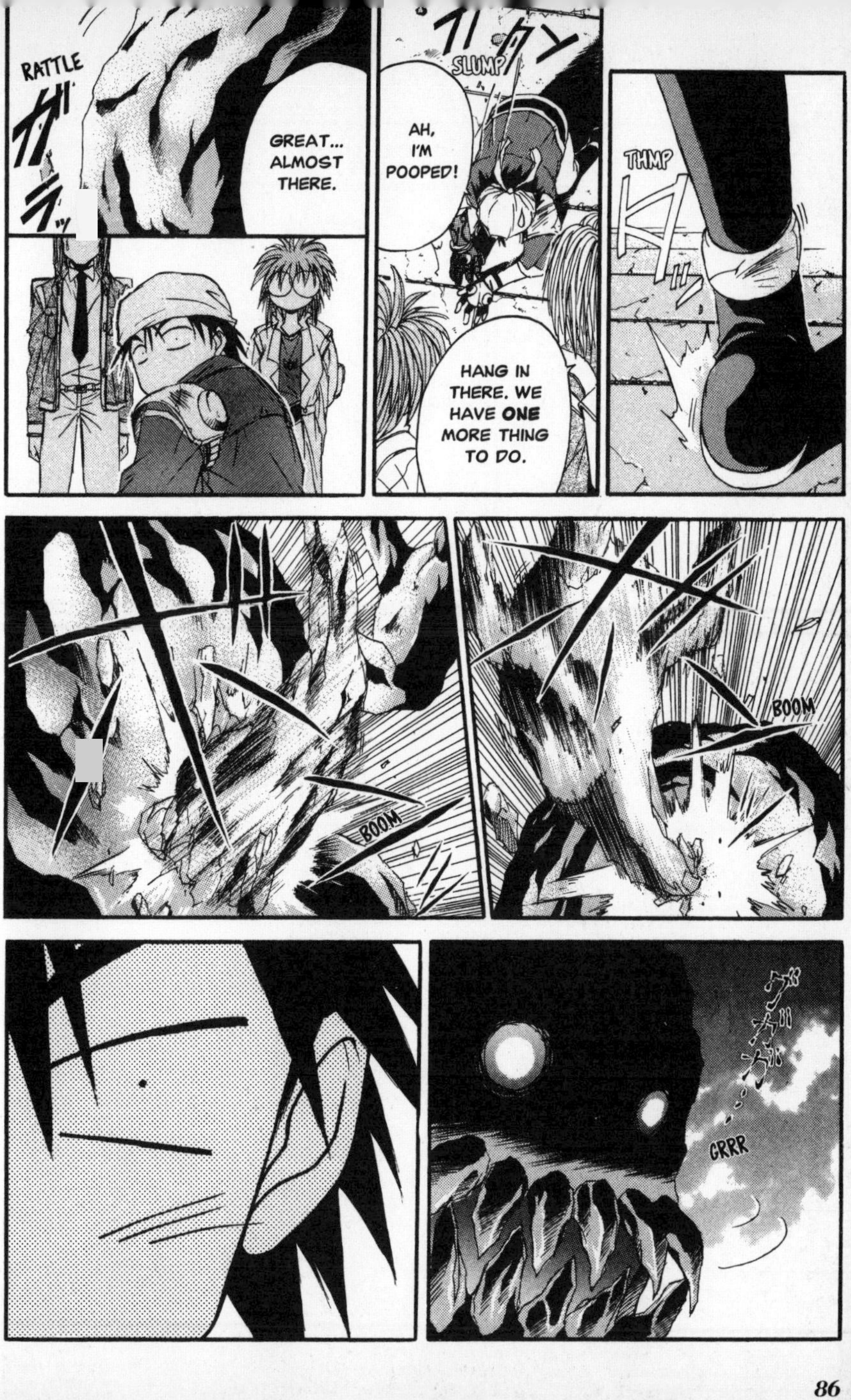
THMP
SLUMP
AH, I'M POOPED!
HANG IN THERE. WE HAVE ONE MORE THING TO DO.
RATTLE
GREAT... ALMOST THERE.
BOOM
BOOM
GRRR

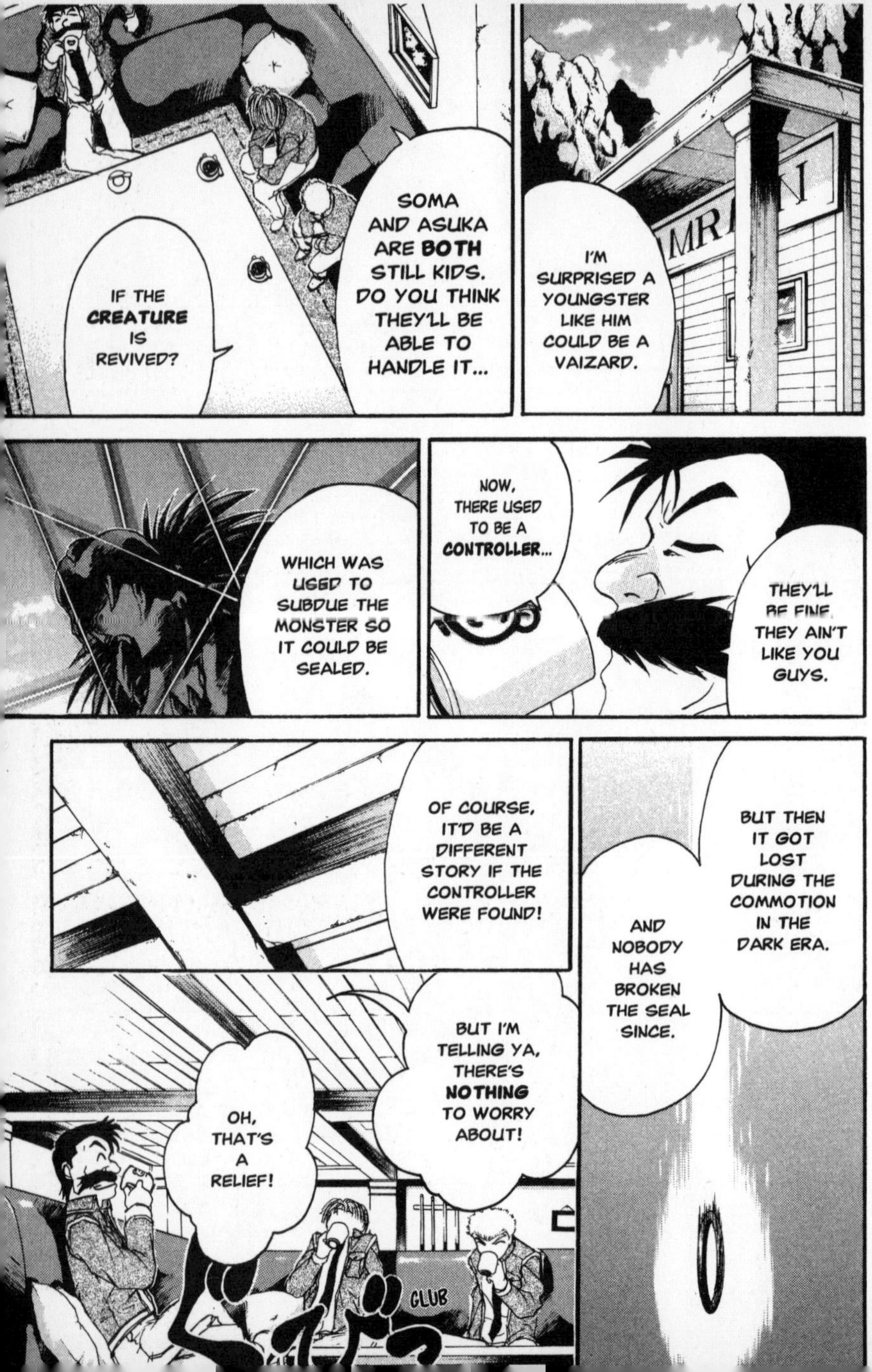
I'M SURPRISED A YOUNGSTER LIKE HIM COULD BE A VAIZARD.
SOMA AND ASUKA ARE **BOTH** STILL KIDS. DO YOU THINK THEY'LL BE ABLE TO HANDLE IT...
IF THE **CREATURE** IS REVIVED?
THEY'LL BE FINE. THEY AIN'T LIKE YOU GUYS.
NOW, THERE USED TO BE A **CONTROLLER**...
WHICH WAS USED TO SUBDUE THE MONSTER SO IT COULD BE SEALED.
BUT THEN IT GOT LOST DURING THE COMMOTION IN THE DARK ERA.
AND NOBODY HAS BROKEN THE SEAL SINCE.
OF COURSE, IT'D BE A DIFFERENT STORY IF THE CONTROLLER WERE FOUND!
BUT I'M TELLING YA, THERE'S **NOTHING** TO WORRY ABOUT!
OH, THAT'S A RELIEF!
GLUB

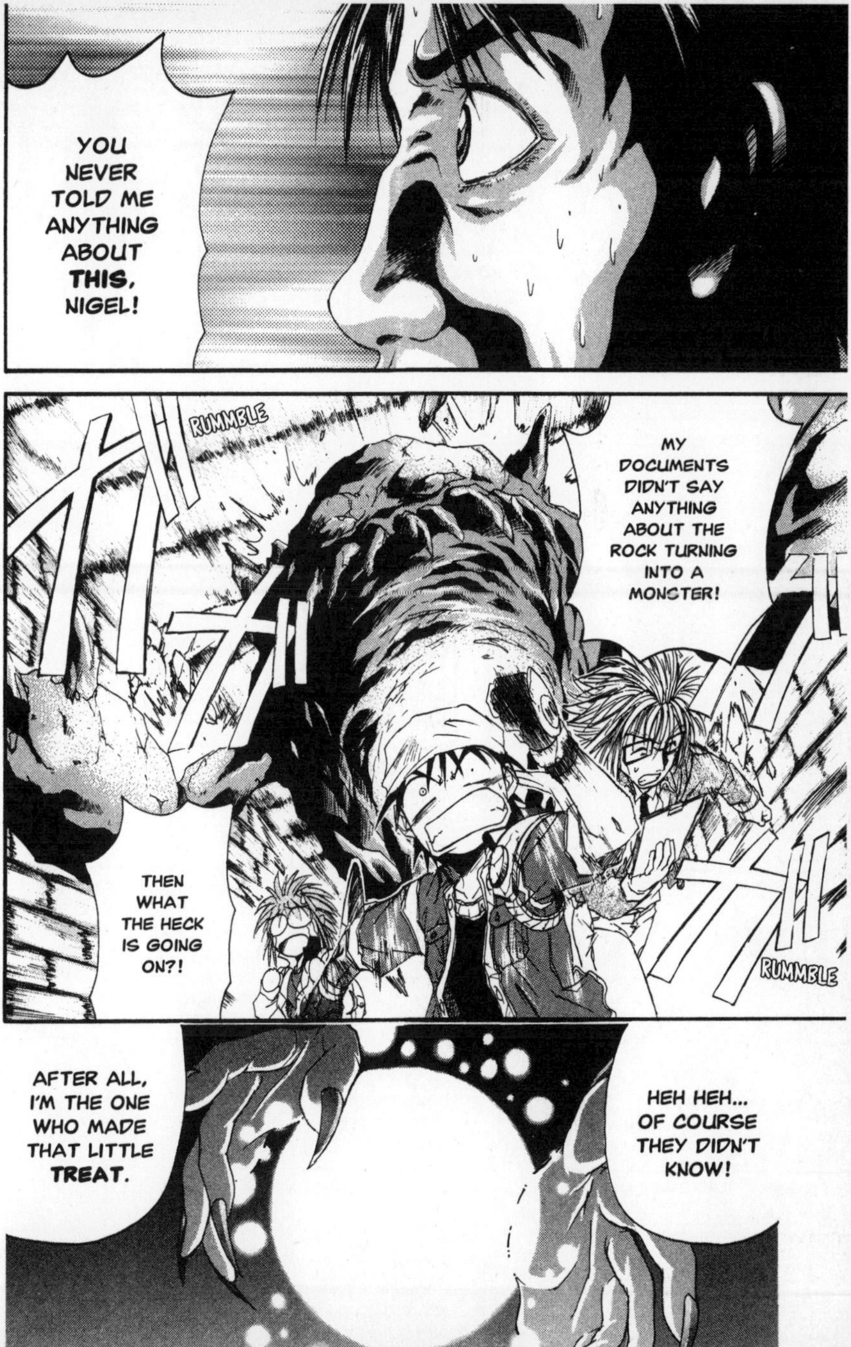
YOU NEVER TOLD ME ANYTHING ABOUT THIS, NIGEL!
RUMMBLE
MY DOCUMENTS DIDN'T SAY ANYTHING ABOUT THE ROCK TURNING INTO A MONCTER!
THEN WHAT THE HECK IS GOING ON?!
RUMMBLE
HEH HEH... OF COURSE THEY DIDN'T KNOW!
AFTER ALL, I'M THE ONE WHO MADE THAT LITTLE TREAT.

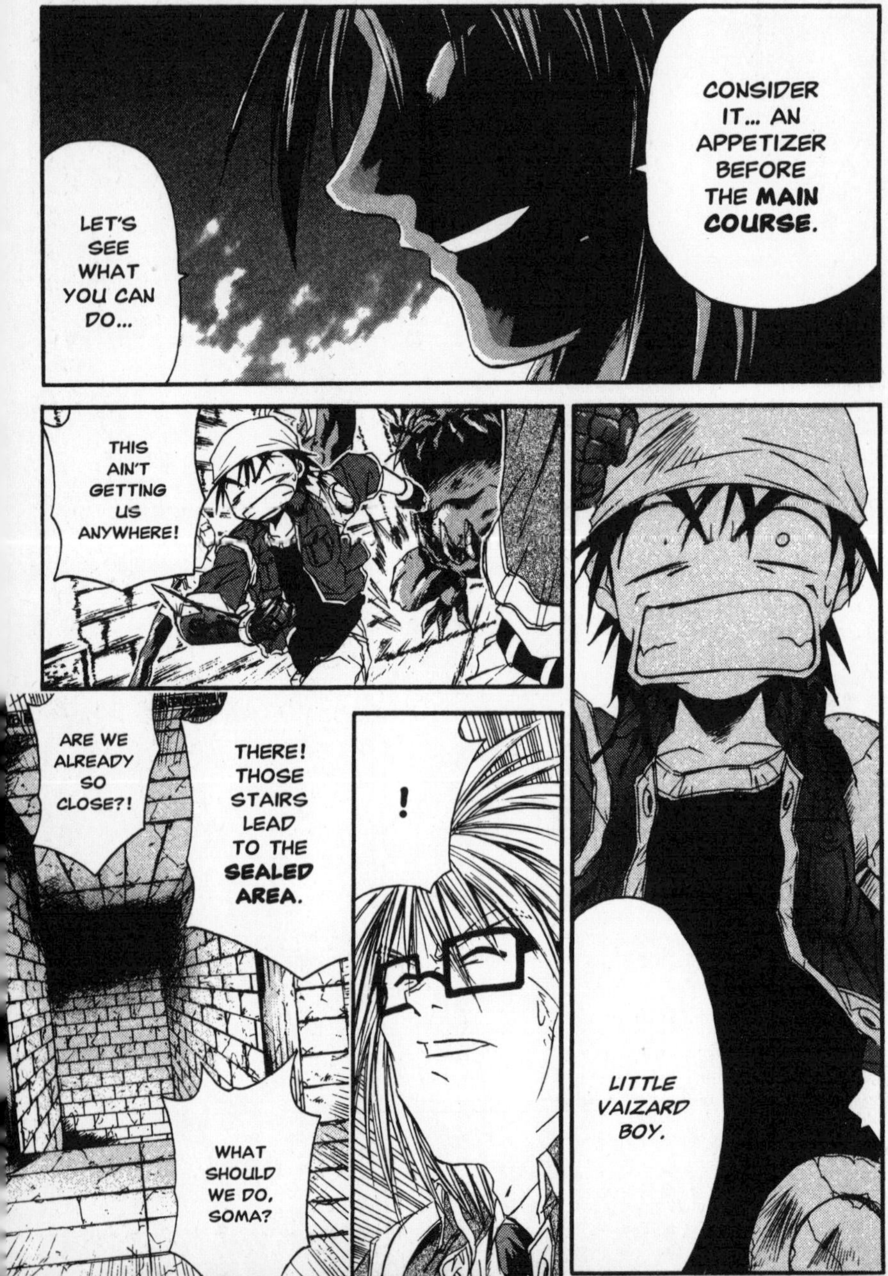
CONSIDER IT... AN APPETIZER BEFORE THE **MAIN COURSE**.
LET'S SEE WHAT YOU CAN DO...
LITTLE VAIZARD BOY.
THIS AIN'T GETTING US ANYWHERE!
!
THERE! THOSE STAIRS LEAD TO THE **SEALED AREA**.
ARE WE ALREADY SO CLOSE?!
WHAT SHOULD WE DO, SOMA?

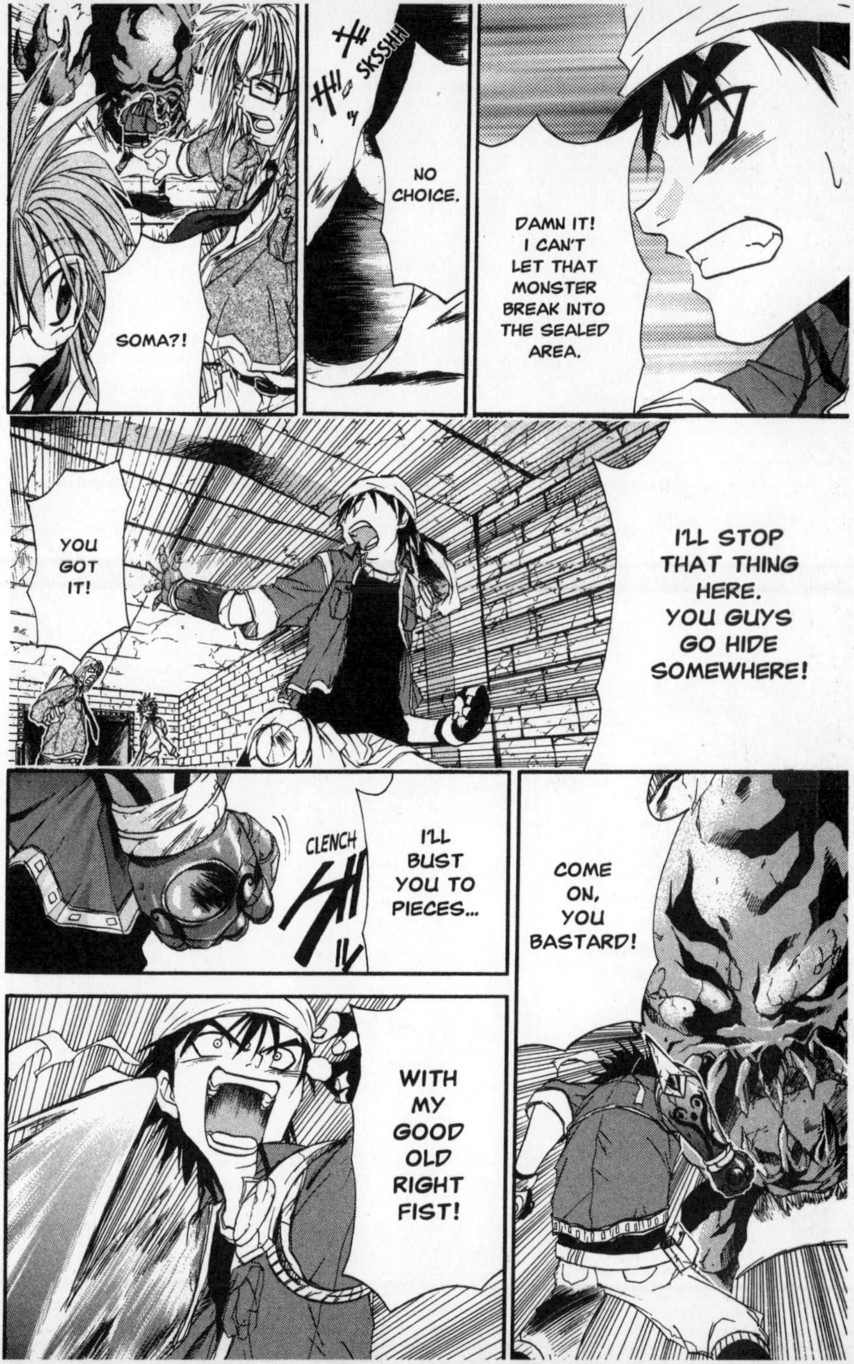
SKSSHH
NO CHOICE.
SOMA?!
DAMN IT! I CAN'T LET THAT MONSTER BREAK INTO THE SEALED AREA.
I'LL STOP THAT THING HERE. YOU GUYS GO HIDE SOMEWHERE!
YOU GOT IT!
CLENCH
I'LL BUST YOU TO PIECES...
COME ON, YOU BASTARD!
WITH MY GOOD OLD RIGHT FIST!

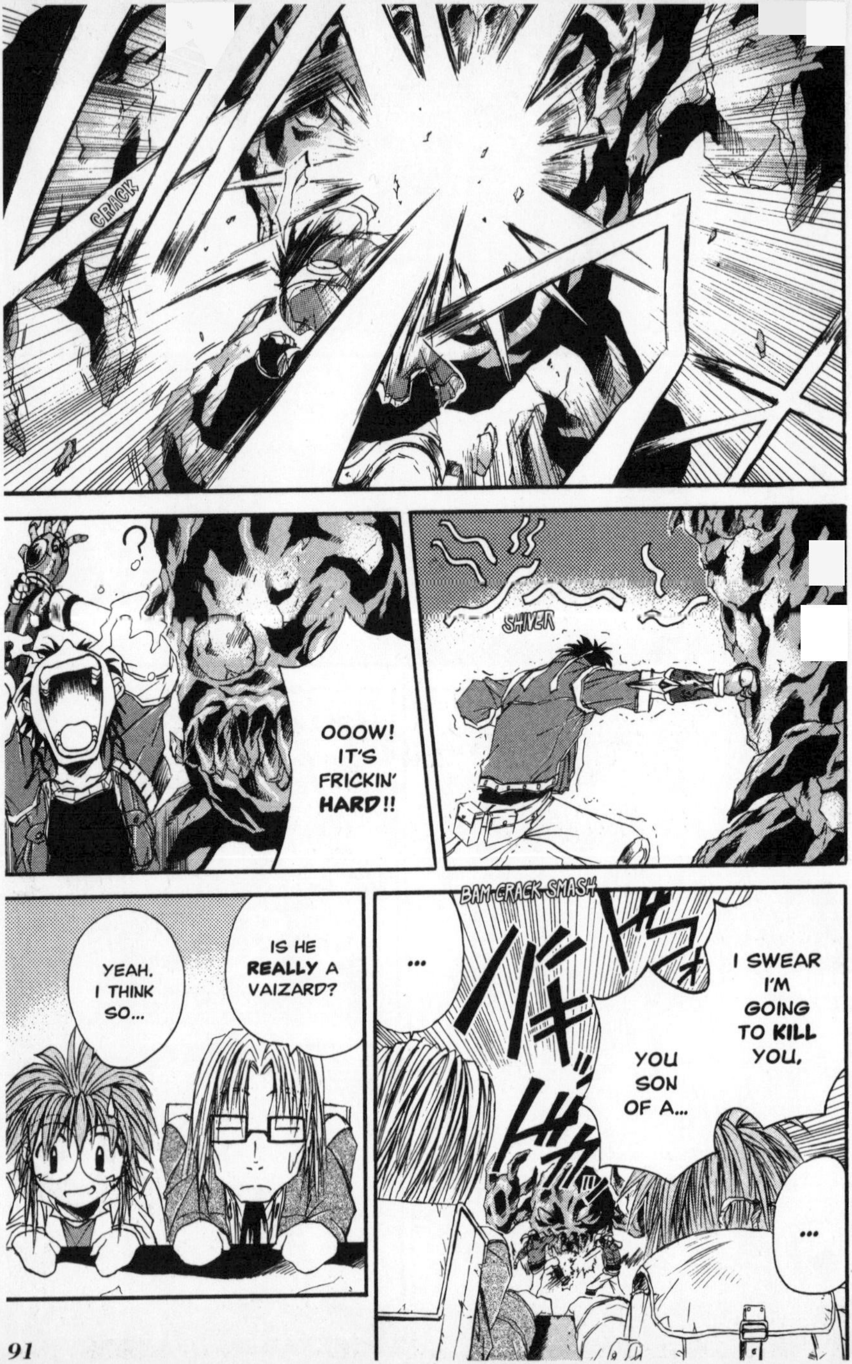

CRACK
OOOW! IT'S FRICKIN' **HARD**!!
SHIVER
BAM CRACK SMASH
I SWEAR I'M GOING TO **KILL** YOU,
YOU SON OF A...
...
...
IS HE **REALLY** A VAIZARD?
YEAH. I THINK SO...

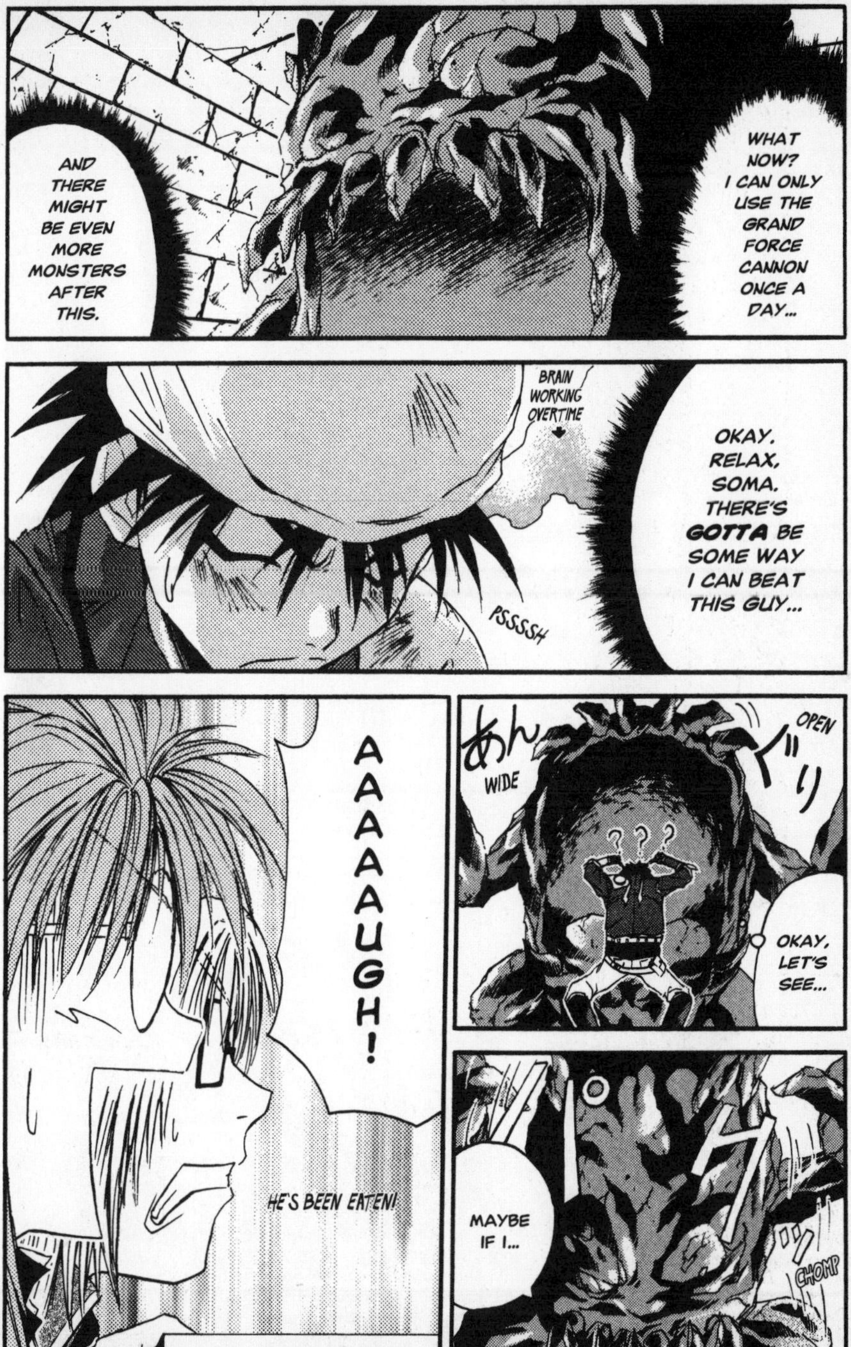
WHAT NOW? I CAN ONLY USE THE GRAND FORCE CANNON ONCE A DAY...
AND THERE MIGHT BE EVEN MORE MONSTERS AFTER THIS.
OKAY. RELAX, SOMA. THERE'S **GOTTA** BE SOME WAY I CAN BEAT THIS GUY...
BRAIN WORKING OVERTIME
PSSSSH
ぐり
OPEN
あん
WIDE
OKAY, LET'S SEE...
MAYBE IF I...
CHOMP
AAAAAAUGH!
HE'S BEEN EATEN!

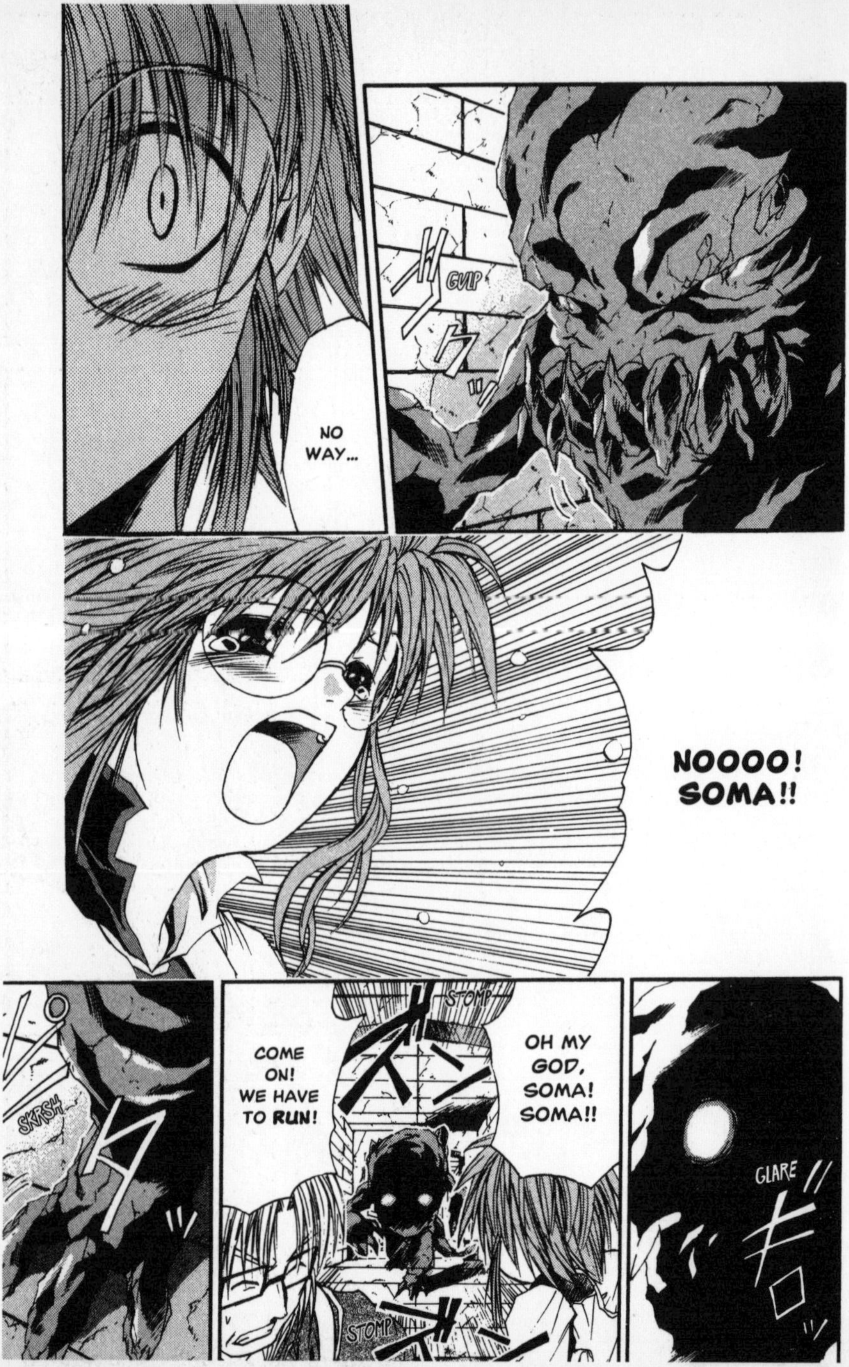
GULP
NO WAY...
NOOOO! SOMA!!
OH MY GOD, SOMA! SOMA!!
STOMP
COME ON! WE HAVE TO RUN!
STOMP
SKRSH
GLARE

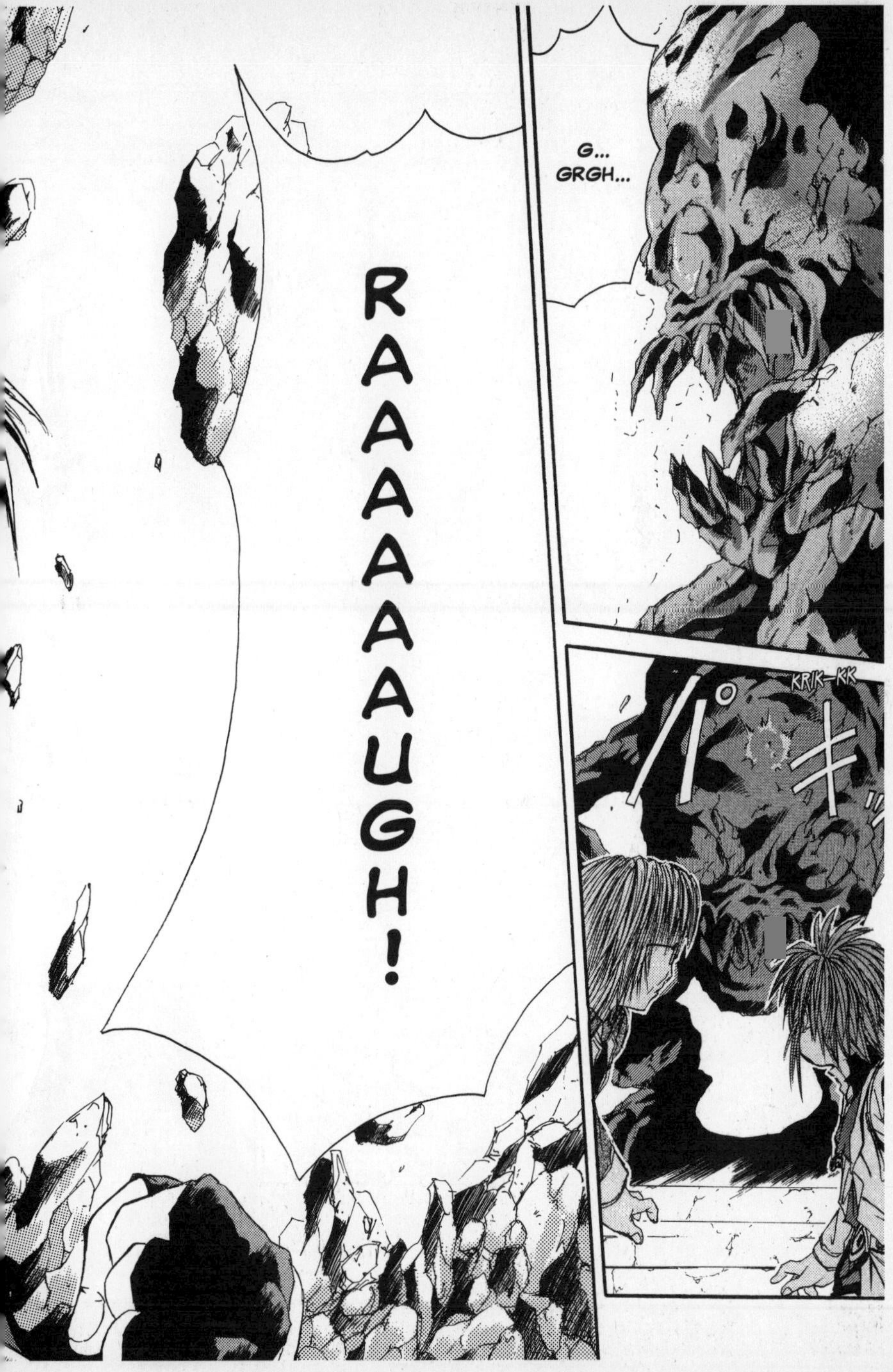
G...
GRGH...
KRIK-KK
RAAAAAAUGH!

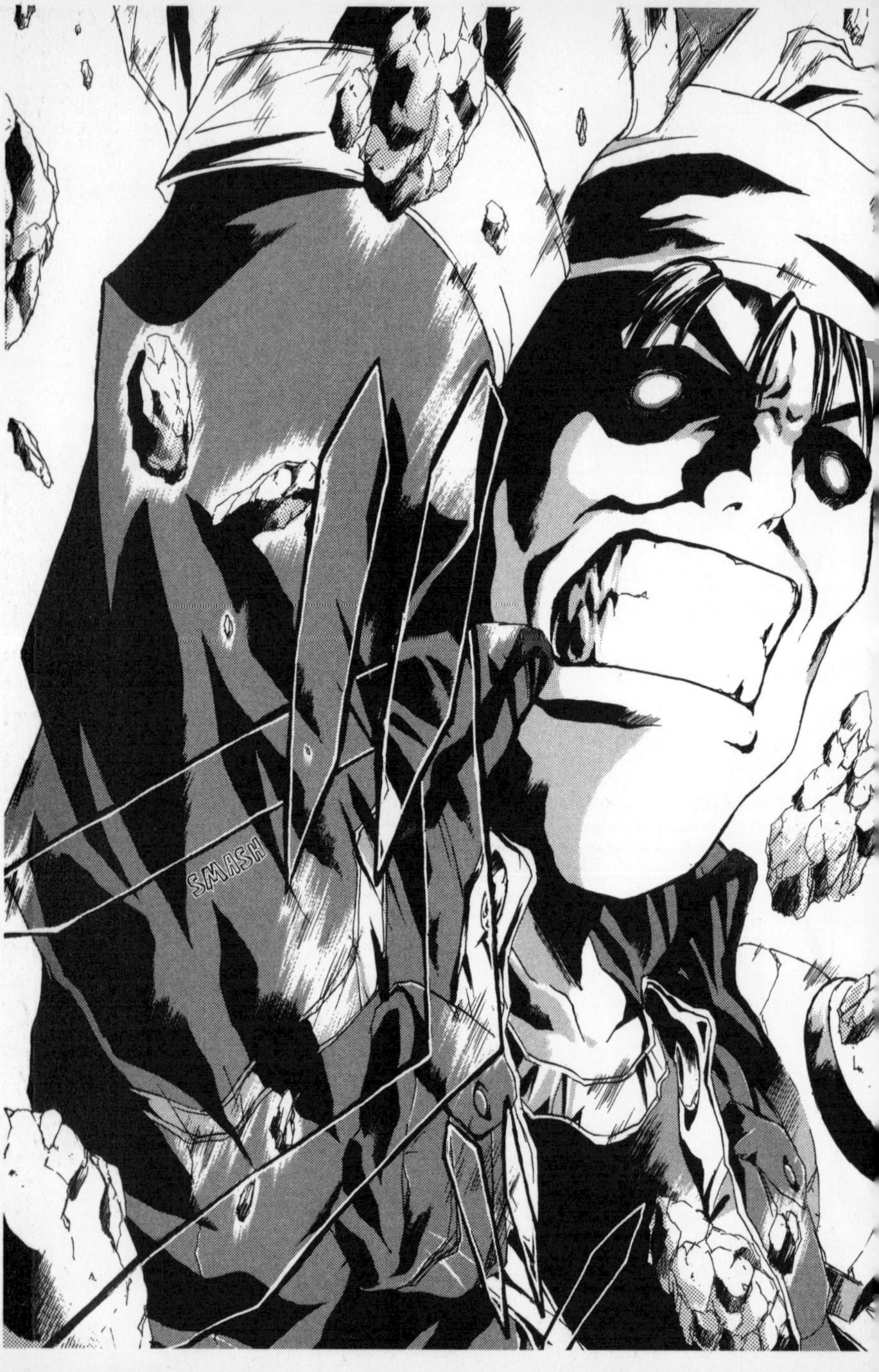
SMASH

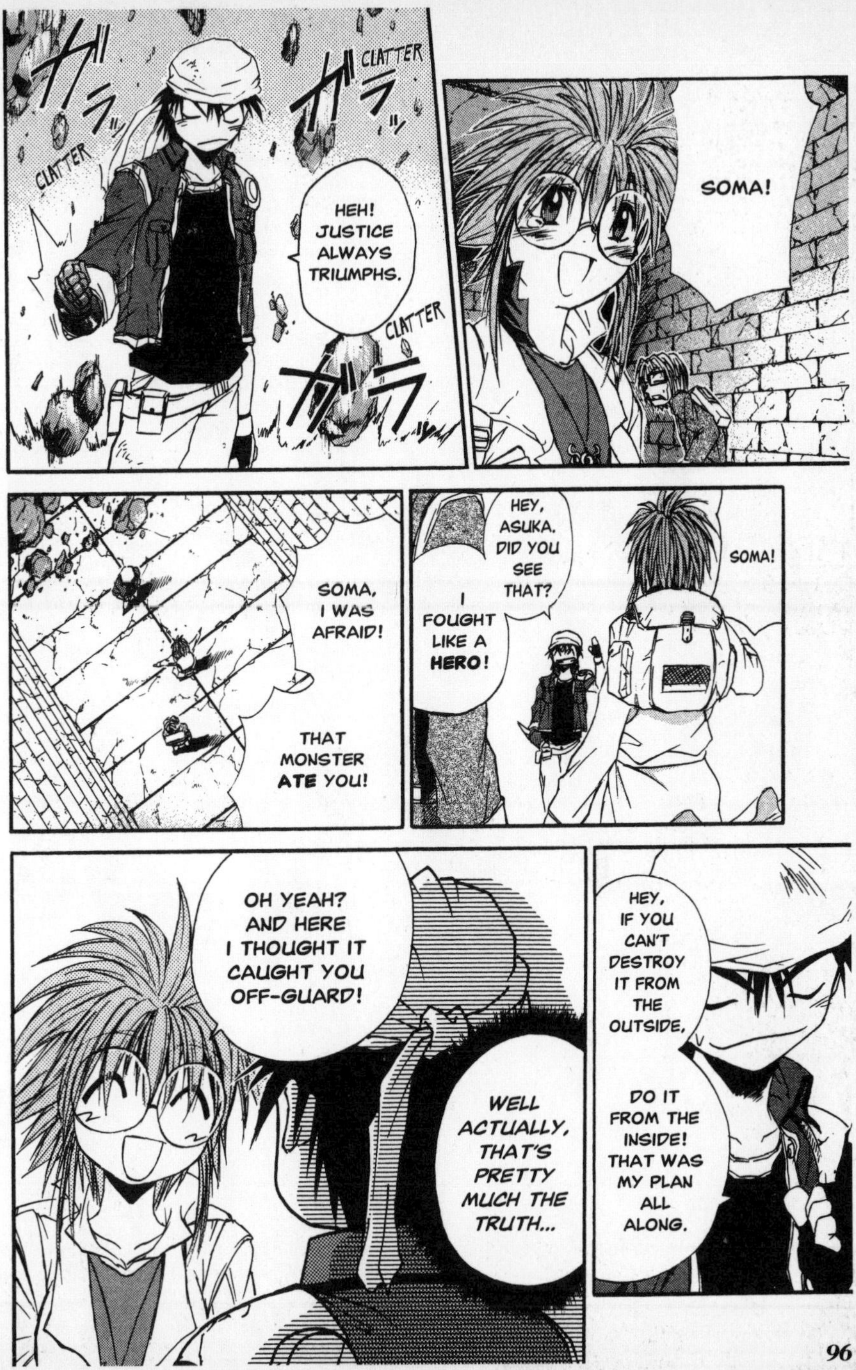
SOMA!
CLATTER
CLATTER
HEH! JUSTICE ALWAYS TRIUMPHS.
CLATTER
SOMA!
HEY, ASUKA. DID YOU SEE THAT?
I FOUGHT LIKE A **HERO**!
SOMA, I WAS AFRAID!
THAT MONSTER **ATE** YOU!
HEY, IF YOU CAN'T DESTROY IT FROM THE OUTSIDE,
DO IT FROM THE INSIDE! THAT WAS MY PLAN ALL ALONG.
OH YEAH? AND HERE I THOUGHT IT CAUGHT YOU OFF-GUARD!
WELL ACTUALLY, THAT'S PRETTY MUCH THE TRUTH...

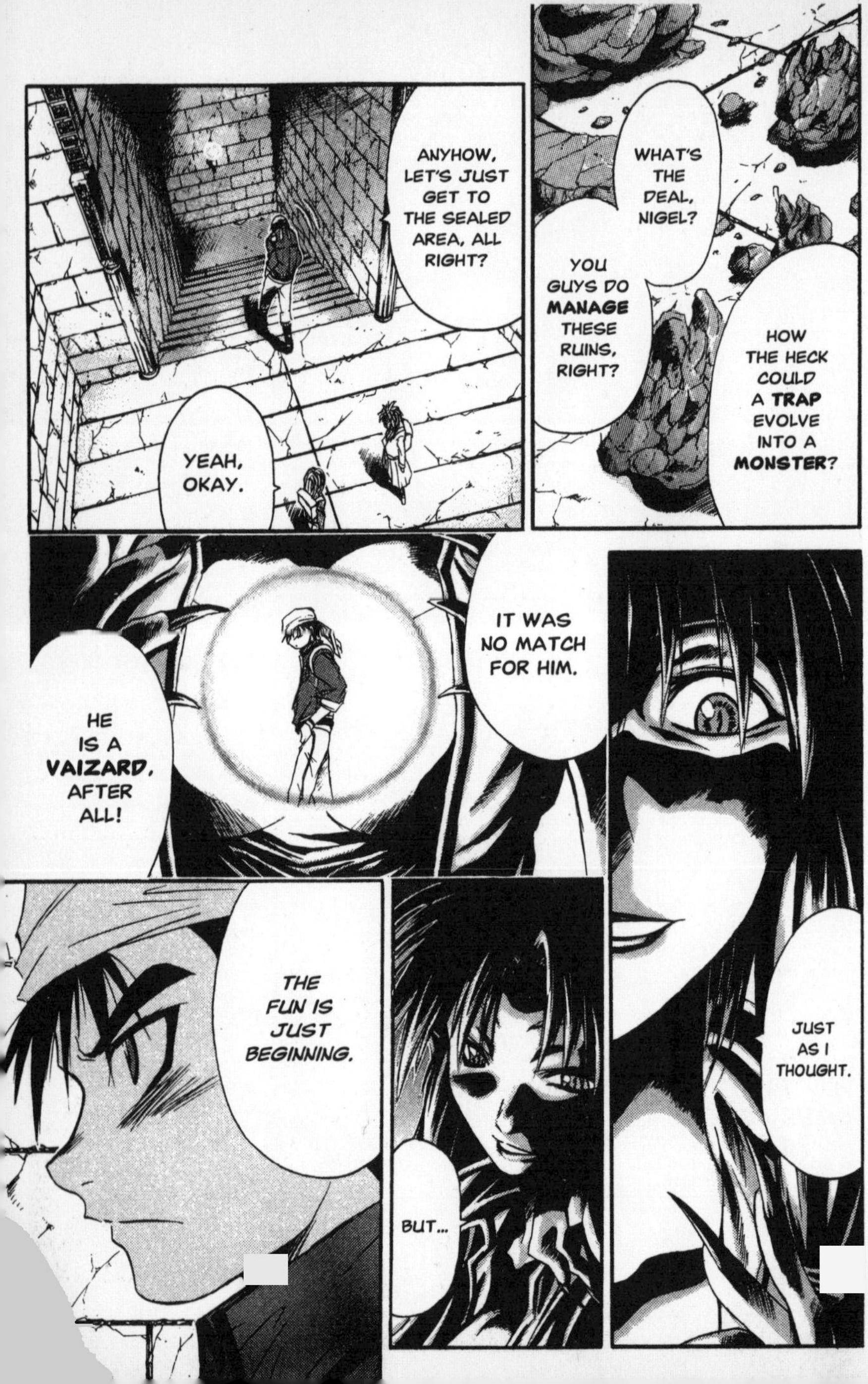
HOW THE HECK COULD A TRAP EVOLVE INTO A MONSTER?
WHAT'S THE DEAL, NIGEL?
YOU GUYS DO MANAGE THESE RUINS, RIGHT?
ANYHOW, LET'S JUST GET TO THE SEALED AREA, ALL RIGHT?
YEAH, OKAY.
IT WAS NO MATCH FOR HIM.
HE IS A VAIZARD, AFTER ALL!
JUST AS I THOUGHT.
BUT...
THE FUN IS JUST BEGINNING.

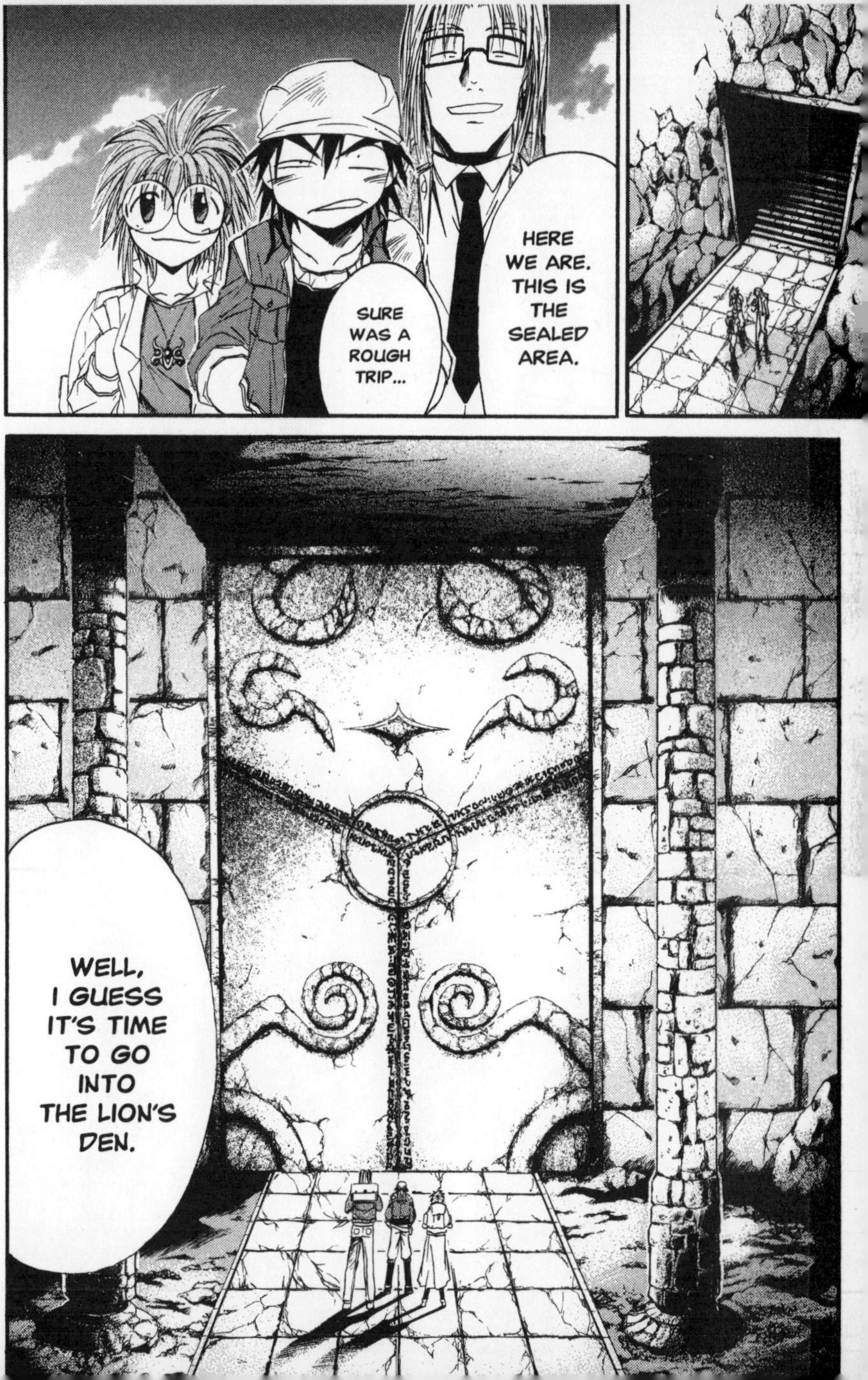
HERE WE ARE. THIS IS THE SEALED AREA.
SURE WAS A ROUGH TRIP...
WELL, I GUESS IT'S TIME TO GO INTO THE LION'S DEN.

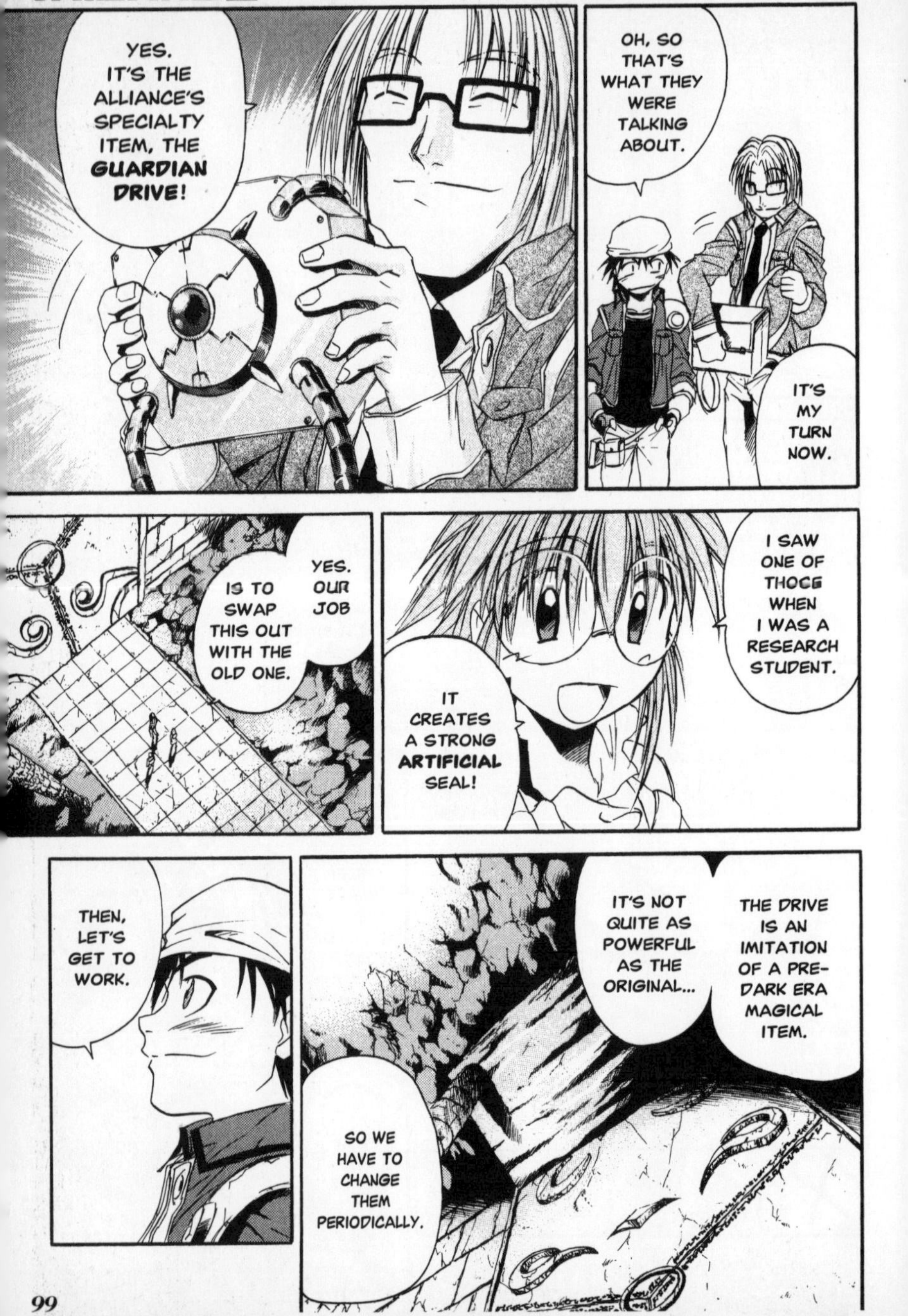
OH, SO THAT'S WHAT THEY WERE TALKING ABOUT.
IT'S MY TURN NOW.
YES. IT'S THE ALLIANCE'S SPECIALTY ITEM, THE **GUARDIAN DRIVE**!
I SAW ONE OF THOCE WHEN I WAS A RESEARCH STUDENT.
IT CREATES A STRONG **ARTIFICIAL** SEAL!
YES. OUR JOB IS TO SWAP THIS OUT WITH THE OLD ONE.
THE DRIVE IS AN IMITATION OF A PRE-DARK ERA MAGICAL ITEM.
IT'S NOT QUITE AS POWERFUL AS THE ORIGINAL...
SO WE HAVE TO CHANGE THEM PERIODICALLY.
THEN, LET'S GET TO WORK.

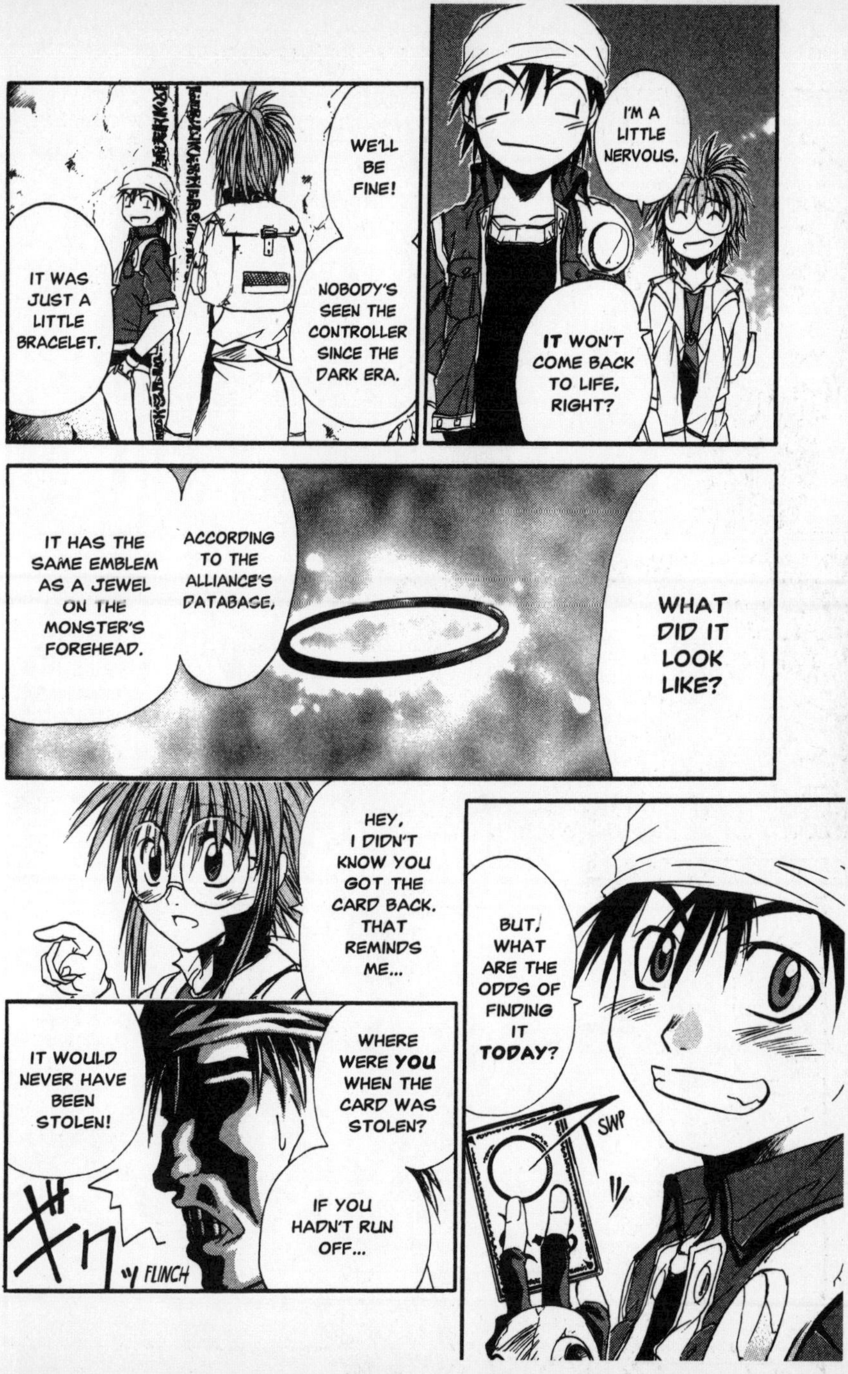
I'M A LITTLE NERVOUS.
IT WON'T COME BACK TO LIFE, RIGHT?
WE'LL BE FINE!
NOBODY'S SEEN THE CONTROLLER SINCE THE DARK ERA.
IT WAS JUST A LITTLE BRACELET.
WHAT DID IT LOOK LIKE?
ACCORDING TO THE ALLIANCE'S DATABASE,
IT HAS THE SAME EMBLEM AS A JEWEL ON THE MONSTER'S FOREHEAD.
BUT, WHAT ARE THE ODDS OF FINDING IT TODAY?
SWP
HEY, I DIDN'T KNOW YOU GOT THE CARD BACK. THAT REMINDS ME...
WHERE WERE YOU WHEN THE CARD WAS STOLEN?
IF YOU HADN'T RUN OFF...
IT WOULD NEVER HAVE BEEN STOLEN!
FLINCH

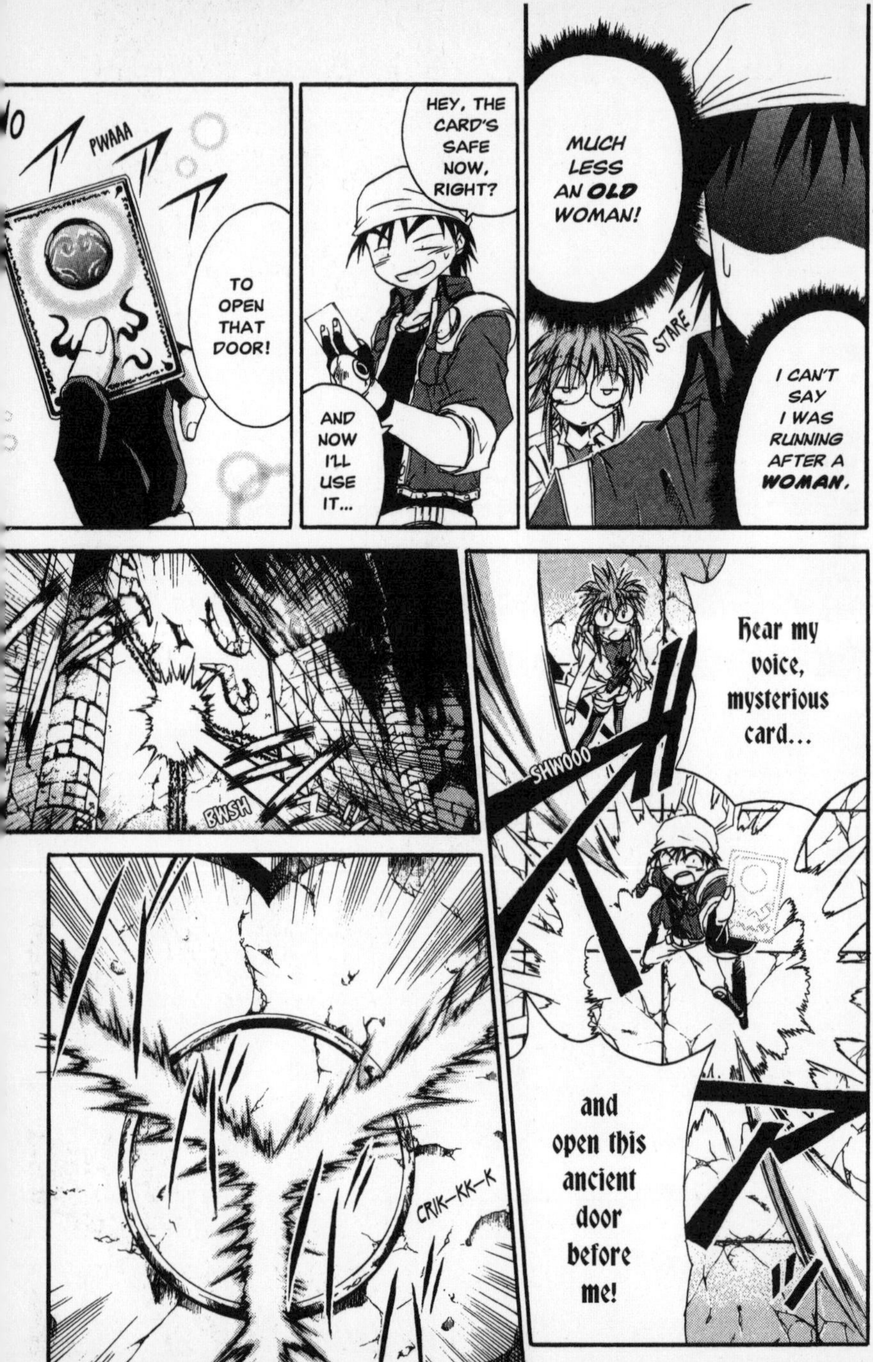
I CAN'T SAY I WAS RUNNING AFTER A WOMAN.
MUCH LESS AN OLD WOMAN!
STARE
HEY, THE CARD'S SAFE NOW, RIGHT?
AND NOW I'LL USE IT...
TO OPEN THAT DOOR!
PWAAA
Hear my voice, mysterious card...
SHWOOO
BWSH
and open this ancient door before me!
CRIK-KK-K

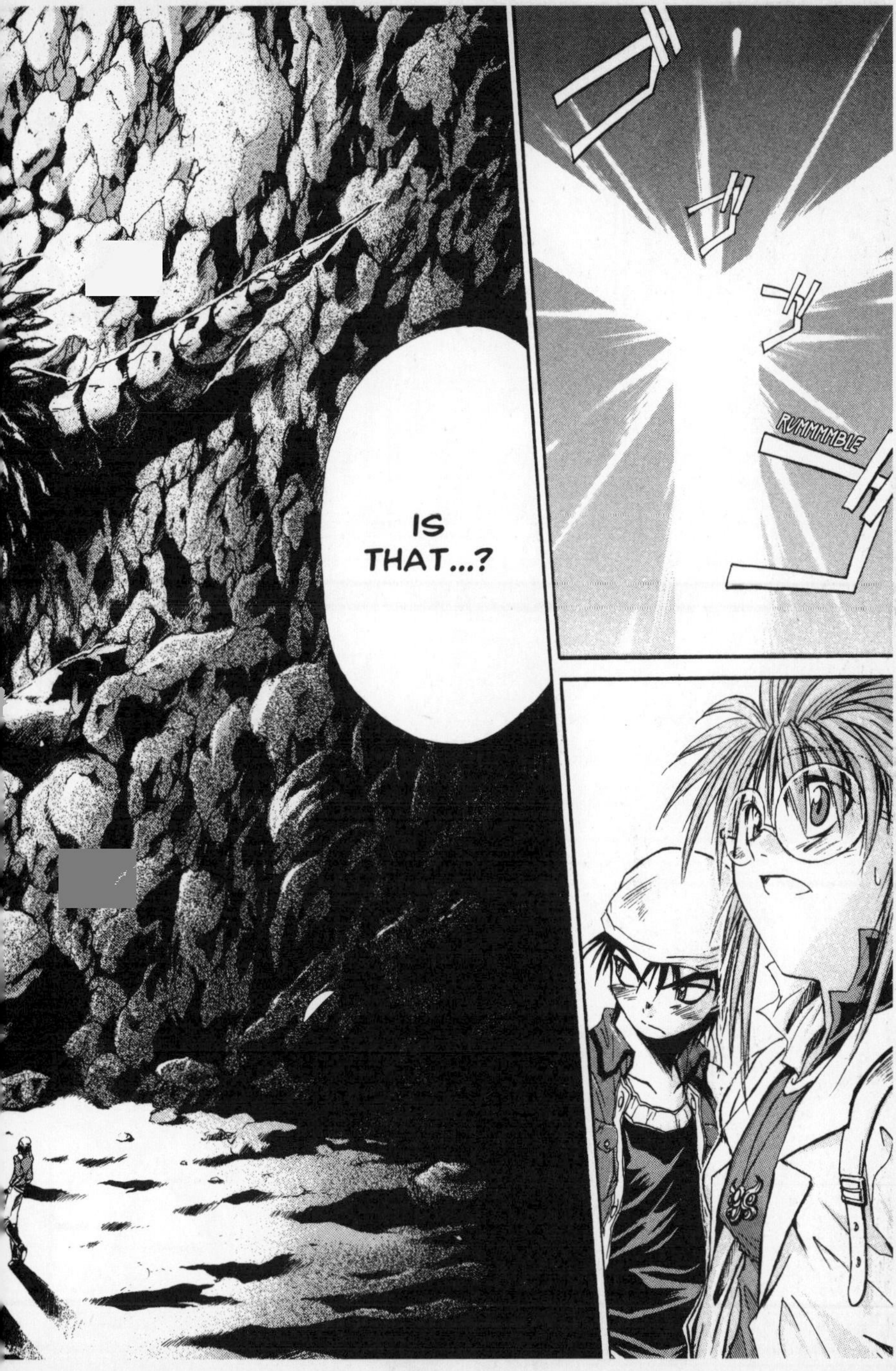
RUMMMMBLE
IS THAT...?

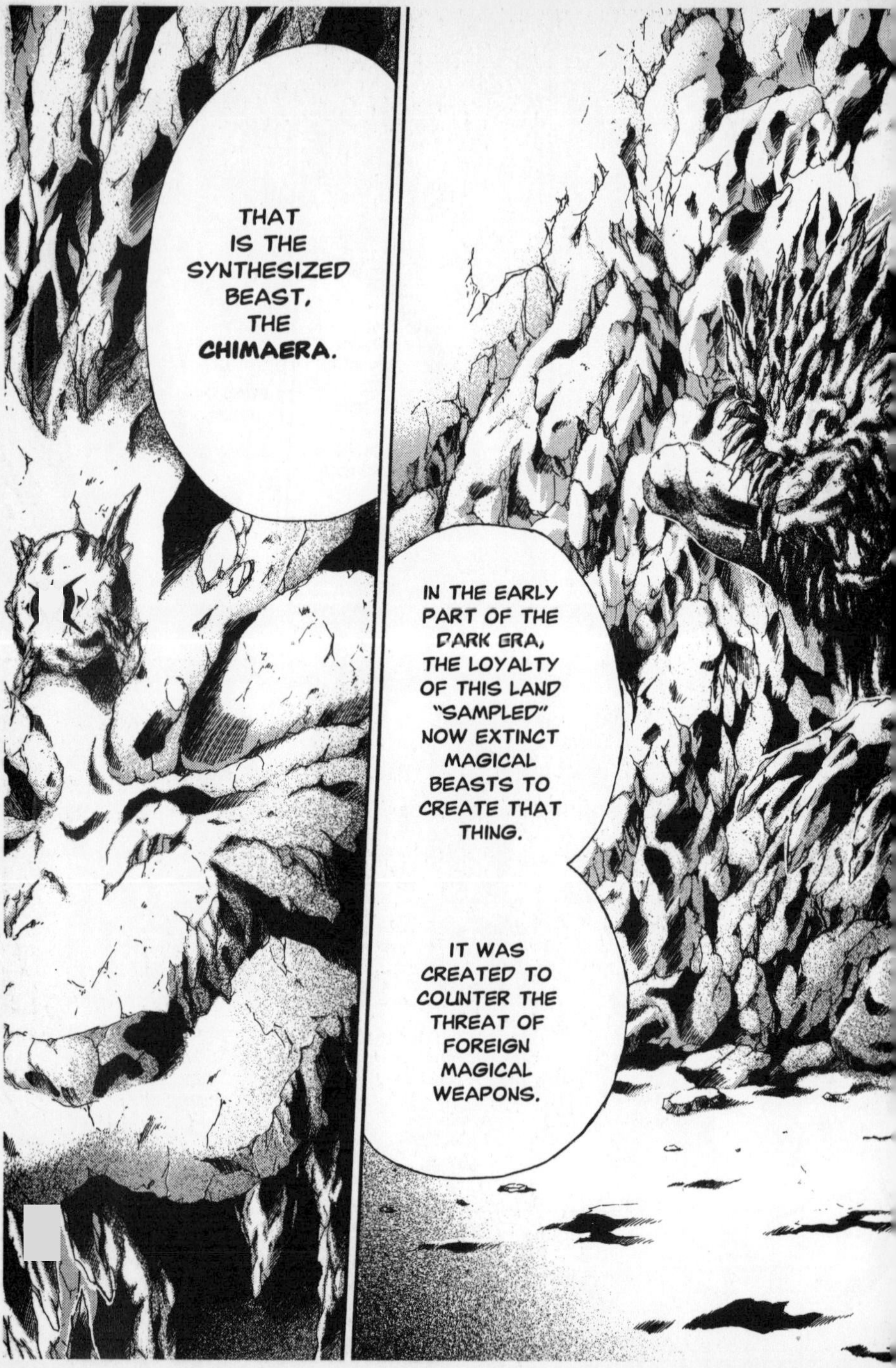
THAT IS THE SYNTHESIZED BEAST, THE CHIMAERA.
IN THE EARLY PART OF THE DARK ERA, THE LOYALTY OF THIS LAND "SAMPLED" NOW EXTINCT MAGICAL BEASTS TO CREATE THAT THING.
IT WAS CREATED TO COUNTER THE THREAT OF FOREIGN MAGICAL WEAPONS.

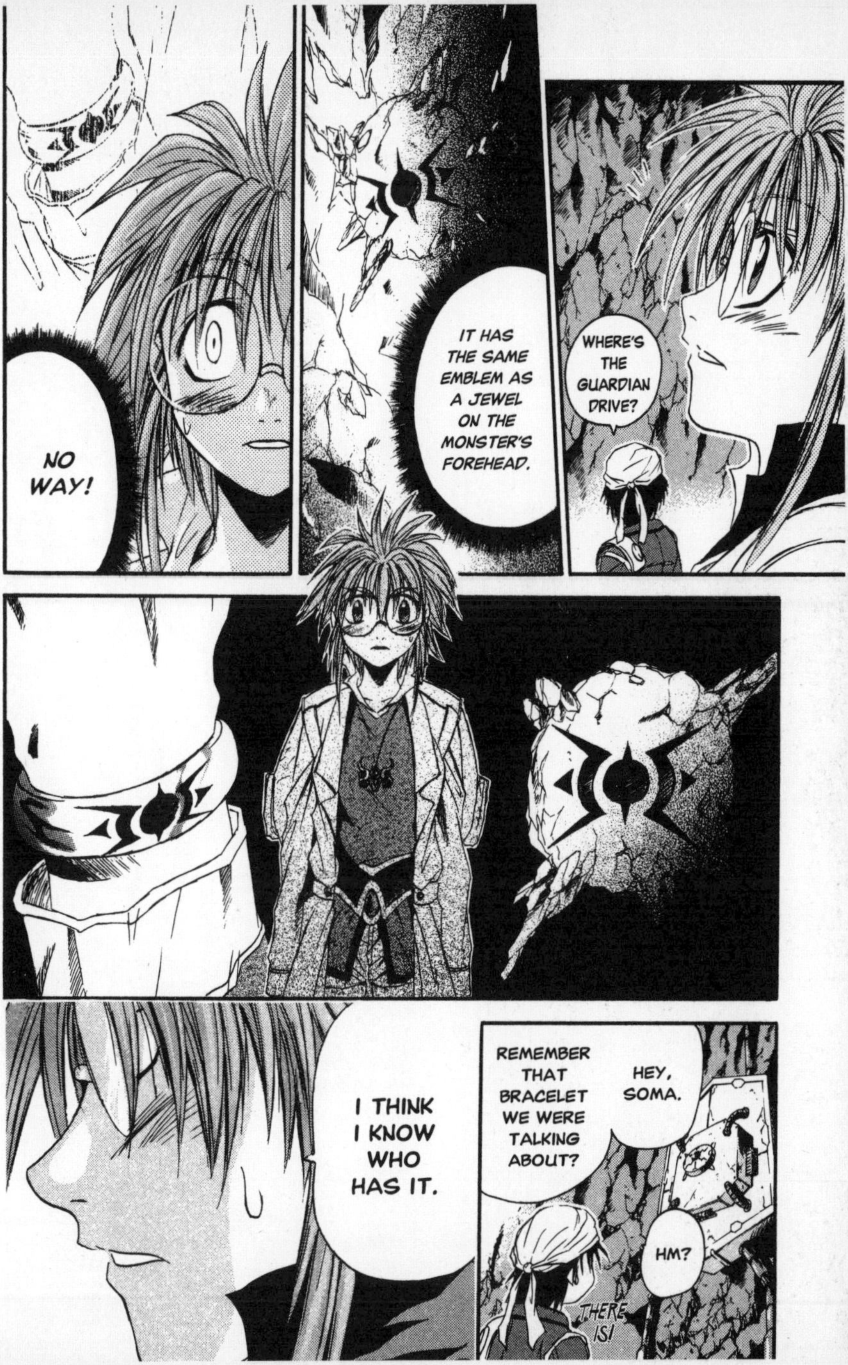
WHERE'S THE GUARDIAN DRIVE?
IT HAS THE SAME EMBLEM AS A JEWEL ON THE MONSTER'S FOREHEAD.
NO WAY!
HEY, SOMA.
REMEMBER THAT BRACELET WE WERE TALKING ABOUT?
HM?
THERE IS!
I THINK I KNOW WHO HAS IT.

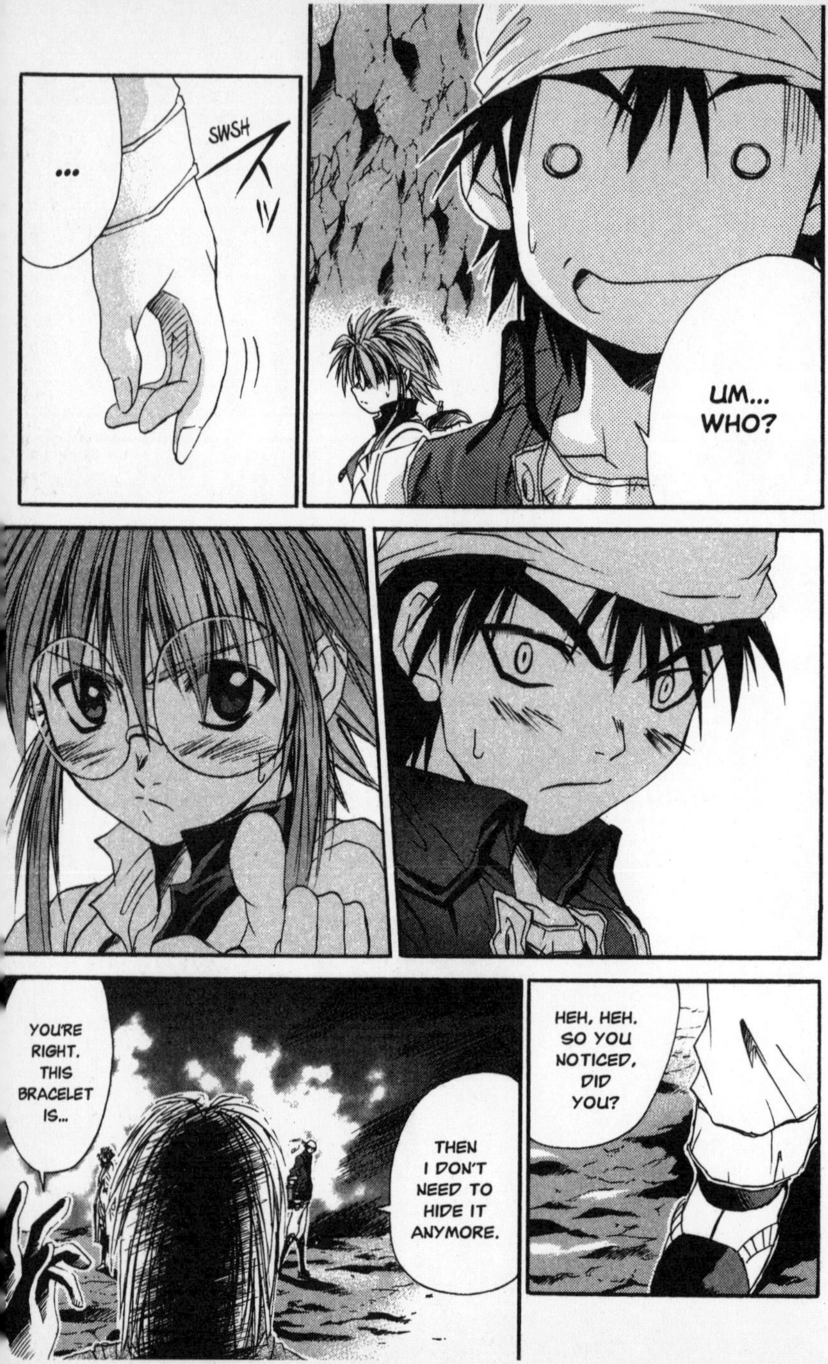
UM... WHO?
SWSH
...
HEH, HEH. SO YOU NOTICED, DID YOU?
THEN I DON'T NEED TO HIDE IT ANYMORE.
YOU'RE RIGHT. THIS BRACELET IS...

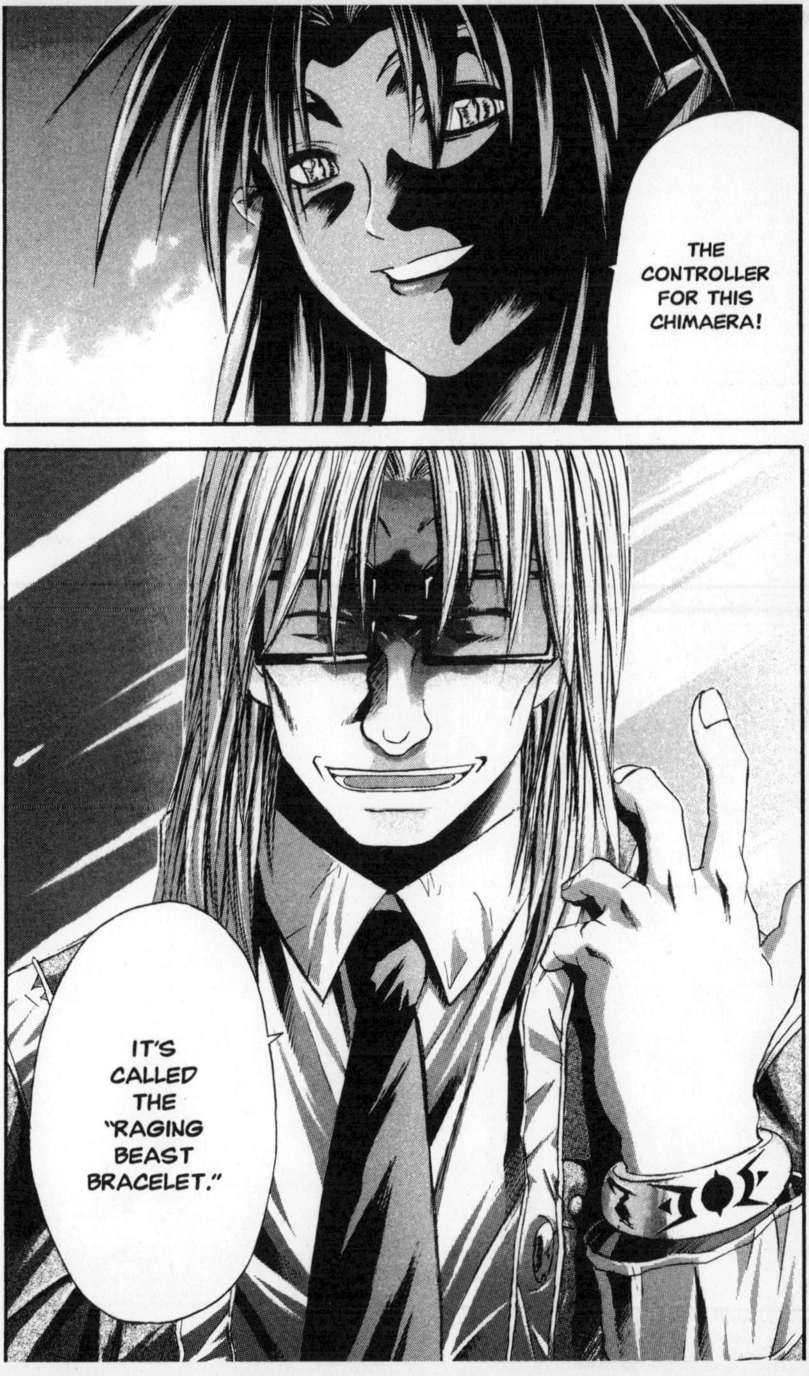
THE CONTROLLER FOR THIS CHIMAERA!
IT'S CALLED THE "RAGING BEAST BRACELET."

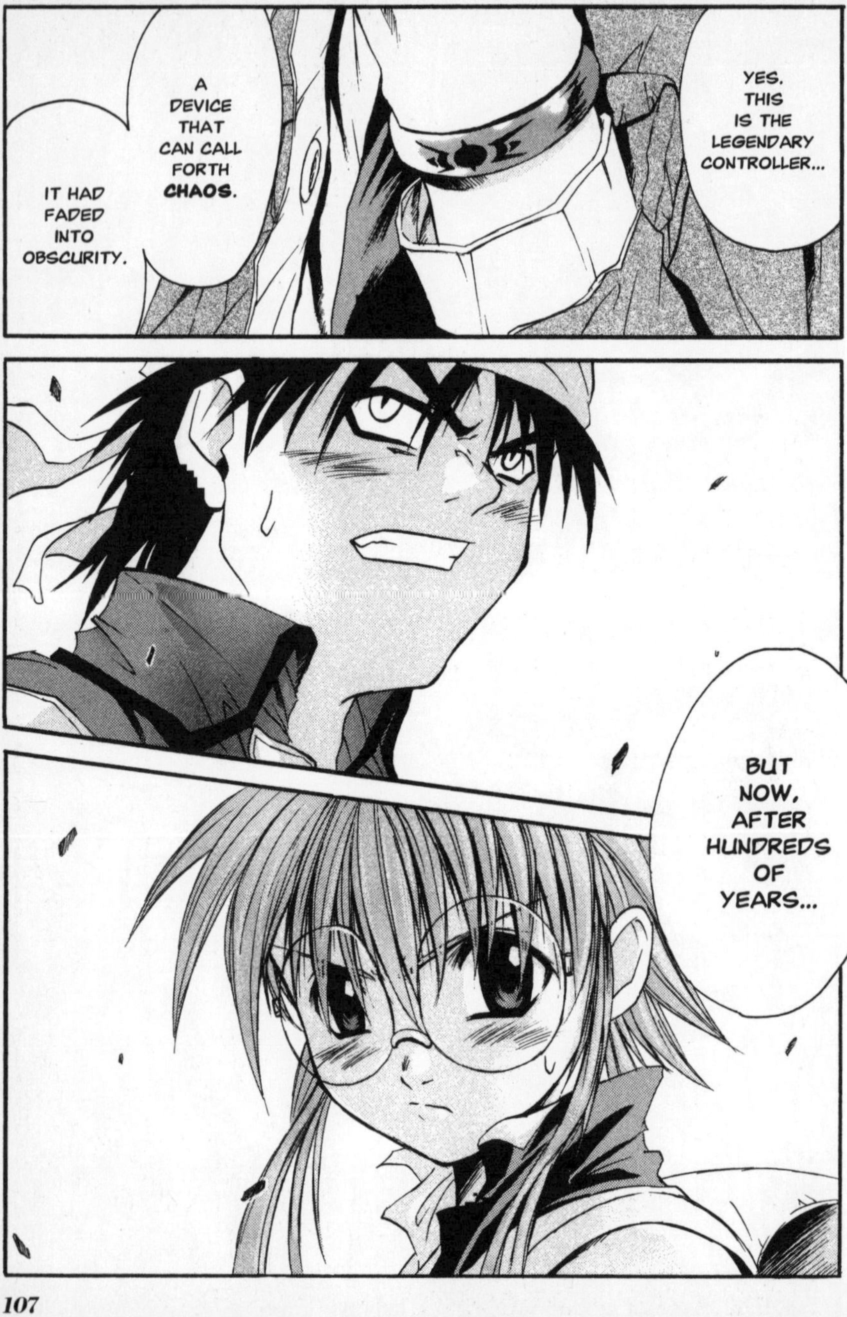
YES. THIS IS THE LEGENDARY CONTROLLER...
A DEVICE THAT CAN CALL FORTH **CHAOS**.
IT HAD FADED INTO OBSCURITY.
BUT NOW, AFTER HUNDREDS OF YEARS...

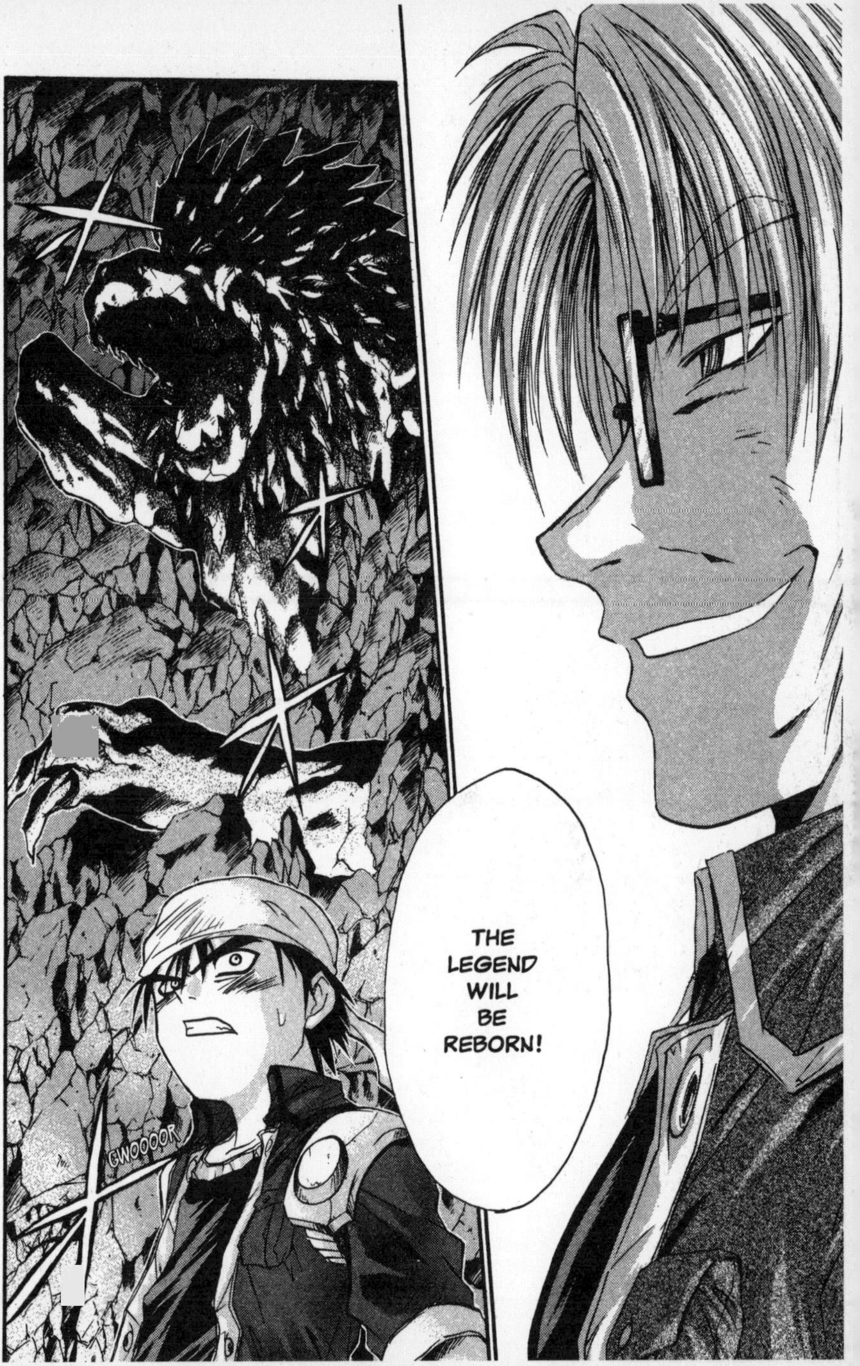
THE LEGEND WILL BE REBORN!
GWOOOOR

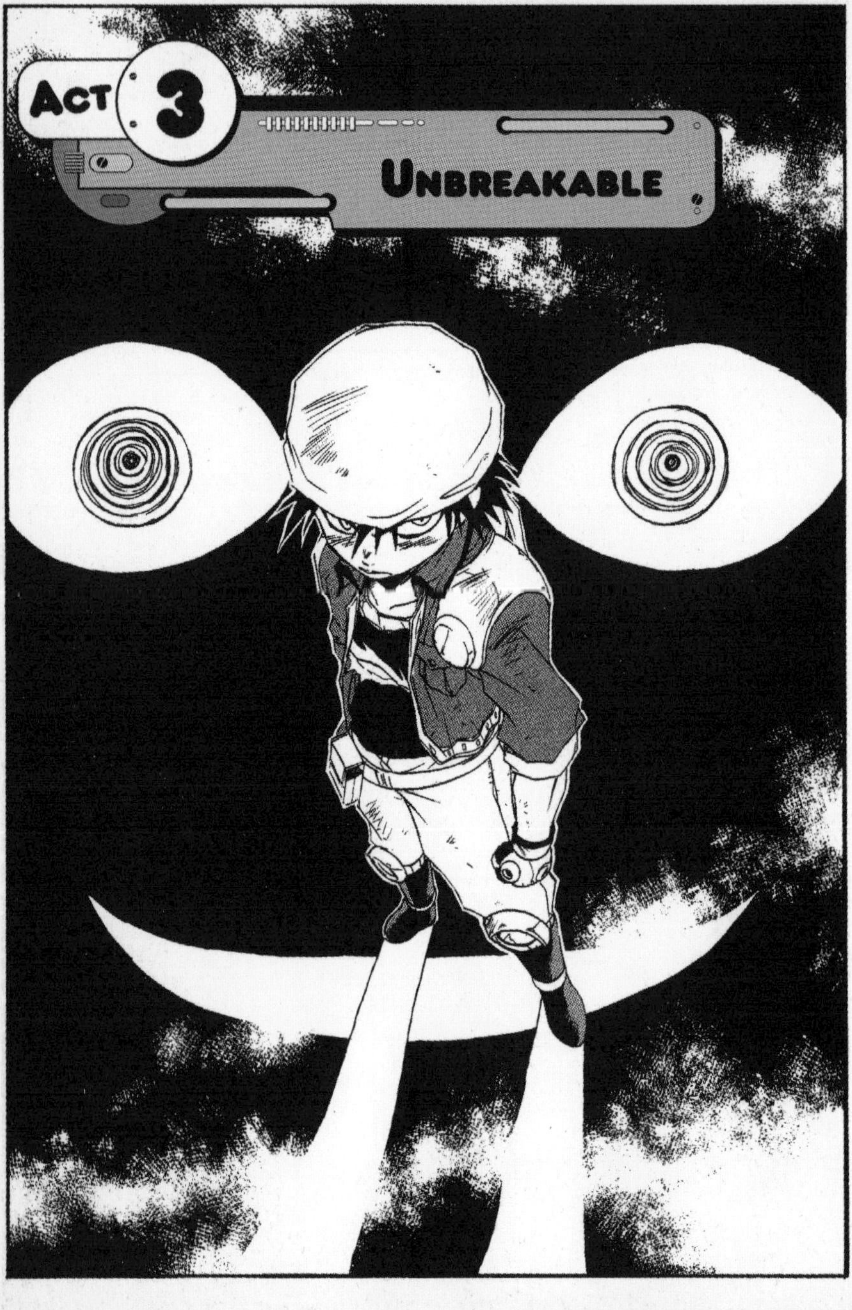
ACT 3
UNBREAKABLE

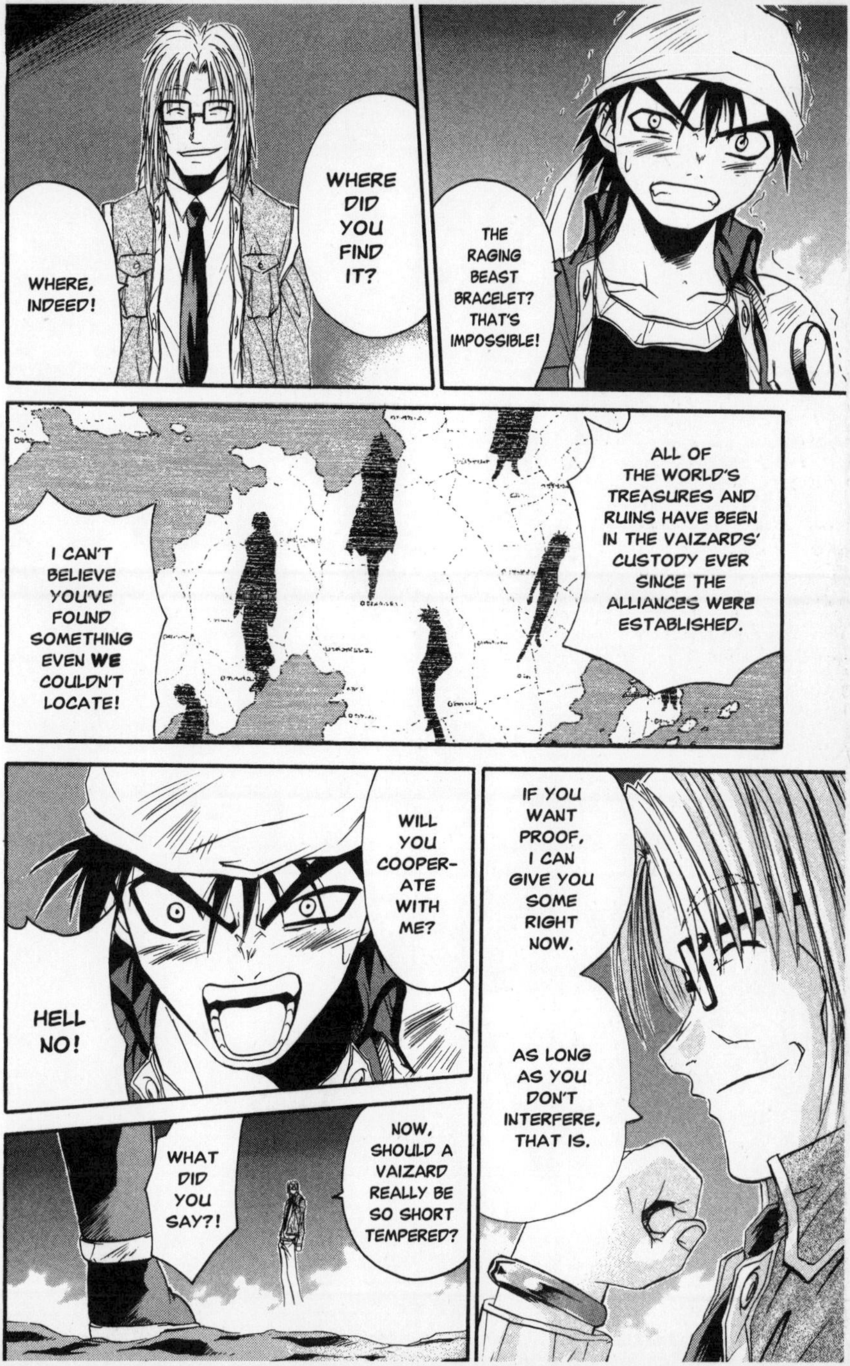
THE RAGING BEAST BRACELET? THAT'S IMPOSSIBLE!
WHERE DID YOU FIND IT?
WHERE, INDEED!
ALL OF THE WORLD'S TREASURES AND RUINS HAVE BEEN IN THE VAIZARDS' CUSTODY EVER SINCE THE ALLIANCES WERE ESTABLISHED.
I CAN'T BELIEVE YOU'VE FOUND SOMETHING EVEN WE COULDN'T LOCATE!
IF YOU WANT PROOF, I CAN GIVE YOU SOME RIGHT NOW.
AS LONG AS YOU DON'T INTERFERE, THAT IS.
WILL YOU COOPER-ATE WITH ME?
HELL NO!
NOW, SHOULD A VAIZARD REALLY BE SO SHORT TEMPERED?
WHAT DID YOU SAY?!

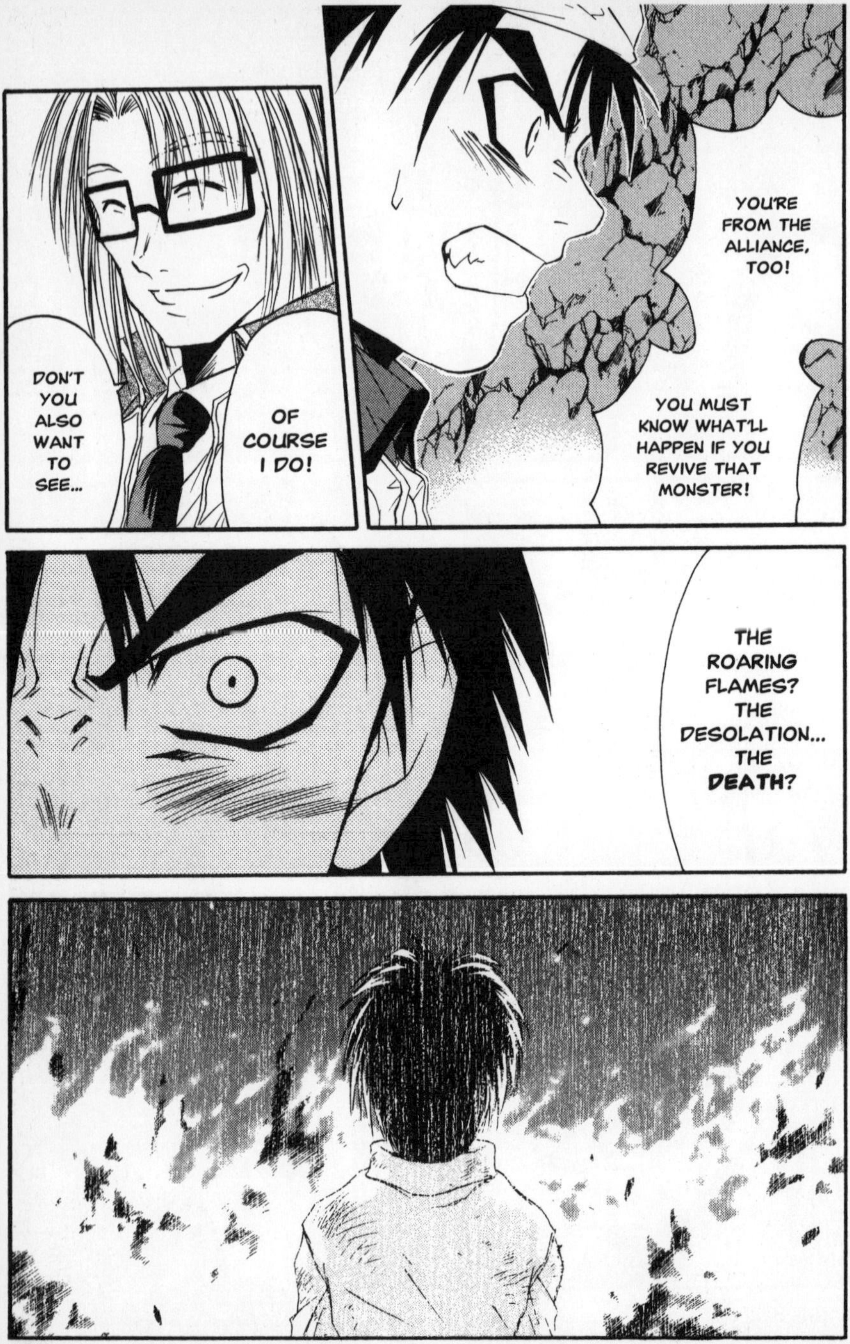
YOU'RE FROM THE ALLIANCE, TOO!
YOU MUST KNOW WHAT'LL HAPPEN IF YOU REVIVE THAT MONSTER!
OF COURSE I DO!
DON'T YOU ALSO WANT TO SEE...
THE ROARING FLAMES? THE DESOLATION... THE **DEATH**?

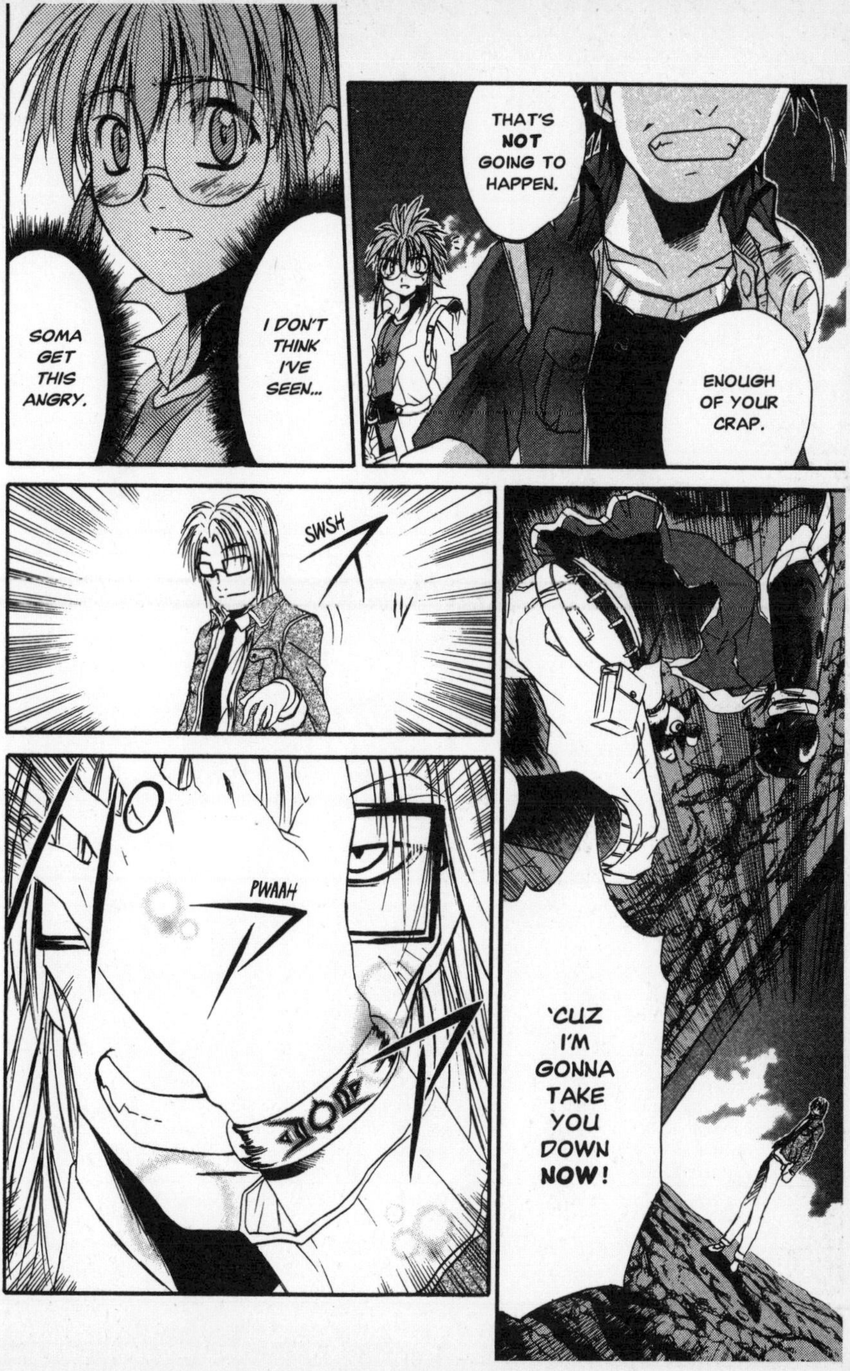
THAT'S NOT GOING TO HAPPEN.
ENOUGH OF YOUR CRAP.
I DON'T THINK I'VE SEEN...
SOMA GET THIS ANGRY.
SWSH
'CUZ I'M GONNA TAKE YOU DOWN NOW!
PWAAH

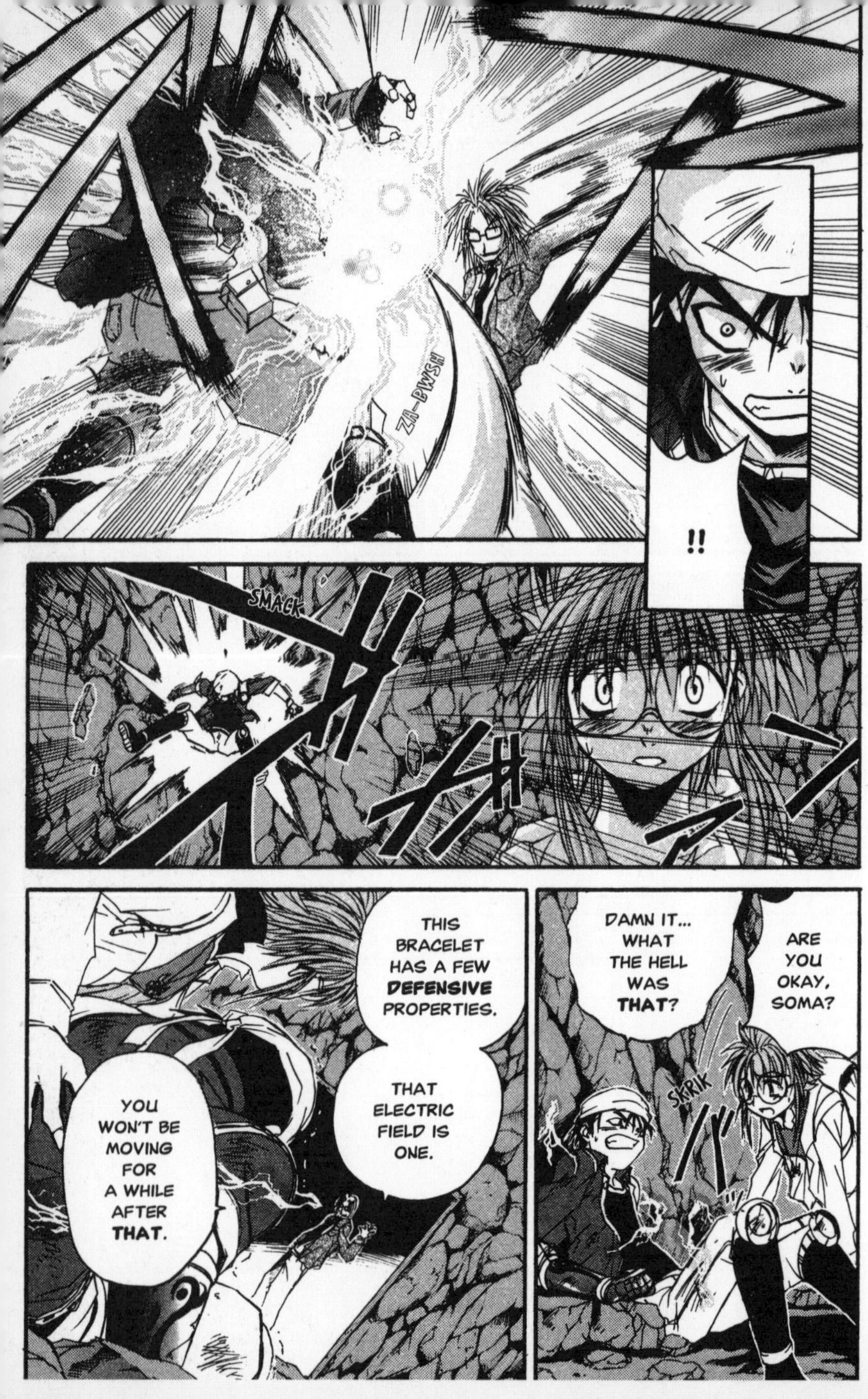
ZA-BWSH
!!
SMACK
ARE YOU OKAY, SOMA?
DAMN IT... WHAT THE HELL WAS THAT?
SKRIK
THIS BRACELET HAS A FEW DEFENSIVE PROPERTIES.
THAT ELECTRIC FIELD IS ONE.
YOU WON'T BE MOVING FOR A WHILE AFTER THAT.

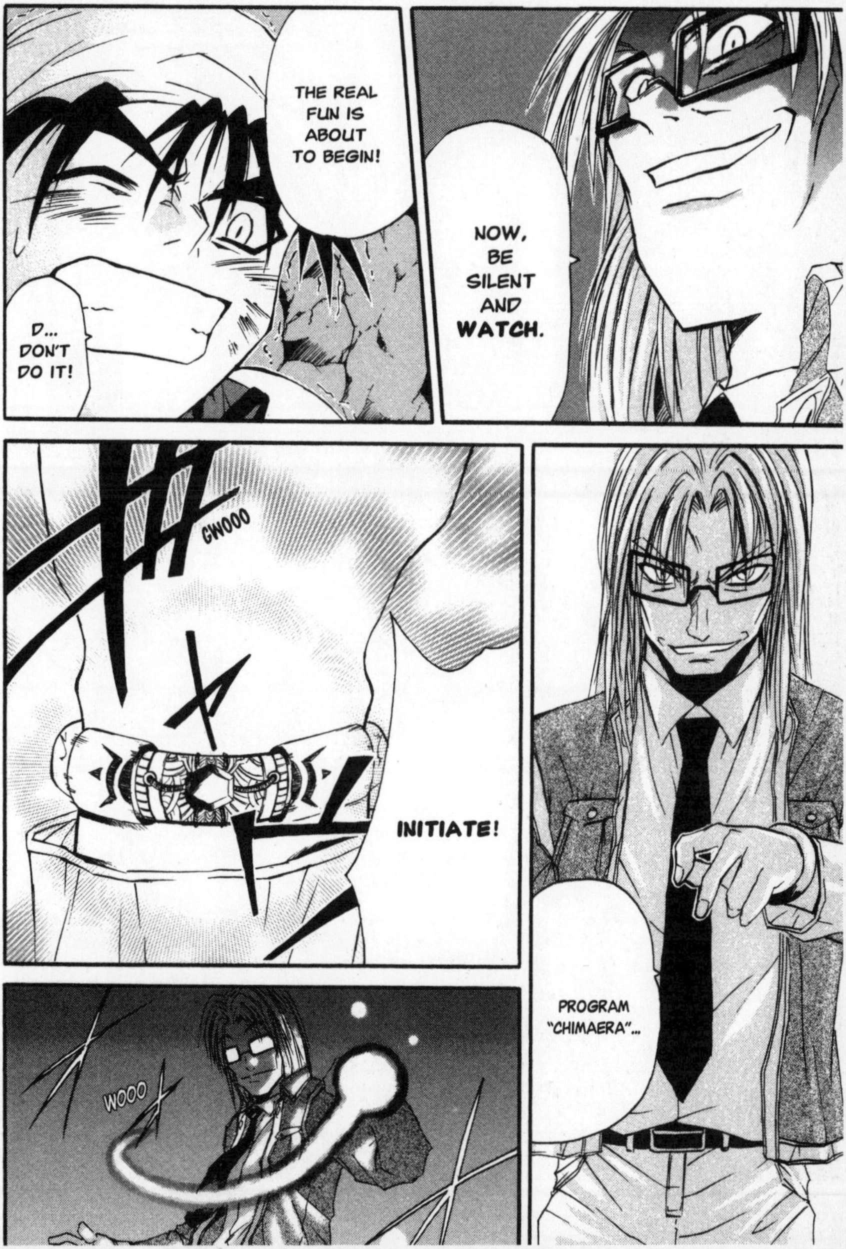
NOW, BE SILENT AND WATCH.
THE REAL FUN IS ABOUT TO BEGIN!
D... DON'T DO IT!
PROGRAM "CHIMAERA"...
GWOOO
INITIATE!
WOOO

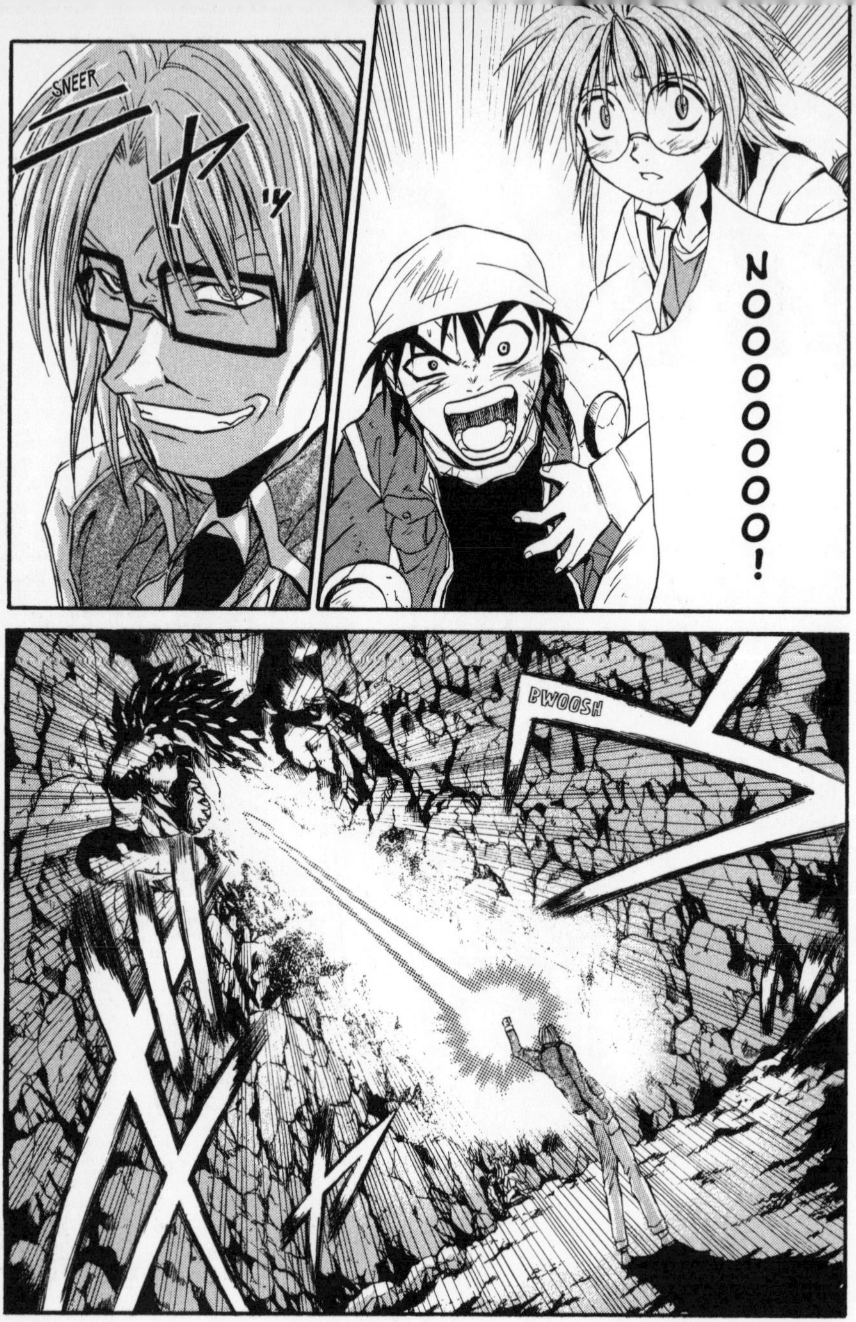
NOOOOOOO!
SNEER
BWOOSH

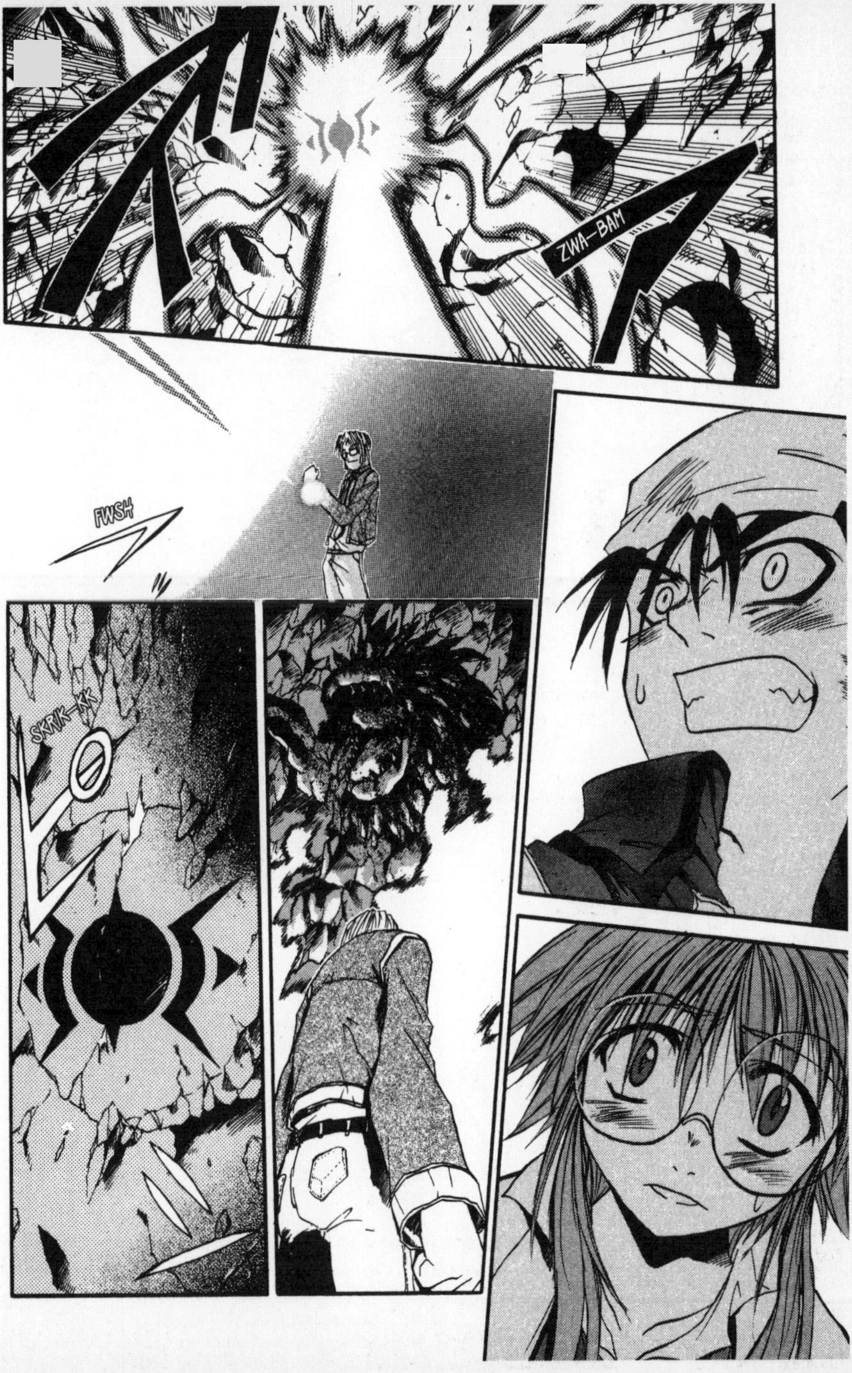
ZWA-BAM
FWSH
SKRIK-KK

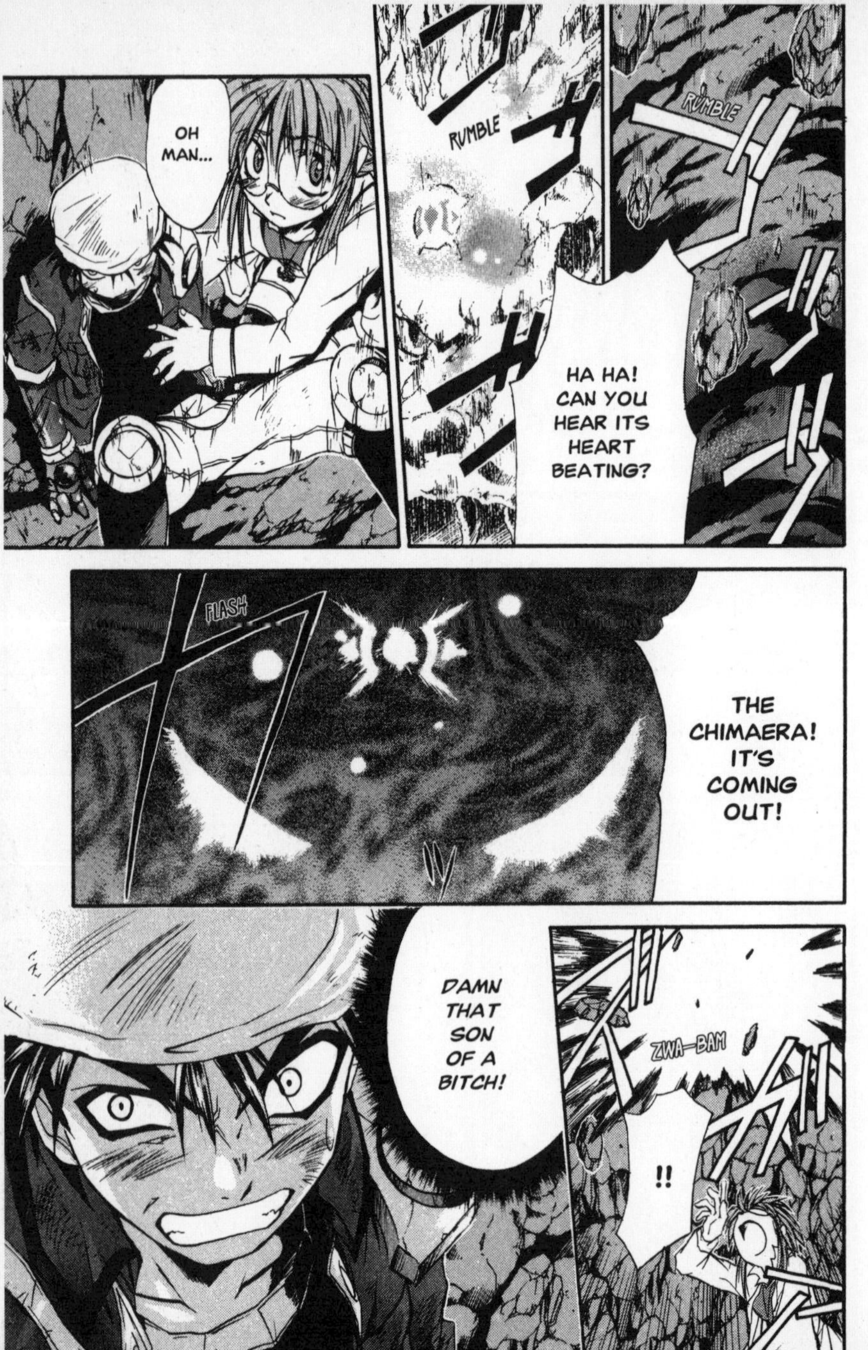
RUMBLE
RUMBLE
HA HA! CAN YOU HEAR ITS HEART BEATING?
OH MAN...
FLASH
THE CHIMAERA! IT'S COMING OUT!
ZWA-BAM
!!
DAMN THAT SON OF A BITCH!

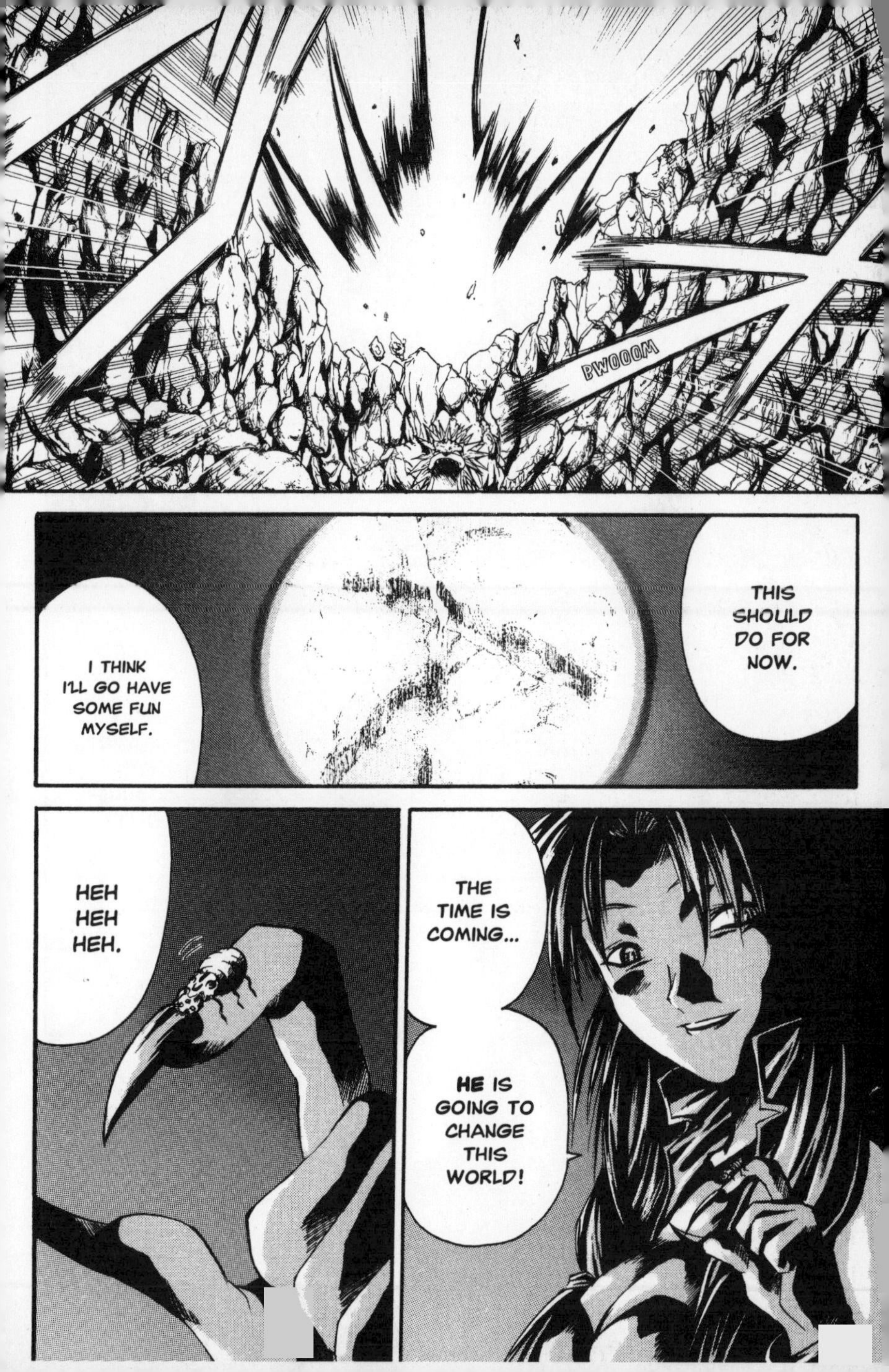
BWOOOM
THIS SHOULD DO FOR NOW.
I THINK I'LL GO HAVE SOME FUN MYSELF.
THE TIME IS COMING...
HE IS GOING TO CHANGE THIS WORLD!
HEH HEH HEH.

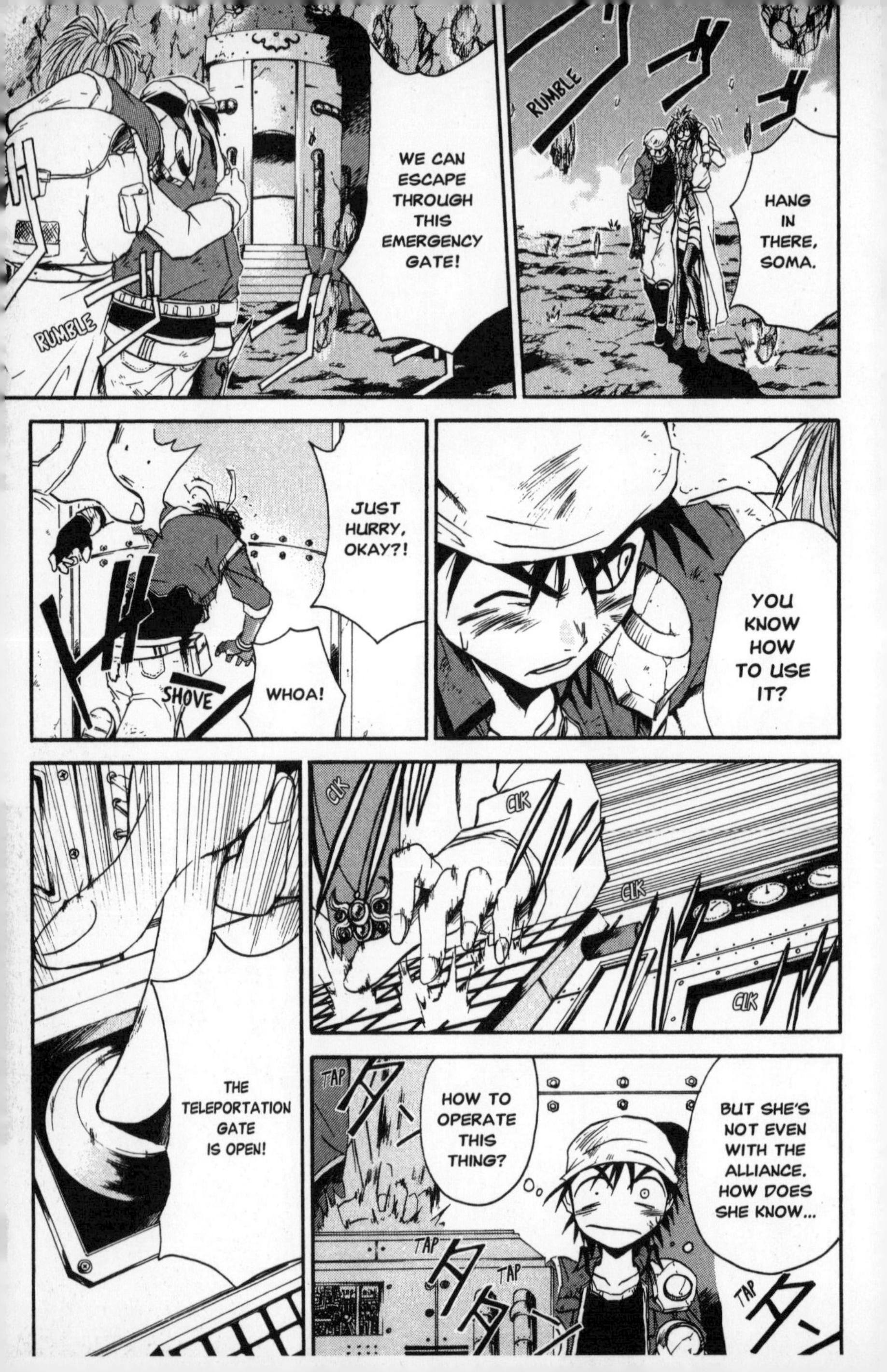
RUMBLE
HANG IN THERE, SOMA.
WE CAN ESCAPE THROUGH THIS EMERGENCY GATE!
RUMBLE
YOU KNOW HOW TO USE IT?
JUST HURRY, OKAY?!
SHOVE
WHOA!
CLK
CLK
CLK
CLK
THE TELEPORTATION GATE IS OPEN!
BUT SHE'S NOT EVEN WITH THE ALLIANCE. HOW DOES SHE KNOW...
HOW TO OPERATE THIS THING?
TAP
TAP
TAP
TAP

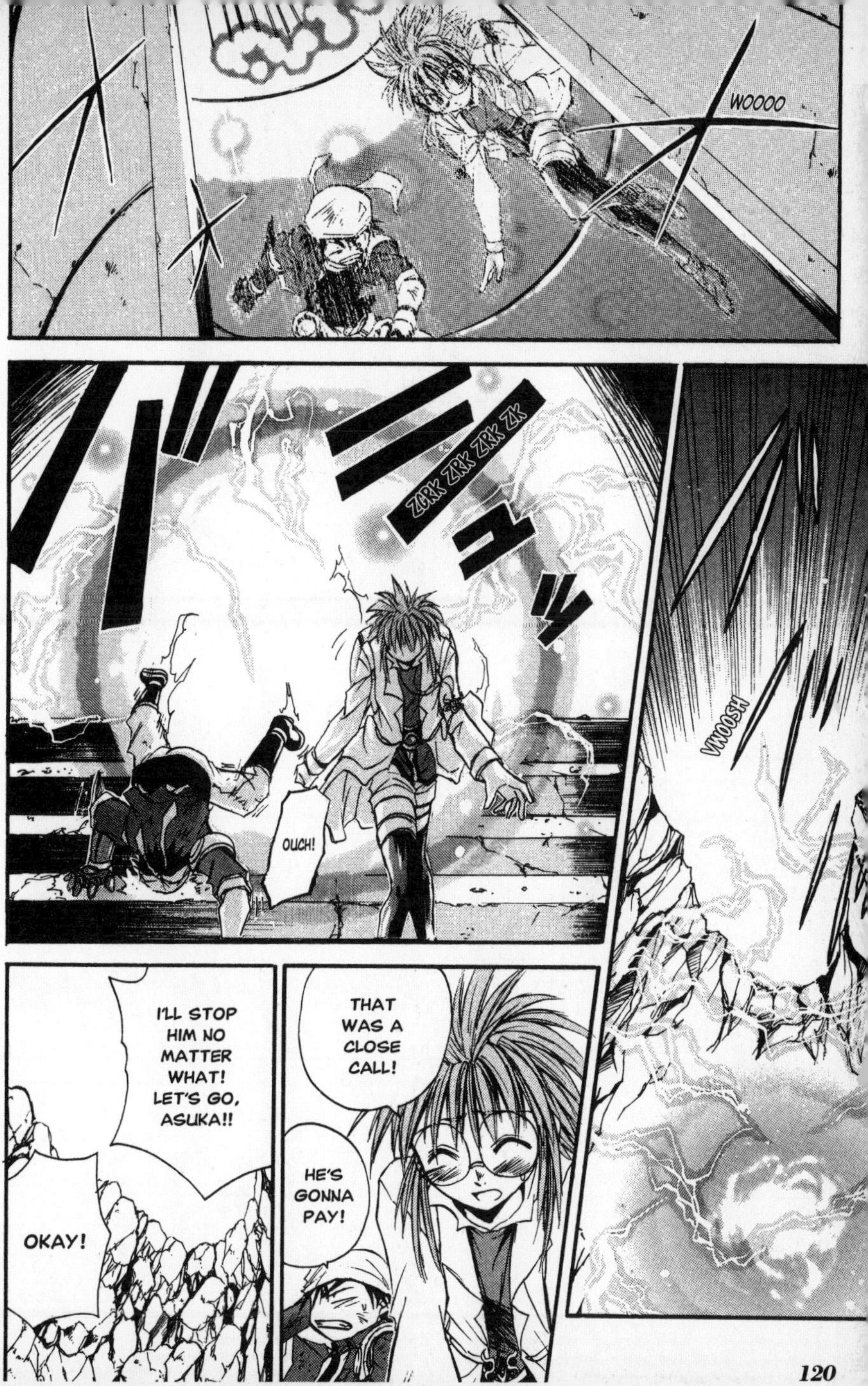
WOOOO
VWOOSH
ZZRK ZRK ZRK ZK
OUCH!
THAT WAS A CLOSE CALL!
HE'S GONNA PAY!
I'LL STOP HIM NO MATTER WHAT! LET'S GO, ASUKA!!
OKAY!

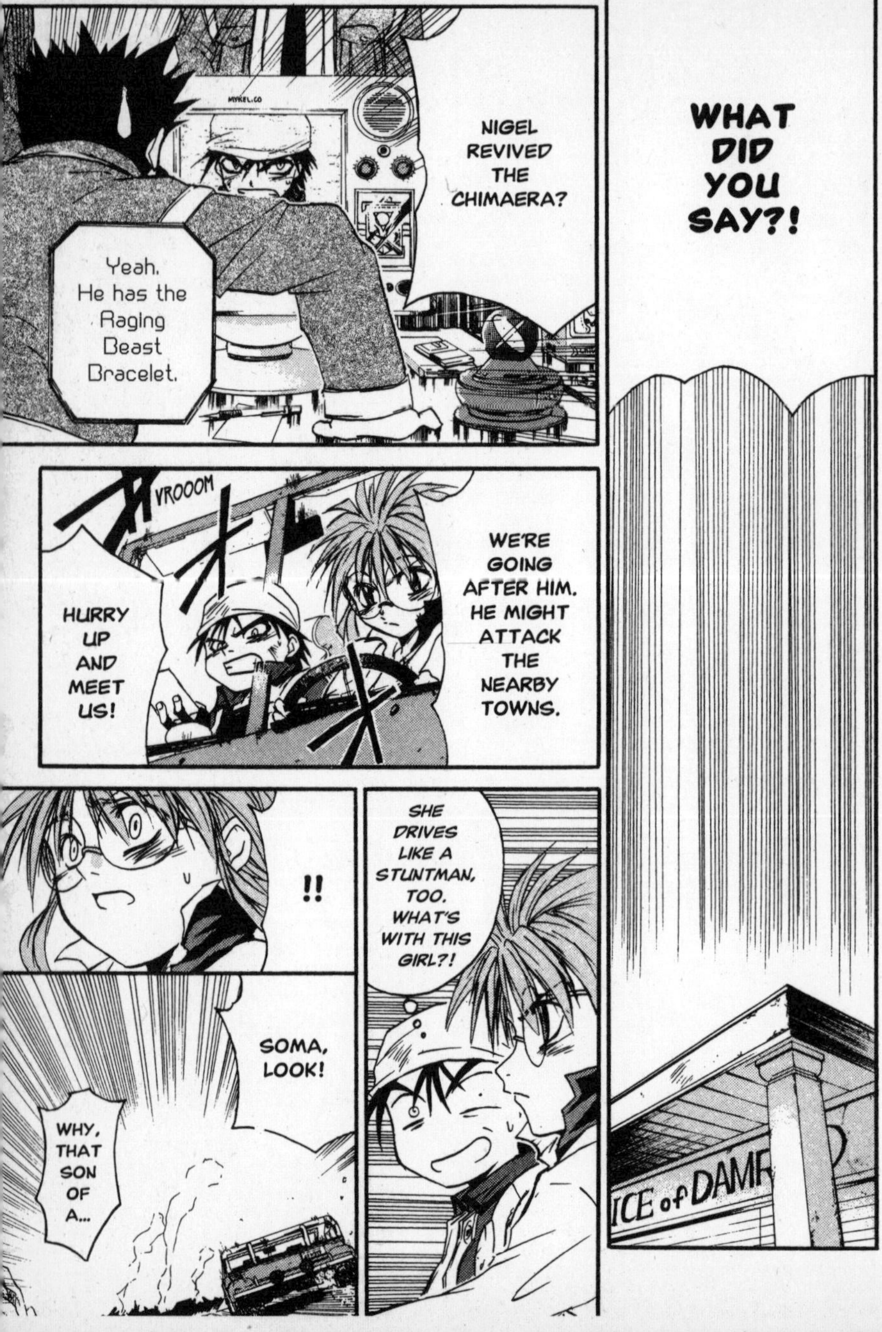
WHAT DID YOU SAY?!
ICE of DAMR
NIGEL REVIVED THE CHIMAERA?
MYKEL.CO
Yeah. He has the Raging Beast Bracelet.
WE'RE GOING AFTER HIM. HE MIGHT ATTACK THE NEARBY TOWNS.
HURRY UP AND MEET US!
VROOOM
SHE DRIVES LIKE A STUNTMAN, TOO. WHAT'S WITH THIS GIRL?!
!!
SOMA, LOOK!
WHY, THAT SON OF A...

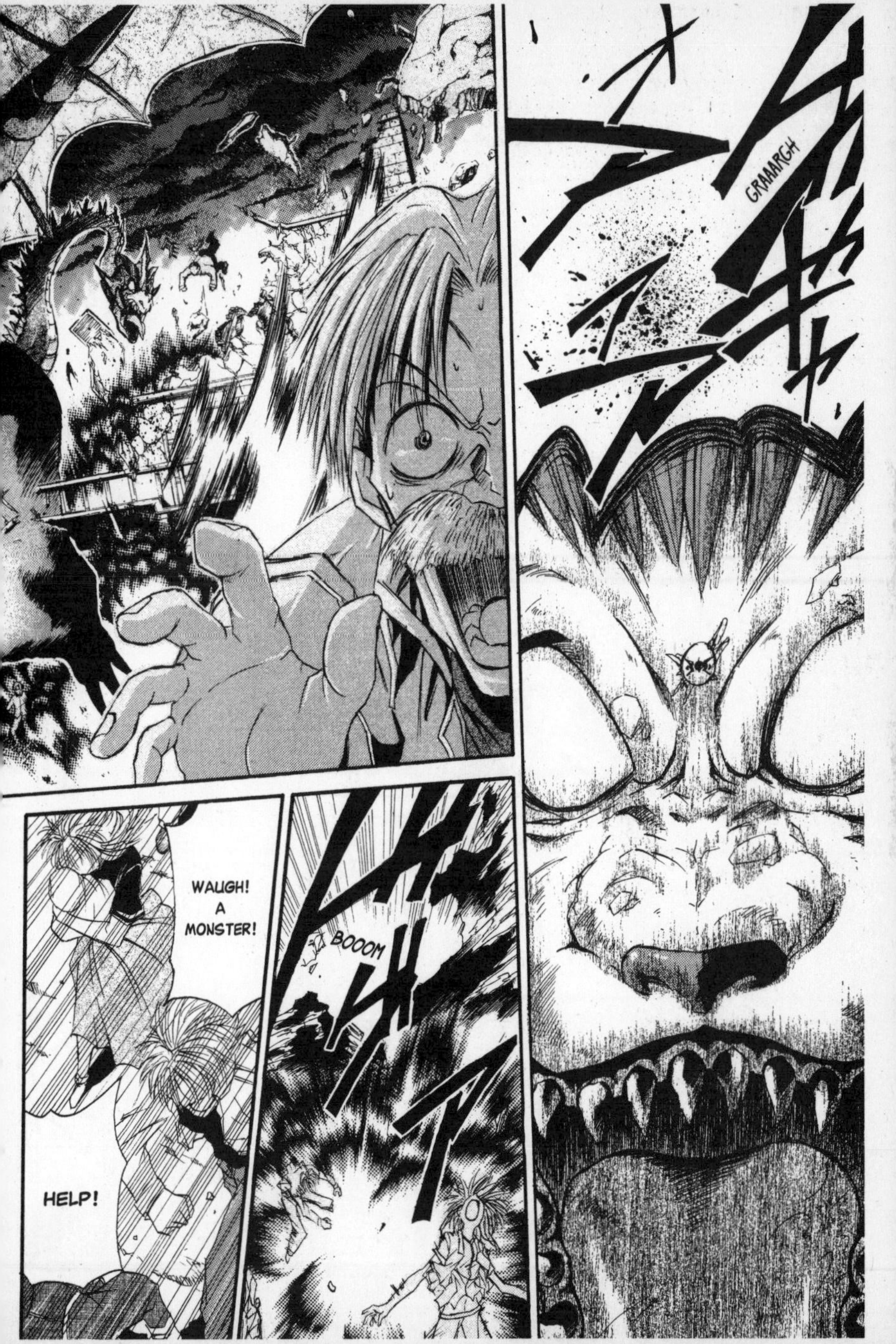
GRAAARGH
BOOOM
WAUGH! A MONSTER!
HELP!

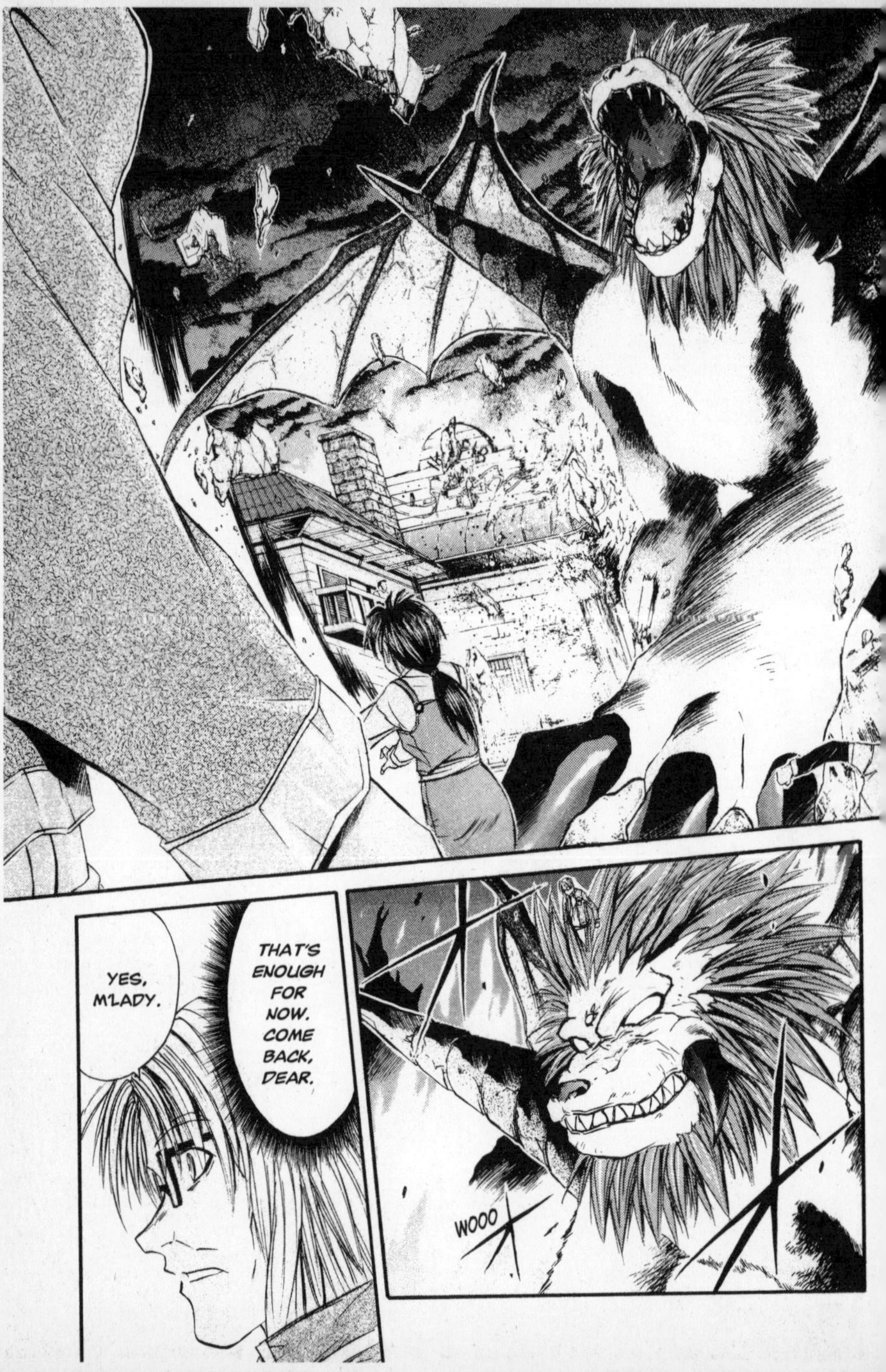
THAT'S ENOUGH FOR NOW. COME BACK, DEAR.
YES, M'LADY.
WOOO

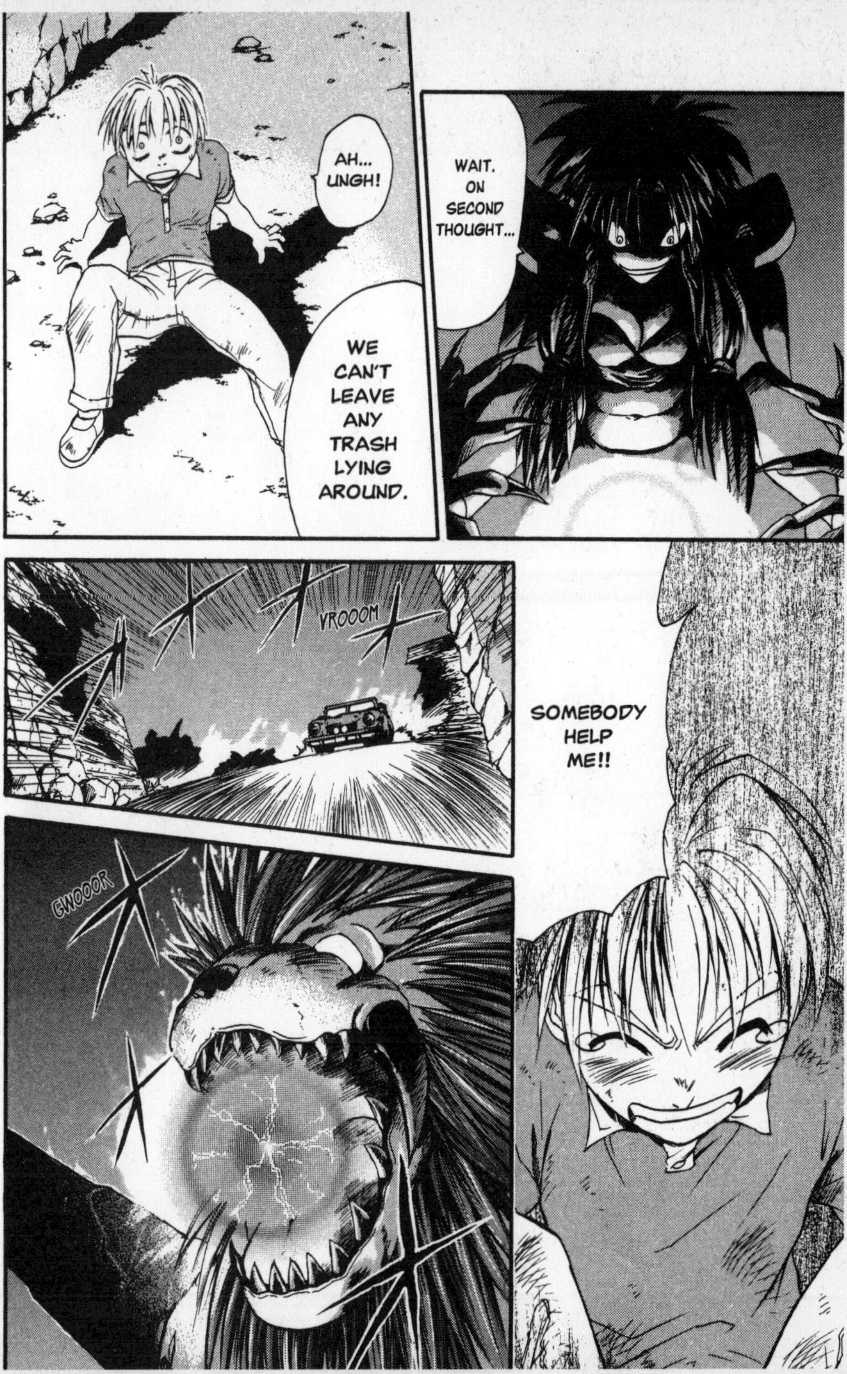
AH... UNGH!
WAIT. ON SECOND THOUGHT...
WE CAN'T LEAVE ANY TRASH LYING AROUND.
VROOOM
SOMEBODY HELP ME!!
GWOOOR

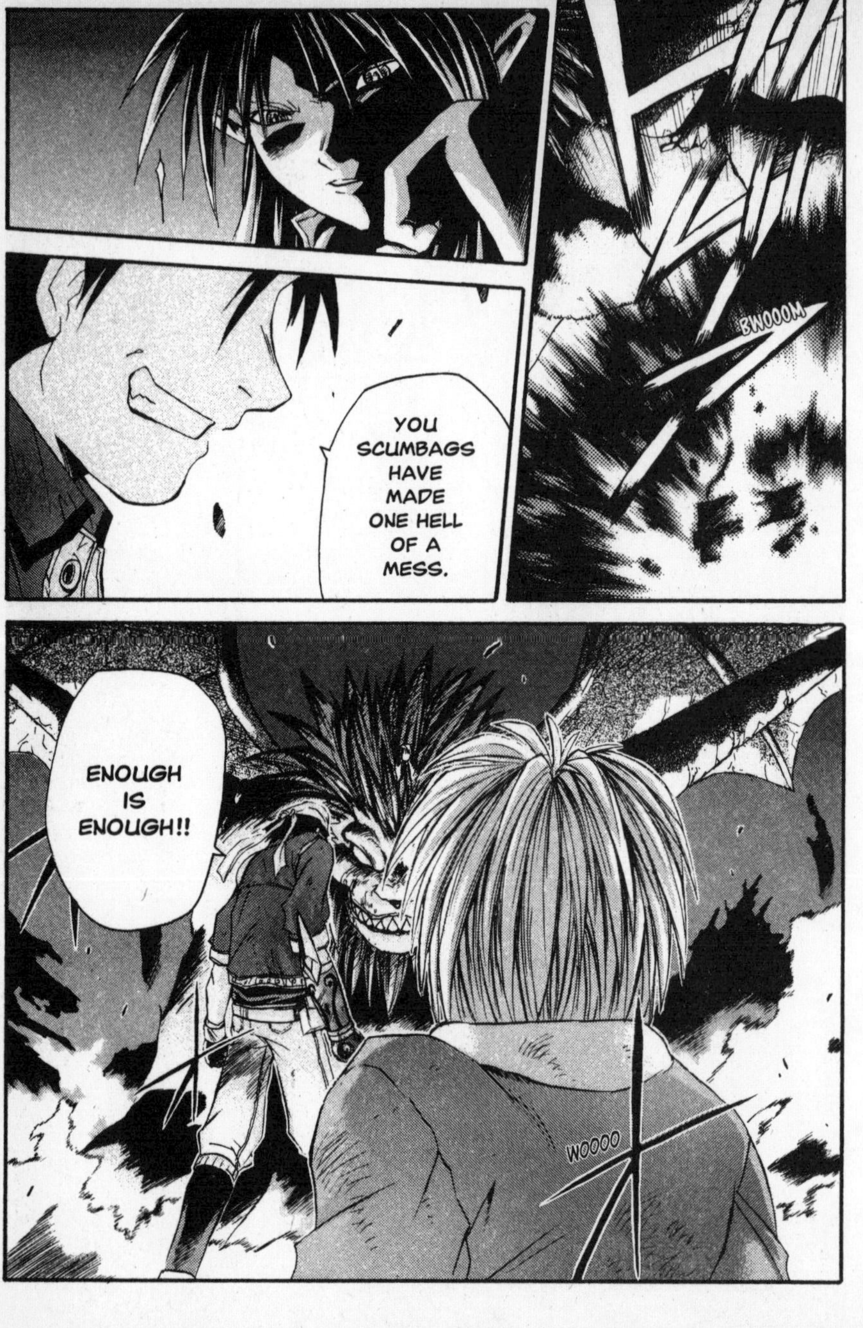
BWOOOM
YOU SCUMBAGS HAVE MADE ONE HELL OF A MESS.
ENOUGH IS ENOUGH!!
WOOOO

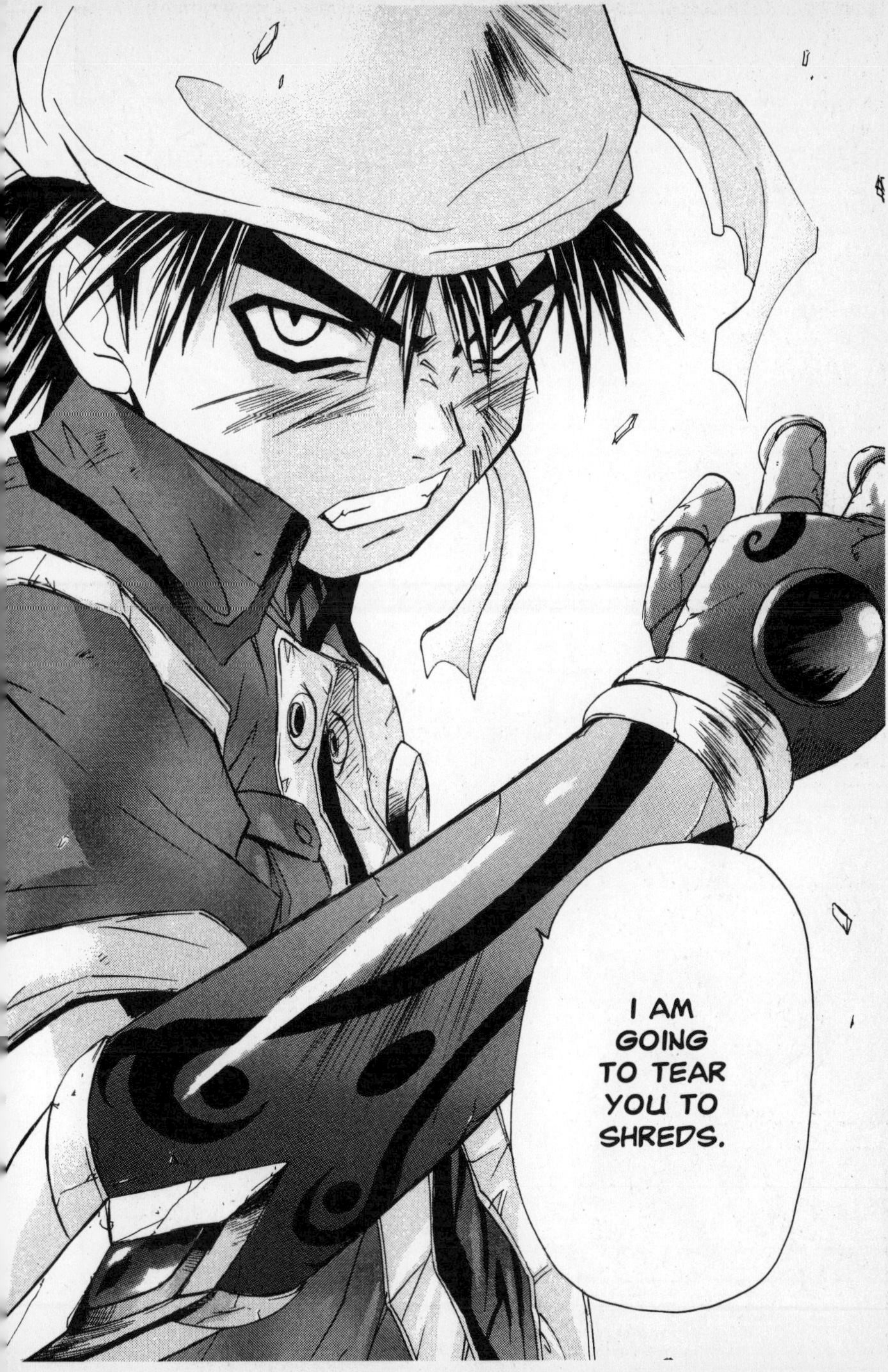
I AM GOING TO TEAR YOU TO SHREDS.

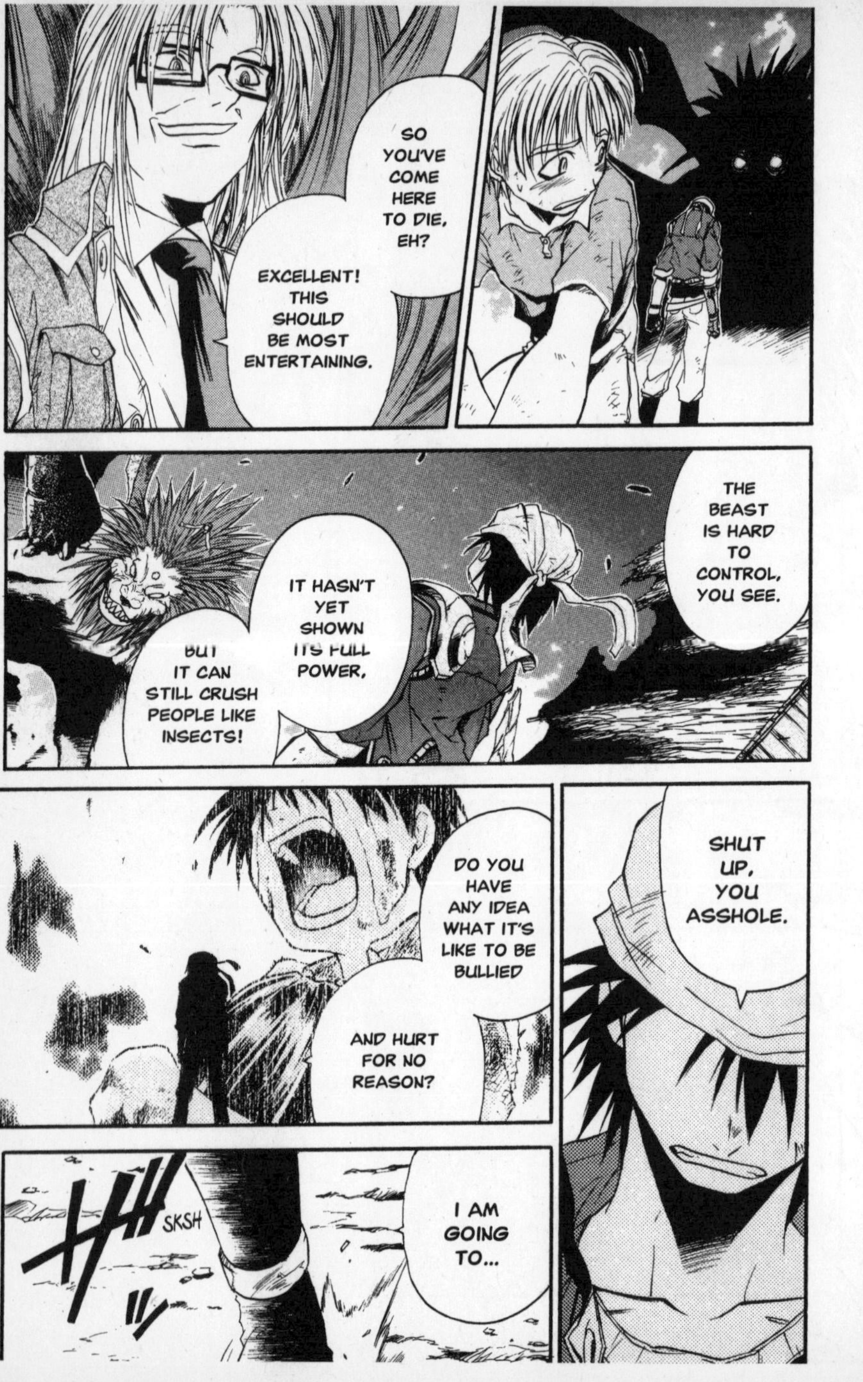
SO YOU'VE COME HERE TO DIE, EH?
EXCELLENT! THIS SHOULD BE MOST ENTERTAINING.
THE BEAST IS HARD TO CONTROL, YOU SEE.
IT HASN'T YET SHOWN ITS FULL POWER,
BUT IT CAN STILL CRUSH PEOPLE LIKE INSECTS!
SHUT UP, YOU ASSHOLE.
DO YOU HAVE ANY IDEA WHAT IT'S LIKE TO BE BULLIED
AND HURT FOR NO REASON?
I AM GOING TO...
SKSH

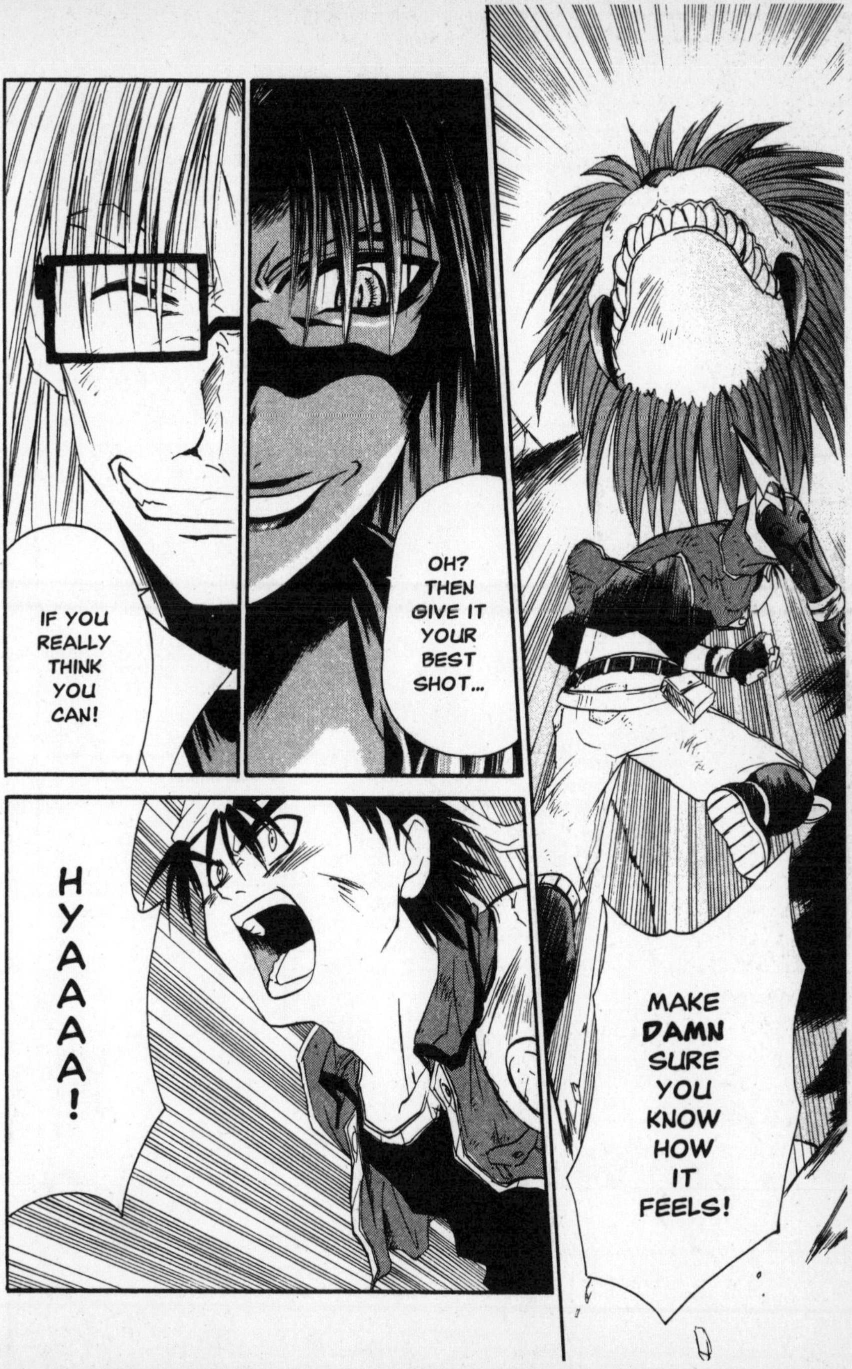
MAKE DAMN SURE YOU KNOW HOW IT FEELS!
OH? THEN GIVE IT YOUR BEST SHOT...
IF YOU REALLY THINK YOU CAN!
HYAAAAA!

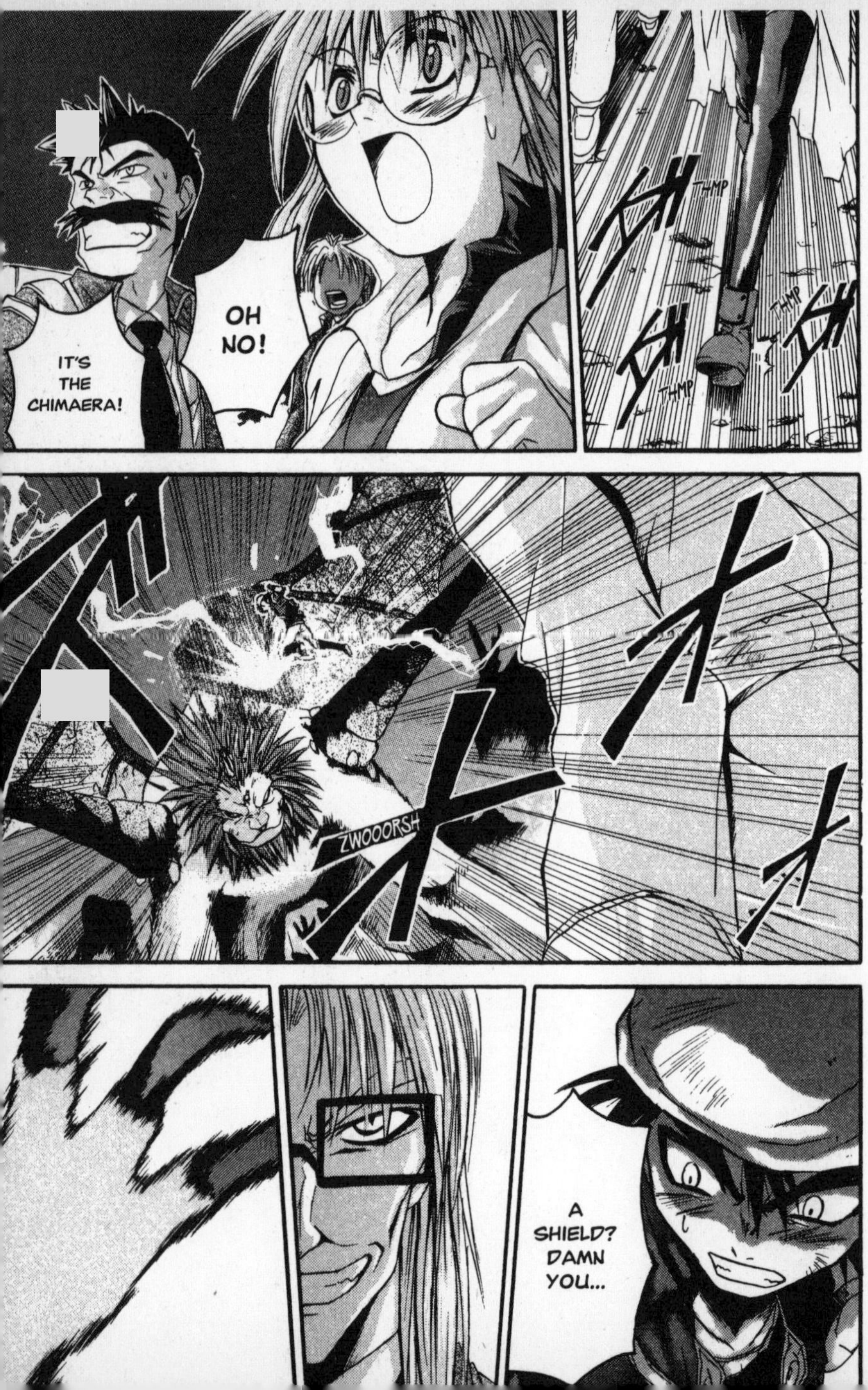
THMP
THMP
THMP
OH NO!
IT'S THE CHIMAERA!
ZWOOORSH
A SHIELD? DAMN YOU...

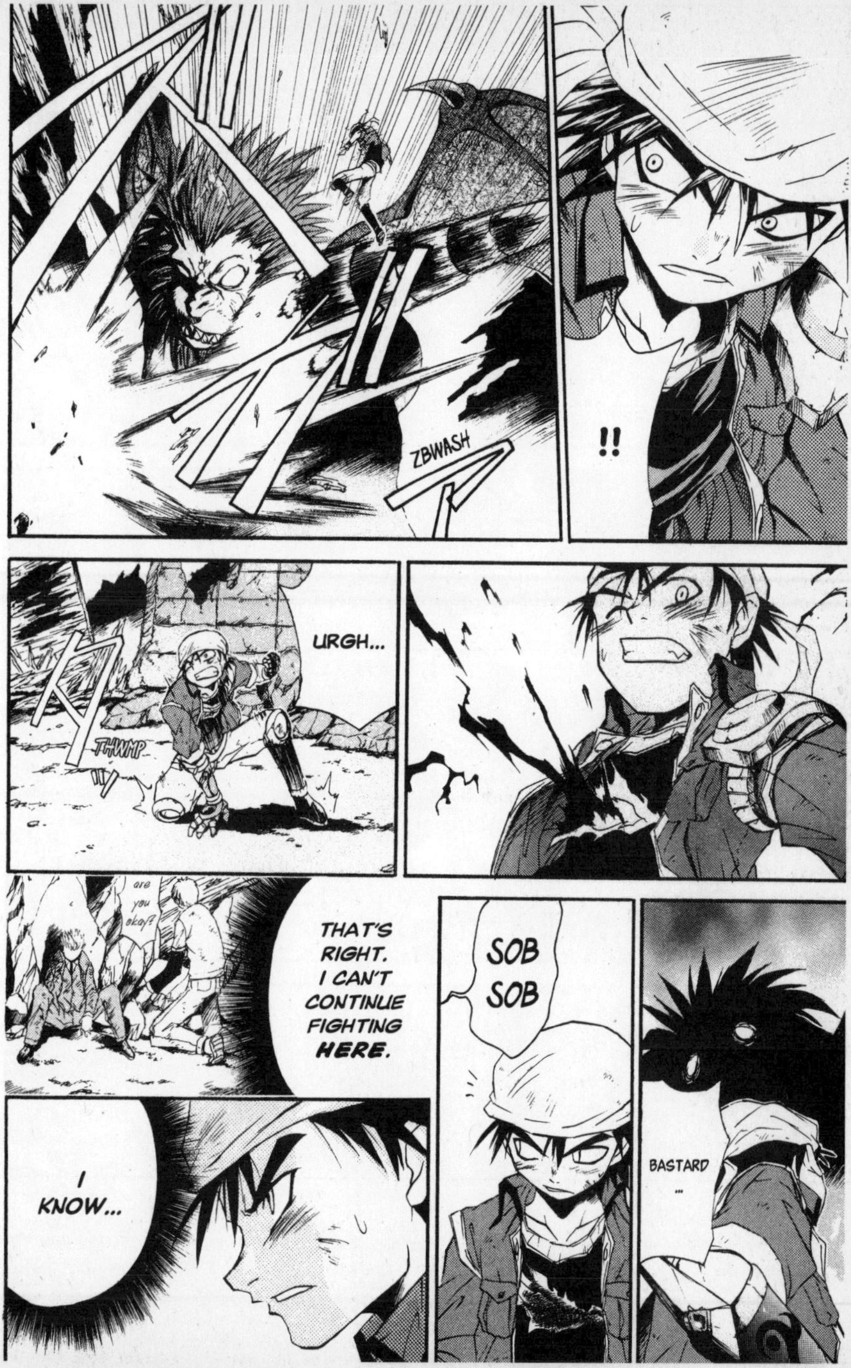

!!
ZBWASH
URGH...
THWMP
BASTARD ...
SOB SOB
THAT'S RIGHT. I CAN'T CONTINUE FIGHTING HERE.
are you okay?
I KNOW...

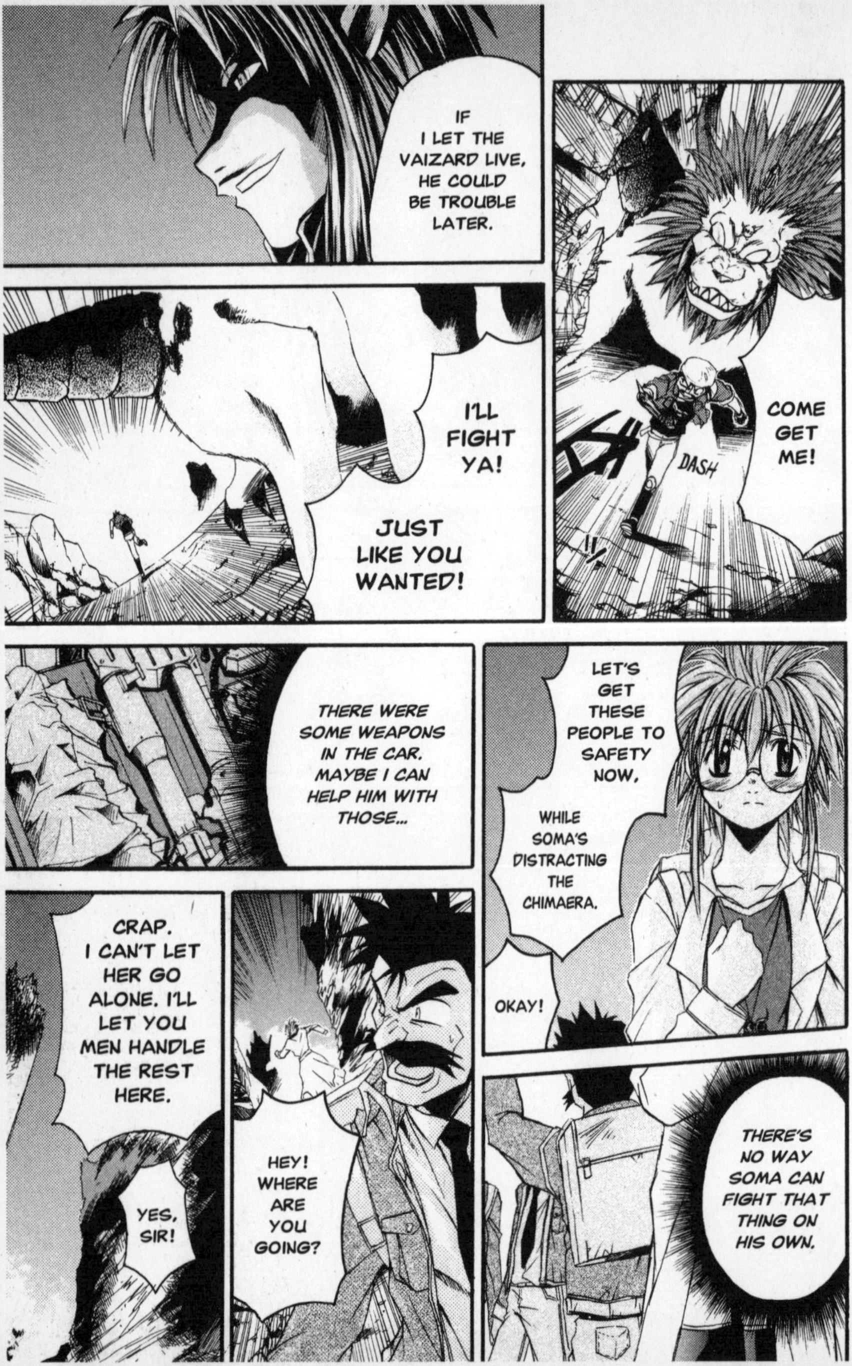
IF I LET THE VAIZARD LIVE, HE COULD BE TROUBLE LATER.
COME GET ME!
DASH
I'LL FIGHT YA!
JUST LIKE YOU WANTED!
LET'S GET THESE PEOPLE TO SAFETY NOW,
WHILE SOMA'S DISTRACTING THE CHIMAERA.
OKAY!
THERE WERE SOME WEAPONS IN THE CAR. MAYBE I CAN HELP HIM WITH THOSE...
THERE'S NO WAY SOMA CAN FIGHT THAT THING ON HIS OWN.
HEY! WHERE ARE YOU GOING?
CRAP. I CAN'T LET HER GO ALONE. I'LL LET YOU MEN HANDLE THE REST HERE.
YES, SIR!

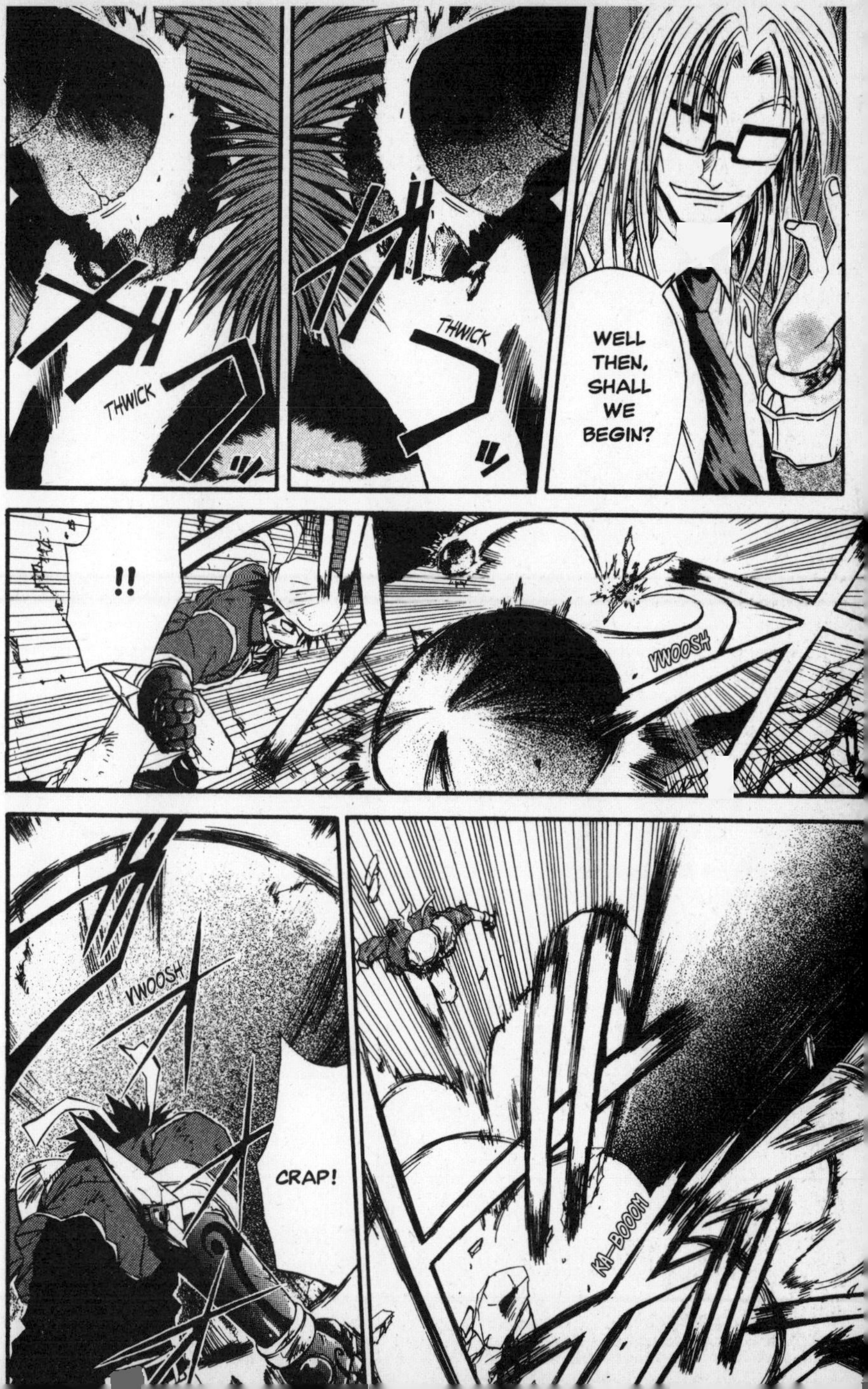
WELL THEN, SHALL WE BEGIN?
THWICK
THWICK
!!
YWOOSH
KA-BOOOM
CRAP!
YWOOSH

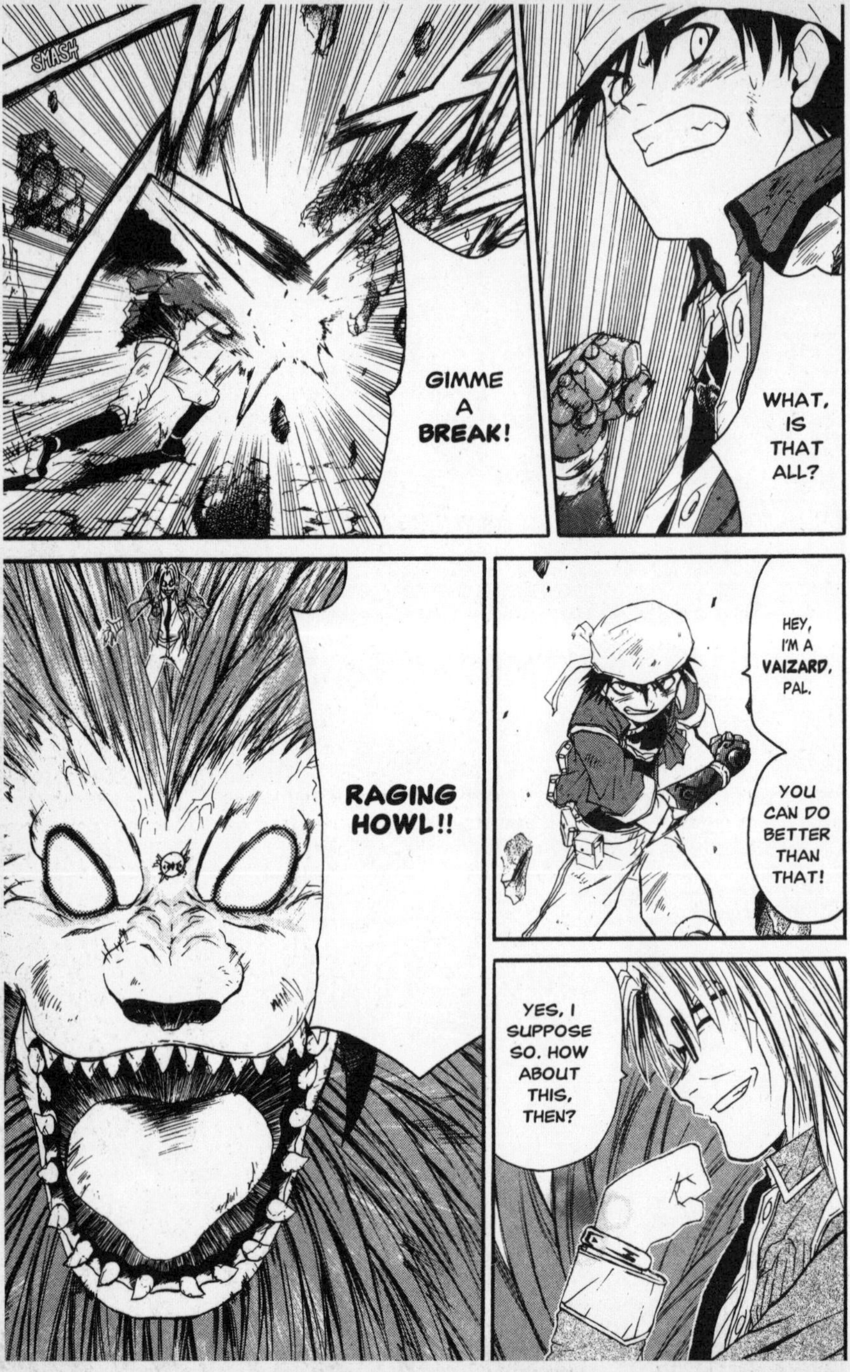
WHAT, IS THAT ALL?
SMASH
GIMME A BREAK!
HEY, I'M A VAIZARD, PAL.
YOU CAN DO BETTER THAN THAT!
YES, I SUPPOSE SO. HOW ABOUT THIS, THEN?
RAGING HOWL!!

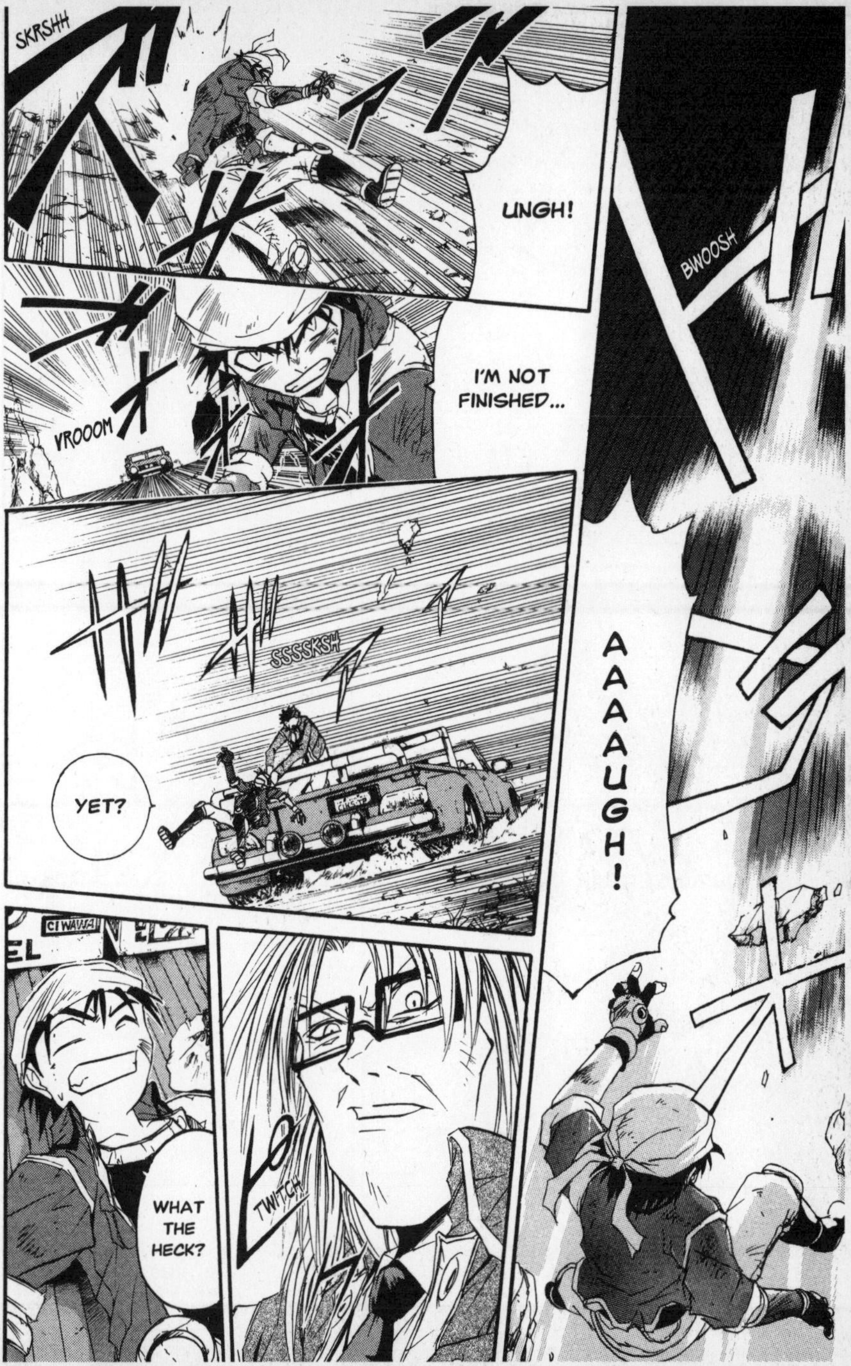BWOOSH
AAAAAUGH!
SKRSHH
UNGH!
I'M NOT FINISHED...
VROOOM
SSSSKSH
YET?
CIWAWA
TWITCH
WHAT THE HECK?

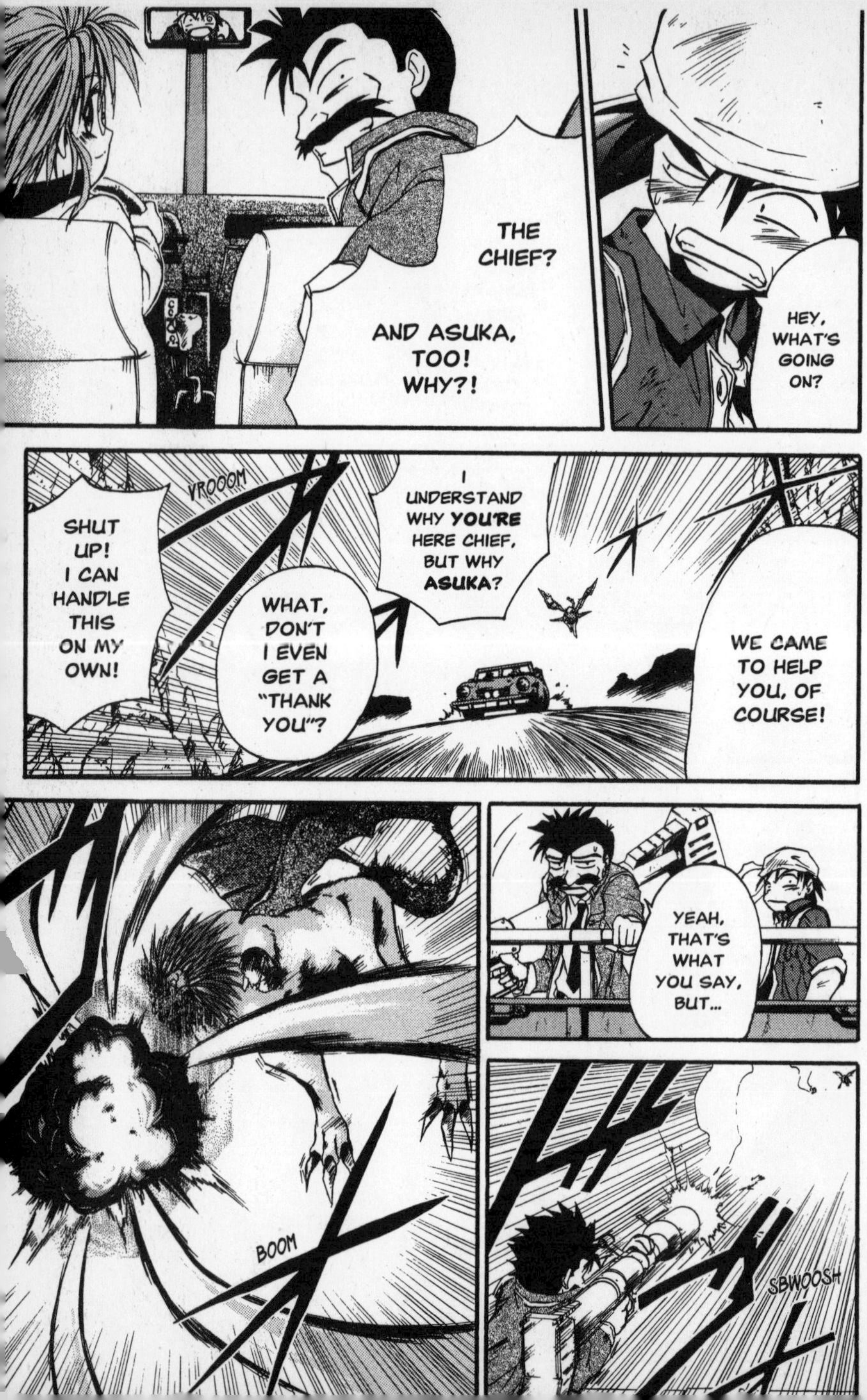
THE CHIEF?
AND ASUKA, TOO! WHY?!
HEY, WHAT'S GOING ON?
VROOOM
I UNDERSTAND WHY YOU'RE HERE CHIEF, BUT WHY ASUKA?
WE CAME TO HELP YOU, OF COURSE!
WHAT, DON'T I EVEN GET A "THANK YOU"?
SHUT UP! I CAN HANDLE THIS ON MY OWN!
YEAH, THAT'S WHAT YOU SAY, BUT...
BOOM
SBWOOSH

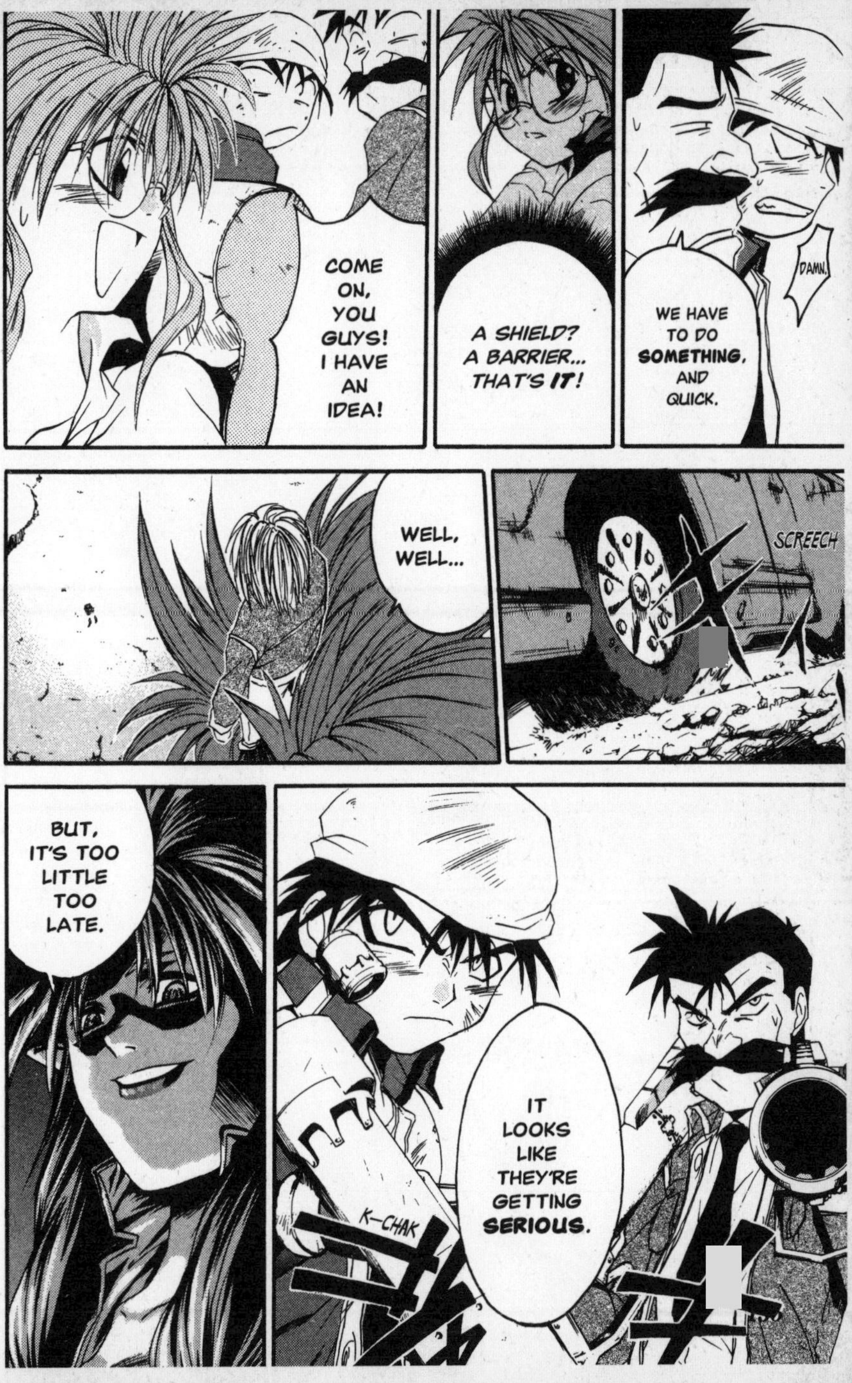

DAMN.
WE HAVE TO DO SOMETHING, AND QUICK.
A SHIELD? A BARRIER... THAT'S IT!
COME ON, YOU GUYS! I HAVE AN IDEA!
SCREECH
WELL, WELL...
IT LOOKS LIKE THEY'RE GETTING SERIOUS.
K-CHAK
BUT, IT'S TOO LITTLE TOO LATE.

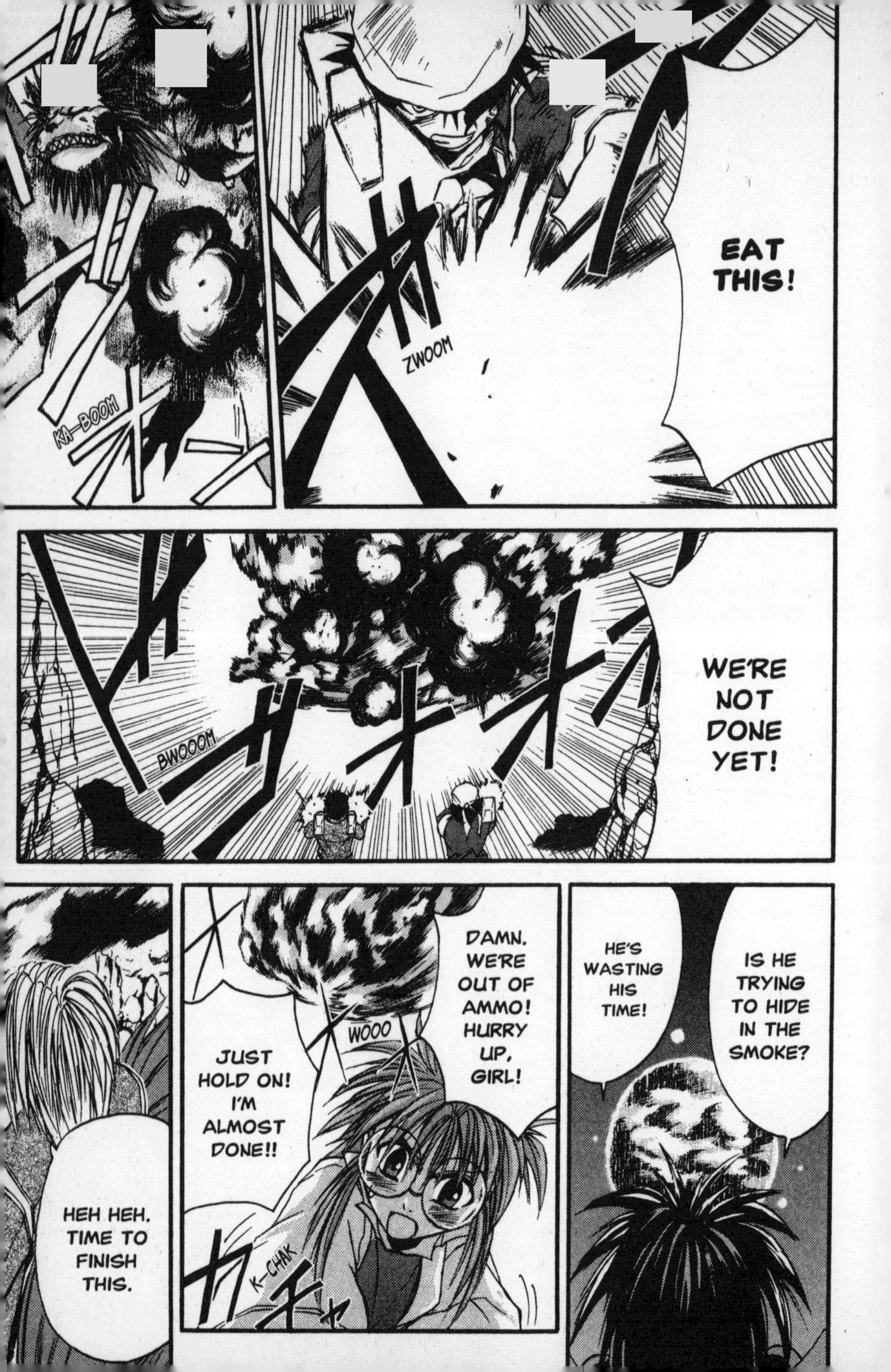
EAT THIS!
ZWOOM
KA-BOOM
WE'RE NOT DONE YET!
BWOOOM
IS HE TRYING TO HIDE IN THE SMOKE?
HE'S WASTING HIS TIME!
DAMN. WE'RE OUT OF AMMO! HURRY UP, GIRL!
WOOO
JUST HOLD ON! I'M ALMOST DONE!!
K-CHAK
HEH HEH. TIME TO FINISH THIS.

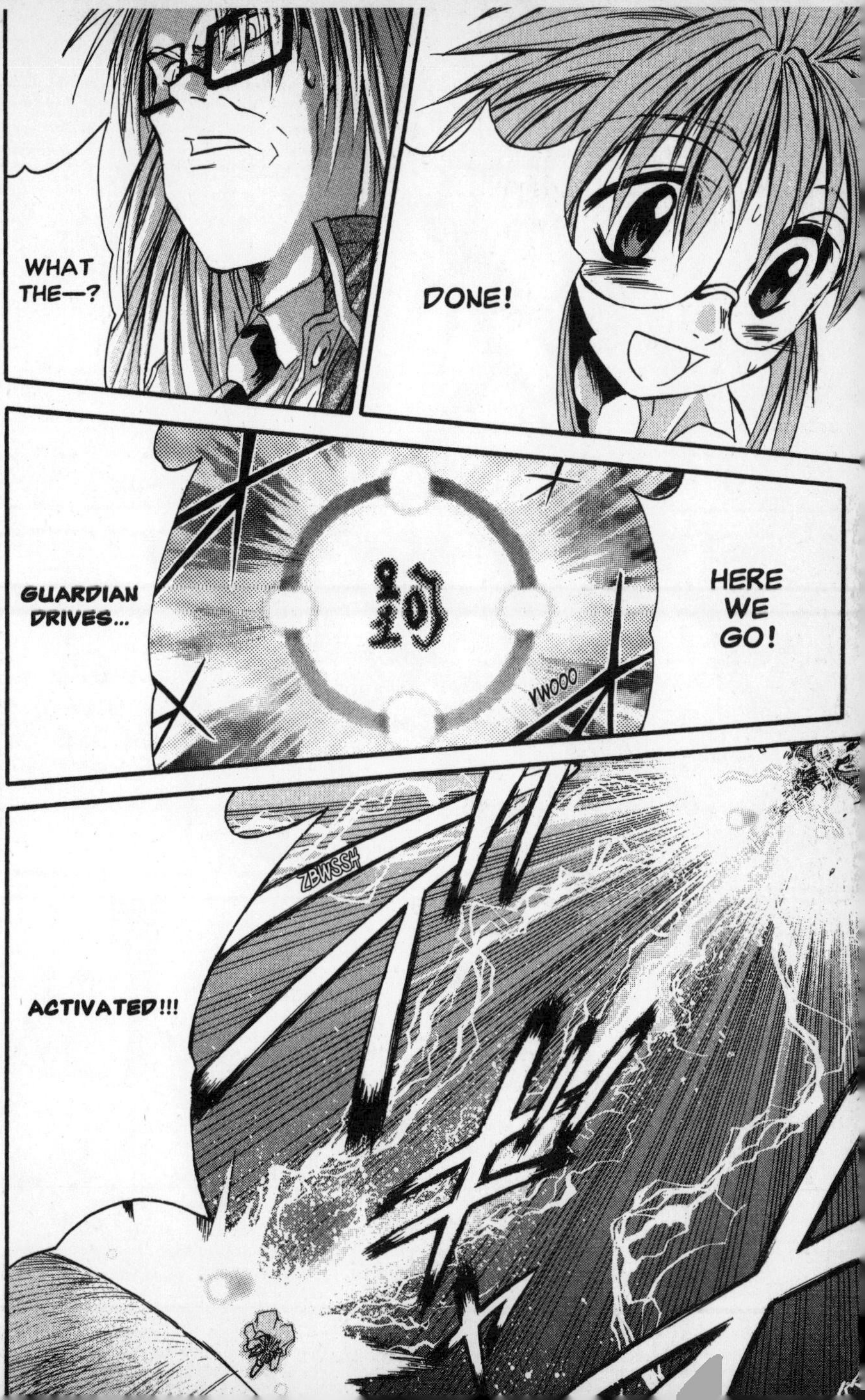
DONE!
WHAT THE—?
HERE WE GO!
GUARDIAN DRIVES...
YWOOO
ZBWSSH
ACTIVATED!!!

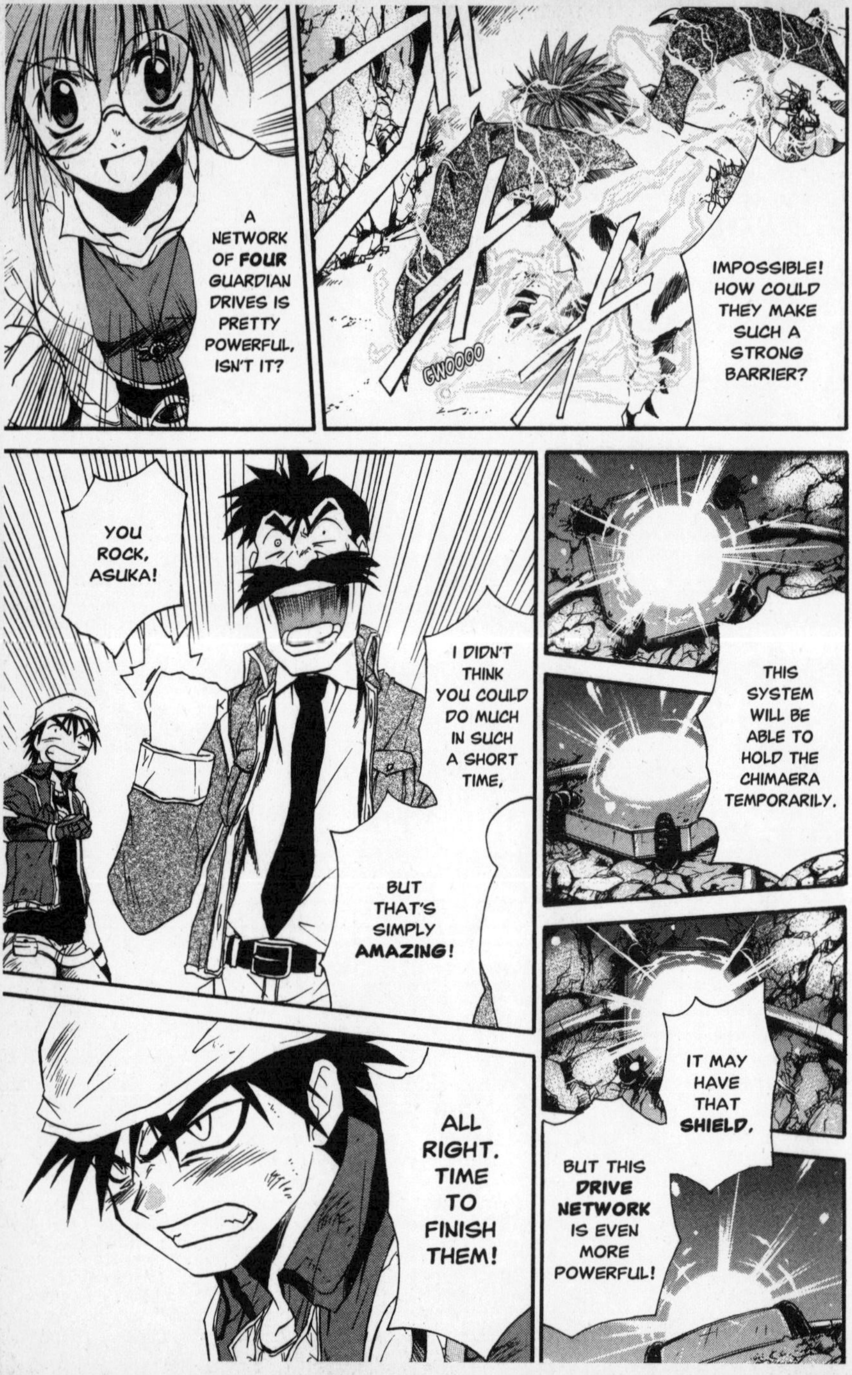
A NETWORK OF FOUR GUARDIAN DRIVES IS PRETTY POWERFUL, ISN'T IT?
IMPOSSIBLE! HOW COULD THEY MAKE SUCH A STRONG BARRIER?
GWOOOO
YOU ROCK, ASUKA!
I DIDN'T THINK YOU COULD DO MUCH IN SUCH A SHORT TIME,
BUT THAT'S SIMPLY AMAZING!
THIS SYSTEM WILL BE ABLE TO HOLD THE CHIMAERA TEMPORARILY.
ALL RIGHT. TIME TO FINISH THEM!
IT MAY HAVE THAT SHIELD,
BUT THIS DRIVE NETWORK IS EVEN MORE POWERFUL!

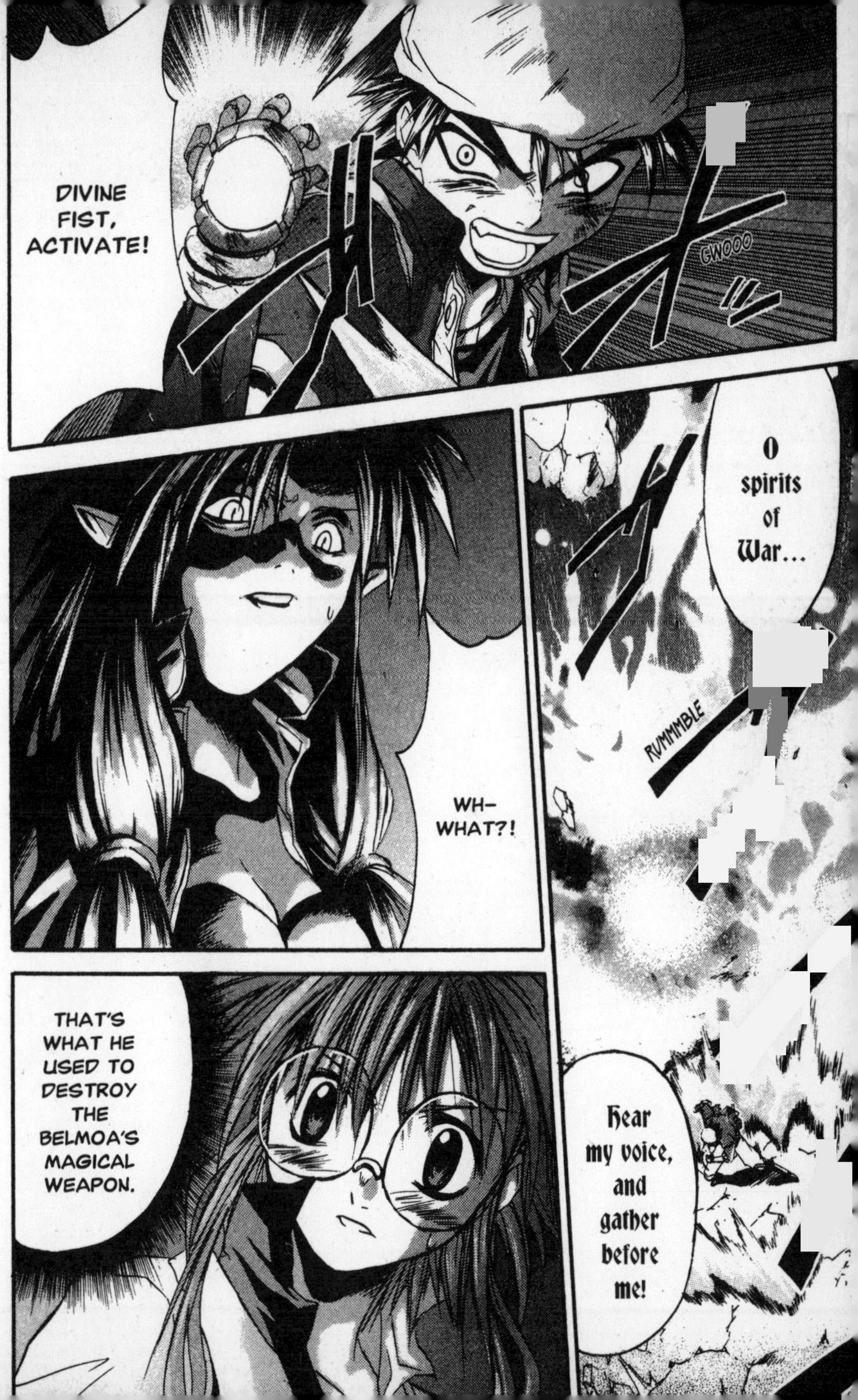
DIVINE FIST, ACTIVATE!
GWOOO
O spirits of War...
RUMMMBLE
Hear my voice, and gather before me!
WH- WHAT?!
THAT'S WHAT HE USED TO DESTROY THE BELMOA'S MAGICAL WEAPON.

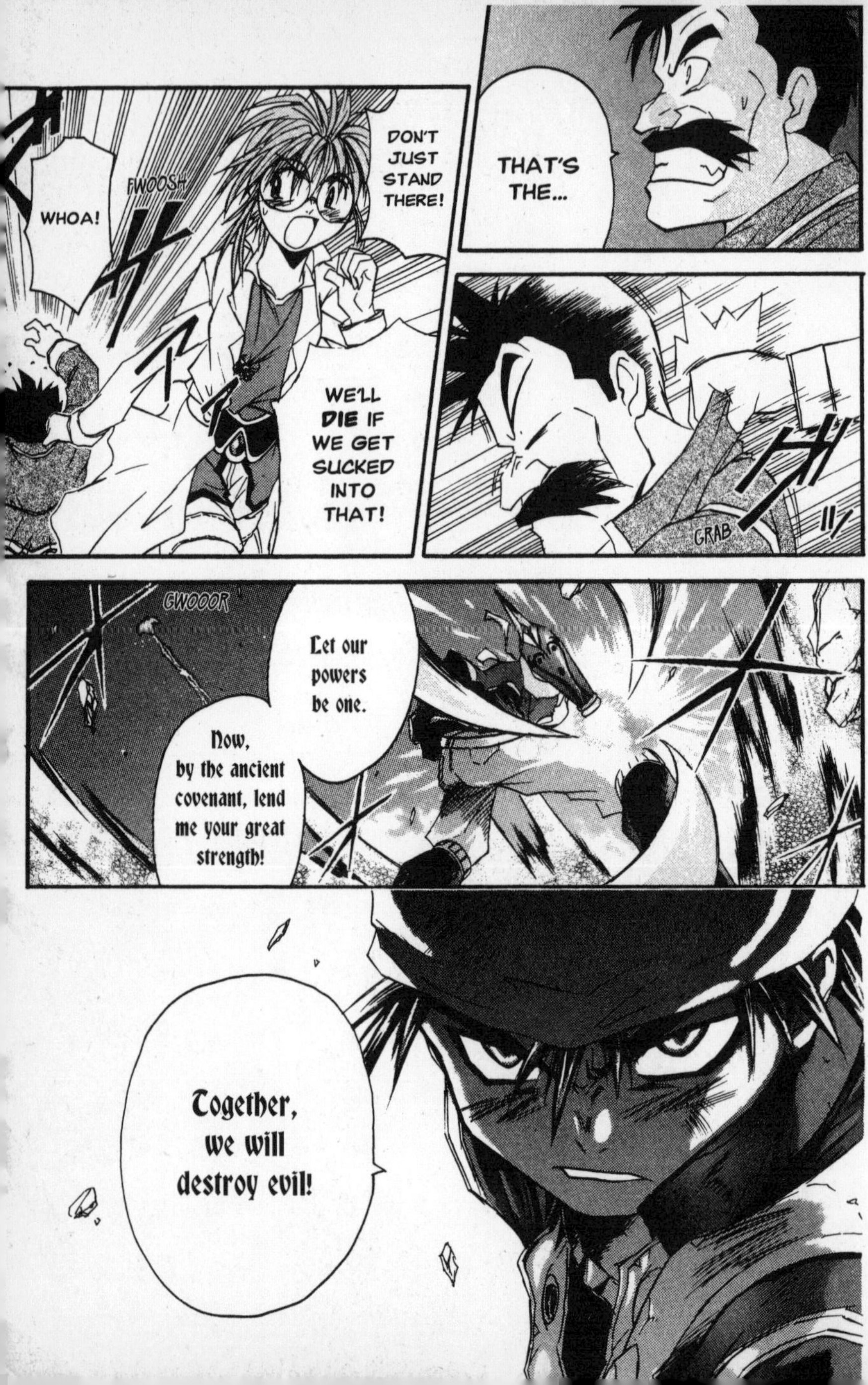
THAT'S THE...
GRAB
DON'T JUST STAND THERE!
WE'LL DIE IF WE GET SUCKED INTO THAT!
FWOOSH
WHOA!
GWOOOR
Let our powers be one.
Now, by the ancient covenant, lend me your great strength!
Together, we will destroy evil!

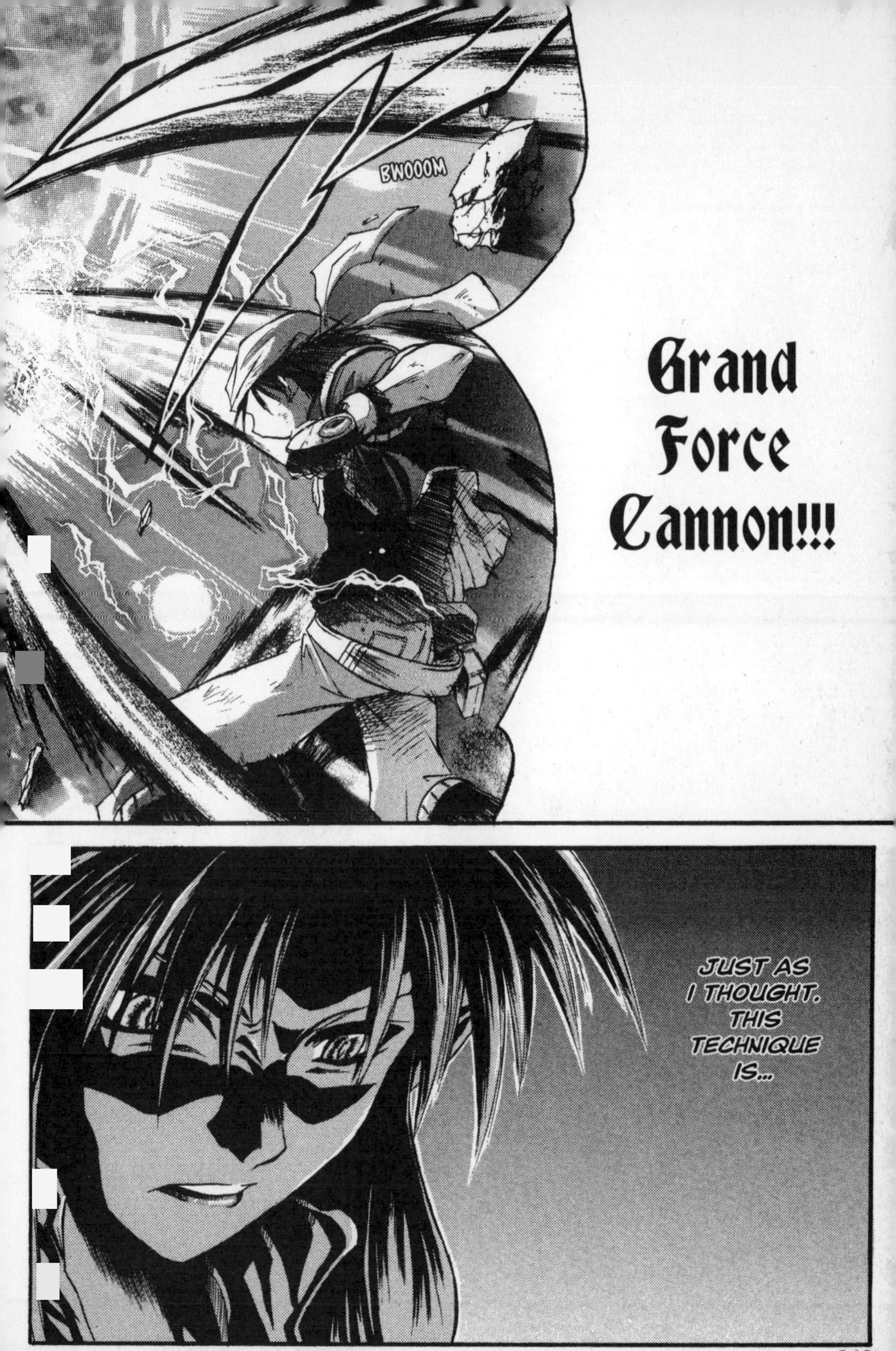
BWOOOM
Grand Force Cannon!!!
JUST AS I THOUGHT. THIS TECHNIQUE IS...

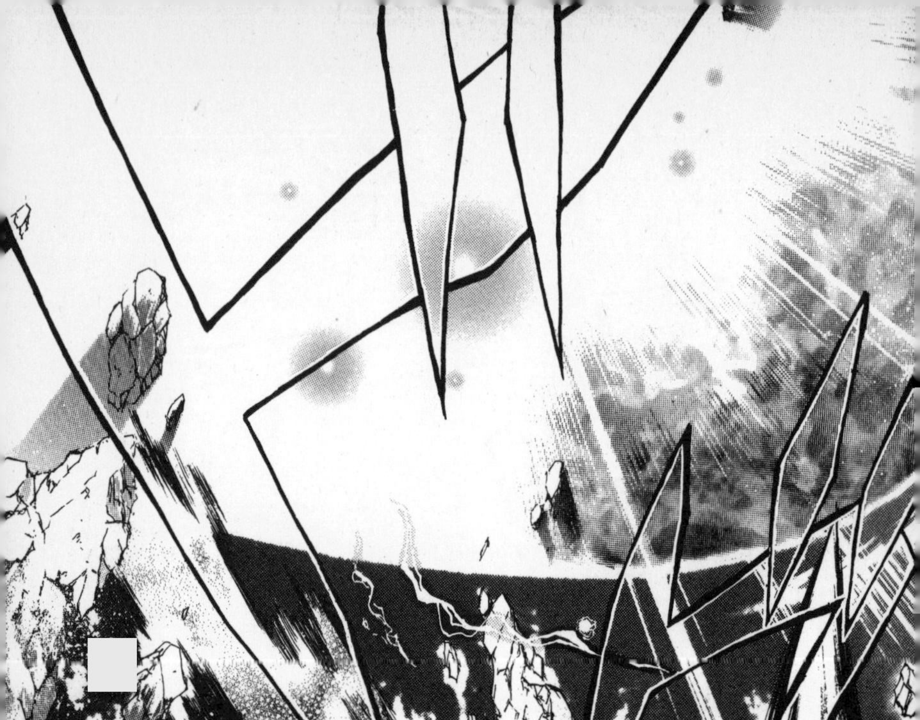
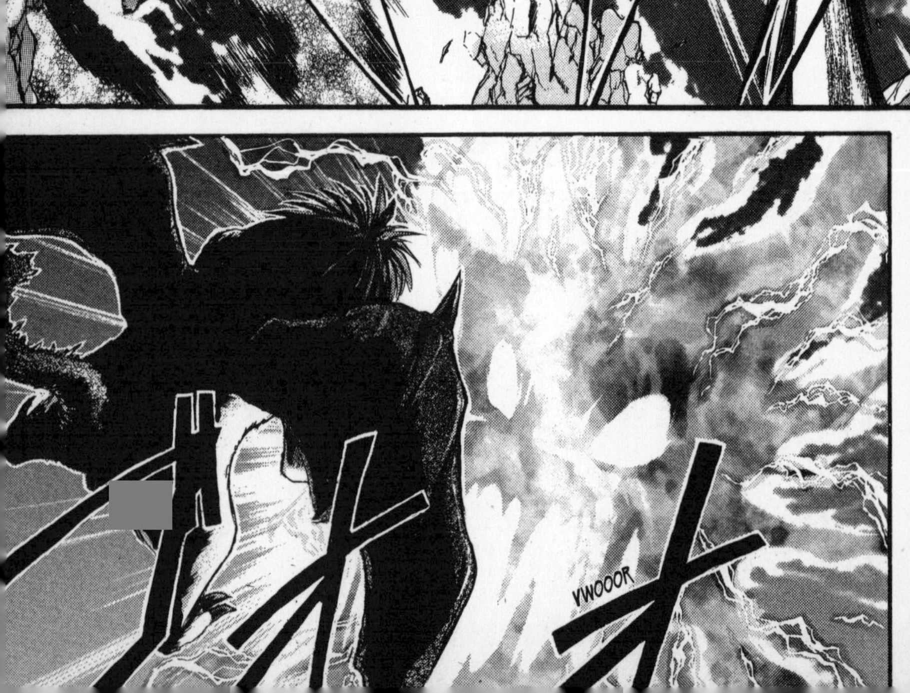
VWOOOR

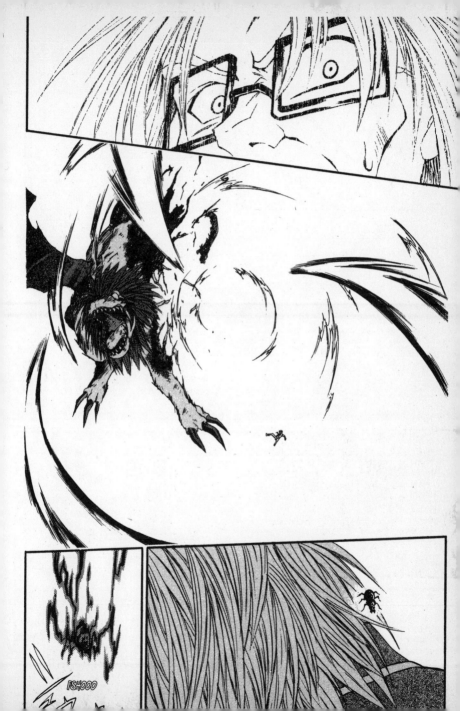

FSHOOO

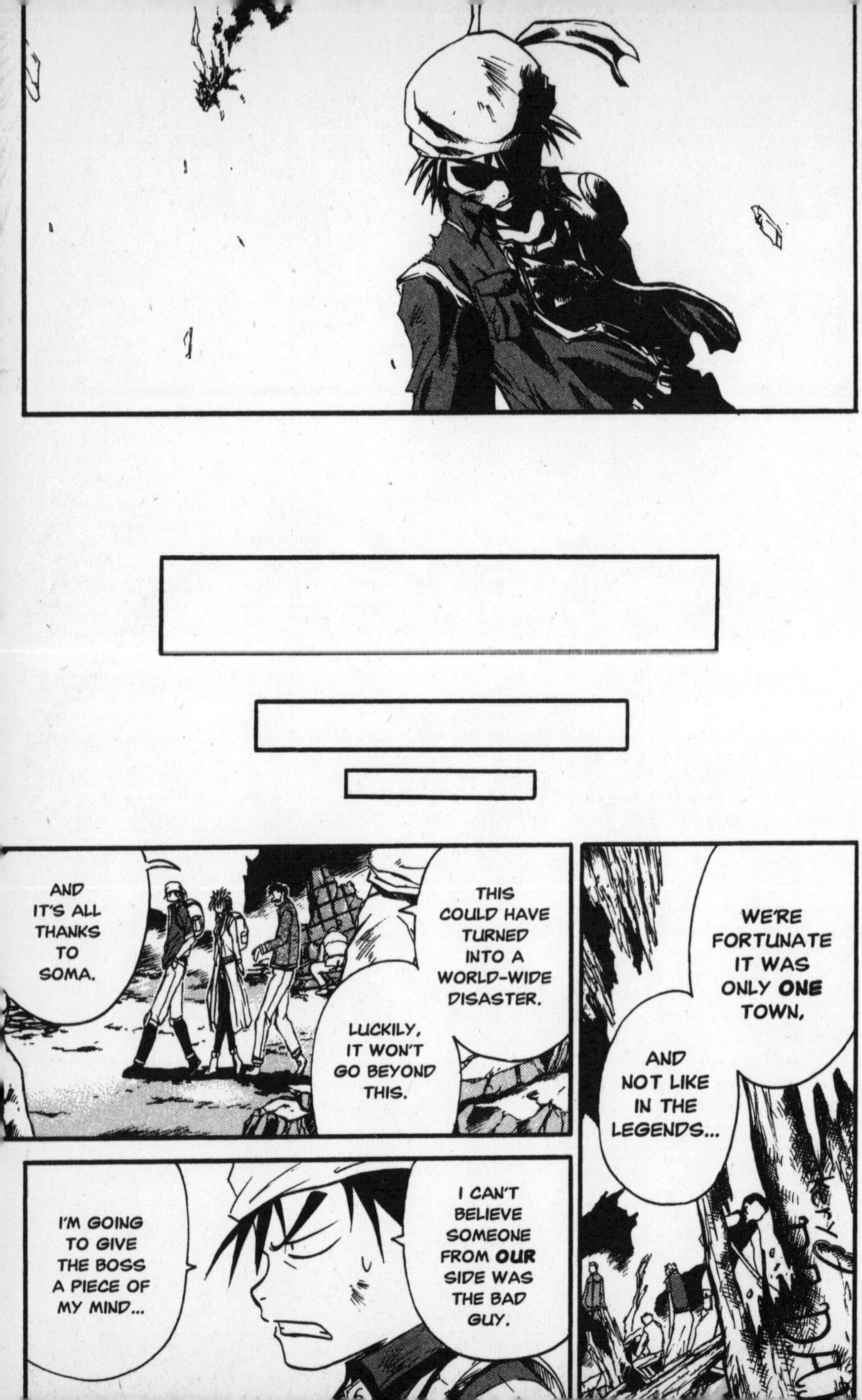
WE'RE FORTUNATE IT WAS ONLY ONE TOWN,
AND NOT LIKE IN THE LEGENDS...
THIS COULD HAVE TURNED INTO A WORLD-WIDE DISASTER.
LUCKILY, IT WON'T GO BEYOND THIS.
AND IT'S ALL THANKS TO SOMA.
I CAN'T BELIEVE SOMEONE FROM OUR SIDE WAS THE BAD GUY.
I'M GOING TO GIVE THE BOSS A PIECE OF MY MIND...

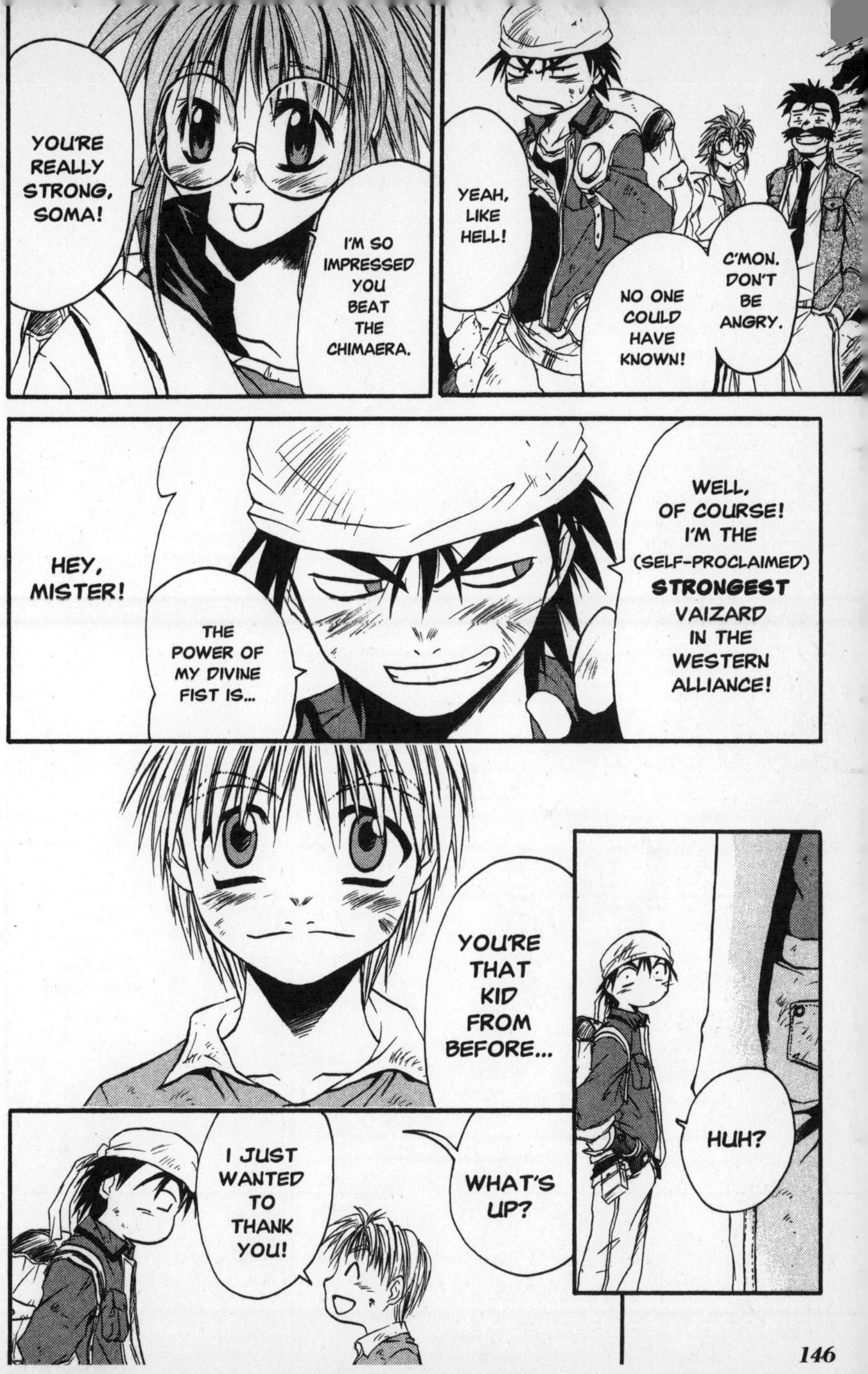
YOU'RE REALLY STRONG, SOMA!
I'M SO IMPRESSED YOU BEAT THE CHIMAERA.
YEAH, LIKE HELL!
C'MON. DON'T BE ANGRY.
NO ONE COULD HAVE KNOWN!
WELL, OF COURSE! I'M THE (SELF-PROCLAIMED) STRONGEST VAIZARD IN THE WESTERN ALLIANCE!
THE POWER OF MY DIVINE FIST IS...
HEY, MISTER!
HUH?
YOU'RE THAT KID FROM BEFORE...
WHAT'S UP?
I JUST WANTED TO THANK YOU!

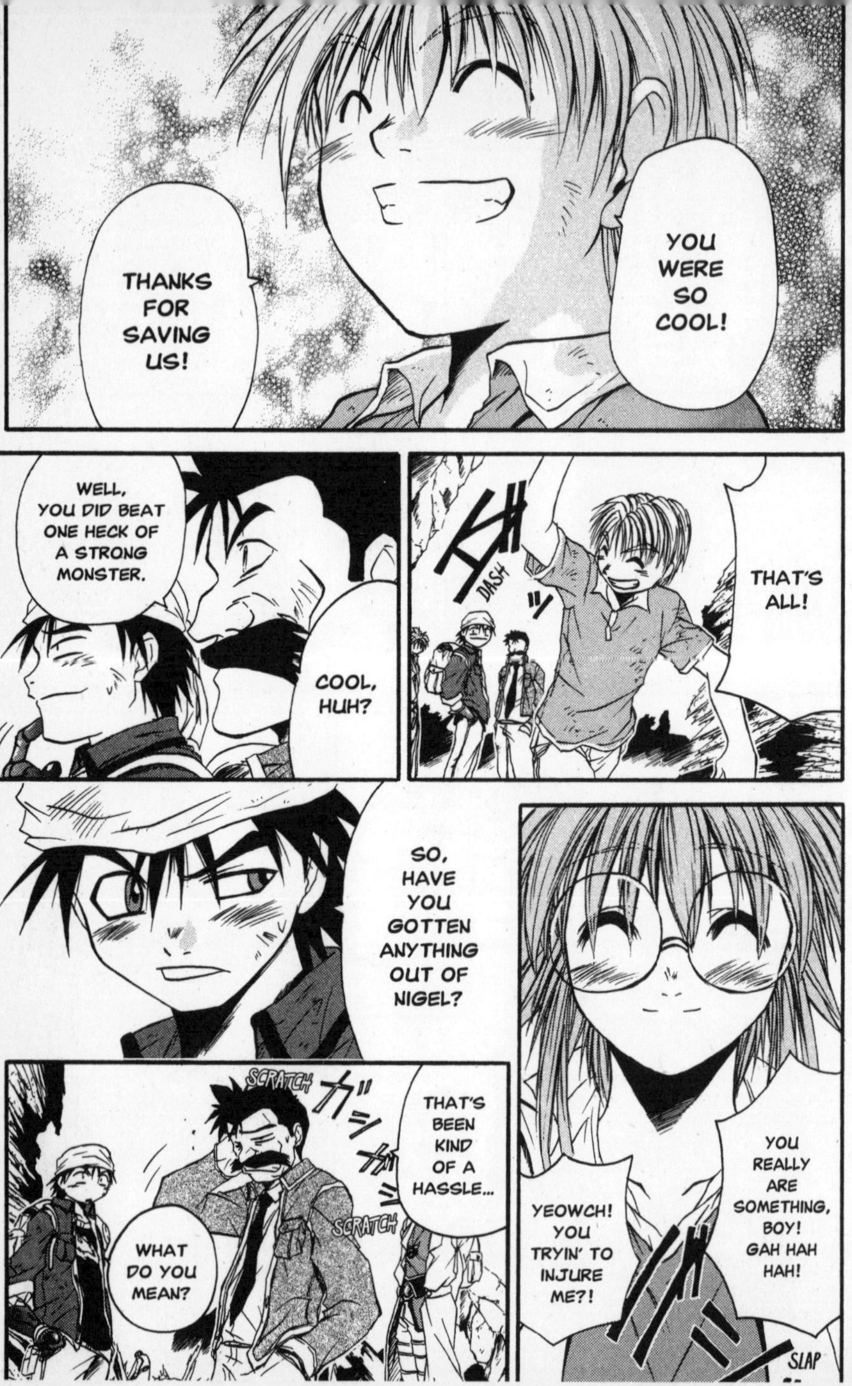
YOU WERE SO COOL!
THANKS FOR SAVING US!
DASH
THAT'S ALL!
WELL, YOU DID BEAT ONE HECK OF A STRONG MONSTER.
COOL, HUH?
YOU REALLY ARE SOMETHING, BOY! GAH HAH HAH!
SLAP
YEOWCH! YOU TRYIN' TO INJURE ME?!
SO, HAVE YOU GOTTEN ANYTHING OUT OF NIGEL?
SCRATCH
SCRATCH
THAT'S BEEN KIND OF A HASSLE...
WHAT DO YOU MEAN?

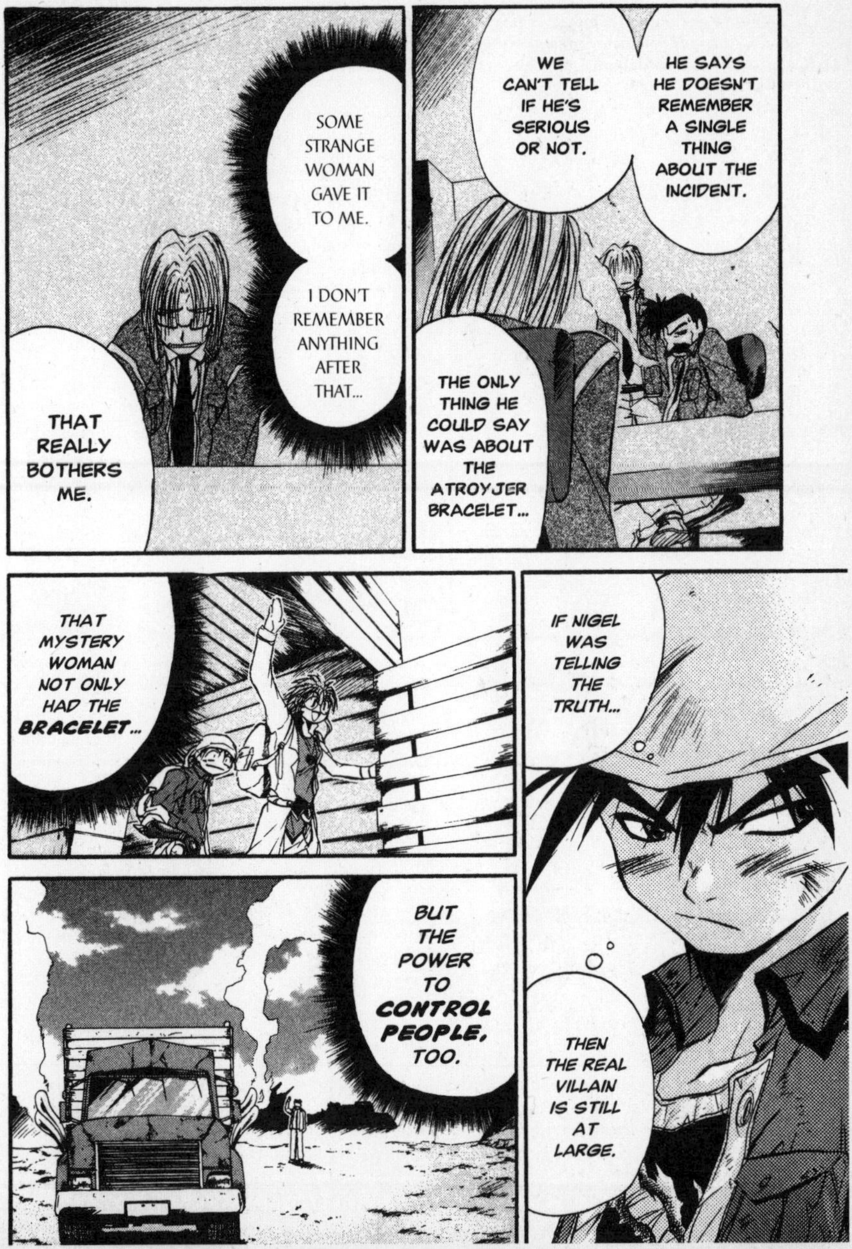
HE SAYS HE DOESN'T REMEMBER A SINGLE THING ABOUT THE INCIDENT.
WE CAN'T TELL IF HE'S SERIOUS OR NOT.
THE ONLY THING HE COULD SAY WAS ABOUT THE ATROYJER BRACELET...
SOME STRANGE WOMAN GAVE IT TO ME.
I DON'T REMEMBER ANYTHING AFTER THAT...
THAT REALLY BOTHERS ME.
IF NIGEL WAS TELLING THE TRUTH...
THAT MYSTERY WOMAN NOT ONLY HAD THE BRACELET...
BUT THE POWER TO CONTROL PEOPLE, TOO.
THEN THE REAL VILLAIN IS STILL AT LARGE.

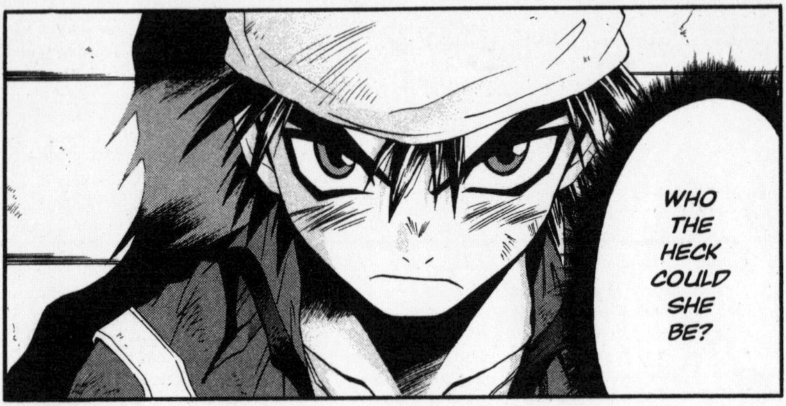
WHO THE HECK COULD SHE BE?

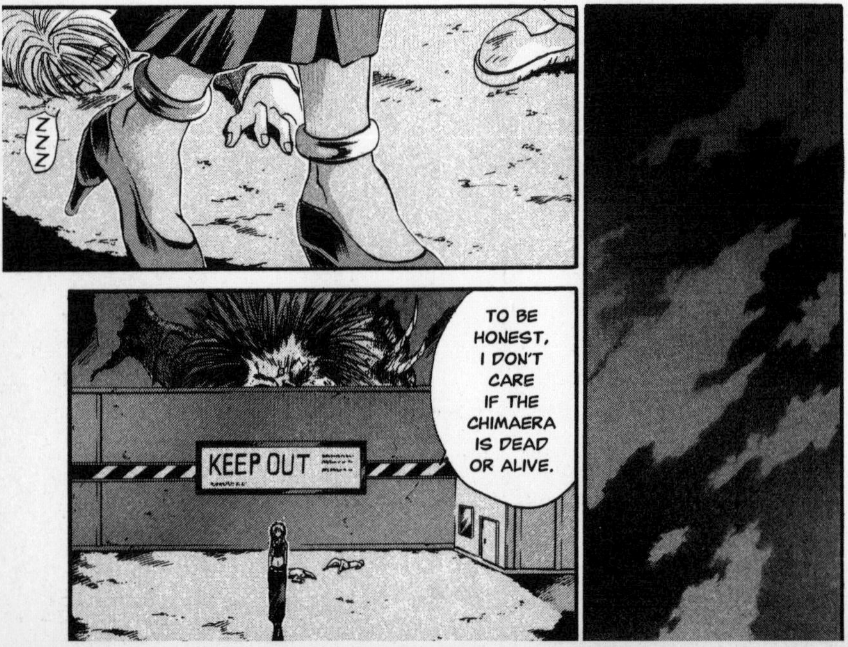
ZZZ
TO BE HONEST, I DON'T CARE IF THE CHIMAERA IS DEAD OR ALIVE.
KEEP OUT

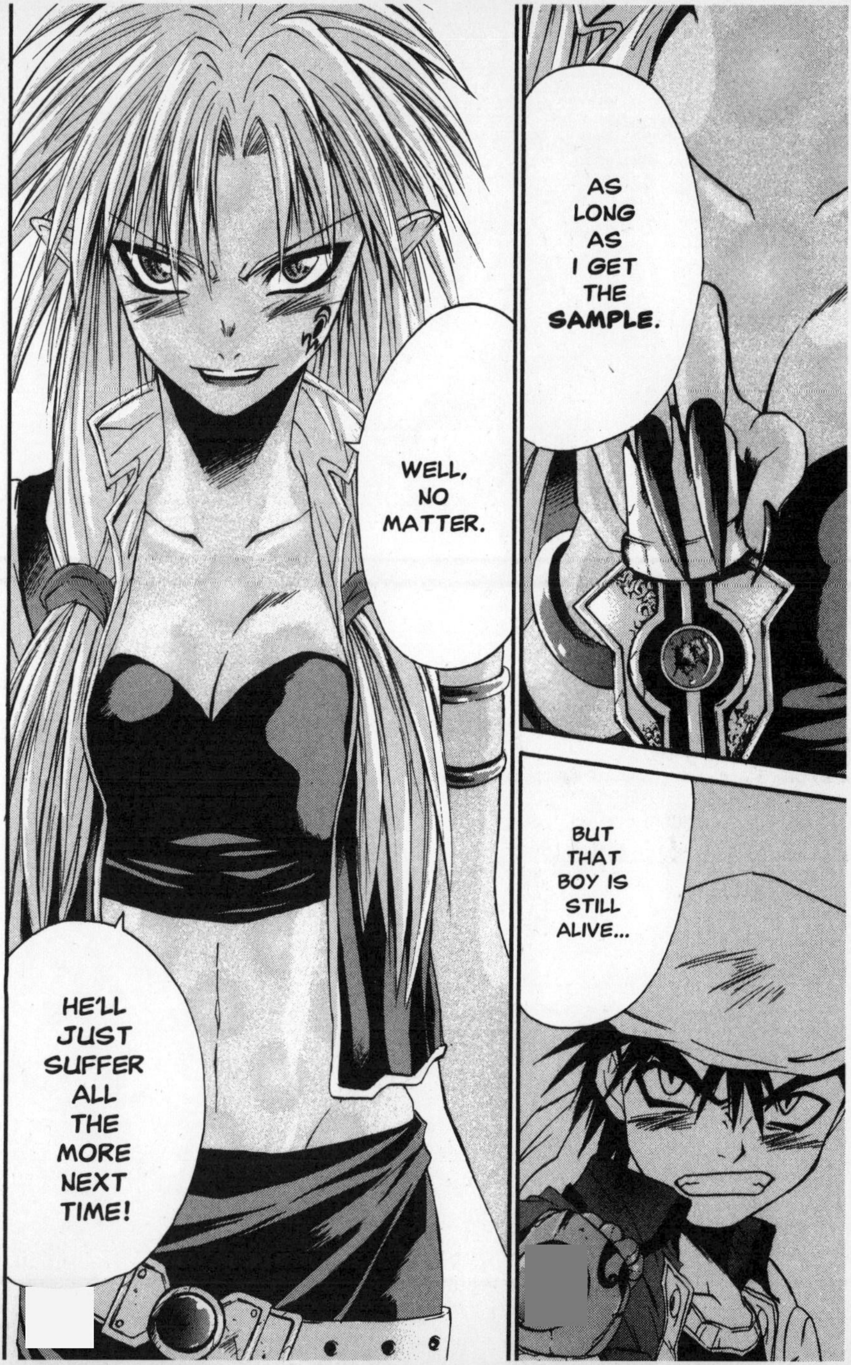
WELL, NO MATTER.
AS LONG AS I GET THE SAMPLE.
BUT THAT BOY IS STILL ALIVE...
HE'LL JUST SUFFER ALL THE MORE NEXT TIME!

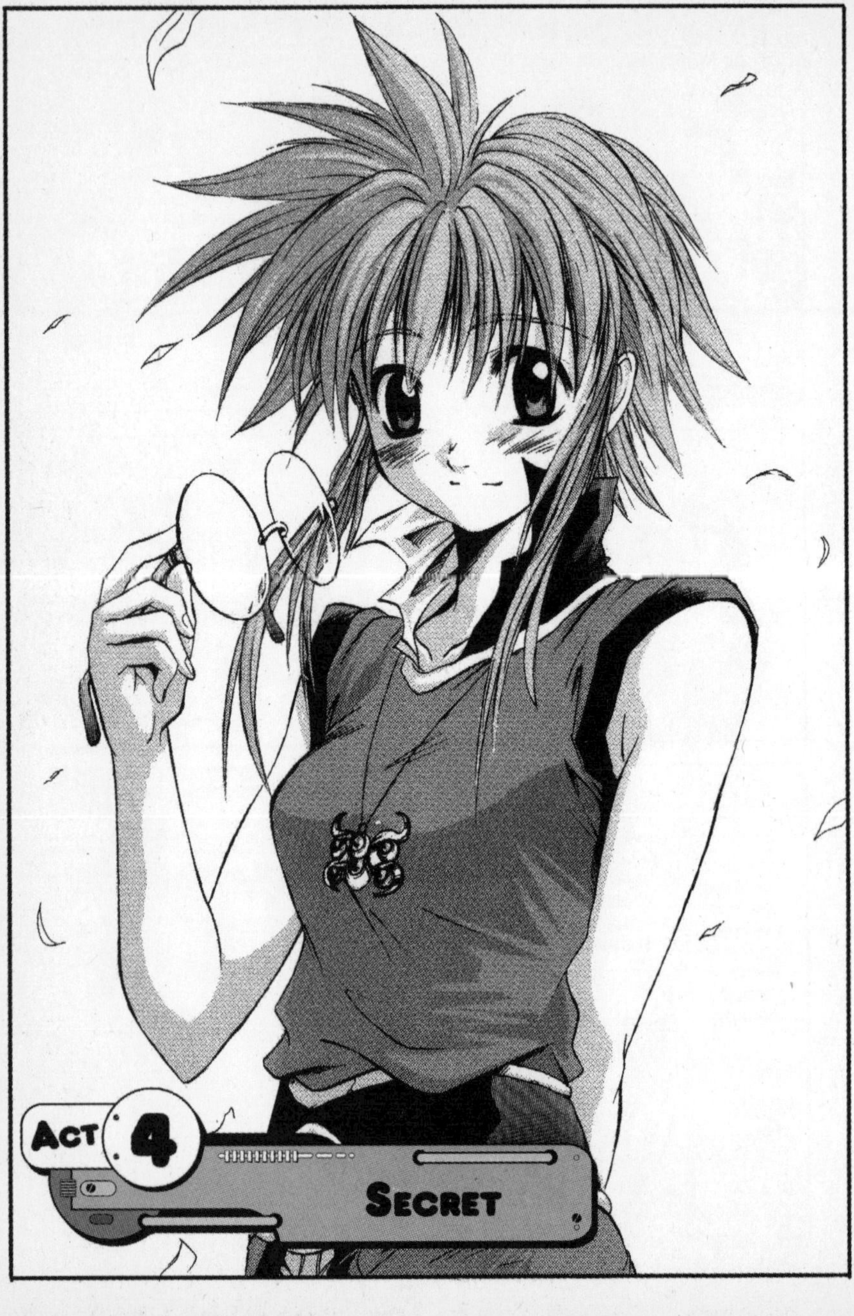
ACT 4
SECRET

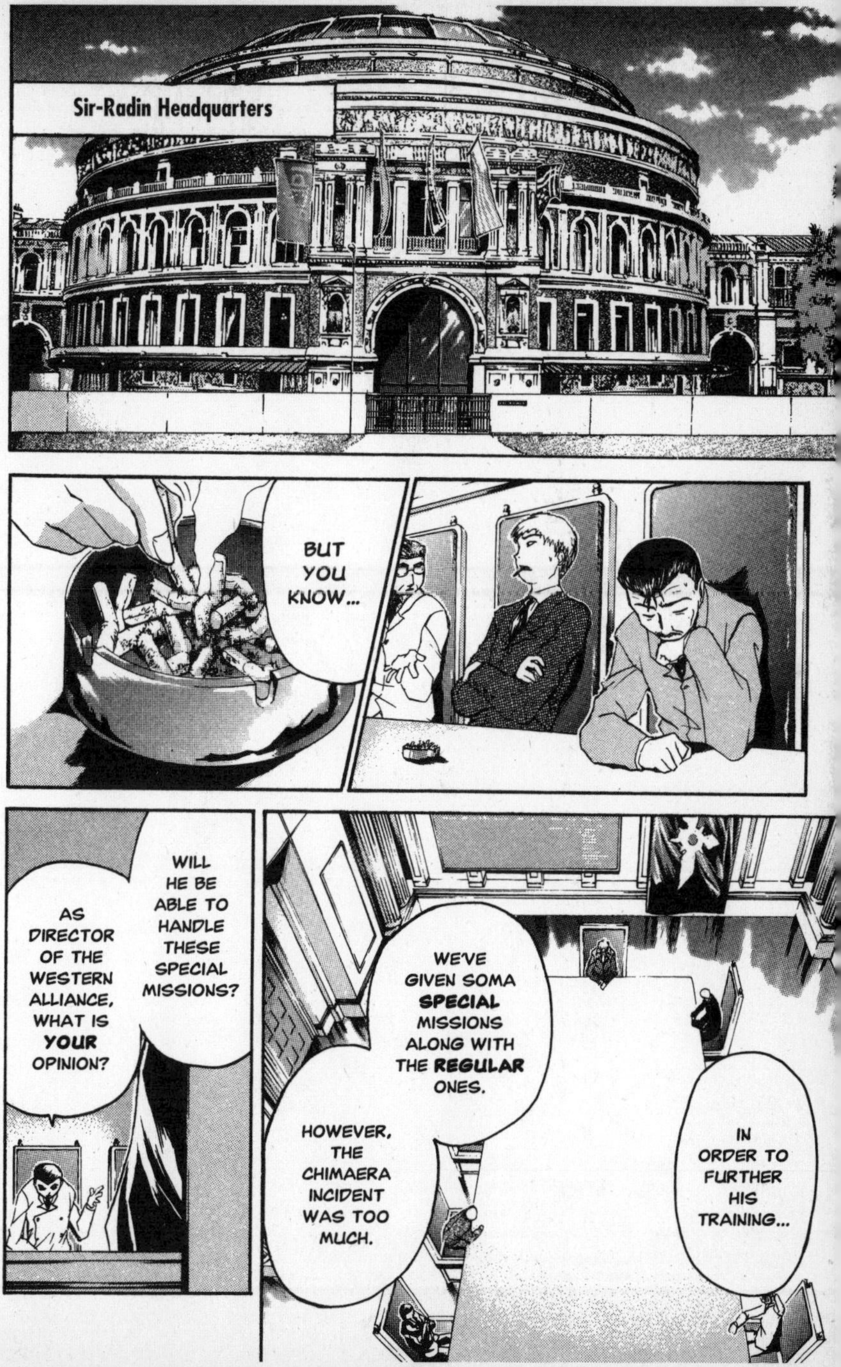
Sir-Radin Headquarters
BUT YOU KNOW...
WE'VE GIVEN SOMA SPECIAL MISSIONS ALONG WITH THE REGULAR ONES.
IN ORDER TO FURTHER HIS TRAINING...
HOWEVER, THE CHIMAERA INCIDENT WAS TOO MUCH.
WILL HE BE ABLE TO HANDLE THESE SPECIAL MISSIONS?
AS DIRECTOR OF THE WESTERN ALLIANCE, WHAT IS YOUR OPINION?

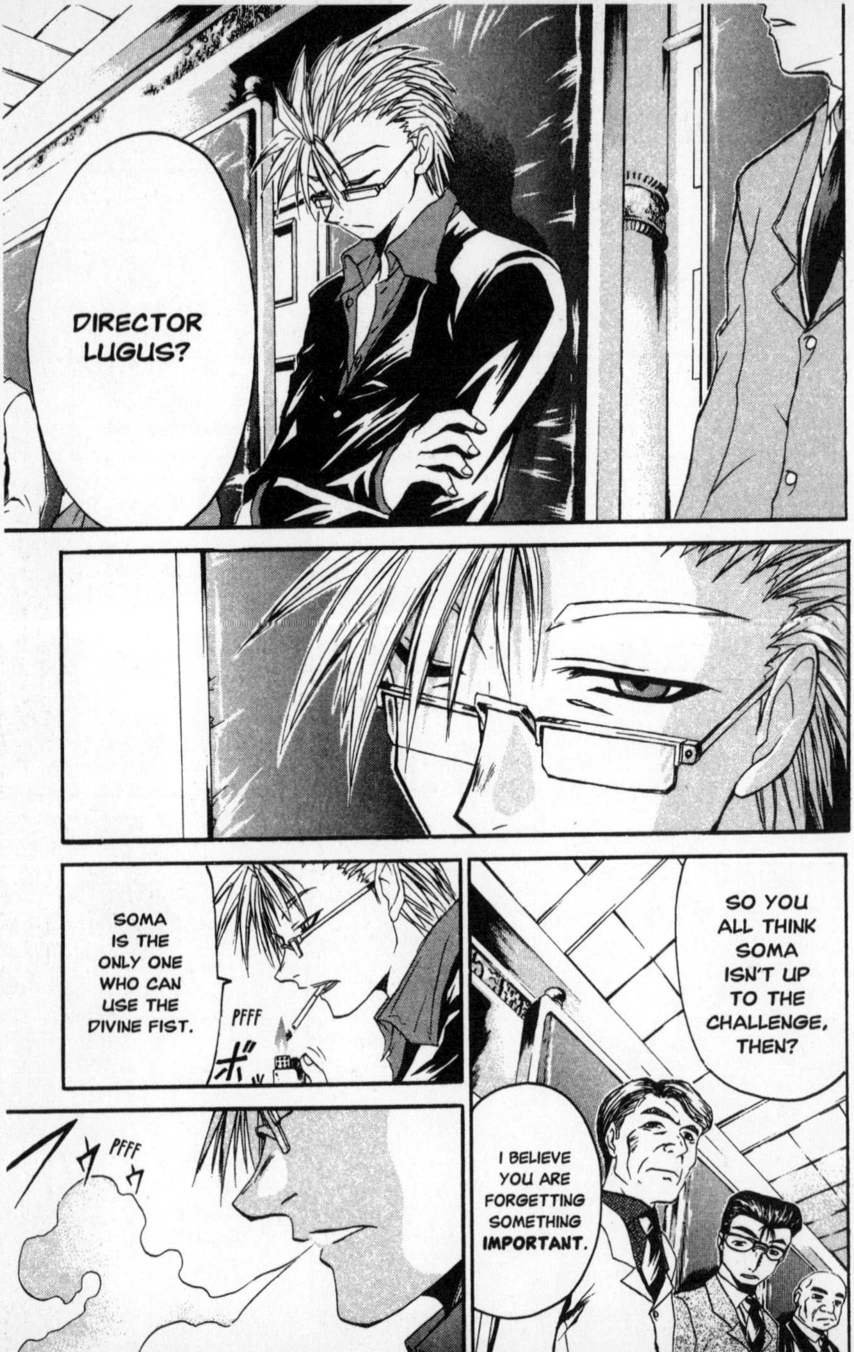
DIRECTOR LUGUS?
SO YOU ALL THINK SOMA ISN'T UP TO THE CHALLENGE, THEN?
SOMA IS THE ONLY ONE WHO CAN USE THE DIVINE FIST.
PFFF
ボッ
I BELIEVE YOU ARE FORGETTING SOMETHING IMPORTANT.
PFFF

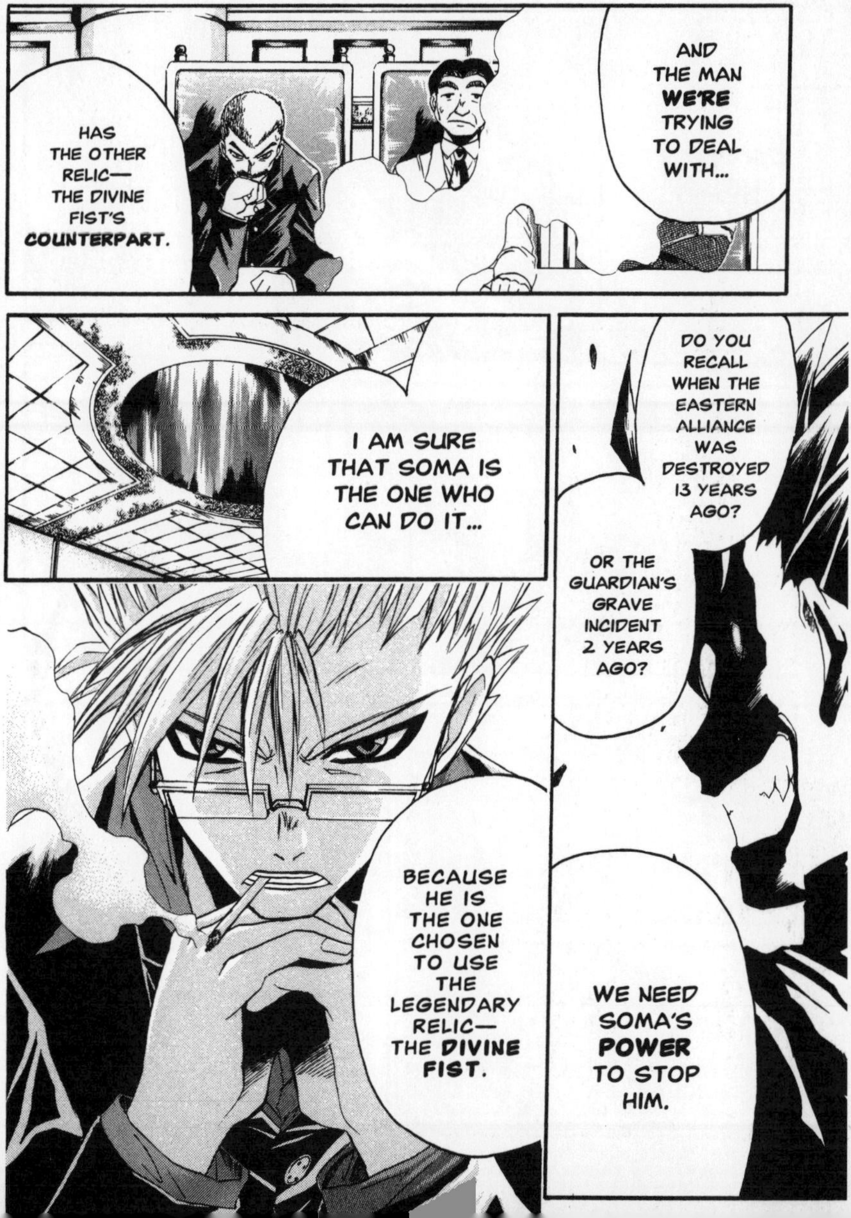
AND THE MAN WE'RE TRYING TO DEAL WITH...
HAS THE OTHER RELIC—THE DIVINE FIST'S COUNTERPART.
DO YOU RECALL WHEN THE EASTERN ALLIANCE WAS DESTROYED 13 YEARS AGO?
OR THE GUARDIAN'S GRAVE INCIDENT 2 YEARS AGO?
WE NEED SOMA'S POWER TO STOP HIM.
I AM SURE THAT SOMA IS THE ONE WHO CAN DO IT...
BECAUSE HE IS THE ONE CHOSEN TO USE THE LEGENDARY RELIC—THE DIVINE FIST.

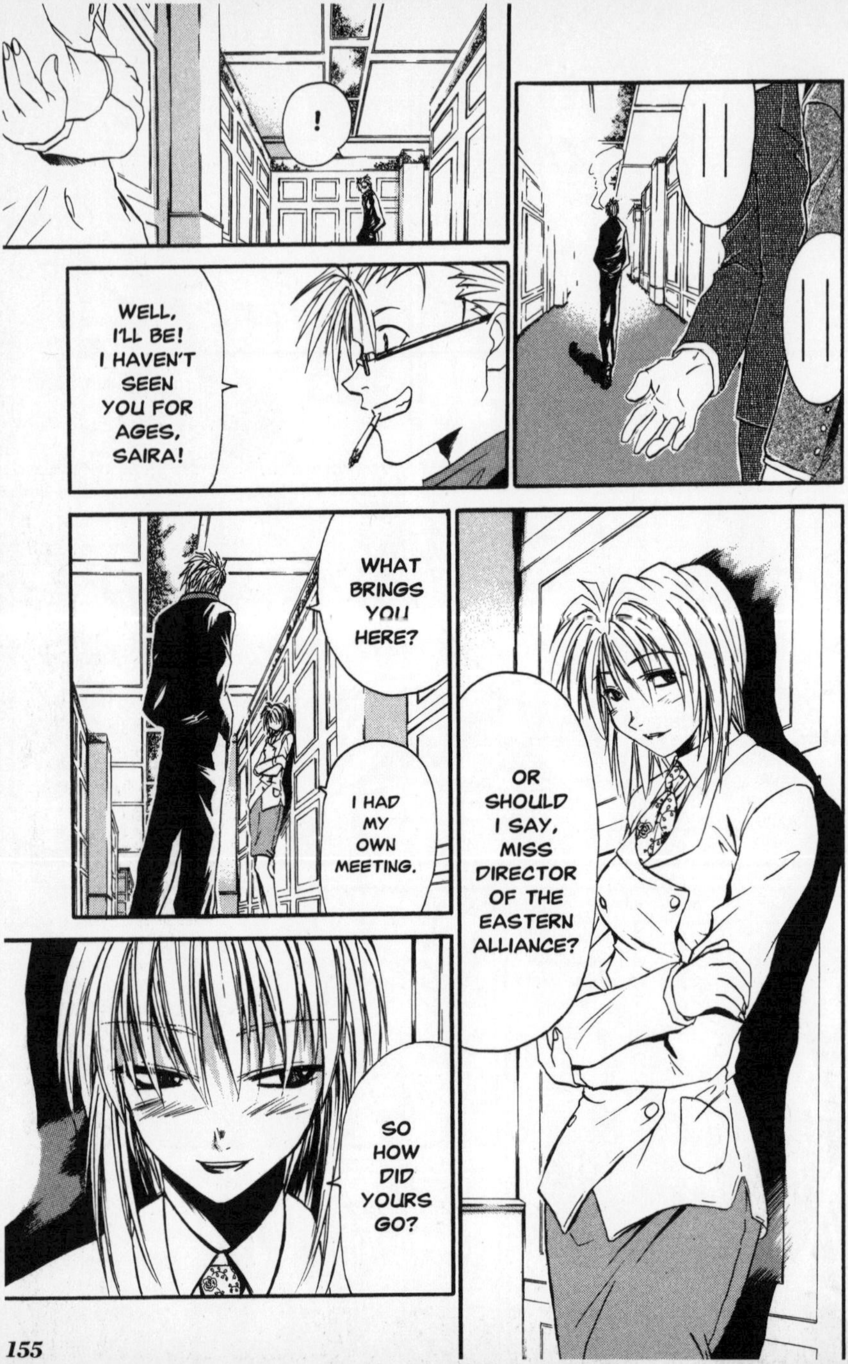
!
WELL, I'LL BE! I HAVEN'T SEEN YOU FOR AGES, SAIRA!
WHAT BRINGS YOU HERE?
I HAD MY OWN MEETING.
OR SHOULD I SAY, MISS DIRECTOR OF THE EASTERN ALLIANCE?
SO HOW DID YOURS GO?

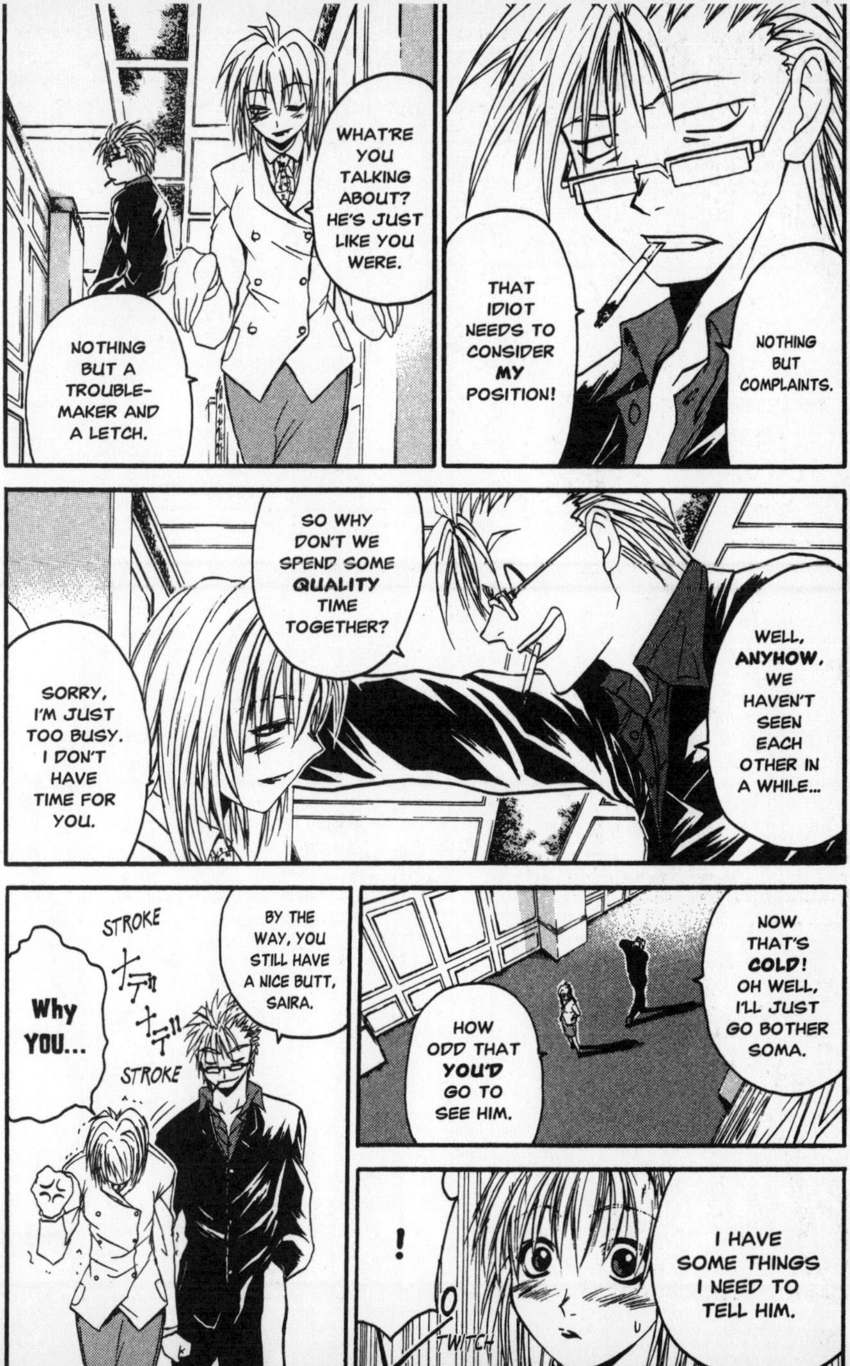
NOTHING BUT COMPLAINTS.
THAT IDIOT NEEDS TO CONSIDER MY POSITION!
WHAT'RE YOU TALKING ABOUT? HE'S JUST LIKE YOU WERE.
NOTHING BUT A TROUBLE-MAKER AND A LETCH.
WELL, ANYHOW, WE HAVEN'T SEEN EACH OTHER IN A WHILE...
SO WHY DON'T WE SPEND SOME QUALITY TIME TOGETHER?
SORRY, I'M JUST TOO BUSY. I DON'T HAVE TIME FOR YOU.
NOW THAT'S COLD! OH WELL, I'LL JUST GO BOTHER SOMA.
HOW ODD THAT YOU'D GO TO SEE HIM.
I HAVE SOME THINGS I NEED TO TELL HIM.
!
TWITCH
BY THE WAY, YOU STILL HAVE A NICE BUTT, SAIRA.
STROKE
STROKE
Why YOU...

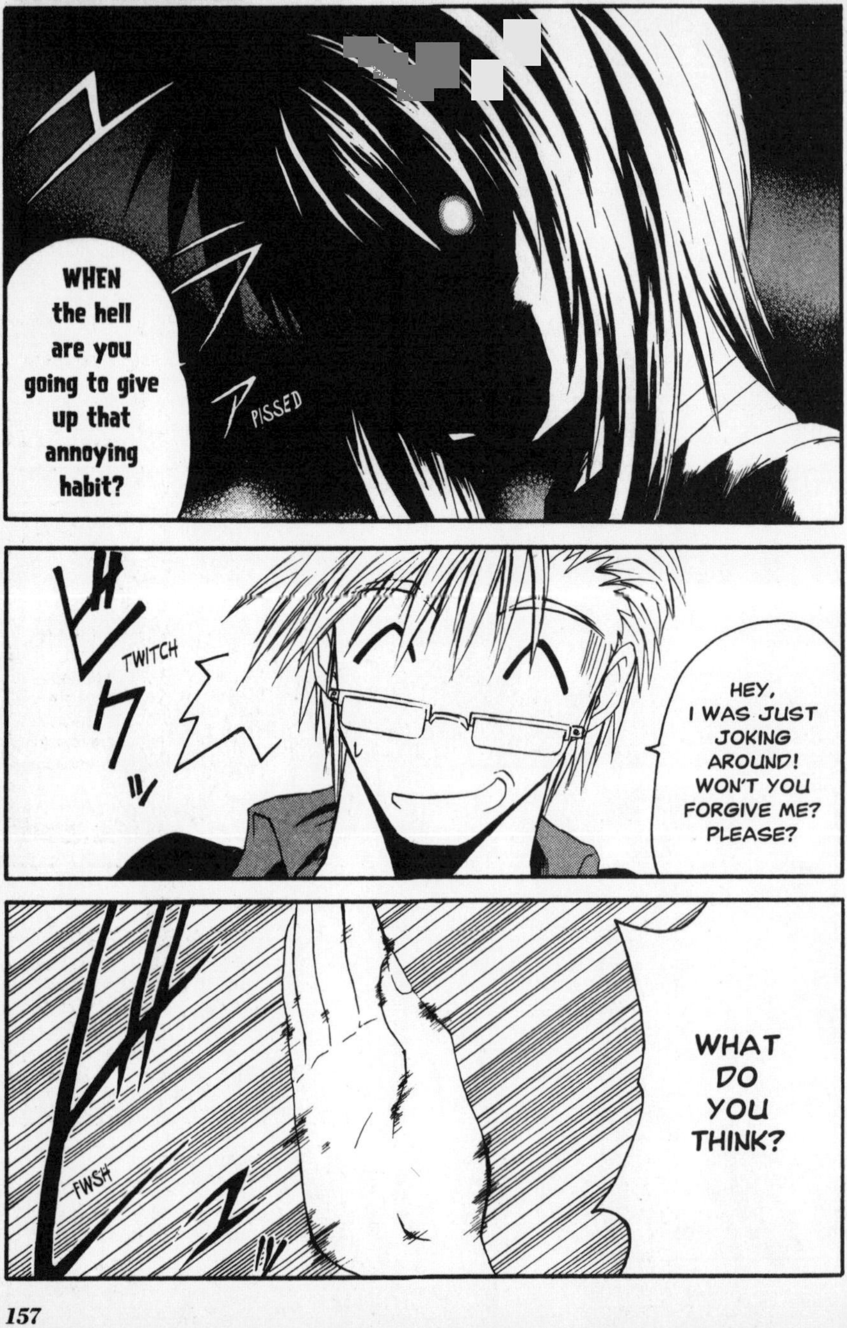
WHEN the hell are you going to give up that annoying habit?
PISSED
HEY, I WAS JUST JOKING AROUND! WON'T YOU FORGIVE ME? PLEASE?
TWITCH
WHAT DO YOU THINK?
FWSH

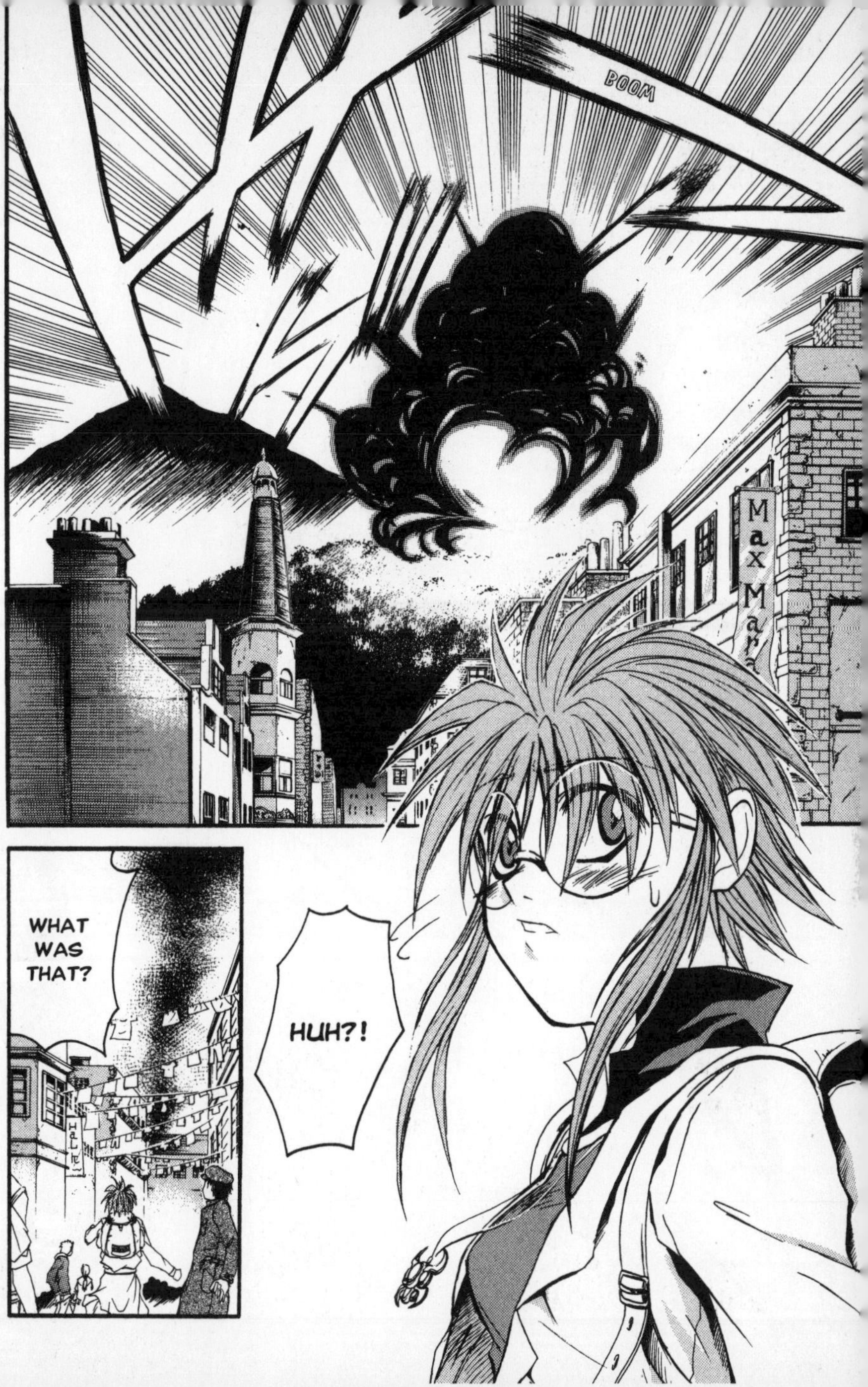
BOOM
HUH?!
WHAT WAS THAT?

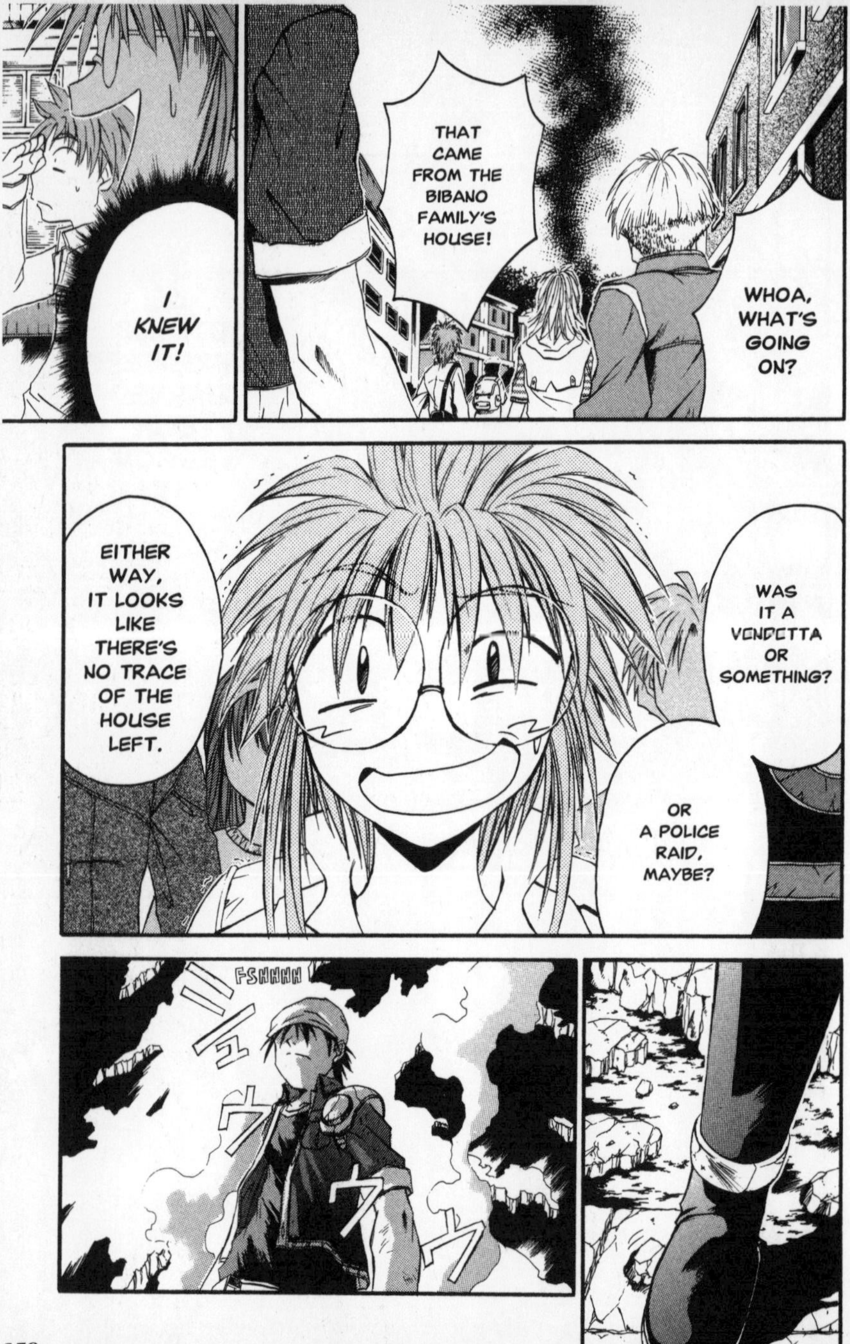
WHOA, WHAT'S GOING ON?
THAT CAME FROM THE BIBANO FAMILY'S HOUSE!
I KNEW IT!
WAS IT A VENDETTA OR SOMETHING?
OR A POLICE RAID, MAYBE?
EITHER WAY, IT LOOKS LIKE THERE'S NO TRACE OF THE HOUSE LEFT.
FSHHHH

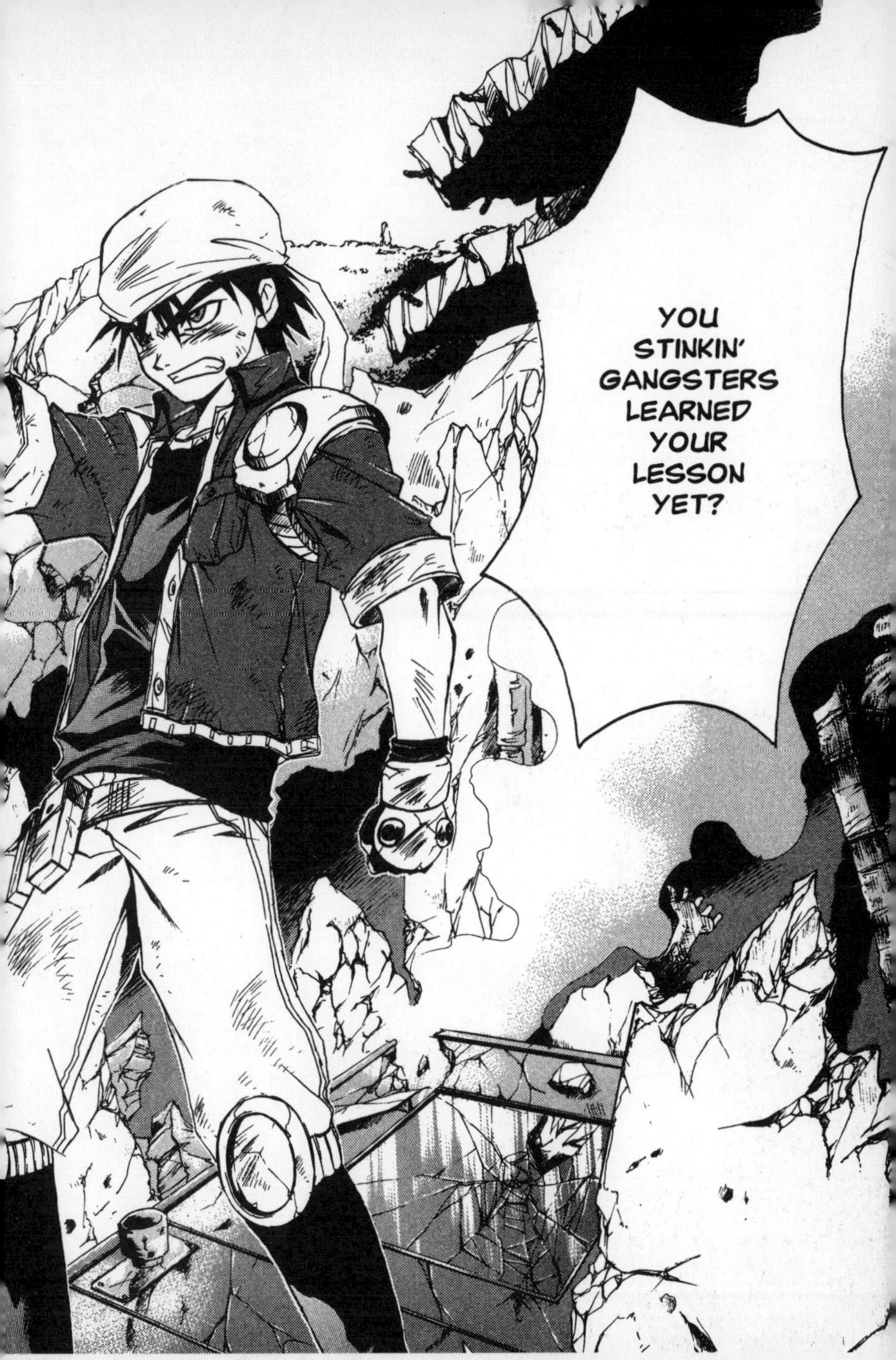
YOU STINKIN' GANGSTERS LEARNED YOUR LESSON YET?

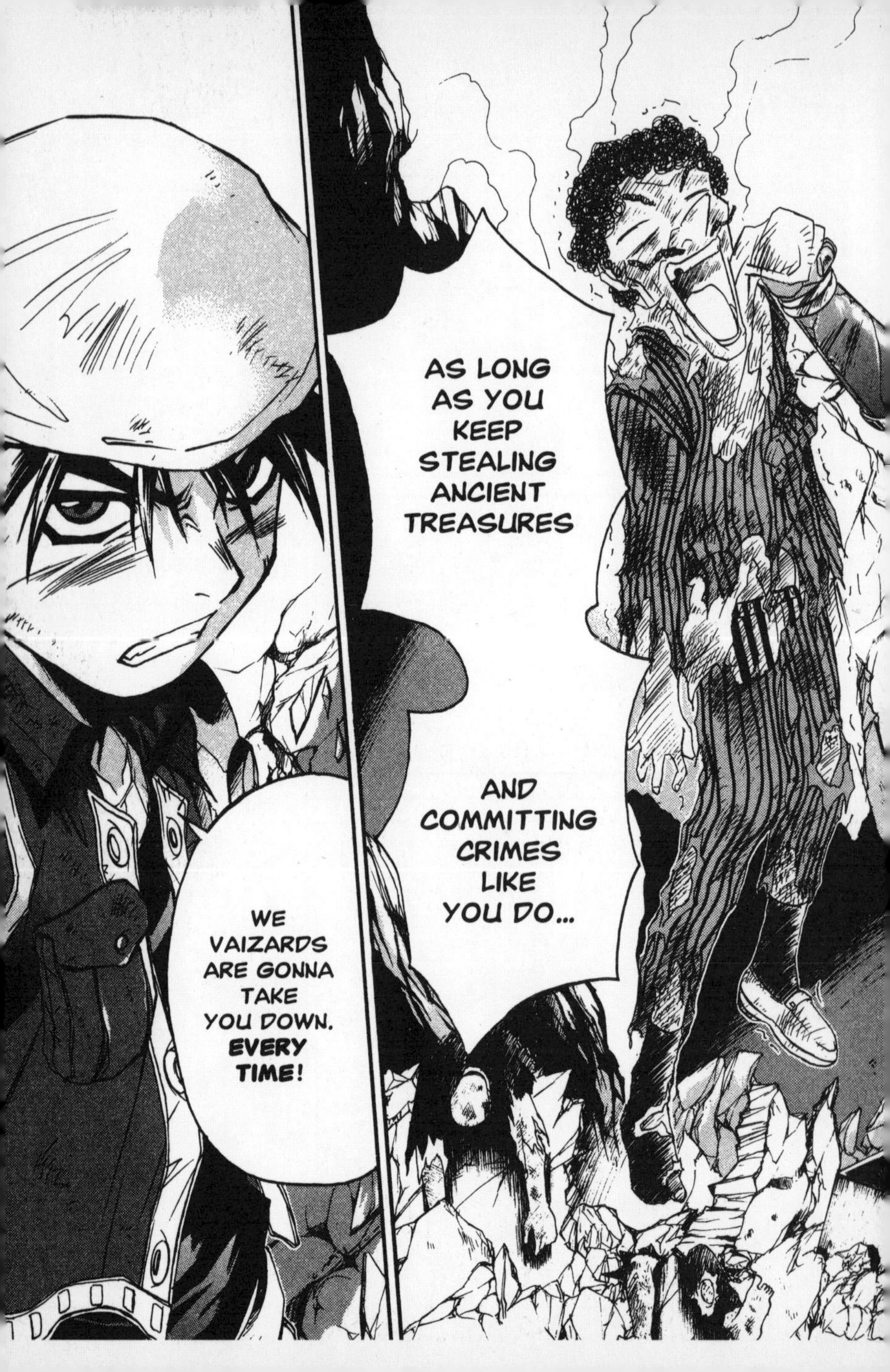
AS LONG AS YOU KEEP STEALING ANCIENT TREASURES
AND COMMITTING CRIMES LIKE YOU DO...
WE VAIZARDS ARE GONNA TAKE YOU DOWN. EVERY TIME!

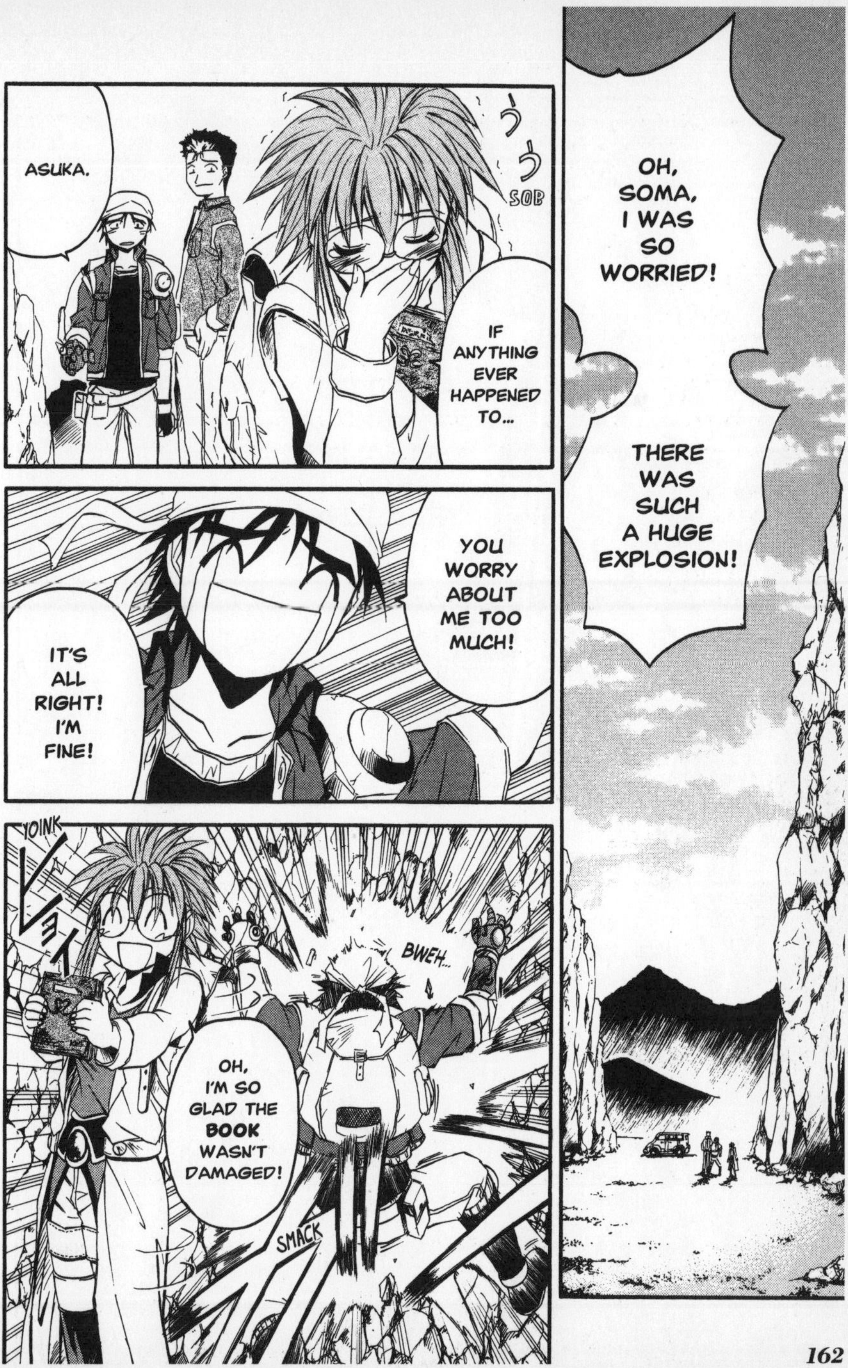
OH, SOMA, I WAS SO WORRIED!
THERE WAS SUCH A HUGE EXPLOSION!
SOB
IF ANYTHING EVER HAPPENED TO...
ASUKA.
YOU WORRY ABOUT ME TOO MUCH!
IT'S ALL RIGHT! I'M FINE!
YOINK
BWEH...
OH, I'M SO GLAD THE **BOOK** WASN'T DAMAGED!
SMACK

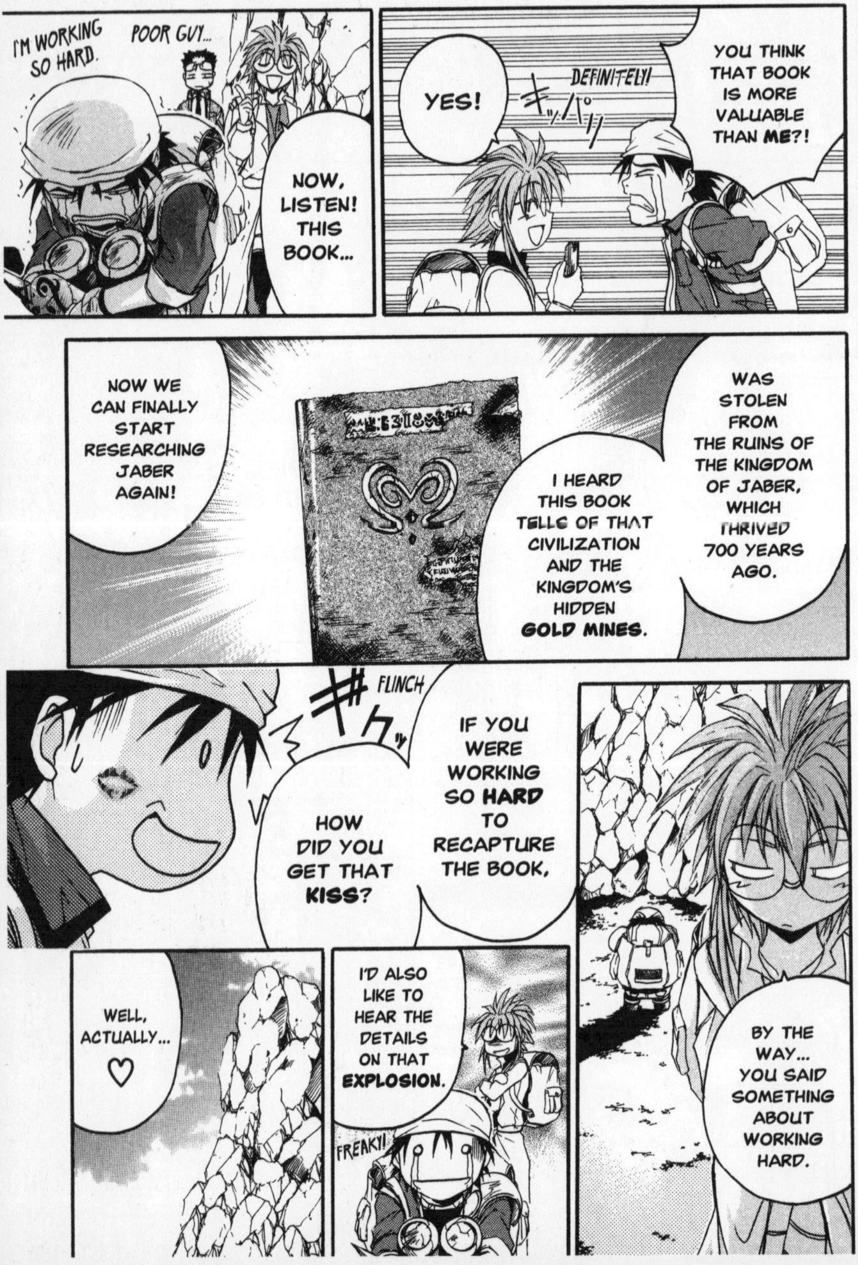
YOU THINK THAT BOOK IS MORE VALUABLE THAN **ME**?!
DEFINITELY!
キッパリ
YES!
NOW, LISTEN! THIS BOOK...
I'M WORKING SO HARD.
POOR GUY...
WAS STOLEN FROM THE RUINS OF THE KINGDOM OF JABER, WHICH THRIVED 700 YEARS AGO.
I HEARD THIS BOOK TELLS OF THAT CIVILIZATION AND THE KINGDOM'S HIDDEN **GOLD MINES**.
NOW WE CAN FINALLY START RESEARCHING JABER AGAIN!
BY THE WAY... YOU SAID SOMETHING ABOUT WORKING HARD.
FLINCH
ギクッ
IF YOU WERE WORKING SO **HARD** TO RECAPTURE THE BOOK,
HOW DID YOU GET THAT **KISS**?
I'D ALSO LIKE TO HEAR THE DETAILS ON THAT **EXPLOSION**.
FREAKY!
WELL, ACTUALLY... ♡

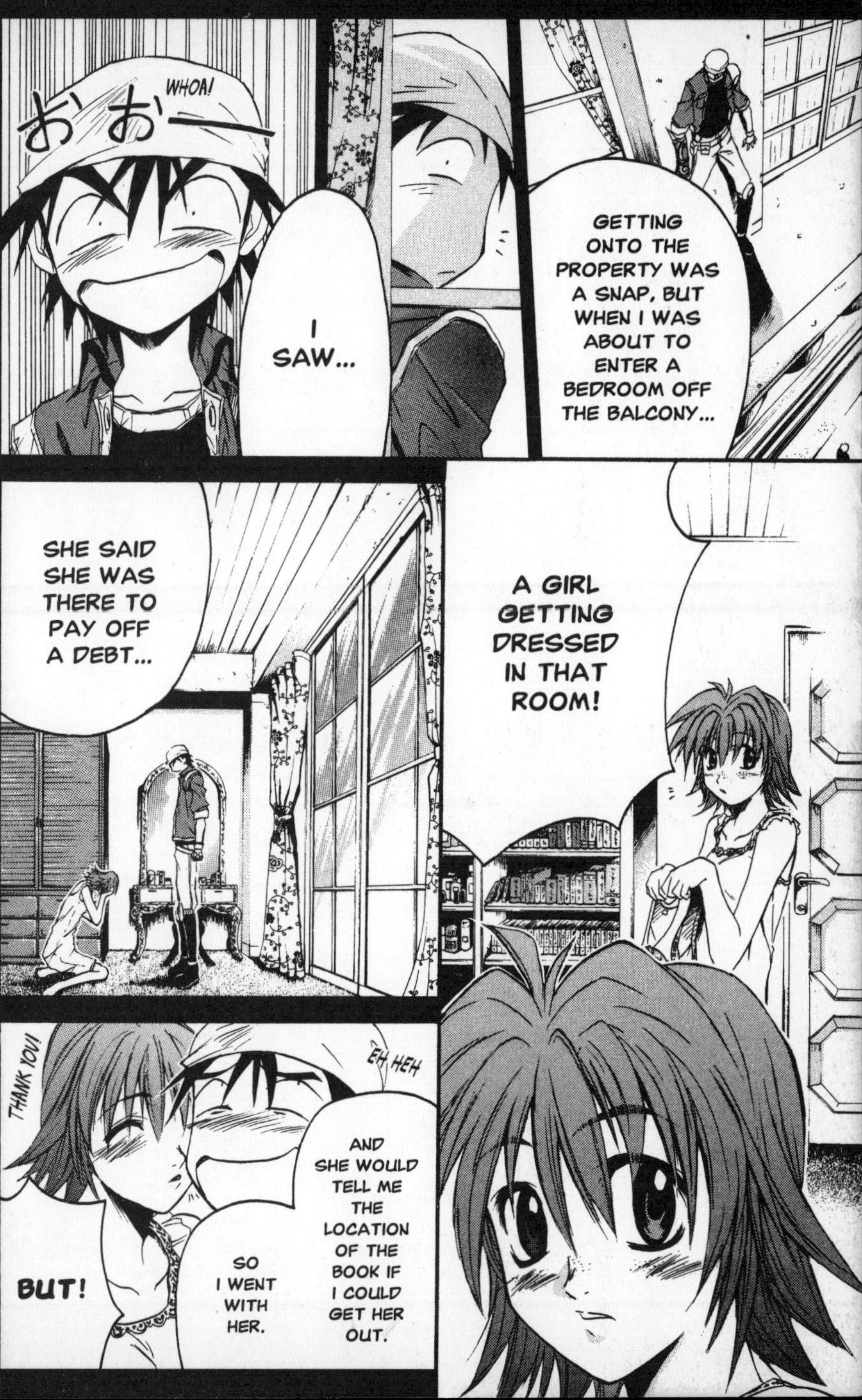
GETTING ONTO THE PROPERTY WAS A SNAP, BUT WHEN I WAS ABOUT TO ENTER A BEDROOM OFF THE BALCONY...
I SAW...
おおーー
WHOA!
A GIRL GETTING DRESSED IN THAT ROOM!
SHE SAID SHE WAS THERE TO PAY OFF A DEBT...
AND SHE WOULD TELL ME THE LOCATION OF THE BOOK IF I COULD GET HER OUT.
EH HEH
SO I WENT WITH HER.
THANK YOU!
BUT!

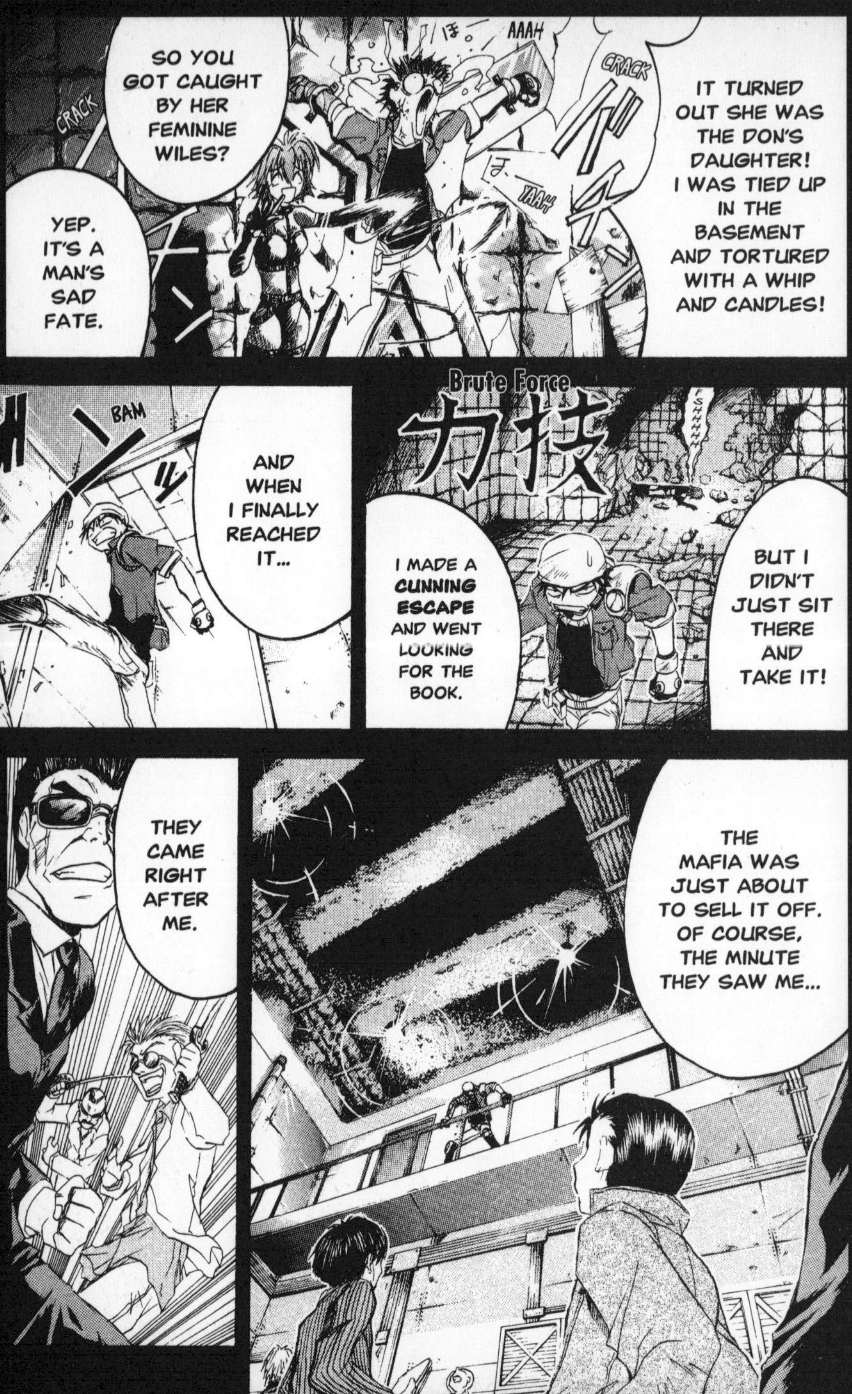
AAAH
CRACK
IT TURNED OUT SHE WAS THE DON'S DAUGHTER! I WAS TIED UP IN THE BASEMENT AND TORTURED WITH A WHIP AND CANDLES!
YAAH
SO YOU GOT CAUGHT BY HER FEMININE WILES?
CRACK
YEP. IT'S A MAN'S SAD FATE.
Brute Force
力技
FSHHHHHH
BUT I DIDN'T JUST SIT THERE AND TAKE IT!
I MADE A CUNNING ESCAPE AND WENT LOOKING FOR THE BOOK.
BAM
AND WHEN I FINALLY REACHED IT...
THE MAFIA WAS JUST ABOUT TO SELL IT OFF. OF COURSE, THE MINUTE THEY SAW ME...
THEY CAME RIGHT AFTER ME.

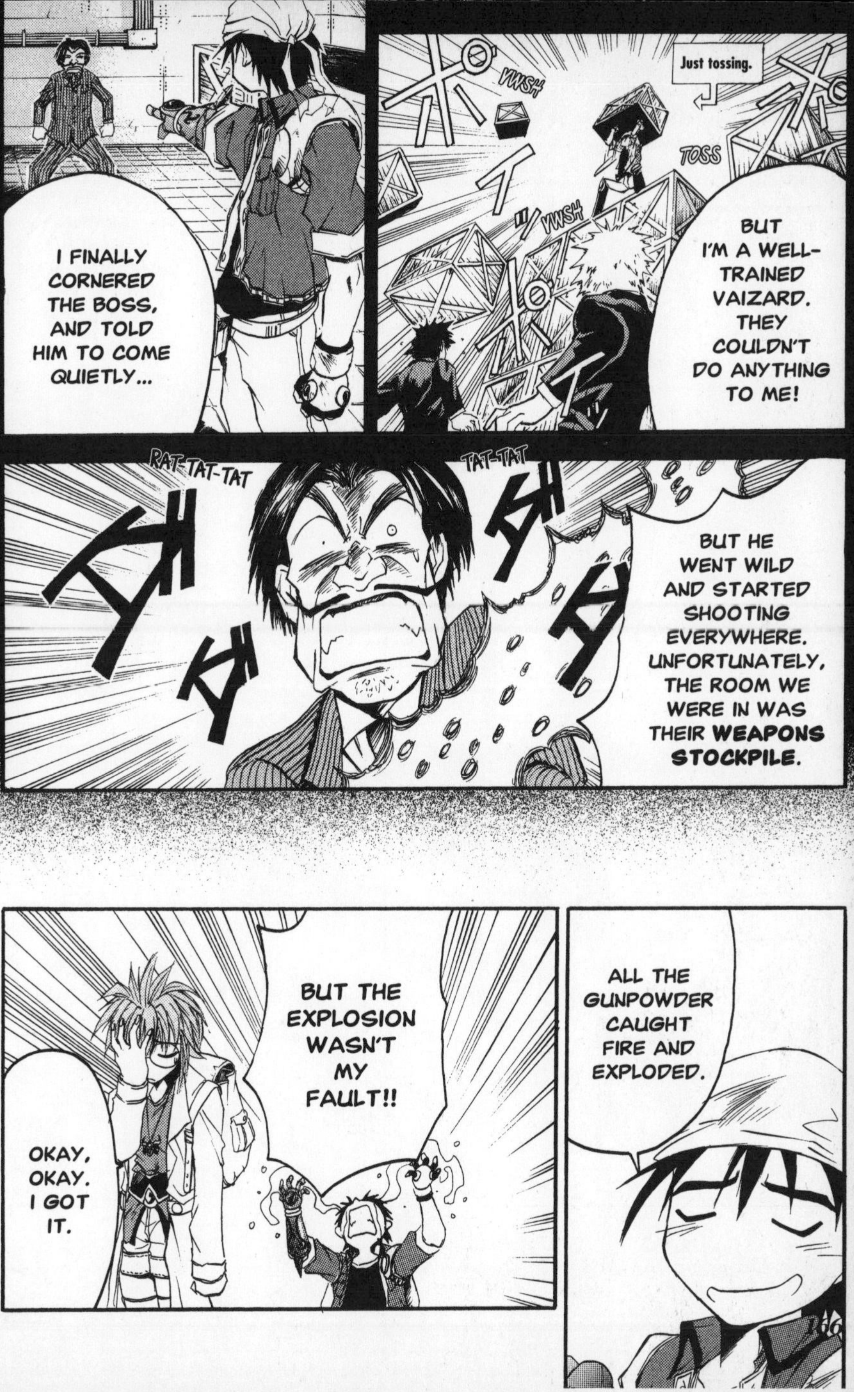

I FINALLY CORNERED THE BOSS, AND TOLD HIM TO COME QUIETLY...
YWSH
Just tossing.
TOSS
YWSH
BUT I'M A WELL-TRAINED VAIZARD. THEY COULDN'T DO ANYTHING TO ME!
RAT-TAT-TAT
TAT-TAT
BUT HE WENT WILD AND STARTED SHOOTING EVERYWHERE. UNFORTUNATELY, THE ROOM WE WERE IN WAS THEIR WEAPONS STOCKPILE.
ALL THE GUNPOWDER CAUGHT FIRE AND EXPLODED.
BUT THE EXPLOSION WASN'T MY FAULT!!
OKAY, OKAY. I GOT IT.

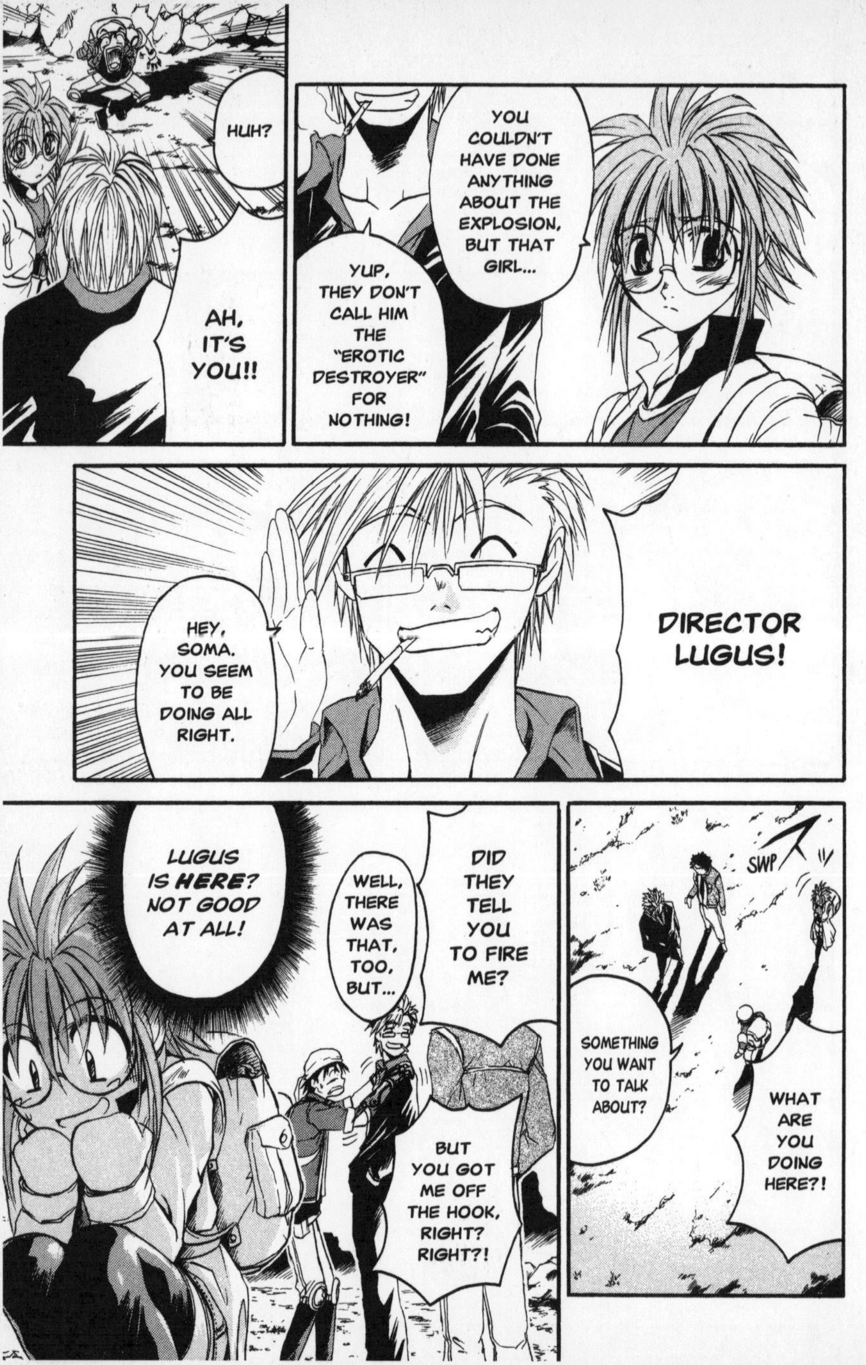
YOU COULDN'T HAVE DONE ANYTHING ABOUT THE EXPLOSION, BUT THAT GIRL...
YUP, THEY DON'T CALL HIM THE "EROTIC DESTROYER" FOR NOTHING!
HUH?
AH, IT'S YOU!!
DIRECTOR LUGUS!
HEY, SOMA. YOU SEEM TO BE DOING ALL RIGHT.
SWP
WHAT ARE YOU DOING HERE?!
SOMETHING YOU WANT TO TALK ABOUT?
DID THEY TELL YOU TO FIRE ME?
WELL, THERE WAS THAT, TOO, BUT...
BUT YOU GOT ME OFF THE HOOK, RIGHT? RIGHT?!
LUGUS IS HERE? NOT GOOD AT ALL!

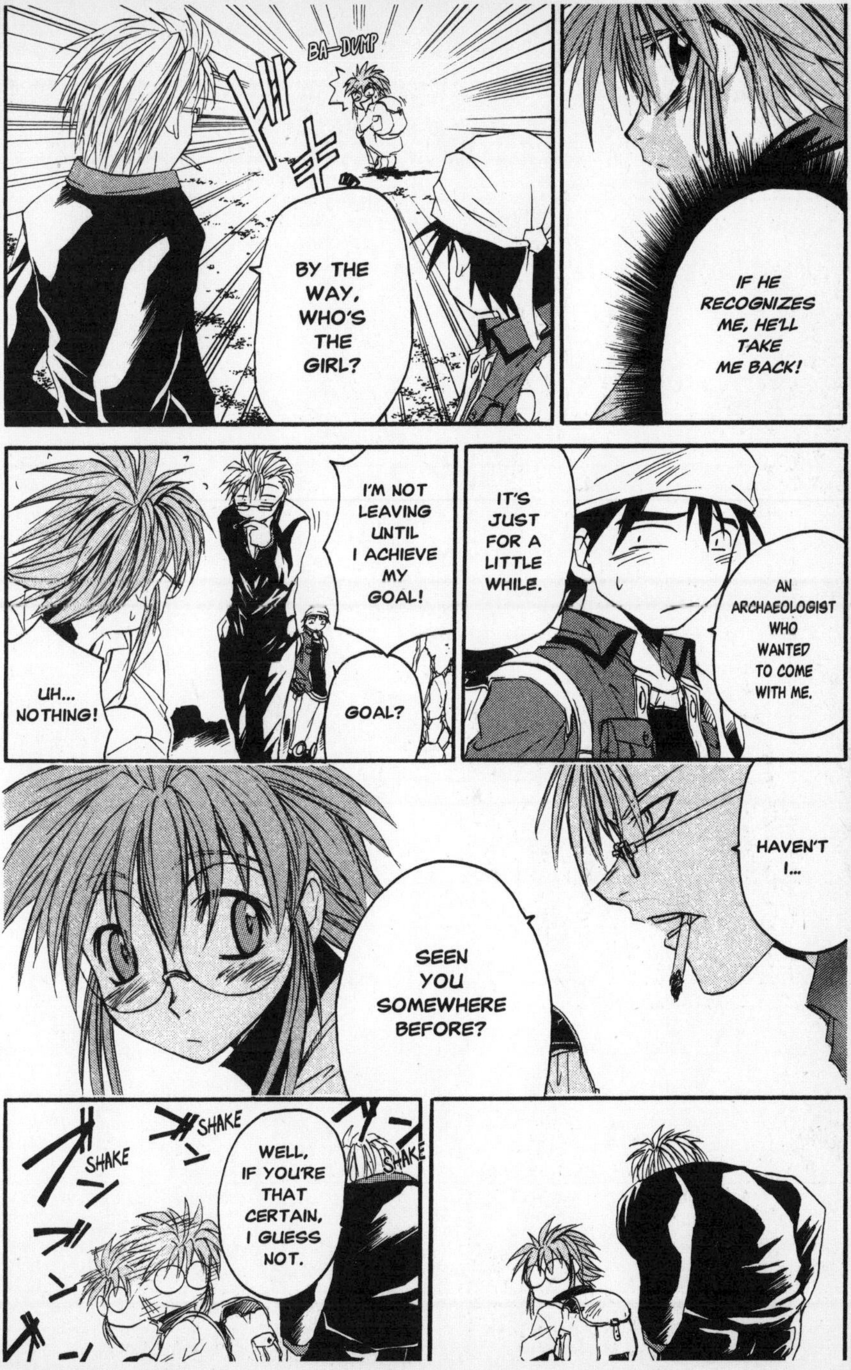

BA-DUMP
BY THE WAY, WHO'S THE GIRL?
IF HE RECOGNIZES ME, HE'LL TAKE ME BACK!
I'M NOT LEAVING UNTIL I ACHIEVE MY GOAL!
GOAL?
UH... NOTHING!
AN ARCHAEOLOGIST WHO WANTED TO COME WITH ME.
IT'S JUST FOR A LITTLE WHILE.
HAVEN'T I...
SEEN YOU SOMEWHERE BEFORE?
SHAKE
SHAKE
SHAKE
WELL, IF YOU'RE THAT CERTAIN, I GUESS NOT.

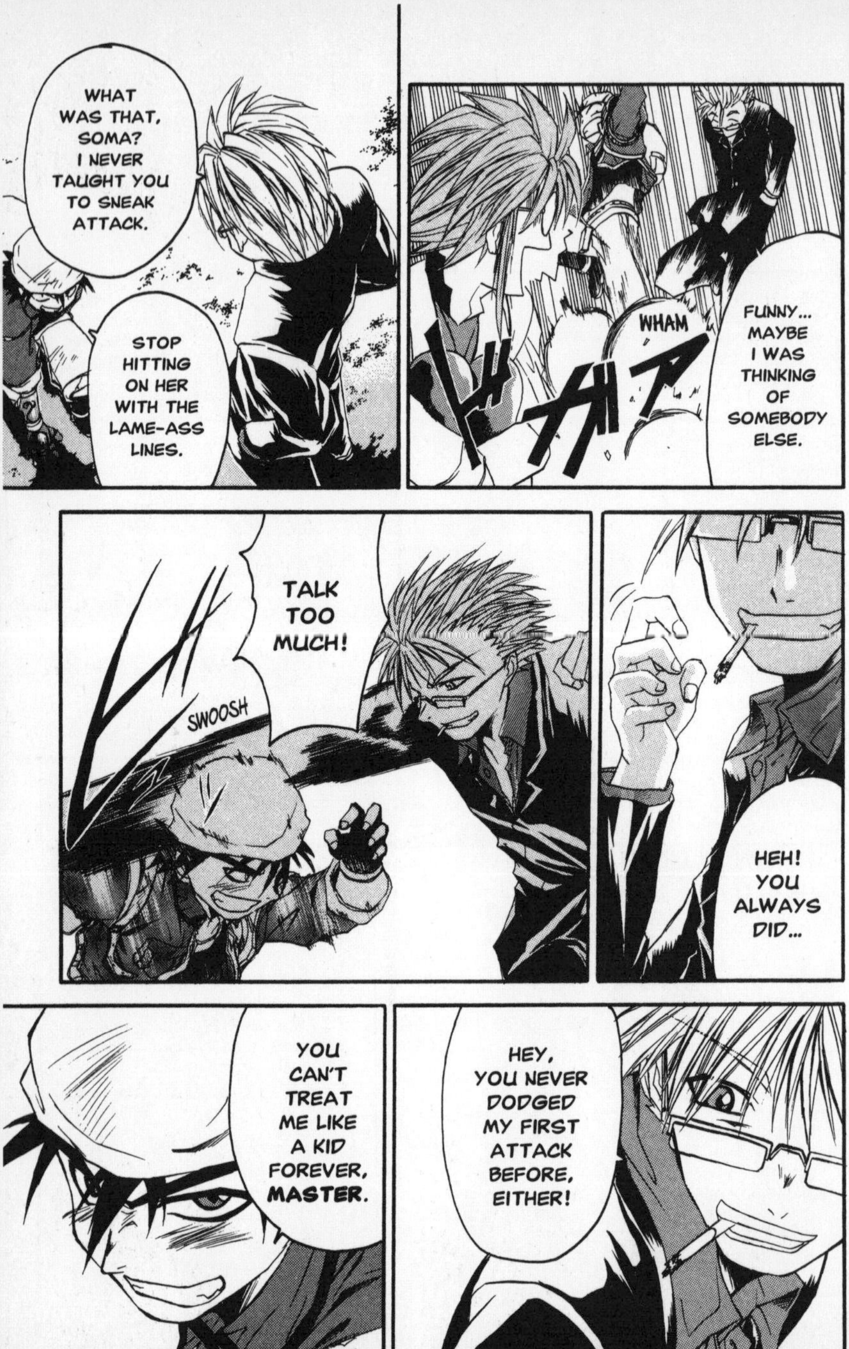
WHAT WAS THAT, SOMA? I NEVER TAUGHT YOU TO SNEAK ATTACK.
STOP HITTING ON HER WITH THE LAME-ASS LINES.
WHAM
FUNNY... MAYBE I WAS THINKING OF SOMEBODY ELSE.
TALK TOO MUCH!
SWOOSH
HEH! YOU ALWAYS DID...
YOU CAN'T TREAT ME LIKE A KID FOREVER, **MASTER**.
HEY, YOU NEVER DODGED MY FIRST ATTACK BEFORE, EITHER!

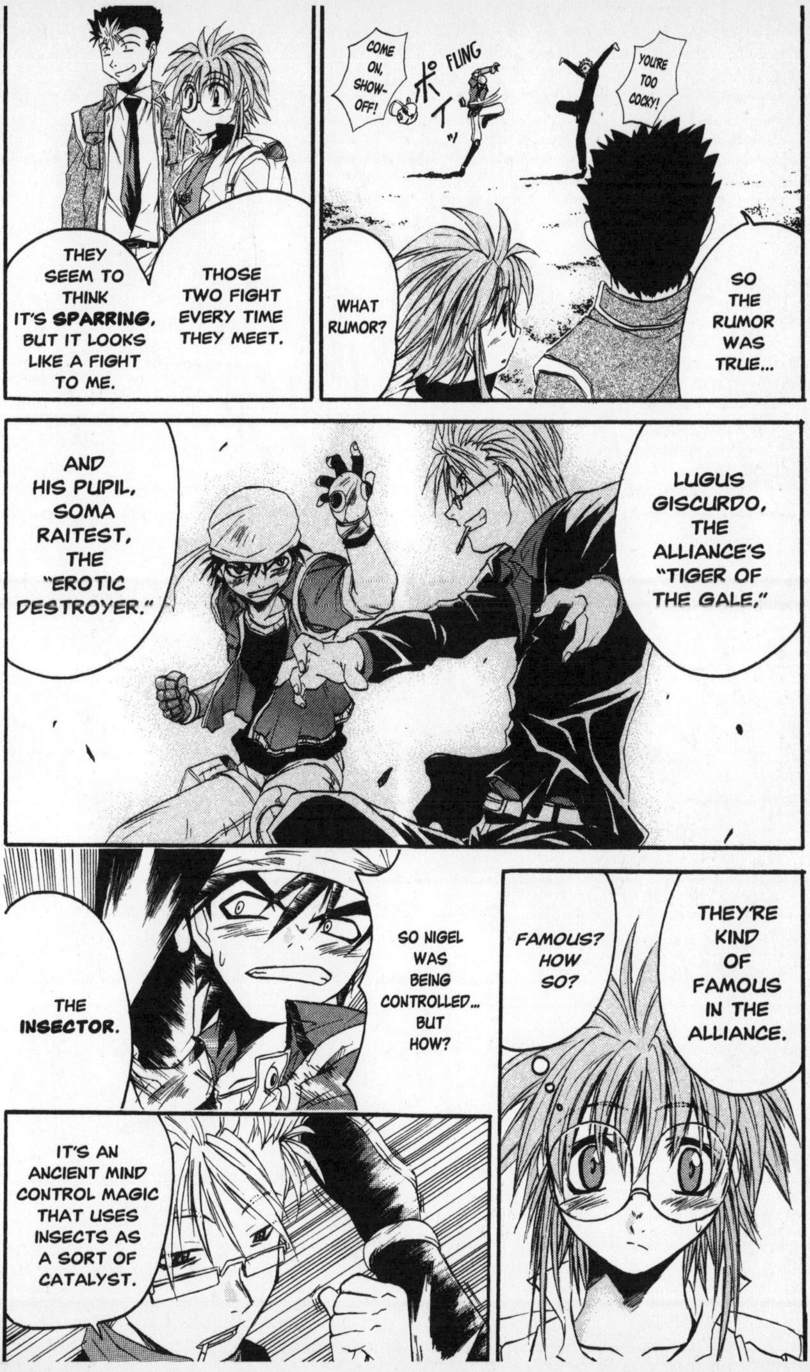

YOU'RE TOO COCKY!
COME ON, SHOW-OFF!
FLING
ポイッ
SO THE RUMOR WAS TRUE...
WHAT RUMOR?
THOSE TWO FIGHT EVERY TIME THEY MEET.
THEY SEEM TO THINK IT'S **SPARRING**, BUT IT LOOKS LIKE A FIGHT TO ME.
LUGUS GISCURDO, THE ALLIANCE'S "TIGER OF THE GALE,"
AND HIS PUPIL, SOMA RAITEST, THE "EROTIC DESTROYER."
THEY'RE KIND OF FAMOUS IN THE ALLIANCE.
FAMOUS? HOW SO?
SO NIGEL WAS BEING CONTROLLED... BUT HOW?
THE **INSECTOR**.
IT'S AN ANCIENT MIND CONTROL MAGIC THAT USES INSECTS AS A SORT OF CATALYST.

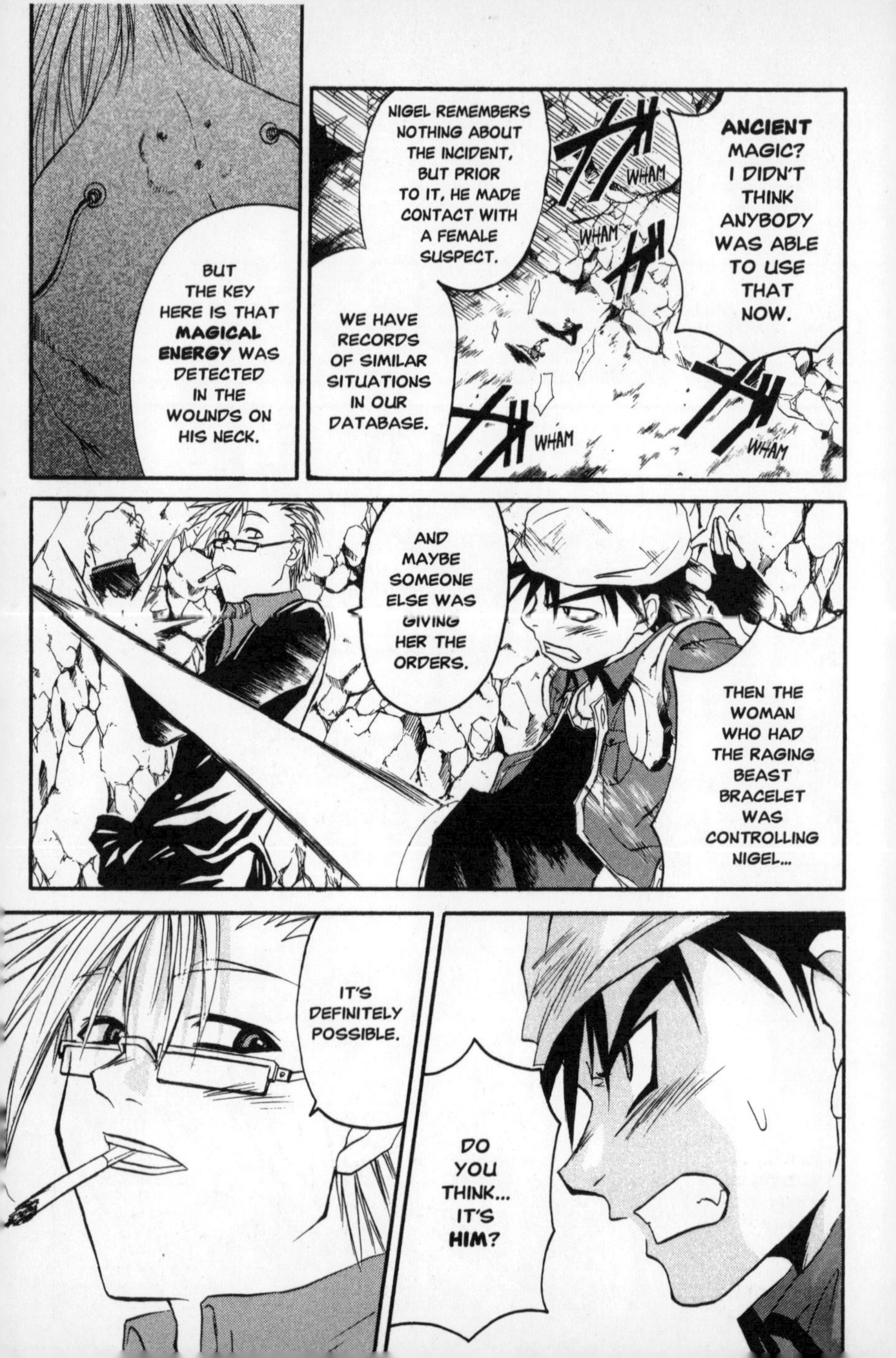
ANCIENT MAGIC? I DIDN'T THINK ANYBODY WAS ABLE TO USE THAT NOW.
WHAM
WHAM
NIGEL REMEMBERS NOTHING ABOUT THE INCIDENT, BUT PRIOR TO IT, HE MADE CONTACT WITH A FEMALE SUSPECT.
WHAM
WHAM
WE HAVE RECORDS OF SIMILAR SITUATIONS IN OUR DATABASE.
BUT THE KEY HERE IS THAT MAGICAL ENERGY WAS DETECTED IN THE WOUNDS ON HIS NECK.
THEN THE WOMAN WHO HAD THE RAGING BEAST BRACELET WAS CONTROLLING NIGEL...
AND MAYBE SOMEONE ELSE WAS GIVING HER THE ORDERS.
DO YOU THINK... IT'S HIM?
IT'S DEFINITELY POSSIBLE.

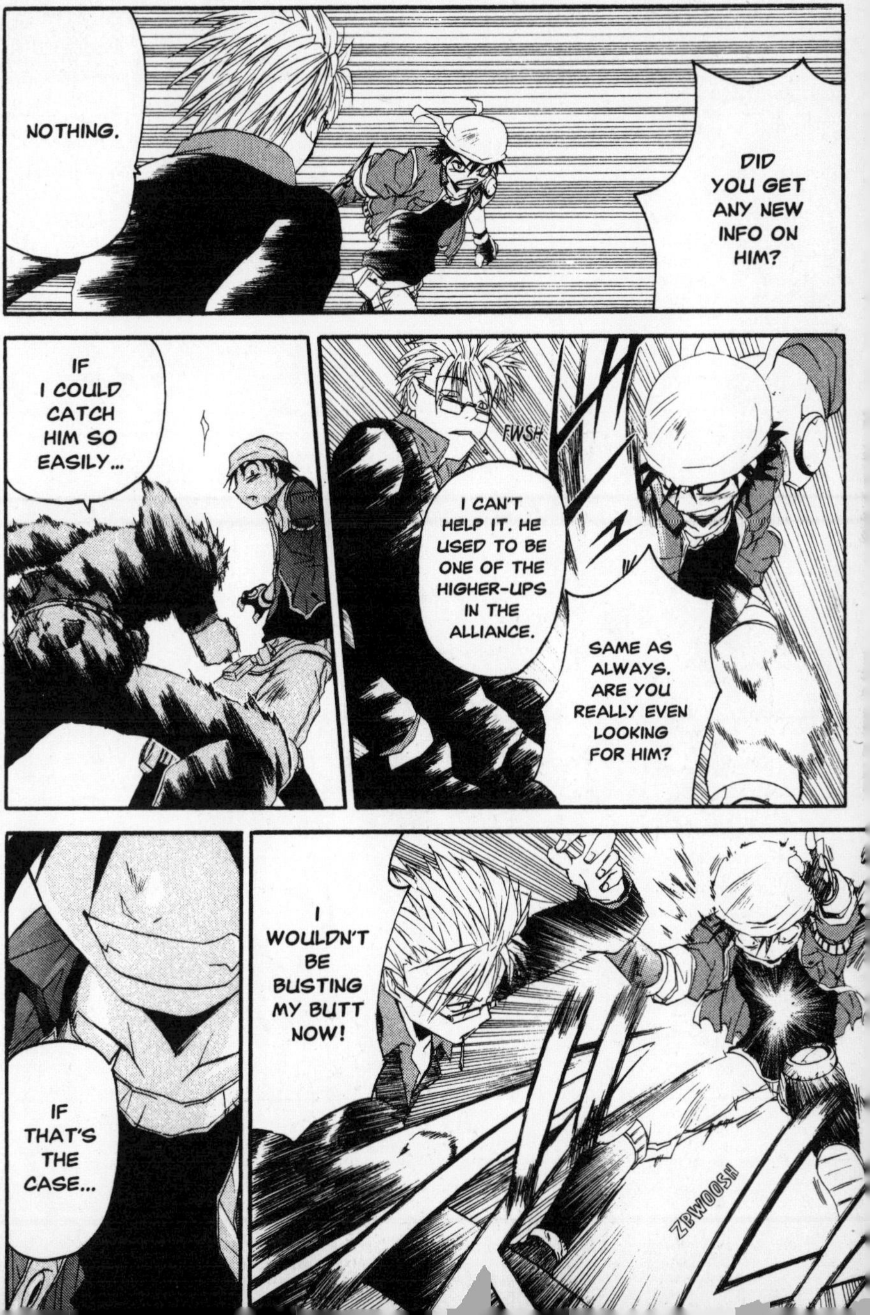
DID YOU GET ANY NEW INFO ON HIM?
NOTHING.
SAME AS ALWAYS. ARE YOU REALLY EVEN LOOKING FOR HIM?
FWSH
I CAN'T HELP IT. HE USED TO BE ONE OF THE HIGHER-UPS IN THE ALLIANCE.
IF I COULD CATCH HIM SO EASILY...
I WOULDN'T BE BUSTING MY BUTT NOW!
ZBWOOSH
IF THAT'S THE CASE...

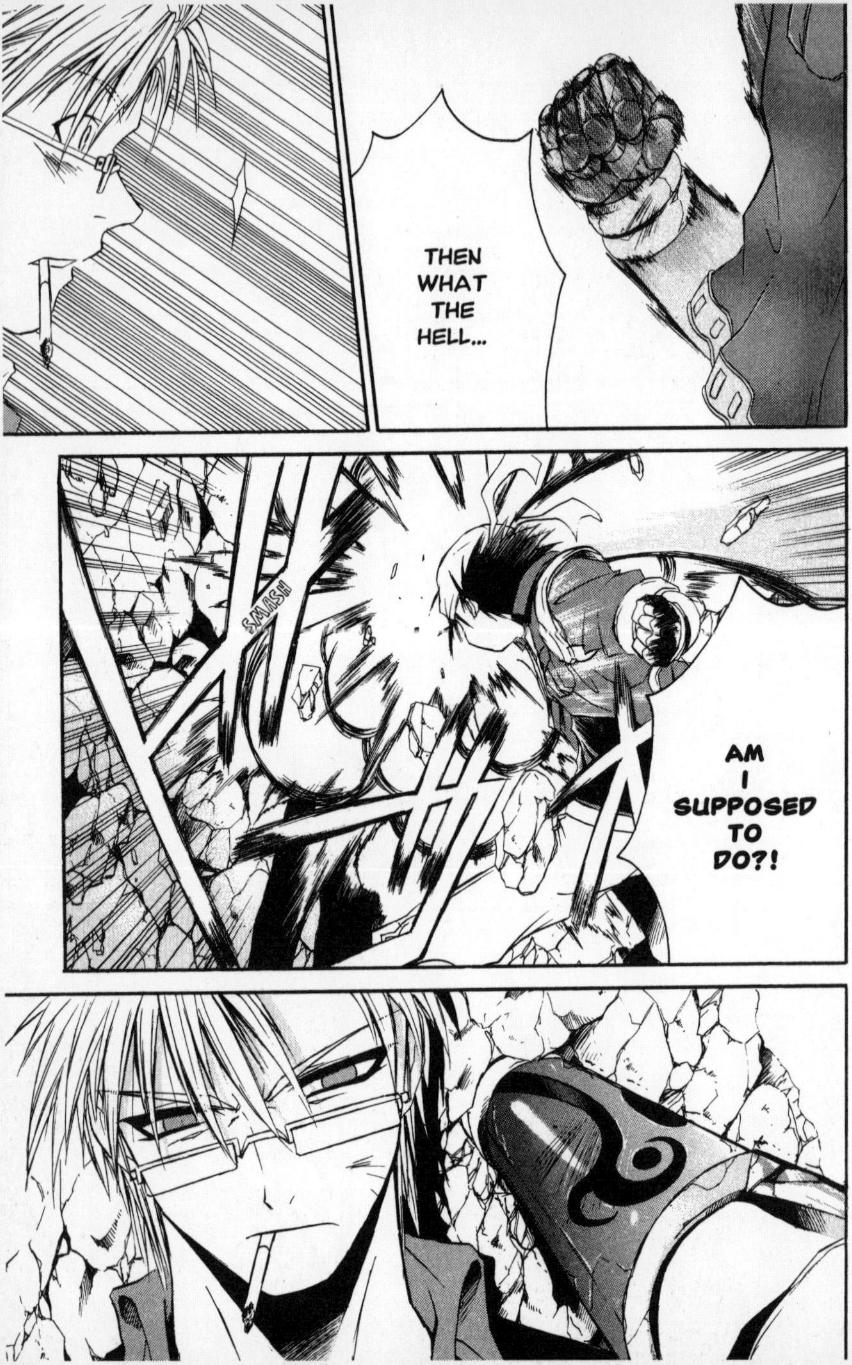
THEN WHAT THE HELL...
SMASH
AM I SUPPOSED TO DO?!

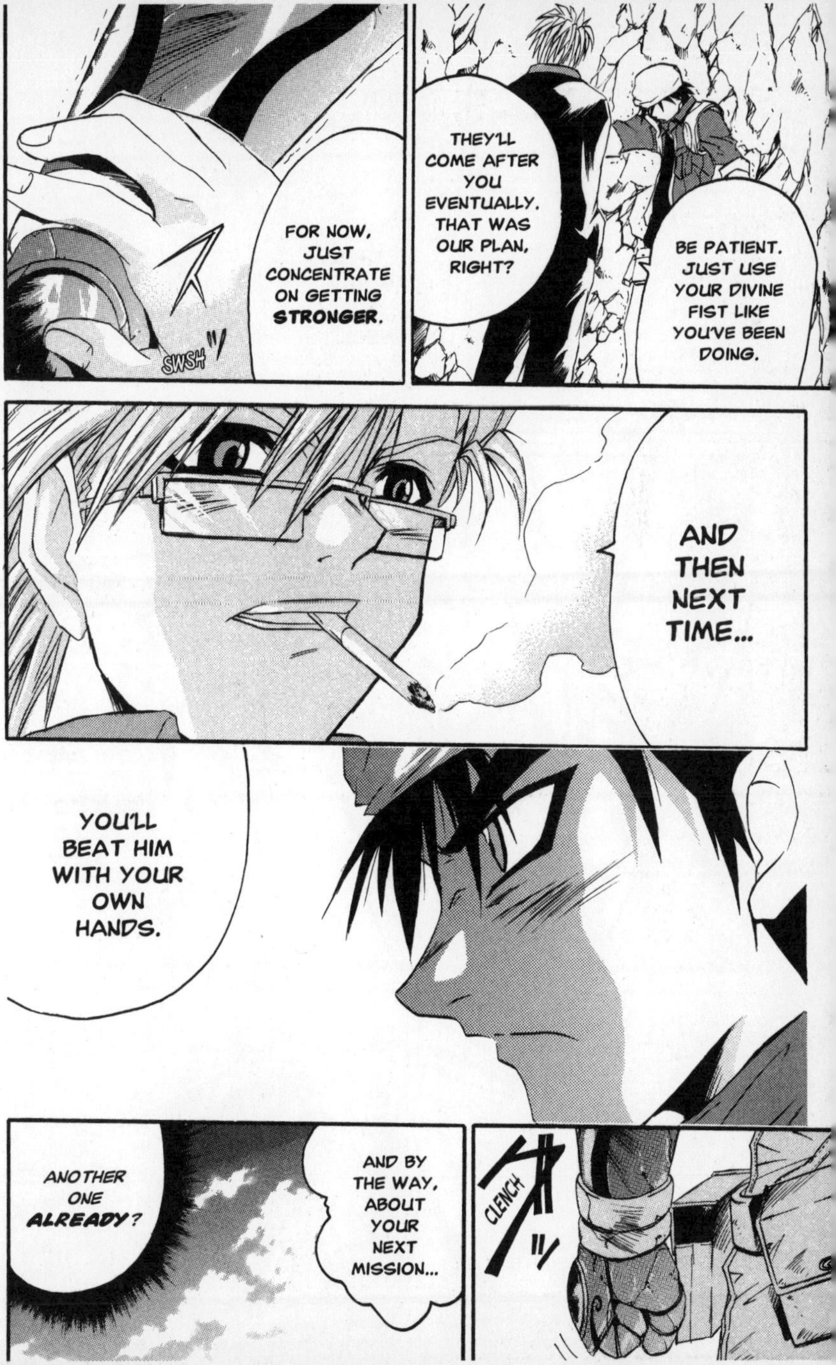
BE PATIENT. JUST USE YOUR DIVINE FIST LIKE YOU'VE BEEN DOING.
THEY'LL COME AFTER YOU EVENTUALLY. THAT WAS OUR PLAN, RIGHT?
FOR NOW, JUST CONCENTRATE ON GETTING **STRONGER**.
SWSH
AND THEN NEXT TIME...
YOU'LL BEAT HIM WITH YOUR OWN HANDS.
CLENCH
AND BY THE WAY, ABOUT YOUR NEXT MISSION...
ANOTHER ONE ***ALREADY*****?**

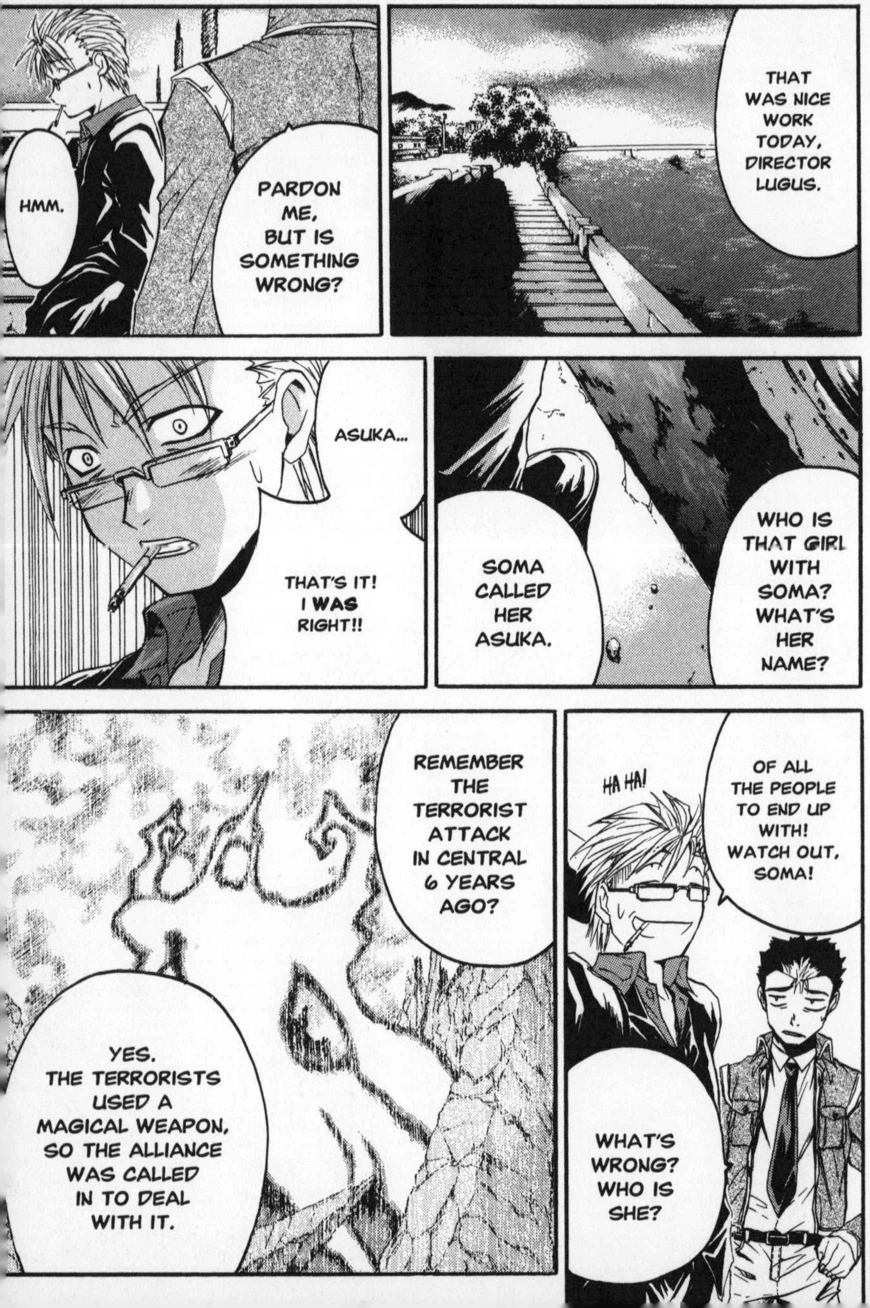
THAT WAS NICE WORK TODAY, DIRECTOR LUGUS.
PARDON ME, BUT IS SOMETHING WRONG?
HMM.
WHO IS THAT GIRL WITH SOMA? WHAT'S HER NAME?
SOMA CALLED HER ASUKA.
ASUKA...
THAT'S IT! I WAS RIGHT!!
HA HA!
OF ALL THE PEOPLE TO END UP WITH! WATCH OUT, SOMA!
WHAT'S WRONG? WHO IS SHE?
REMEMBER THE TERRORIST ATTACK IN CENTRAL 6 YEARS AGO?
YES. THE TERRORISTS USED A MAGICAL WEAPON, SO THE ALLIANCE WAS CALLED IN TO DEAL WITH IT.

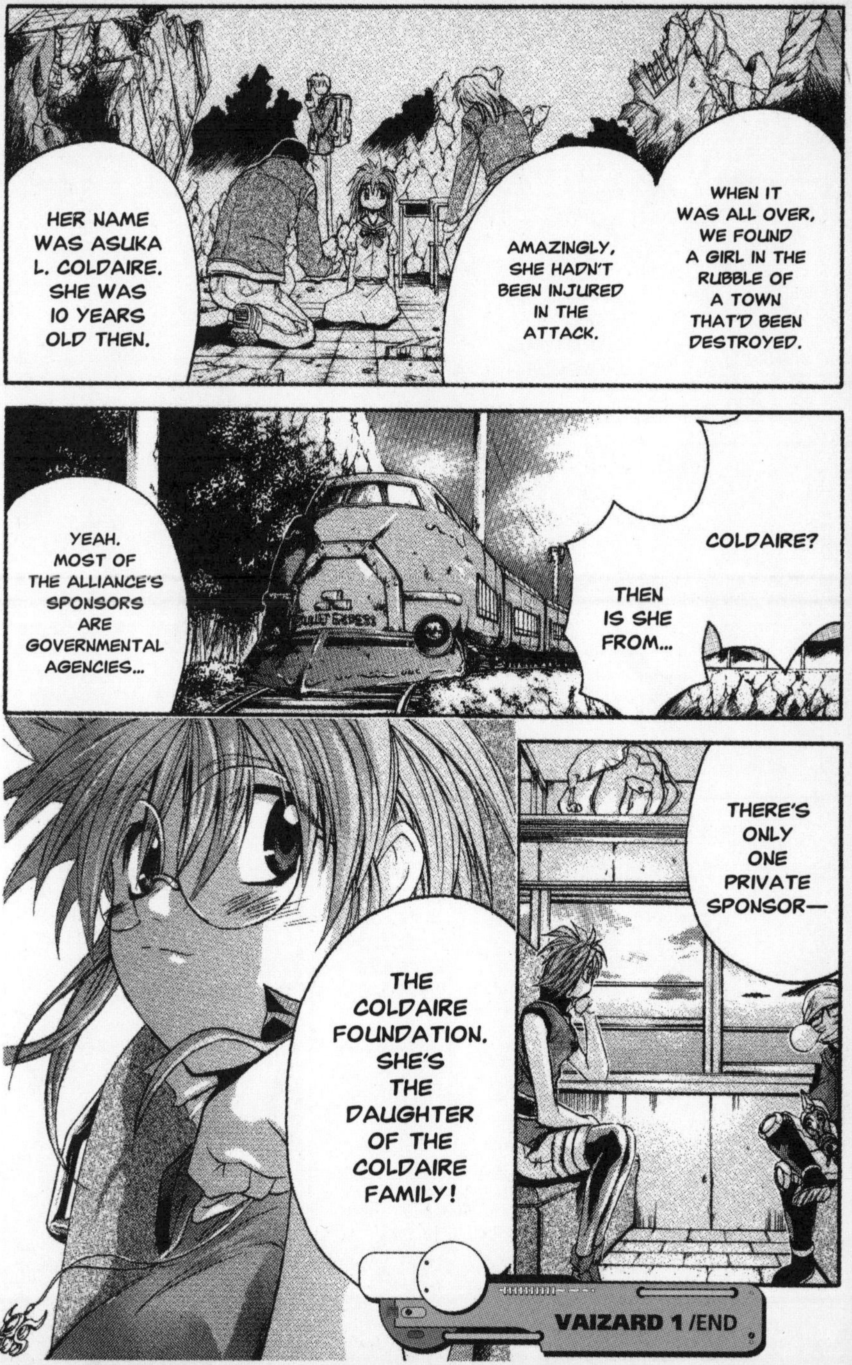
WHEN IT WAS ALL OVER, WE FOUND A GIRL IN THE RUBBLE OF A TOWN THAT'D BEEN DESTROYED.
AMAZINGLY, SHE HADN'T BEEN INJURED IN THE ATTACK.
HER NAME WAS ASUKA L. COLDAIRE. SHE WAS 10 YEARS OLD THEN.
COLDAIRE?
THEN IS SHE FROM...
YEAH. MOST OF THE ALLIANCE'S SPONSORS ARE GOVERNMENTAL AGENCIES...
THERE'S ONLY ONE PRIVATE SPONSOR—
THE COLDAIRE FOUNDATION. SHE'S THE DAUGHTER OF THE COLDAIRE FAMILY!
VAIZARD 1 /END